Little Mother of Russia

*

A BIOGRAPHY OF THE EMPRESS MARIE FEODOROVNA

'HAPPY THE MAN, AND HAPPY HE ALONE,
HE, WHO CAN CALL TO-DAY HIS OWN;
HE, WHO SECURE WITHIN, CAN SAY,
TOMORROW DO THY WORST FOR I HAVE LIVED TODAY,
COME FAIR OR FOUL, OR RAIN OR SHINE,
THE JOYS THAT I HAVE POSSESSED, IN SPITE OF FATE, ARE MINE.
NOT HEAVEN ITSELF OVER THE PAST HAS POWER,
AND WHAT HAS BEEN HAS BEEN, AND I HAVE HAD MY HOUR'.

– John Dryden (1631-1700)

To the memory of my parents
Peggy and Ernie Bawcombe
and to
Charles and Matilda Woodcock,
buried at Novo-Saratov,
Alexandrovskoe, St Petersburg

Little Mother of Russia

*

A BIOGRAPHY OF THE EMPRESS
MARIE FEODOROVNA
(1847-1928)

CORYNE HALL

HOLMES & MEIER

First published in the United States of America 2001 by
Holmes & Meier Publishers, Inc.
P.O. Box 943, Teaneck, NJ 07666
www.holmesandmeier.com
Paperback edition, revised 2006

First published in 1999 by
Shepheard-Walwyn (Publishers) Ltd

Library of Congress Cataloging-in-Publication Data
Hall, Coryne.
    Little mother of Russia: a biography of Empress Marie Feodorovna
    (1847-1928)/Coryne Hall.
        p. cm.
    Includes bibliographical references and index.
    ISBN 0-8419-1422-2 (paperback : alk. paper)
    1. Marie Feodorovna. Empress, consort of Alexander III, Emperor of
Russia, 1847-1928. 2. Empresses—Russia—Biography. 3. Russia—
History—1801-1917. I. Title.

DK236.A2.H35 2001
947.08'2'092—dc21
[B]   2001024538

Typeset by Alacrity
Banwell Castle, Weston-super-Mare
Printed in Great Britain through Print Solutions, Wallington, Surrey

Contents

List of Illustrations

Author's Note

Russian dates present their own problems. Russia used the Old Style Julian Calendar until 1st February 1918. This was twelve days behind the west in the nineteenth century and thirteen days behind in the twentieth century. Many sources do not even state which style dating they have used, which adds to the confusion, and sometimes it is not even possible to establish whether they have used Old Style or New Style. I have used the Gregorian, New Style, Calendar but any dates given according to the Russian Calendar are indicated O.S.

I have used the spelling of Russian names most familiar to English-speaking readers. Where there is an option I have used my own preference. The Empress Marie Feodorovna was always called Princess Dagmar or 'Kejserinde Dagmar' in Scandinavia. I have followed this custom and called her Dagmar throughout. Her sister is Alexandra or 'Alix'; the Empress' daughter-in-law, the Empress Alexandra Feodorovna, is 'Alicky' or Empress Alexandra, to avoid confusion.

The titles Emperor, Tsar, Empress, Tsarina, are all correct and are used interchangeably. The wife of the Tsarevitch was the Tsarevna.

Russians have three names – their Christian name, patronymic (their father's name) and their surname. Alexander III's daughter Olga was therefore Olga Alexandrovna, his son was Nicholas Alexandrovitch. Nicholas II's daughter Olga was Olga Nicholaievna. The surname is hardly used at all.

Acknowledgements

I would like to acknowledge the gracious permission of Her Majesty the Queen for permission to publish material from the Royal Archives. My thanks to the staff there for their unfailing courtesy and efficiency. Crown copyright material from the Public Record Office is reproduced by permission of the Controller of Her Majesty's Stationery Office.

Special thanks are due to Marlene Eilers, for supplying me with valuable information and contacts; to Robin Piguet, for all his help and for introducing me to many interesting people; and to Anthony Summers, for encouragement, advice and documents.

Information has been drawn from a variety of sources, including Preben Ulstrup's article 'Marie Feodorovna Through Diaries and Personal Letters' in the Christiansborg Exhibition Catalogue, and Inger-Lise Klausen's book *Dagmar: Zarina fra Danmark*, from both of which works I was not permitted to quote.

This book would not have been possible without the help of a large number of people. I would like to express my thanks to them all here:

In Britain: Lord Brabourne & the Trustees of the Broadlands Archives; Professor M.A. Branch, School of Slavonic & East European Studies; Mrs Mollie Chalk, Archivist at Broadlands; William Clark; Jim Cockburn; Mike Colenso, the University of Surrey; Rosemary & Donald Crawford; the Danish Tourist Board; Karen Davies; Richard Davies, Archivist, the Brotherton Library, Leeds University Russian Archive; Frances Dimond, Curator, the Royal Photographic Collection, Windsor; David Downes; the staff of Guildford & Bordon Public Libraries; Elaine Hart, *The Illustrated London News*; Dr Peter Gill, Forensic Science Service, Birmingham; Fiona Harris; Lone Hensen; Pauline Holdrup; Sylvia Leone, the University of Surrey Languages Department; Mrs Terttu Leney; Christopher Macdonald, Hennell of Bond Street Ltd; Rosie Mitchell, the Public Record Office; Geoffrey Munn, Wartski Ltd; The British Library Newspaper Library, Colindale; Dr Michael Occleshaw; Monika Ridby-Hopper; Sue Woolmans; Marion Wynn; Charlotte Zeepvat.

In Canada: the late Tihon Kulikovsky-Romanoff.

In Denmark: Tonny Andersen, B. & W. Museum; Jørgen O. Bjerregaard & Lillian Stehr, Ballerup Egnsmuseum; Anne Dyhr & Jacob Thomsen, Det Kongelige Bibliotek; Major Jesper Gram-Andersen, Curator, Det

Livgardens Historisk Samling, who not only provided the information but translated it into English; Jørgen Hein, the Rosenborg Museum; H.M. Queen Ingrid; Janni Jakobsen, for her help with the translations; Professor Bent Jensen, Odense University; Paul Edward Kulikovsky; the Royal Danish Ministry of Foreign Affairs; Ove Mogensen; Hans Neerbek; Gerda Petri, Curator, Christian VIII's Palace, the Amalienborg; Sigurd Rambusch and the staff of the Rigsarkivet; Keld Wincklemann, Curator, Roskilde Domkirke; and to the people of Denmark, whose warm, friendly manner did so much to help us on our way during two bitterly cold December trips to Copenhagen.

In Finland: Ragnar Backström, Curator, the Langinkoski Imperial Fishing Lodge Museum; Helsinki University Library; and the Finnish group who kindly allowed me to join their tour of the Anitchkov Palace in St Petersburg, particularly Kirsti Makela who translated for me as we went round.

In France: Jacques Ferrand.

In Germany: Brigitte Leipold, Kulturreferentin, Schloss Mainau.

In Malta: Major A.E. Abela; Margaret, Baroness von Brockdorff; Joseph Caruana, National Archives of Malta; Norbert Dalli; Mr Achille Mizzi, Secretary to H.E. the President of Malta.

In Russia: Zoia Belyakova & Leonid Belyakov; Irina Konopatchskaya; Professor Julia Kudrina, Russian Academy of Sciences, Moscow; Elena Yablochkina & Sergei Yablochkin.

In Spain: H.H. Prince Michael Feodorovitch Romanoff.

In Sweden: Ted Rosvall.

In Switzerland: H.H. Prince Nicholas Romanoff; Karen Roth-Nicholls; H.M. Queen Anne of Roumania; Eric Nassbaum, Curator, Cartier, Geneva.

In the United States of America: Ronald M. Bulatoff, the Hoover Institution on War, Revolution & Peace; Senta Driver; Brien Horen; Greg King; Peter Kurth; Dr Ronald Moe; Stanford University, California; Dr Idris Traylor, Jnr.

My thanks to Stewart Velzian, for teaching me how to 'surf the net', and to his staff, especially Neil Dobner and Tom Nugent. They bailed me out when things went wrong on obscure Russian websites, unjammed the printer and kept me going with cups of tea. Thanks also to Roger Collard, who allowed me to use the facility.

Every effort has been made to trace all copyright holders. We will be happy to correct any errors and make suitable acknowledgement in a future edition.

Last, but by no means least, special thanks to my husband Colin. He carried the bags, read the maps, coped with the currency, corrected the drafts and edited every line. Without his constant support and encouragement the book would never have been completed.

THE DANISH ROYAL FAMILY

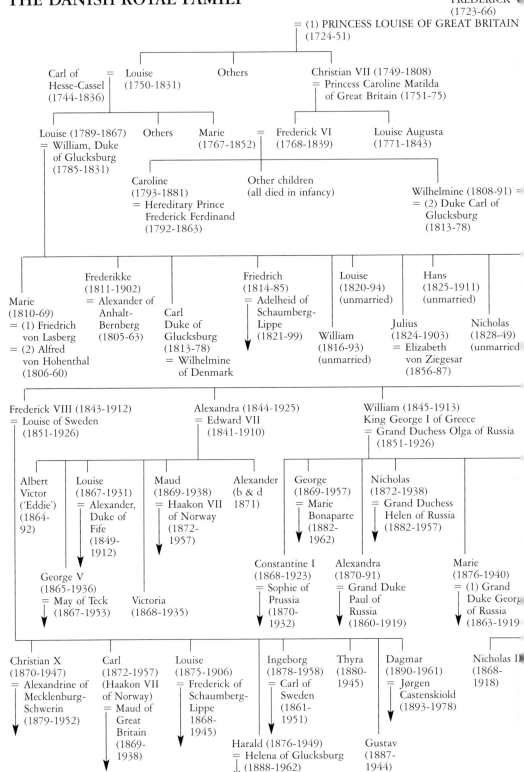

OF DENMARK

= (2) JULIANA OF BRUNSWICK-WOLFENBÜTTEL
(1729-96)

rederick (1753-1805)
Crown Prince of Denmark
= Sophie of Mecklenburg-Schwerin
(1758-94)

Christian VIII (1768-1848)
= (1) Charlotte of Mecklenburg-Schwerin
(1784-1840)
= (2) Caroline of Augustenburg (1796-1881)

) Frederick VII (1808-63) = (2) Caroline of Mecklenburg-
Strelitz (1821-76)
(3) Louise Rasmussen (1815-74)
Created Countess Danner

Louise Charlotte
(1789-1864)
= William, Landgrave
of Hesse-Cassel
(1787-1867)

**Hereditary Prince
Frederick Ferdinand**
(1792-1863)
= Caroline, daughter
of Frederick VI
(1793-1881)

---

hristian IX = Louise
818-1906)   (1817-98)

Caroline
(1811-29)

Marie
(1814-95)
= Frederick of
Anhalt-Dessau
(1799-1864) ↓

Frederick
(1820-84)
= (1) Grand Duchess
Alexandra of Russia
(1825-44)
= (2) Anna of Prussia
(1836-1918) ↓

Augusta
(1823-89)
= Carl Frederick,
Baron Blixen-
Finecke
(1822-73)

Sophie
(b & d
1827)

Dagmar (1847-1928)
(Marie Feodorovna)
= Alexander III of Russia
1845-94)

Thyra (1853-1933)
= Ernst August,
Duke of Cumberland
(1845-1923)

Waldemar
(1858-1939)
= Marie of
Orleans
(1865-1909)

ndrew
882-1944)
= Alice of
Battenberg
(1885-
1969)

Christopher
(1888-1940)
= (2) Françoise
of Orleans
(1902-53) ↓

Marie Louise
(1879-1948)
= Max of Baden
(1867-1929) ↓

Alexandra
(1882-1963)
= Frederick
Franz IV of
Mecklenburg-
Schwerin
(1882-1945) ↓

Christian
(1885-
1901)

George
(1880-
1912)

Olga
(1884-
1958)

Ernst August,
Duke of Brunswick-
Lüneburg
(1887-1953)
= Victoria Louise,
daughter of
Kaiser William II
(1892-1980) ↓

George
(1871-
99)

Michael
(1878-
1918)

Olga
(1882-
1960)

Aage
(1887-1940)
= Mathilde
Calvi di
Bergolo
(1885-
1949) ↓

Axel
(1888-1964)
= Margaretha
of Sweden
(1899-
1977) ↓

Erik
(1890-1950)
= Lois
Booth
(1897-
1941) ↓

Viggo
(1893-1970)
= Eleanor
Green
(1895-
1966)

Margrethe
(1895-1992)
= René of
Bourbon-
Parma
(1894-
1962) ↓

lexander
869-70)

Xenia
(1875-
1960)

Coryne Hall, 1999

THE RUSSIAN IMPERIAL FAMILY

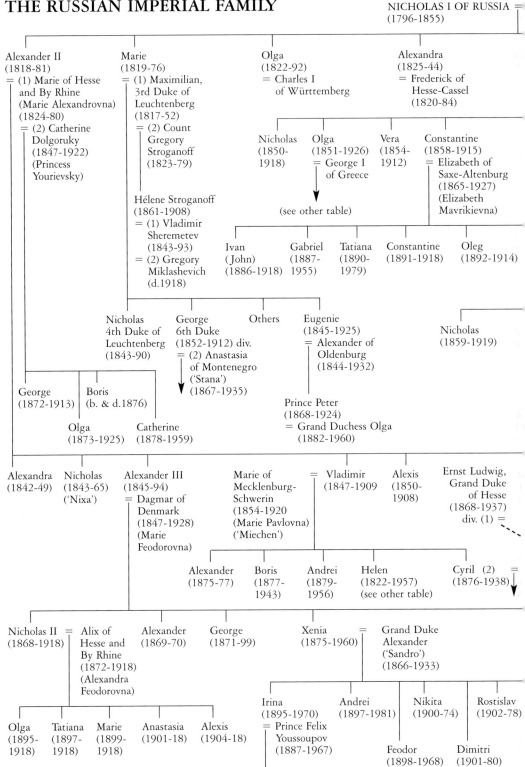

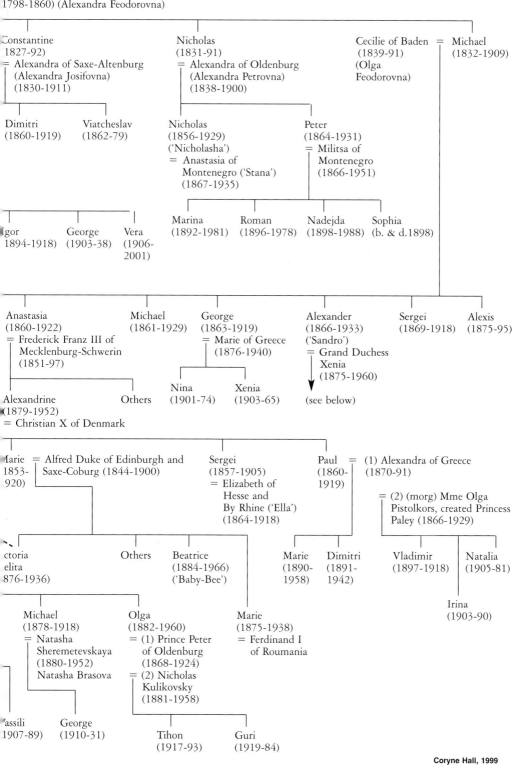

CHARLOTTE OF PRUSSIA
(1798-1860) (Alexandra Feodorovna)

Constantine
(1827-92)
= Alexandra of Saxe-Altenburg
  (Alexandra Josifovna)
  (1830-1911)

Dimitri   Viatcheslav
(1860-1919)   (1862-79)

Igor   George   Vera
1894-1918) (1903-38)   (1906-
                         2001)

Nicholas
(1831-91)
= Alexandra of Oldenburg
  (Alexandra Petrovna)
  (1838-1900)

Nicholas   Peter
(1856-1929)   (1864-1931)
('Nicholasha')   = Militsa of
  = Anastasia of   Montenegro
  Montenegro ('Stana')   (1866-1951)
  (1867-1935)

Marina   Roman   Nadejda   Sophia
(1892-1981) (1896-1978) (1898-1988)   (b. & d.1898)

Cecilie of Baden = Michael
  (1839-91)   (1832-1909)
  (Olga
  Feodorovna)

Anastasia   Michael   George   Alexander   Sergei   Alexis
(1860-1922)   (1861-1929)   (1863-1919)   (1866-1933)   (1869-1918)   (1875-95)
= Frederick Franz III of   = Marie of Greece ('Sandro')
  Mecklenburg-Schwerin   (1876-1940)   = Grand Duchess
  (1851-97)   Xenia
                                    Nina   Xenia   (1875-1960)
Alexandrine   (1901-74) (1903-65)   (see below)
(1879-1952)   Others
= Christian X of Denmark

Marie = Alfred Duke of Edinburgh and   Sergei   Paul = (1) Alexandra of Greece
1853-   Saxe-Coburg (1844-1900)   (1857-1905)   (1860-   (1870-91)
920)   = Elizabeth of   1919)
                                             Hesse and   = (2) (morg) Mme Olga
                                             By Rhine ('Ella')   Pistolkors, created Princess
                                             (1864-1918)   Paley (1866-1929)

ctoria   Others   Beatrice   Marie   Dimitri   Vladimir   Natalia
elita   (1884-1966)   (1890-   (1891-   (1897-1918)   (1905-81)
876-1936)   ('Baby-Bee')   1958)   1942)
                                                                                        Irina
      Michael   Olga   Marie   (1903-90)
      (1878-1918)   (1882-1960)   (1875-1938)
      = Natasha   = (1) Prince Peter = Ferdinand I
        Sheremetevskaya   of Oldenburg   of Roumania
        (1880-1952)   (1868-1924)
        Natasha Brasova   = (2) Nicholas
                            Kulikovsky
                            (1881-1958)

Vassili   George   Tihon   Guri
1907-89)   (1910-31)   (1917-93)   (1919-84)

Coryne Hall, 1999

Introduction

In the autumn of 1928 the tattered remnants of Imperial Russia converged on Copenhagen. Grand Dukes and Grand Duchesses, princes who once owned large estates and now drove taxis in Paris, impoverished officers, their uniforms taken out of mothballs for the occasion – many of them now working as Paris waiters or chauffeurs – all came to pay their respects to the memory of a Danish princess who had become the symbol of Tsarist Russia.

For one day the glory of Imperial Russia shone again. From their places of exile came Grand Duke Cyril, self-styled 'Guardian of the Russian Throne' and Prince Felix Youssoupov, the murderer of Rasputin, with his glamorous wife Princess Irina. Among the foreign representatives was Prince Albert, Duke of York, who had left the Duchess and baby Princess Elizabeth in London in order to attend the funeral of his great-aunt Minny.

Inside the twelfth-century Roskilde Cathedral rested the coffin of the last surviving Empress of Russia draped with the Imperial flag. The icon of the Chevalier Guards, of whom she had been Honorary Colonel, lay on the catafalque, which was guarded by the Cossack bodyguards who had faithfully followed her into exile – but nothing could disguise the fact that, with the death of the eighty-one-year-old Dowager Empress, Imperial Russia had also died.

It was the end of an era. The Empress Marie Feodorovna, formerly Princess Dagmar of Denmark, had spent over fifty years in Russia and gained the love and respect of all classes of people. How did this poor, Cinderella princess from a junior branch of the Danish Royal House rise to become the Empress of mighty Russia and, during her ten years of exile, keep most of the Romanov family united?

She was undoubtedly a woman of considerable, if discreet, influence although later her counsel was not always heeded. If her son Nicholas II had listened to her wise advice there would have been no Rasputin and the history of the twentieth century might have been very different. After the revolution her word was law among the émigrés and her position as head of the Imperial family ensured that her influence was paramount among the Romanovs. She had truly become *Matoushka*, the 'mother of her people'.[1]

For many years rumours persisted that the Imperial family did not die at Ekaterinburg and these stories had one very notable devotee – the Empress Marie Feodorovna. The Empress said that she knew the family were all alive – and she steadfastly maintained this attitude in public until her death, always refusing to meet the young woman who claimed to be Anastasia.

My interest in Imperial Russia began when I discovered that my great-grandmother was born in St Petersburg and was an almost exact contemporary of Nicholas II. Although her parents, Charles and Matilda Woodcock, were English, the story fired my interest. It has taken many years of patient searching to find the record of Alice Woodcock's birth in Alexandrovskoe, where her father was a teacher. Sadly, the same register also recorded the deaths of her brother and sister in childhood and they were buried 'in the Germany colony' at Novo-Saratov.

When I visited Russia for the second time in July 1998 I found that the cemetery is still in existence. Our guides, Elena Yablochkina and Sergei Yablochkin, very kindly went down to Novo-Saratov before we even arrived in St Petersburg and took photographs for us to show the family in England. Sadly, there was no sign of the children's graves. I was unable to go myself, as our tour schedule was very hectic. That week Tsar Nicholas II and his family were being re-buried in St Petersburg.

In 1985 Mikhail Gorbachev became President of the Soviet Union and began a policy of perestroika (reform). Glasnost (openness) was now the order of the day. Four years later the Berlin Wall came down. Communist governments all over eastern Europe fell and communist rule in Russia also came to an end. Boris Yeltsin became president of the new Russian Federation, Leningrad reverted to its old Imperial name of St Petersburg and the town of Sverdlovsk became Ekaterinburg once more.

I first visited Russia in 1991, when Mikhail Gorbachev was still in power and the Russian people had only recently been told about the Tsar's death. With the fall of communism, Russians are eager to rediscover their past. Consequently there is a resurgence of interest in the monarchy, especially the last three tsars, Alexander II, Alexander III, Nicholas II and their families, who were taboo subjects for over seventy years. Only recently has this restriction been lifted. Monarchist movements are springing up; the red flag has been replaced by the tsarist red, white and blue; and in 1991 the pretender to the Russian throne, Grand Duke Vladimir, was invited to visit Russia. When he died during a Miami press conference in May 1992 he was given a funeral in the SS Peter & Paul Cathedral in St Petersburg – unthinkable even a couple of years earlier – and his parents Grand Duke and Grand Duchess Cyril have also been reburied in the cathedral.

With all this interest in Imperial Russia it came as no surprise to my family when I decided to write a book. When I began my research many years ago the Soviet archives were closed to westerners. I found that the lives of Nicholas II's parents had been sadly neglected and I decided that it was time to redress the situation. Many books about Nicholas scarcely mention his mother at all.

There have been only two biographies of her in English – Vladimir Poliakoff's *The Empress Marie of Russia & Her Times*, written during the Empress' lifetime; and E.E.P. Tisdall's *Marie Feodorovna, Empress of Russia*, written in 1957. She also appears in books about her family and it was Theo Aronson's *A Family of Kings* (1976) which first inspired me and led to my research into the life of Princess Dagmar of Denmark. More recently, the *Maria Feodorovna, Empress of Russia* exhibition catalogue from Christiansborg Slot in Copenhagen (published in Danish and English), although not a full biography, does give a new insight into certain periods of her life. In Denmark, there is H.C. Clausen's *Kejserinde Dagmar*, which covers her association with Finland; Hans Neerbek's *Søstrenes Slot*, the story of her Danish villa, Hvidøre; Inger-Lise Klausen's *Dagmar: Zarina fra Danmark*, dealing with her life from 1864; and Bent Jensen's *Zarmoder blandt Zarmordere*, covering the period 1917-1928. The full story of her life has never been told in English before and I have pieced it together from a variety of sources.

Despite the fall of communism and the policy of glasnost, much work remains to be done on translating the vast wealth of information on Imperial Russia, especially the archive material relating to the Empress Marie Feodorovna. Unfortunately, the Danish Royal Archives are closed to researchers.

Marie Feodorovna has been called the Empress who 'lived one of the most dramatic lives of anyone to wear a crown in Russia'.[2] Everything she held most dear was destroyed before her eyes. Her husband died in his prime and two of her sons died young. Russia was engulfed in revolution, leading to the destruction of the dynasty and the Church. Many members of her family, including her remaining two sons and five of her grandchildren, disappeared or were murdered in the subsequent Red Terror.

The Empress Marie ended her life as a tragic relic of a bygone age. When she died the émigré movement lost its focal point and the Romanov family, by now divided over who should become head of the family, remain so to this day.

Seventy years after her death, the time has come for a new study of this fascinating woman.

Coryne Hall
1999

PART 1

PRINCESS
OF DENMARK

(1847-1866)

CHAPTER 1

Changing Fortunes

'IN DENMARK I WAS BORN, THERE I BELONG' – Danish song

MOST DIPLOMATS accredited to Copenhagen remembered the terrible winter cold. 'The wind was something terrific and the sea was frozen a dingy green, in thick, unequal lumps ...', wrote the British Minister's wife. 'It was a joke with the Danish Royal Family that the wind was *round*, because one always meets it ...'[1] She also noticed that the country was very unsophisticated. This was hardly surprising.

In the nineteenth century Denmark was a poor country crippled by debt after the Napoleonic Wars. Large areas of Copenhagen had been destroyed by the bombardment of the British fleet in 1807. The capitulation and surrender of the Danish fleet to the British was followed by national bankruptcy in 1813 and the loss of Norway (joined to the Danish Crown for 450 years) to Sweden. After this humiliation Denmark was determined to recover her prestige and ensure that the tiny kingdom was not reduced in size any further.

The redistribution of territory after Napoleon's defeat ruined many people, including a junior relation of Denmark's ruling house, Duke William of Schleswig-Holstein-Sonderburg-Beck, who was left with little money and a growing family. His wife's sister Princess Marie of Hesse-Cassel had married King Frederick VI of Denmark. Although the King allowed him to exchange his German property of Beck for the Danish castle and Dukedom of Glucksborg in 1824, William retained a strong liking for everything German.

When Duke William died in 1831 he left ten children with no prospects. The sixth child, thirteen-year-old Christian, was sent to Copenhagen and placed in the guardianship of his uncle King Frederick, who treated him like a son and enrolled him in the Cadets' Academy. In 1835 he was confirmed and appointed a Captain in the Royal Danish Horse Guards.

Two years later he was sent to London to present the King's congratulations to the eighteen-year-old Queen Victoria on her accession. His modesty, good manners and smart appearance were generally admired and

3

when he returned for the coronation the following year it seemed that this handsome, popular young man was all that the young Queen could desire.

It was not to be. Victoria married Prince Albert of Saxe-Coburg-Gotha and Prince Christian went to Bonn University to study history and law. While he was there the childless King Frederick VI of Denmark died and was succeeded by his cousin Christian VIII.

In 1841 Prince Christian proposed to his cousin Princess Louise. Her father, the extremely rich Landgrave William of Hesse-Cassel, was Governor of Copenhagen and her mother Princess Charlotte of Denmark was a sister of King Christian VIII. The Landgrave was not pleased that his daughter wished to marry a penniless prince but the wedding took place at his home, the Brockdorffe Palace (part of the King's palace, the Amalienborg), on 26th May 1842 with King Christian and Queen Caroline Amalie as guests of honour.

They made their home at the Yellow Mansion, a grace and favour residence in Copenhagen given to them by the King. It was actually No 18 Amaliegade, a town house, small by royal standards whose name derived from the colour of its outside walls.

Louise, a small, slim, pretty woman with a deep religious faith, was clever and ambitious for the advancement of her family. She began to take an interest in politics and maintained a regular correspondence with her relatives all over Europe. A more forceful personality than Christian, she soon became the centre of the household.

Despite financial help from the Landgrave of Hesse-Cassel and Prince Christian's aunt the widowed Queen Marie, they lived very modestly. Their first four years of married life passed quietly and happily. The birth of a son, Frederick, in 1843 was followed by Alexandra in 1844 and William George in 1845. In 1847 a second daughter joined the other children in the palace nursery.

*

Princess Marie Sophia Frederikke Dagmar of Schleswig-Holstein-Sonderburg-Glucksborg was born at the Yellow Mansion on 26th November 1847. Known to her family as Minny, she was always called Dagmar ('bringer of light') by the Danish people, to remind them of the virtuous thirteenth-century Queen Dagmar who is immortalised in popular ballads.

Legend says that King Valdemar II was far away when his young wife Queen Dagmar, taken suddenly ill, realised she was dying. Summoning her page, she told him to find her husband and beg him to return quickly if he wished to see her alive. The King galloped swiftly home, praying as he rode:

Forbid it God our Father in Heaven
That Dagmar die so young! ...

As he neared the castle he heard the tolling of the church bells and realised he was too late. Dagmar's body was lying in state, surrounded by candles. Grief-stricken, he prayed to God to give her back to him. At that moment the Queen sat up. She had been permitted, she said, to return for a few moments to say farewell. Her soul had been in purgatory – if she had not broken the Sabbath it would have been in heaven. She asked the king to proclaim a general pardon and then, after a few loving words, she died.[2]

At the beginning of 1848 Christian VIII was succeeded by his son, Frederick VII. At Dagmar's christening in the Royal Chapel of Christiansborg Slot on 7th March the new King was among the impressive list of godparents, who included the Dowager Queen Caroline Amalie; the heir presumptive Prince Ferdinand (King Frederick's uncle) and his wife Princess Caroline; Dagmar's grandfather Landgrave William of Hesse-Cassel and his son Prince Frederick; Prince Ernst of Hesse-Philipsthal-Barchfeldt (Prince Christian's uncle) and Prince Ludwig of Bentheim-Steinfurth. Unlike her elder sister, whose godmothers included the Empress of Russia, Dagmar had no godparents from the Russian Imperial family.[3]

In 1853 Louise gave birth to another daughter, Thyra but from her earliest days the person closest to Dagmar was Alexandra. The two little girls shared a tiny room on the top floor of the Yellow Mansion with scarcely room for more than their beds and a chest of drawers. Here their nurse, Anne Larsen from Roskilde, watched over them.[4] There were no bathrooms. In winter they had to make do with a weekly wash-down in a tub but in summer they bathed in the sea at nearby Klampenborg.

With only Prince Christian's officer's pay of about £800 a year to live on there was nothing to spare for luxuries. Although by royal standards they were poor, they were a happy, united family. Dagmar and Alix soon formed a special bond with Willie, which lasted all their lives. There was never the same close relationship between these three and their eldest brother Freddie. Dagmar, dark-haired with huge dark eyes, was smaller and altogether more vivacious than her elder sister. In a neat summing-up by their parents Alexandra was pronounced the most beautiful, Dagmar the cleverest, Thyra the sweetest-tempered and Willie the cutest.

Louise supervised much of their early education, teaching her daughters needlework and ensuring they would be proficient housekeepers. They were always plainly dressed and as they grew older made their own clothes. Shortage of money meant they had to change their smarter clothes immediately after outings so that nothing would be spoilt.

Music was taught by Miss Tuxen, piano and the harp by the composer F. Kuhlau. Although Alexandra and Thyra were more musical, Dagmar painted better and loved drawing. With her mother and sisters she took drawing lessons from Professor Buntzen and painting lessons from a variety of tutors including the flower painter I.L. Jensen.

Although the family spoke Danish among themselves, Dagmar also learnt German, Swedish and 'Scandinavian', a mixture of Swedish, Danish and Norwegian. Miss Mathilde Knudsen joined the household in 1858 to teach the children English. In 1863 their Swiss governess was replaced by Mlle Sidonie L'Escaille, a 'humane and sympathetic' Belgian lady recommended by the Empress of Russia, who taught Dagmar French and was still her confidante in 1921.[5] In a family completely lacking in intellectual interests Dagmar was the only one of the daughters who showed any inclination to read a book. Apart from a sound knowledge of religion, taught by Archdeacon Paulli, priest of the Royal Chapel at Christiansborg Slot, and history, taught by Professor Petersen, the girls received little else in the way of a formal education.

Throughout their lives all the girls loved dancing. They were lively and exceptionally athletic. Their father taught them gymnastics, handstands and cartwheels and all retained a supple figure into old age. In winter when snow lay thick upon the ground they skated along the canals, tobogganed or made up sleighing parties, warming themselves afterwards with doughnuts and hot punch. They loved all outdoor sports, especially riding at which Dagmar excelled. Louise insisted on them sleeping with open windows and being outdoors as much as possible, regardless of the weather. If they were ill she nursed them herself.

The children were well-known around Copenhagen and were often seen walking in the city, looking in shops whose goods were too expensive for them to buy, sitting down by the Nyhavn listening to the sailors tell their tales, or strolling through the Old Market where the women wore colourful national costumes. Dagmar and Alix particularly loved the long promenade of the Langeline by the Yacht Club. Their favourite pleasures were excursions to the sea or the woods, followed by coffee at a local inn. They were especially fond of feeding the swans and the herd of deer at the Dyrehaven (Deer Park) and were always surrounded by their small dogs and other pets.

The Yellow Mansion had a resident staff of six, including the governess, a nurse and two parlourmaids. Mme Marie von Flotow, who came from a rich and distinguished German family, was for a time Princess Louise's head lady's maid and there was also a lady's maid from Hesse.[6] The front door was opened by a maid, who showed visitors straight to Prince Christian. A frequent visitor was Hans Christian Andersen, who wrote many of his fairy tales for the children. Later in life they remembered his stories as one of the highlights of their childhood.

Meals were plain and simple. Usually there was a substantial breakfast of Øllebrød – black bread boiled in black beer, poured over a layer of brown sugar and mixed with thick cream. In summer there was Rødgrød – red fruit cooked with potato flour, swamped with sugar and cream. At lunchtime they helped themselves. On the servants' days off Dagmar and Alexandra waited at table, helped in the kitchen and assisted their mother in the running of the modest household. Louise supervised all the household books and accounts. Discipline was strict and good manners and punctuality were insisted upon especially at meals, although time-keeping was not the strong point of either Dagmar or Alix. Latecomers had to stand behind their chair during the first course, a punishment they minded less than the teasing of the servants afterwards. The children had a rough-and-tumble kind of humour and a liking for practical jokes which remained with them all their lives.

By the time Louise gave birth to her last child, Prince Waldemar, in 1858, the family's status had changed dramatically. Frederick VII was childless and the problem of the succession was urgent; Denmark was running out of heirs. The King's only male heir was his childless uncle Ferdinand and, on his death, the Duchies of Schleswig, Holstein and Lauenberg would revert to the Dukes of Augustenberg and Glucksburg, the German relatives of Dagmar's father. The Danes would then lose almost half of their kingdom. Schleswig, Holstein and Lauenberg were governed by Salic Law and, by ancient decree, must always remain united. The Duchies lay in the narrow strip of land between Denmark and Germany. Although they were administered by Denmark, Holstein, with its largely German population, was part of the German Confederation while Schleswig, with a predominantly Danish population, was not.

The Schleswig-Holstein question was very involved. Lord Palmerston once remarked that only three people had ever understood it: a German professor, who had gone mad; the Prince Consort, who was dead; and himself, who had forgotten all about it. Frederick VII therefore faced serious problems.

Twice-divorced Frederick was popular with the people but it was common knowledge that he was incapable of fathering children. King Louis Philippe of France, hearing a rumour that Frederick's wife was expecting a child, is said to have retorted, 'Well, God bless the father, whoever he is!'[7] He had been living happily for some years with his mistress, Louise Rasmussen, a former dancer, whom he married morganatically in 1850 and created Countess Danner. Society ostracized her because of the scandal and her presence killed off all Court life. The King's failure to provide an heir was to have a profound effect on Dagmar's childhood.

Soon after his accession in 1848 Frederick issued a United Constitution which ruled that Denmark, including the Duchies of Schleswig, Holstein and Lauenberg, should henceforth have one law of succession which could pass through the female line. The result was civil war between Holstein and Denmark. This was particularly painful for Prince Christian, whose family supported Holstein but, conscious of his duty, the prince sided with Denmark. In contrast Princess Louise's father and brother threw in their lot with Holstein, resigned their posts and left Copenhagen. Denmark defeated the rebels but throughout the following year the Duchies seethed with unrest.

In June 1848 the Danish Government altered the Law of Succession to exclude the Augustenburg and Glucksburg lines who had sided with the rebels. 'The Government would accept a son of the Grand Duke of Oldenburg who lives in Russia', reported the French Minister, 'or the son of Prince Christian of Glucksborg, who lives in Copenhagen and is the only one of his family who has taken Denmark's side'.[8] For the first time, Prince Christian's family figured in the dynastic question.

In 1849 Denmark became a constitutional, instead of an absolute, monarchy. After the King's uncle Ferdinand, the next heirs were Princess Charlotte and her son Prince Frederick of Hesse-Cassel, the mother and brother of Princess Louise, who were unpopular for siding with Holstein. Prince Christian's claim to the throne was through the female line but he had the support of Tsar Nicholas I of Russia who, as a Duke of Holstein-Gottorp, also had to be consulted. Finally, all the members of the Hesse-Cassel family including Princess Louise, who had a strong claim to the throne through her mother, were persuaded to renounce their rights to the Danish crown without knowing who would be the chosen successor. Louise canvassed tirelessly for her husband, writing to influential people all over Europe. Finally, on 8th May 1852, a settlement by the Great Powers guaranteed that the Duchies would remain attached to the Crown of Denmark and nominated Prince Christian heir to the throne after Prince Ferdinand.

In 1853 the King created Christian and his family Princes and Princesses of Denmark. Waldemar was thus the first child to be born a Prince of Denmark for fifty years. The King attended his christening and raised the family to the rank of Royal Highnesses.

One of the benefits Prince Christian received after becoming heir presumptive was the use of Bernstorff, a small, elegant eighteenth-century palace in a large park ten miles from Copenhagen. Its well-kept gardens and magnificent avenues of lime trees were ideal places for the children to play. Dagmar spent the long, happy summers of her childhood picnicking in the woods or riding for hours through the forest with Alexandra. They mixed with the local villagers, played with the children and accompanied their mother on visits to the old, sick or needy. As they grew older they were each given a small garden to cultivate. On Sundays the prince and his family walked to the service in the little red brick church at Gentofte, where they sat in high-backed wooden pews. Afterwards Dagmar and her brothers and sisters went down to the beach to play with the children of Copenhagen's burghers.

Apart from visits to Prince Christian's mother Duchess Louise at Louiselund and a short stay in Dieppe in the summer of 1855, Dagmar's only holidays were spent at Schloss Rumpenheim on the River Main near Frankfurt. The eighteenth-century castle had been the home of Princess Louise's grandfather, Landgrave Frederick of Hesse-Cassel, who left it equally to his six children with the proviso that they and their families reunite there every two years.

Each family, often twenty to thirty members plus servants, lived in one of the self-contained apartments and usually the modest sized Schloss was unbearably overcrowded. It was a very unsophisticated, cosmopolitan gathering of an affectionate family who enjoyed gossip, childish jokes, flirtations and matrimonial intrigues. To the members of Dagmar's family it was a place remembered with a thrill of nostalgia and the later family gatherings at Bernstorff and Fredensborg can be traced back to the influence of Rumpenheim. The atmosphere was best described by the German word 'gemutlich', comfortable.

Members of the family came from almost every part of Europe. Dagmar had the opportunity to meet her cousins, including the Duchess of Cambridge's two daughters Princess Augusta, Duchess of Mecklenburg-Strelitz and Princess Mary Adelaide, later the Duchess of Teck. Mary Adelaide wrote that she had 'completely lost [her] ... heart' to Louise's children[9] but Augusta seems to have developed a dislike for Dagmar.

The girls knew how to fight. Bernhard von Bulow, a childhood playmate of Dagmar and Alexandra and later Chancellor of Germany, recalled their rough treatment. Alexandra was already becoming a beauty but Dagmar, although lively and clever, impressed him as being 'a more vivid personality' and 'desperately hard-headed and obstinate'.[10]

In a life of simple pleasures all the children enjoyed the excitement of Christmas. On Christmas Eve the family assembled in the drawing room of the Yellow Mansion where there was a large Christmas tree with lights and ornaments. Each child had a smaller tree loaded with presents but, because of the tight budget, home-made gifts figured prominently. Later in the evening they gathered round the piano and sang traditional

Danish hymns. As they grew older, Dagmar, Alexandra and Thyra also took their turn as accompanists and from these humble beginnings sprang the eight-handed arrangements on two grand pianos with which Louise and her daughters delighted guests in later years. Christian and Louise, wrote one of the family, 'were the centre of everything'.[11]

There is a story that one day Dagmar and her sisters were discussing the future and each made a wish. Dagmar wished for power and influence; Thyra wished to be clever; and Alexandra to be loved. Dagmar's wish was granted but she had yet to learn that power and influence do not always bring happiness. Growing up in provincial Copenhagen far from the great world, without even a personal maid, Dagmar and Alexandra were both totally unprepared for the life fate had decreed for them.

*

By 1859 Prince and Princess Christian had already begun to discuss suitable marriages for their daughters. The first of these plans concerned fifteen-year-old Alexandra, who was blossoming into one of the most beautiful princesses in Europe. This was the beginning of the extraordinary elevation of the family which would place their descendants on Europe's thrones.

Thirteen-year-old Dagmar's chief attraction was her dark brown, velvety eyes. She was 'a dear little thing with a pretty figure and a very plain face – all excepting her eyes which are very pretty'.[12] Her elfin-like, sparkling face with a wide flashing smile had less regular features than Alix's and, although never a classic beauty, she was slender with the same flair for clothes as her sister. She was also more intelligent and quick-witted, with wider interests. Both had what Queen Victoria described as pretty manners but it was chiefly due to Alexandra's grace and beauty that the family's first dynastic achievement occurred.

Queen Victoria and Prince Albert were anxious to find a German bride for the Prince of Wales. They enlisted the aid of their eldest daughter Victoria ('Vicky') the Crown Princess of Prussia but she was having difficulty in finding a suitable princess who was both beautiful and charming, the qualities her brother Albert Edward ('Bertie') most admired.

Lady Walburga Paget, the young wife of the British Minister in Copenhagen, was a close friend and former lady-in-waiting of Vicky; her uncle, Count Alfred Hohenthal, was married to Prince Christian's sister. One evening at Windsor 'Wally' Paget found herself seated next to Prince Albert at dinner. She knew Prince Christian's family well and her glowing account of Alexandra so impressed him that he repeated it to the Queen, who asked Lady Paget to obtain a photograph and make some enquiries.

Queen Victoria had been against a Danish marriage from the beginning. There was increasing tension between Denmark and Germany over Schleswig-Holstein. The Queen's sympathies were pro-German. She particularly distrusted the gatherings at Rumpenheim and dreaded the influence of Princess Louise's mother and sisters, whom she considered immoral. 'The mother's family are bad – the father's foolish', she said. It would never do to have one of the 'Danish Camp' in the family.[13] Suddenly, swayed by Wally's eloquence, she changed her mind.

In May 1861 Vicky travelled to Neu-Strelitz, where Louise and her daughters were staying with Grand Duchess Augusta. 'Graceful, bewitching, indescribably charming' was her verdict on Alexandra, while to Wally she wrote, 'little Dagmar is a darling'.[14] The Queen was particularly anxious that the Duchess of Cambridge should not hear what was afoot, although the Cambridges 'always made more of ... Dagmar, who you say is plain but who they thought so very pretty'.[15]

On 24th September Prince Christian and his family set out from Rumpenheim for Speyer Cathedral. To Dagmar and the others it was just another outing but, unknown to them, the Crown Prince and Princess of Prussia were also heading for Speyer that day, with the Prince of Wales. The two parties met in the cathedral as if by chance and Bertie and Alexandra were discreetly left alone.

The astute Princess Louise now took over the Danish end of the negotiations. Although Dagmar was not quite fourteen, Louise hinted to her German relations that Tsar Alexander II of Russia was considering one of her daughters as a bride for the Tsarevitch. Then, in December, Prince Albert died and Louise's uncertainty increased as thoughts of Bertie's marriage were put aside. She had already rejected a tentative proposal from the Tsar (without, of course, consulting her daughter) and began to wonder whether she should have kept this ace up her sleeve.

Queen Victoria was determined that the marriage would go ahead as Albert had planned. Nevertheless, early in 1862 Vicky dashed off a warning: 'I hear that the Emperor of Russia has not given up his intention of asking for Alexandra or Dagmar for his son. Princess Christian feels very nervous now for fear that Bertie should not be in earnest after all, and for that case she would still wish to have the Tsarevitch in reserve'.[16] Louise was unwilling to let the Tsarevitch go without a firm proposal for either daughter from elsewhere.

Dagmar had already been rejected as a future daughter-in-law of Queen Victoria without even realising it. The Queen's handsome seventeen-year-old second son Alfred (who would one day succeed his uncle Ernst as Duke of Coburg) was serving in the Royal Navy. Naturally Victoria wanted a German marriage for him and in 1862, when touring the Scandinavian

Courts, he was pointedly told to avoid Copenhagen. Her wish that he should not meet Countess Danner cannot have been the Queen's only concern. Vicky now suggested Dagmar as his bride. 'I should be sorry if anything were decided for Dagmar before you had seen her as it would be one chance less for Affie', she wrote, 'and it is surely to be desired he should have as large a choice as possible'.[17]

The Queen vetoed this idea. 'Let the Emperor have her', she replied. Besides the undesirability of two brothers marrying two sisters, there had been such an outcry in Germany against Bertie's marriage 'that to go and make Affie, the future Duke of Coburg, take the other sister would be really courting abuse and enmity ...'[18]

Later that summer the British Chargé d'Affairs in Copenhagen reported that Prince and Princess Christian had taken their family to Ostend. This holiday, paid for by King Leopold of Belgium, was a pretext to meet his niece Queen Victoria at Laeken, the King's home. The meeting passed off well and just before lunch the prince and princess presented their daughters. 'Alexandra is lovely', wrote the Queen, 'such a beautiful, refined profile, and quiet, lady-like manner ... Dagmar is quite different, with fine brown eyes. Princess Christian must have been quite good-looking. She is unfortunately very deaf ...'[19] Later, while their parents talked alone, the Danish princesses had the opportunity to make friends with two of the Queen's daughters, Louise and Helena. A few days later the Prince of Wales proposed to Alix. There was no doubt that she would accept.

As she helped Alexandra with her trousseau, fifteen-year-old Dagmar must have wondered what fate had in store. There was still talk of Prince Alfred, although Queen Victoria would have none of it – but a much more glittering prize awaited Dagmar.

*

In February 1863 Prince Christian's family travelled to England for Alexandra's wedding. When the steamer left it was Dagmar who waved, smiled and chatted gaily while Alexandra sadly watched the shores of her native country fade into the distance. To the Danish children, who teased Alexandra remorselessly, the journey was one huge lark.

From Gravesend, where they were met by the Prince of Wales, carriages took them to Paddington Station. When the procession entered Hyde Park the crowds mistook Dagmar for the prince's bride and they began to cheer wildly before realising their mistake. All along the route they received an enthusiastic welcome and the tired travellers were several hours late by the time their train reached Windsor in pouring rain that evening. It was in a mood of excitement and curiosity that Dagmar followed her family into the castle where they were received by Queen

Victoria. Later Dagmar renewed her friendship with Louise, the Queen's daughter nearest in age to herself.

Despite the fact that the wedding was overshadowed by the Queen's mourning and she had used this excuse to exclude all but the very closest relatives – even the King of Denmark was not invited – the occasion was Dagmar's first taste of the pageantry that would become a way of life. After the ceremony she was among the forty-six witnesses who signed the marriage register. A notable absentee was Prince Alfred. Dagmar therefore missed the opportunity to meet the prince to whom she might have been betrothed.

While the newlyweds had a short honeymoon Dagmar and her family stayed at a London hotel. Prince and Princess Christian attended society balls and the children enjoyed themselves at the zoo. Before they returned to Denmark they tried to raise their spirits by holding a farewell party at Buckingham Palace. Dagmar was especially sad as Alexandra was her closest friend and confidante. From then on they wrote to each other every week, the forty volumes of letters written between 1867 and 1917 bearing silent witness to the bond between them, Alexandra's in an illegible hand that 'would have disgraced an intoxicated spider'.[20]

*

The next stage in the elevation of Dagmar's family occurred soon afterwards. The Greeks gained independence from the Ottoman Empire in 1830 and chose Prince Otto of Bavaria as their King. In 1862 a revolution forced King Otto off the throne and Greece was looking for a new ruler. This was proving difficult because of the turbulent state of the nation's politics but Greece's guaranteeing powers (France, Russia and Britain) finally agreed on seventeen-year-old Prince William of Denmark. The Greeks, hoping that a choice suggested by Britain would give them back the Ionian Islands, a British protectorate since 1815, readily accepted.

Once again Princess Louise took over the negotiations, ensuring that her son would receive double the proposed income, a pension if the Greeks deposed him and that he would not be required to convert to Orthodoxy. With matters finalised, on 30th March 1863 William was proclaimed King of the Hellenes.

He chose to reign as King George I and on 6th June Dagmar was present in the crowded throne room of Christiansborg Slot for the formal ceremony of acceptance, followed by a banquet. That year Punch published a cartoon showing a gang of Greek bandits, all armed to the teeth, guarding a mountain path. The caption read: 'Too bad for him. The first man who passes, we'll make him King!'[21]

*

A few weeks later the Hereditary Prince Ferdinand died, leaving Prince Christian heir to the Danish throne. His allowance was increased and Freddie was sent to Oxford University for a year to equip him for his future position.

That autumn Dagmar stayed with Alexandra and Bertie at Sandringham, in the flat countryside of Norfolk, which reminded the sisters so much of Denmark. Alexandra was expecting her first baby and there was much for them to talk about.

While Dagmar was there news arrived of the death of King Frederick on 15th November and the accession of her father as King Christian IX. Now, as the daughter of the King of Denmark and the sister of the King of Greece and the Princess of Wales, she was suddenly one of the most eligible princesses in Europe. Her marriage prospects were bright indeed.

CHAPTER 2

Two Brothers

'HE IS AT PEACE, FOUND WORTHY
OF ANOTHER AND FINER CROWN ...
NOT OF THIS WORLD, THIS HERITAGE,
HE, OUR JOY SINCE BIRTH, HE WAS NOT OURS,
HE BELONGED TO GOD ...'
                    – Feodor Tiutchev (1803-73)

Dagmar and her family spent a miserable Christmas. They all missed Willie, now in Greece and Alix, awaiting her confinement in England. Then, on 9th January 1864 news arrived that Alix had prematurely given birth to a son, Albert Victor, the previous evening. There was anxiety about her condition and it was several days before reassuring news arrived.

Meanwhile, the Schleswig-Holstein crisis had grown more acute and King Christian was preparing for war. When Frederick VII died he left an unsigned joint constitution which would incorporate Schleswig (but not Holstein) into the Danish kingdom. When King Christian reluctantly signed the document soon after his accession, a storm of protest erupted in the Duchies. He withdrew his troops from Holstein, making it clear that he was prepared to fight for Schleswig. Prussian troops occupied Holstein and it was soon apparent that neither William I of Prussia nor his Minister-President, Bismarck, had any desire for peace. Bismarck was starting on his policy of 'blood and iron' and had decided that the duchies should belong to Prussia. As a first step he allowed the Duke of Augustenburg to proclaim himself Duke Frederick VIII of Schleswig-Holstein.

On 1st February Prussian and Austrian troops invaded Denmark. Neither England nor any of the other Great Powers would come to the aid of the beleagured Danes. Alix was ill with worry over the plight of her family and country; Dagmar feared she would never be able to visit England again.

Dagmar was old enough to appreciate the suffering caused to her parents and to the Danish people as the carts of wounded arrived. On

5th February, having already abandoned Holstein and Lauenberg to the Germans without firing a shot, the Danes were forced to abandon the Dannevirke, the strongly fortified wall built as a defence against Germany. The people remembered King Christian's German blood, calling him a traitor, or 'the German' and riots broke out in Copenhagen. By the end of February, Prussian and Austrian troops had overrun Danish Schleswig and by March part of Jutland was occupied.

This was a difficult time for all the Royal family. To add to their sorrow, Dagmar's grandmother Princess Charlotte, the Landgravine of Hesse-Cassel, died. The atmosphere in the capital was ugly. One Sunday morning as they drove home from church Dagmar and Thyra were taunted by the crowd and Freddie was spat upon.

In April a conference was held in London to arrange an armistice but the Prussians wanted nothing less than complete political independence for the Duchies. When Denmark refused, the war was renewed and Sonderburg fell. In June the Prussians conquered Als and occupied the whole of Jutland. King Christian had no choice but to submit to the terms of the Allied powers. He sent his brother Prince Hans to Brussels to beg for King Leopold's help as intermediary at the Vienna Peace Conference.

*

During 1864 Dagmar and her family moved to their new summer home Fredensborg, 'Castle of Peace', set in a vast park near Copenhagen. It reminded Queen Louise of 'an enchanted castle in its century-long sleep'.[1]

The State Apartments had been renovated by Frederick VII. The outstanding feature was the big square hall under the cupola in the main building. All the first floor rooms opened onto a gallery overlooking this hall where the family assembled for dinner. Their private apartments were very simply furnished but at least sixteen-year-old Dagmar now had her own room with a view across the park. Although Freddie had been recalled from Oxford, life had become rather dull for her since Alix and Willie left home. As there had been no Queen of Denmark for some years, Dagmar helped her mother revive Court etiquette.

The apparent weakness of King Christian's position now had dynastic advantages. Tsar Alexander II was looking for a bride for the Tsarevitch but he wanted a marriage that would be considered non-political. During June 1864, with Denmark soundly trounced by Prussia, the diplomats earnestly began to discuss the possibility of Dagmar's marriage to Tsarevitch Nicholas. Nobody could conceivably see any political advantage in this match. The Emperor was no stranger to King Christian, who had met him several times when he stayed in Russia during his youth;

Queen Louise's brother Frederick had been briefly married to the Tsar's sister Alexandra, who died in childbirth.

In August the Empress Marie Alexandrovna informed the Danish Court that, as part of his European tour, her eldest son would be arriving at Fredensborg the following month. The astute and ambitious Queen Louise immediately recognised the significance of this visit even if her daughter did not and it was therefore with some embarrassment that she had to welcome another suitor for Dagmar's hand. Alexandra's stunning beauty was the talk of Europe, so it was hardly surprising that other unmarried princes should look towards Denmark.

Twenty-year-old Crown Prince Umberto of Italy was also in search of a bride. Although he was impressed with Dagmar he was not the kind of man to turn a young girl's head. He received no encouragement and, to Louise's relief, no proposal was forthcoming. With one daughter married to the future King of England, Louise saw no reason why Dagmar should marry anyone less than the Tsarevitch.

Nicholas ('Nixa') was a 'romantic figure'. Almost twenty-one he was tall, handsome, slim, intelligent and accomplished, quite unlike his lusty, rugged brothers. He was well-read, wrote poetry and had travelled widely. His father saw a worthy successor in this favourite son, who had inherited something of his own mind and liberal tendencies, although Nicholas was against the emancipation of the serfs, telling his father prophetically that 'it will never bring anything but misfortune to the country'.[2] His doting mother supervised every step of his education, often to the detriment of her other children.

Dagmar would be seventeen in November and had not been confirmed into the Lutheran Church. The princess would be free to convert to Orthodoxy, as she would be required to do before marrying the Tsarevitch. 'Dagmar is cleverer [than Alexandra]', wrote Queen Victoria, 'and would I am sure be very fit for the position in Russia; she is a very nice girl'.[3] Nicholas had been given Dagmar's photograph as long ago as 1860, when she was twelve and the Tsar had made the first tentative feelers about the possibility of a marriage. He had fallen in love with her from afar and had been collecting pictures of her ever since.

It was almost a foregone conclusion that Dagmar would be attracted to Nicholas; he, in turn, found himself enchanted by 'charming Minny', the tiny, vivacious princess with her hair in a neat chignon, who greeted him in a light summer dress under a black pinafore. He found her even prettier than in her photographs. Alexandra gave her sister moral support and helped arrange undisturbed meetings, with the result that Dagmar and Nixa soon fell deeply in love.

In mid-September, having sounded out Freddie about his prospects for a successful outcome, Nixa left for Germany to celebrate his twenty-first birthday with his parents at Heiligenberg and ask permission to propose.

When Nixa returned to ask King Christian for his daughter's hand he was given an encouraging response, although the King insisted he would have to ask Dagmar himself. Christian then explained matters to his daughter, who said she was ready to talk to the Tsarevitch.

The ground thus prepared, on 28th September during the afternoon walk at Bernstorff Dagmar and Nicholas were discreetly allowed to fall behind to allow the young man to make his proposal. She responded with a heartfelt 'yes'. He kissed her and they squeezed each others' hands.

The betrothal was announced at a Court dinner and the Lord High Steward proposed a toast. 'The betrothal took place today', wrote an observer, 'now the Queen is happy'.[4] Nixa's mother had given him a medallion with little horse-shoes to present to his fiancée, which she immediately put around her neck. Later, she added some lines to his letter to the Empress, expressing her happiness.

The next few days were idyllic for Dagmar. They exchanged confidences and she blushed when she saw his large collection of her photographs. Shortly before Nixa left for Germany they carved their names on a window with a diamond ring: 'Nicolai-Dagmar, le 11 Octobre, 1864'. Dagmar's happiness shone through but Lady Paget noticed Nicholas' 'worn, aged face and his pale lustreless blue eyes', in sharp contrast to his fiancée in her 'bright pink barège frock, her eyes sparkling and her shining hair' who seemed 'ill-matched to the delicate Tsarevitch'.[5]

Dagmar's betrothal gifts were a foretaste of what was to come: the Tsar and Tsarina sent her a six-row pearl collar and from her fiancé she received a bracelet with three pearl stars. It had already been decided that on conversion to the Orthodox Church she would take the name Maria, in accordance with Nixa's dearest wish.

Meanwhile the peace conference was underway and Dagmar decided to try and help her father. On 29th October she wrote to the Tsar to enlist his support:

My dear Papa,

Forgive me that I approach you, this time with a request, my first, which I address to you; but when I see my poor Papa and our country bending under the yoke of injustice, I naturally feel drawn towards you, my dear Papa, by bonds of love and trust. Therefore I come as a daughter to her father, and in asking you to use your power to mitigate the terrible conditions which the Germans have brutally forced Papa to accept, I am showing you how deep my trust in you already is, in that, unbeknown to my Father, I am asking you for help and protection, if that is possible, against our dreadful enemies.

I hope, dear Papa, that you will not find your future daughter-in-law too obtrusive, but the sad plight of my fatherland, which makes my heart heavy, has inspired me to turn to you as he who can be our providence. In giving you a sincere kiss, I ask you to kiss my dear Mama's hands, not forgetting the dear brothers and Marie, and I remain your devoted and obedient daughter,

Dagmar Marie.[6]

The letter, Dagmar's first excursion into politics, undoubtedly sent with Queen Louise's consent, had no effect. The peace terms were harsh. Defeated Denmark had to cede Schleswig, Holstein and Lauenberg to Austria and Prussia. Within months of his accession King Christian had been forced to relinquish almost half his kingdom. In November, after the signing of the peace treaty, Dagmar told Nixa that it was not much of a treaty for Denmark. She was sad that her country was enduring such suffering because of the brute force of the Prussians.

From that time onwards Dagmar hated the Germans as a nation and the Hohenzollerns in particular. She never forgave them for plundering her father's kingdom and for his consequent humiliation. When Nixa left Germany she was delighted and, in her letter of 4th November, railed against the 'barbarians' so much that she had to stop, for fear of turning even more nasty. This dislike was general in the family and was to have far-reaching consequences when Dagmar and Alexandra carried their undying hatred to their adopted countries.

*

Nixa continued his European tour through Germany to Italy. For Dagmar's seventeenth birthday he sent her a beautiful medallion encrusted with precious stones which spelt out the words 'For Ever!' in Russian. They wrote to each other twice a week, the words 'Dushka' and 'little darling' appearing frequently in their correspondence.

Only one shadow clouded Dagmar's happiness and that was her fiancé's health. While Nixa was riding with her in Denmark he was forced to slow down because of pains in his back. He had always been delicate and, while still a boy, was frequently taken to German health resorts. Four years earlier he had hurt his spinal column when he fell from his horse and he now began to experience violent pains in his backbone.

On 22nd November he arrived in Florence, where he was confined to bed for six weeks. In her letter of 6th December Dagmar expressed her first worries about his health, although the Empress was still telling her brother that Nixa had rheumatism. As his condition worsened his letters to Dagmar became less frequent.

In her letter of 3rd January 1865 Dagmar wished the Tsar luck for the New Year, but the year was destined to be the unhappiest of her short life. On New Year's Day Nixa left on board a warship to join his mother in the French Riviera, where she had been spending the winter. He had difficulty in walking and lay prostrate on his bed. Nice had always been a favourite haunt of the Imperial family and Russian high society, many of whom owned villas in the aristocratic quarter of Cimiez. The Empress found the mild climate beneficial to her failing health and now, as Nicholas moved into the Villa Diesbach near the sea, she hoped it would have the same effect on her son.[7]

In Denmark, King Christian and Queen Louise had left the Yellow Mansion for their official residence, the Schacks Palace at the Amalienborg. There a courtier arrived from Russia to arrange for Dagmar to meet the Tsarina in Nice and, more optimistically, to discuss the wedding. Dagmar asked if she could select a doctor and a secretary to accompany her to Russia. She also received instruction in the Orthodox religion from Father Yanishev. Although her family were deeply-rooted in the Lutheran faith they were not bigoted. 'When the Grand Duke was here last he frankly raised the religious question in a conversation with the Queen', wrote a courtier. '"We don't, of course, believe all that the common people cling to!" he said …'[8] The Danish clergy were unhappy. Archdeacon Paulli was told he could speak to Dagmar if she wished but the princess declined. She had made up her mind.

Dagmar also started to learn the Russian language and study Russian literature. Five of her notebooks are preserved, which show that she read Pushkin's 'A Winter's Day in St Petersburg', biographies of Turgenev and Gogol and biographical notes on Lermonotov and other prominent Russians. In one of the books are her short answers to historical questions.

Nixa had promised to be back in Denmark for King Christian's birthday in April but in February disquieting reports about his health appeared in the newspapers. 'The King and Queen of Denmark', a diplomat reported, 'are much disturbed in mind and the little Princess very unhappy. Her necessary change of religion diminishes in Danish eyes the glamour of her Russian marriage. The future Grand Duchess is busy learning Russian, but people are wondering whether she will ever need it'.[9]

By March Nixa had moved to the Villa Bermont, which was actually a vast estate with five villas away from the noise of the sea. Dagmar was impatient to see him and begged him not to expose himself to the cold. Her one desire was to be with her angel Nixa, so that she could tell him how much she loved him. Walking with difficulty one day in the Valley of Flowers, Nixa confided to a friend that he loved Dagmar so much he dared not speak of her for fear of losing control of his emotions. She wrote delightedly of a future he dared not contemplate. A photograph of the Anitchkov Palace, which was to be their home, filled her with varying emotions and pictures of a happy family life together.

Although Nixa had his own visions of their future, by 7th March he was so despondent that he told Dagmar poignantly that his dreams were all he had left. Even if only a tenth of their wishes were fulfilled, he wrote, it would ensure that they were happier than anyone else in the world.

For several weeks there was no word from Nixa and on 7th April Dagmar despondently wrote what was to be her last letter to him. She could not understand why she had heard nothing from him since 20th March, when she only lived for his next letter. Perhaps, she continued only half-jokingly, he had fallen in love with a beautiful black-eyed Italian girl and forgotten his Danish fiancée. She followed this the next day with a telegram.

The response was shattering. On Easter Monday Queen Louise received a telegram announcing a deterioration in the Tsarevitch's condition. He had suddenly become nervous, feverish and complained of blurred vision. Soon afterwards he suffered a cerebral haemorrhage, leaving one side of his body temporarily paralysed. After a consultation between the six doctors and Professor Zdekauer, summoned hastily from St Petersburg, the Empress was informed that her son had cerebrospinal meningitis. His condition was serious. 'Hence his whole treatment has been absolutely wrong for months past', she told her brother.[10]

Within hours a second telegram arrived from the Tsar: 'Nicholas has received the Last Rites. Pray for us, and come if you are able to'.[11] Shocked and distraught, Dagmar prepared to leave with her mother and Mlle L'Escaille. At the same time the Tsar and his sons Vladimir and Alexis left Russia to meet Dagmar's party and Freddie at Dijon. The Tsar's second son Alexander (Sasha) had already left for Nice. They raced across Europe, stopping only for a few moments at Lyons where Napoleon III expressed his sympathy. Although all ordinary passenger trains were cancelled to allow them to pass, Dagmar was haunted by the fear that they would not arrive in time.

They reached Nice on Friday. The Villa Bermont was a lovely place, with fountains, cypress groves, masses of parma violets and, it was said, over two hundred thousand orange trees but as Dagmar sat by the bed of her dying fiancé, who only months before had been so full of life, she noticed none of it. Her feelings can scarcely be imagined. Rumours had been flying round – she was to be married to Nicholas on his death-bed; she would marry the next heir to the throne; even that, after the Tsarina's death, the Tsar would marry her himself. Twice the doctors thought the end had come but each time Nixa, dosed with a mixture of musk and champagne, rallied. Dagmar never forgot the smell of musk in the sick-room. At eight o'clock in the evening of 23rd April Dr Oppolzer arrived from Vienna and, after a superficial examination, also diagnosed cerebral meningitis. That morning, as Dagmar came into the room, Nixa whispered to the Tsarina, 'Isn't she just charming?'[12]

The following day, 24th April 1865, as the Russian Orthodox priests chanted prayers, Nixa died, a tear on his cheek.

On 4th May Queen Louise described his death in a moving letter to Queen Victoria:

> Your sympathy gave great pleasure to me and to my child, so severely tried so early in life ... She tells me that she would not for the world have missed the past, short but happy as it was, and his look, as the Tsar led her by the hand up to his bed, I shall never forget! It was of the purest happiness, and he recognised *her* the whole day when he was dying! He said goodbye to her, kissed her and held her hand firmly in his until he died! We had travelled for four days and four nights and she never left his bedside, kneeling by him day and night until 1 o'clock when she kissed him and he breathed away his young life! For me it was terrible, for I loved him very much, and saw all the happiness of the poor young bride-to-be ebbing away ... Minny is at Darmstadt for a day, to see the parents again. The whole dear family is so kind and loving to her that the parting is doubly painful for her.[13]

There is a story that just before his death Nixa called Dagmar and Alexander to his bedside and clasped their hands together, begging them to marry. He told the distraught Dagmar that his brother was a much better man and asked Alexander to make her happy. Although the story is uncorroborated, it is clear from later events that both Sasha and Dagmar thought this was Nixa's wish.

The following few days were particularly trying for Dagmar. The next evening she said her last farewell to the fiancé she would never see again and asked permission to keep the cross from by his bed.

Although she found it painful to write, Dagmar poured out her heart to her father, telling him how glad she was to have seen, and be recognised, by Nixa before he died. Just to remember the look of love on his face was a consolation in her unhappiness. King Christian who, unlike Dagmar, was prepared for Nixa's death, had sent his daughter a letter which touched her deeply. Dagmar was now concerned that, when she returned home, her nervous state and unhappiness would only add to her father's present troubles. She vowed to get a grip on herself.

After the Orthodox Mass in the bedroom of the villa, the coffin was borne by torchlight to the Orthodox Church in the rue Longchamp for a funeral service. On 28th April, covered with flowers, it was transported to Villefranche and placed on board the Russian warship *Alexander Nevsky* for the sad journey back to St Petersburg. The Empress donated Nixa's icon of St Nicholas the Miracle Worker to the Russian Church. There had been no miracle for Nixa.

Queen Louise took her daughter to Rumpenheim for a few days rest.

1. *The death of the Tsarevitch at the Villa Bermont, Nice.*
(Der Kongelige Bibliotek/Illustreret Tidende, Copenhagen)

On 4th May Dagmar and Freddie visited the Tsar and Tsarina at Heiligenberg, the home of the Tsarina's brother Prince Alexander of Hesse and
his family. It was a sad reunion. Sasha was crying because he missed his
brother and felt unprepared to be the heir and there were constant memorial services for Nixa. 'Poor child', the Tsar murmured as Dagmar left.
'Who knows', replied Prince Alexander, 'she may yet become a member
of your family'. To which the Tsar replied, 'she would certainly be
welcome'.[14]

Dagmar returned to Copenhagen in a daze and her family rallied round
to try and ease the blow. Nor did Russia forget her. She received a gift of
a lapis lazuli crucifix and an Orthodox Bible from the ladies of the aristocracy. A letter of sympathy came from the University of Helsingfors in
Finland, where Nixa had been Chancellor.

As the funeral ship came close to the Danish coast the King and Crown
Prince went aboard to pay their respects. Only Freddie attended the
funeral. He carried a letter to the Tsarina from Dagmar and also one from
Queen Louise, which shows that already the plans for Dagmar's future
were being laid. Louise was being cautious and had not mentioned
marriage with Sasha, for fear of ruining their schemes and driving her
daughter away from the new Tsarevitch. As for Sasha, she urged the
Tsarina to show equal caution and give him time to think about it.

Queen Louise and Dagmar maintained a regular correspondence with
the Tsarina (whom she still addressed as 'beloved Mama'), whose dream
now was that Dagmar should marry Sasha. To facilitate this, she wished
Dagmar to come to Russia as soon as possible but Louise refused to be
pressurised, insisting that her daughter's fragile nerves needed rest and
peace. Despite her formal protestations, Louise continued to work behind
the scenes for Dagmar's marriage and it is significant that the Russian
lessons and religious instruction were resumed later in the year.

Dagmar began to write to Sasha as a 'sister and friend' but she was
afraid for the future. Despite her mother's precautions she had already
heard of their plans. On 22nd May she wrote to the Tsar, addressing him
as 'Papa', saying that Sasha must be really certain he wanted to marry her.
She hoped 'Papa' would understand that she did not want to be blamed
later if Sasha was unhappy.

By September Dagmar was ill. She had a high fever, headaches, pains
in the abdomen and was unable to eat. Her nerves were in shreds and her
hair had to be cut short, although many attributed this to ancient mourning ritual. After her recovery she was still very shaky for some time and
did not even want to ride, although it was her favourite pastime. It
reminded her too much of the time Nixa first complained of back pains.

Sympathy for Dagmar was widespread and there was much speculation

2. *The coffin of Tsarevitch Nicholas arriving at the Russian Church in Nice.*
(Det Kongelige Bibliotek/Illustreret Tidende, Copenhagen)

about her future. Rumours still circulated that she would marry the new
Tsarevitch. 'I pity ... poor Princess Dagmar very much as I believe it was
quite a marriage of inclination ...' Lord Clarendon commented. 'I
wonder whether she has finally become Greek in her religion – if so it will
hardly do to turn back to Protestantism ... I have a notion that in the
Greek Church betrothal is an important ceremony and that being made
thereby as good as the wife of the Czarewitch she could not be passed on
to the next Brother ... How the brilliant prospects of that Danish family
have faded away. The King is deprived of half his territory – his son the
King of Greece is likely to be kicked out any moment and his Daughter
instead of being Empress of Russia is simply une demoiselle à marier'.[15]

*

Grand Duke Alexander was a complete contrast to his gifted elder brother.
He and Nicholas had been very close. Sasha, born on 10th March 1845,
was a mere seventeen months younger, but he did not have the same care
taken over his education. As boys they studied together but, as they grew
older, their paths diverged – Nicholas was prepared for his future as
Emperor; Sasha for the army. Not by any means clever, his slow, ponder-
ous brain was nevertheless equipped with sound common sense and a rigid
code of morality. Although he spoke French, English and German he
remained a bad linguist and his spelling, even in Russian, was poor. He
had a deep horror of war which stayed with him all his life and he never
possessed the love of military manoeuvres and parades so evident in the
other Romanovs.

At 6 feet 3 inches he was the tallest Romanov since Peter the Great but
with this height went a heavy build and a complete lack of grace – he
shambled along like a great Russian bear. His physical strength was amaz-
ing. He could straighten horse-shoes with his bare hands, bend iron bars
and smash through doors with his massive shoulders. His health was excellent and his appetite enormous. Behind his somewhat gruff exterior and
rather formidable appearance there was a placid, even-tempered, generous man who was devoted to his family, loved animals and children and
was almost transparently honest. At a ball he responded to the formal
thank you of a German princess: 'Why can't you be honest? It was just a
duty neither of us could have relished. I have ruined your slippers and you
have made me nearly sick with the scent you use'.[16]

As a young Guards officer he was conscientious but, in contrast to other
members of the family, never a really proficient rider. Outside of the
regiment and his family he had few interests. Unsociable in public, the
round of off-duty pleasures associated with, and almost expected of, a
Grand Duke did not appeal to him.

When Nixa died and he realised that his life as a Guards officer was at an end he had to study hard to remedy the defects in his education. Although there were rumours that he would be passed over in favour of his talented younger brother Vladimir, Alexander was formally proclaimed Tsarevitch the day after Nixa's death.

Sasha was a reluctant heir. For some time he had been in love with the beautiful Princess Marie Elimovna Mestchersky, one of his mother's maids of honour but he was now under pressure from his parents to marry Dagmar. As the pressure mounted he tried to stop seeing Marie. 'I still miss M.E.', he confided to his diary on 7th July 1865. 'I was accustomed to seeing her every morning and evening ... Since I came to Peterhof, I have thought more about Dagmar and pray to God every day to arrange this matter, which will mean my happiness for the rest of my life'.[17]

Yet he still wavered between his passion for Marie and his duty and continued to see her. Marie was his first love but by the following spring he had resigned himself to marriage with Dagmar. 'I will say goodbye to M.E., whom I loved as I loved no-one before', he wrote in April 1866. 'So many times I wanted to end this love and sometimes I succeeded for a while, but then everything was the same again. Spring and autumn in 1865 at Tsarskoe Selo will always remain in my memory ...'[18] By May he had changed his mind again. 'I want to refuse to marry Dagmar, whom I cannot love and don't want ... I don't want any wife but M.E. ...'[19]

A few days later he told his father that he could not go to Denmark and did not want to get married. There was an angry scene, during which Sasha said he wanted to renounce his rights to the throne because of his love for Marie. Anyway, he did not feel adequate for the position as heir.

The Tsar was furious. He replied that Marie would be sent away. News of the liaison had reached Denmark and threatened to ruin his plans. He ordered his son to go to Copenhagen. Sasha noted sadly in his diary that he and Marie kissed for the last time and said goodbye in a side room at Tsarskoe Selo. Although he had begged his father not to let Marie suffer because of him, she was packed off to Paris, hastily married to Prince Paul Demidov and died in childbirth in 1868.

In Copenhagen people began to speak more and more about the possibility of Dagmar's marriage to the new Tsarevitch. The idea had first been mentioned in the newspaper *Folkets Avis* early in 1866 and was repeated in *Faedrelandet* on 9th March. Speculation reached its height when, in June, Tsarevitch Alexander arrived at Fredensborg with his brother Vladimir. Dagmar learnt of his imminent arrival with mixed feelings.

Sasha confided to his diary that his heart beat faster when he saw Dagmar again after a year and he realised he wanted to marry her. To his father's delight he wrote saying he was sure he and Dagmar could be happy.

Over the next couple of weeks Sasha was given every opportunity to get to know Dagmar and her family. One evening after dinner she took his hand firmly. Encouraged, he spoke to Freddie and shortly afterwards King Christian gave him permission to propose. In his diary entry for 17th June Sasha wrote of his constant hope that everything would work out as he wished.

Sasha had several opportunities to speak to her but could not bring himself to do so. Finally, on 23rd June, while they were sitting on the sofa in her room reading Nixa's letters and looking at photographs, he plucked up the courage to propose.

He described in his diary how Dagmar almost threw herself at him and embraced him. He asked her if she could ever love him after dear Nixa. Her reply was immediate. Saying that she could never love anyone else, only her beloved, Dagmar embraced and kissed him passionately.

As the family came to congratulate them they both dissolved into tears. Later they all drove to the woods at Hellebaek Strand. Queen Louise had ordered the Hofmarshall to bring champagne and during lunch the King proposed a toast.

Reporting the news to the Empress Marie Alexandrovna, Queen Louise said that the couple shed many tears but thanks to Alexis, Sasha's younger brother, a naval cadet, who had also arrived in Copenhagen, they finished the day happily. She added that Dagmar and Sasha both seemed pleased.

Dagmar also wrote to the Empress, proud to be called her daughter again. Her one wish, she said, was to make Sasha happy and be for him what she had not been permitted to be for Nixa. This, she felt, was also Nixa's wish.

The idea that Nixa wished them to marry seemed to be uppermost in their minds. Sasha told Dagmar that he would always be grateful to Nixa for his happiness, as it was his brother who had given her to him as his bride.

On 28th June Sasha sadly returned home. Two days later Dagmar wrote to her 'Dushka Sasha' saying how unhappy she was to be parted from him and how much she loved him. She longed for his embrace and to hear him call her 'dushka'. He was equally miserable and begged his 'angel Minny' to send him a big picture of her and also one of her wearing a tight riding-habit – like an amazon.

Sasha was now impatient for his bride. The wedding was originally to be in the spring but the Tsar and Tsarina suddenly announced that they wanted it to take place in November. Louise was disappointed. She wanted to take Dagmar to England to see Alix and let her go to Russia in the spring, to avoid the Russian winter. Now Dagmar would have to go to St Petersburg instead. She would also have to learn the customs of the Court and get to know the Imperial family. Coming straight from Copenhagen, where her father still practised rigid economies in his private life, she would have a lot to learn.

Queen Louise and the Empress corresponded about the bride's trousseau. Louise said that Dagmar nearly always wore white. The Queen also requested that Dagmar's Danish maid Sophie, who had cared for her faithfully when she was ill, should remain permanently in Russia. She wanted no repetition of Alexandra's suffering in England, with no-one from home for company. The Empress appointed Mme Marie von Flotow, whom Queen Louise thought highly of, as Dagmar's lady's maid and she came from her home in Mitau, Latvia, to follow the princess to Russia.

Not only Denmark was gripped by Dagmar-fever. In July the Honourable Gustavus Fox, Assistant Secretary of the U.S. Navy, arrived in Copenhagen on the *Miantonomoh* and invited the Royal family to visit the ship. Dagmar, wearing a blue and white striped dress and a pink hat, attracted the most attention, the Americans being keen to see the Tsarevitch's bride. 'She is possessed of more than ordinary personal beauty', wrote Fox. 'She has an oval face, regular in outline, a brilliant complexion, glossy brown hair, and bright intelligent eyes. She conversed with freedom, speaking English fluently and correctly ... and displayed a thorough knowledge of the general topics discussed'. Two days later Fox and his party dined at Bernstorff.[20]

On 7th September there was a Court Ball at Christiansborg Slot. On 19th there was a dinner in her honour at Bernstorff, at which Grand Duke Alexis and thirty members of the Danish Royal family were present. Hans Christian Andersen wrote a poem in Dagmar's honour and theatres, ships and hotels bore her name. Even a fashion paper called *Dagmar* was launched. Deputations from all parts of the country presented wedding gifts. The South Jutland delegates were led by an extremely handsome man who held her hand for a long time. 'Little princess', he said gazing into her eyes, 'put in a good word for us with your father-in-law'.[21]

On 22nd September Dagmar set off for her new country. Danish and Russian flags lined her route from Bernstorff to the Amalienborg. At the harbour a guard of honour was provided by the garrison of Copenhagen and the Commanding Officer of the Royal Danish Life Guards presented her with a photograph album. Although Queen Louise had been invited to accompany her daughter she felt that two leave-takings would be too much. Dagmar therefore left for Russia accompanied by her brother Freddie, her small dog Beauty, her Danish bible and, significantly, all Nixa's letters. Among her large entourage were three ladies' maids,

Doctor Plum, her former governess Sidonie L'Escaille, Queen Louise's Mistress of the Robes Ida Bille-Brahe and, as A.D.C., Lieutenant Wenzel Dineson of the Royal Guards, a cousin of the writer Karen Blixen.[22]

The whole family accompanied Dagmar on board the Royal Yacht *Slesvig* to say goodbye. When the King, Queen, Thyra and Waldemar transferred to a smaller vessel and sailed away, Dagmar locked herself in her cabin and tried to regain her composure. In her diary she described the dreadful, heartbreaking moment of parting. She was comforted a little when the Lord Chamberlain presented her with a parrot. In a letter that Dagmar carried with her, Queen Louise begged the Empress to have patience with her daughter's homesickness and tears. Time, and Dagmar's love for all her new family, would help her to get over it.

When the *Slesvig* reached the limit of territorial waters the Danish escort ship, the *Peder Skram* dropped back and, in a symbolic gesture, the Russian ships steamed past. As the band played the song 'In Denmark I Was Born, There I Belong', one of those on board the yacht heard the princess murmur a hearty 'yes'.

Dagmar must have realised that the informality of her past life was gone for ever. From now on her actions would be governed by the rigid etiquette of the Imperial Court of Russia.

PART 2

TSAREVNA

(1866-1881)

CHAPTER 3

Imperial Russia

'A YOUNG LIFE IS THUS BEING SOLD AND SACRIFICED
TO THE DOCTRINES OF THE GREATER CONVENTIONS'

The Tsar's domains covered one sixth of the land surface of the earth; as the sun set at one end of the Empire it rose again at the other. It was a land of strange contrasts. To the north-west was St Petersburg, the new capital built by Peter the Great; to the east lay the frozen wastes of Siberia, stretching up towards the Arctic.

Over seventy-five per cent of the population were peasants, who lived in small isolated villages and worked the land for six months of the year. When the snow lay thick on the ground, they huddled, starving, inside their log huts. Until 1861 one third of them had been serfs who could be bought, sold and mortgaged like cattle.

Russia was still fighting in the Crimea when Alexander II succeeded his father. A liberal, he instituted a series of reforms. The Emancipation Act of 1861 was followed by the Zemstvo Statute in 1864, providing for elected local government councils and the reorganisation of the judicial system, the introduction of trial by jury and the creation of an independent judiciary. When Alexander abolished serfdom he was hailed as the 'Tsar-Liberator' but there were dangerous undercurrents in the rejoicing. The peasants thought they were being made a gift – riots broke out when they realised they had received only half the land they had previously cultivated, and that they would also have to pay taxes and make redemption payments. Their hatred was not directed against the Tsar, their 'Little Father'. As the ultimate resort of the oppressed, he had always been loved. 'It is very high up to God! It is very far to the Tsar!' ran an old Russian saying.[1]

For these people, most of whom lived and died in the villages where they were born, the Orthodox Church provided the only relief from their monotonous existence. Every cottage had its beautiful corner, an icon with a small lamp burning before it. They stood for hours in the churches, regardless of age or infirmity, while the chanting of the priests and the heady perfume of the incense made the senses soar. In the richly ornamented cathedrals the clergy in gold robes with bejewelled icons, crosses and mitres provided an almost overwhelming display of colour and ritual.

Moscow was the centre of the Orthodox Church, the Holy City. The hub of the city was, as it is now, the Kremlin. With its red brick walls and towers rising from the banks of the Moscow river, its many churches and, predominant, the 266-foot high golden-domed bell tower, it presented a fairy-tale appearance. Just outside, in Red Square, was the Cathedral of St Basil, a fantasy of multi-coloured domes and steeples of various shapes and sizes, 'a masterpiece of caprice', as the Marquis de Custine called it, today almost the image of Russia in western eyes. It was built in the sixteenth century for Ivan the Terrible, who was reputedly so delighted that he had the architects blinded so that they could never build another.

Moscow was a great industrial and artistic centre but, although it was still the city where the Tsars returned to be crowned, it had long since ceased to be the capital of Imperial Russia.

In the early eighteenth century, while still at war with Sweden, Peter the Great built a new capital out of the marshes where the mouth of the River Neva meets the Gulf of Finland. According to legend, St Petersburg owed its beauty on such an unpromising site to the fact that the city was built in the sky, then lowered down to earth in one piece.[2]

Peter had travelled widely in Europe and wanted to wrench Russia from the old traditions and implant western ideas. The symbol of Peter's Russia was to be his new capital, his 'window on the west' as Pushkin described it. Nineteen islands were linked together by a series of immense waterways spanned by 150 bridges. The cost in human labour was appalling. Thousands died, as bogs and marshes were transformed into parks and gardens and 'muddy streams' became 'majestic canals'.[3] It was deliberately planned as a great western city, elegantly classical, with wide straight avenues and enormous squares. Along the three mile long waterfront of the Neva arose splendid baroque palaces designed by Italian architects for the nobility. In 1712 the government offices were transferred from Moscow and the city became the new capital of Russia. It soon came to be known as the 'Venice of the North', one of Europe's most beautiful cities. It was also one of the most cosmopolitan.

In summer there were the 'white nights', when twenty-two hours of daylight kept the city bathed in a soft silvery-pearl haze. In the sub-zero temperatures of winter, cruel icy winds kept people indoors and there were only four hours of daylight. From mid-November until mid-April the Neva became a frozen road; lines of fir trees marked the safest paths across the ice. Shops were barricaded and the street lamps were dim and flickering in the whirling snowflakes. Not until 1874 was St Petersburg illuminated with electric lamps. At night society attended the theatre, the ladies vying with each other over the splendour of their jewels. 'One was judged', wrote Theodore Gautier in 1865, 'according to one's furs'.

The Romanovs' lifestyle was fabulous and their extravagance was legendary. They all had fantastic incomes and indulged their every whim, travelling in luxurious private trains between Biarritz, Italy and the Riviera with a mountain of luggage and an enormous retinue. Wherever they went the men left large tips. They lived in sumptuous palaces and many of them kept a little actress or ballerina. They attended balls given by the aristocracy and afterwards drove wildly through the snow in troikas to St Petersburg's night haunts to hear the gypsies sing. Wild parties at Cubat's Restaurant invariably ended in drunken brawls.

The Winter Palace was the perfect setting for the Russian Court. Built by Rastrelli for Empress Elizabeth in the eighteenth century, this massive dark red building stretched for a third of a mile along the banks of the Neva and had 1,050 rooms, 117 staircases and 1,786 windows. Its lavish interiors surpassed any of the other Russian palaces. Behind 40 foot high wooden doors inlaid with gold were the State Rooms – St George's Hall, the White Hall, the Malachite Room and the Small Throne Room – all decorated with gold, silver, onyx, malachite, lapis-lazuli and marble. Huge chandeliers were suspended from the ceilings and the light from thousands of candles was reflected in the mirrors and the parquet floors. The Nicholas Hall was 180 feet long, its gilded walls set off by two rows of colonnades. The rooms were filled with priceless paintings, objets d'art, gold and silver plate and richly carved furniture with gold inlay. Among the 1,200 servants were scarlet-shirted men who polished the parquet floors by skating along with a hard brush attached to one foot; exotic Circassian chiefs in chain armour; and the Arabs in oriental dress who were the personal attendants of the Emperor.

'The Imperial Court was the most magnificent in Europe', wrote Prince Christopher of Greece. 'There was something still barbaric in its splendour; its ceremonies were based on those of the old Byzantine Empire ...',[4] more Eastern than European.

The apex of Society was Tsar Alexander II. In his youth he toured Europe, bowled over the young Queen Victoria and was the first Romanov to be received by the Pope. While visiting the Grand Duchy of Hesse and by Rhine, Alexander fell head-over-heels in love with Grand Duke Louis' fifteen-year-old daughter Princess Marie. After her conversion to Orthodoxy as the Grand Duchess Marie Alexandrovna they were married in 1841, when the bride was not quite seventeen. Marie was beautiful but very delicate. The cold Russian winters and the frequent births of children undermined her fragile health and by 1866 she was obliged to spend most of her time in the warmer climate of the Crimea, or in Nice. Alexander soon became bored and his love affairs were common knowledge.

Alexander and Marie had eight children. The eldest, Alexandra, who died of tuberculosis when she was two years old, was followed by Nixa and Sasha. The Empress never recovered from Nixa's death and turned increasingly to religion. The third son Grand Duke Vladimir Alexandro-vitch, now nineteen, was considered by many to be the most intelligent member of the family but the Tsar's favourite was his daughter, thirteen-year-old Marie. The younger sons were sixteen-year-old Alexis, a naval cadet, nine-year-old Sergei and six-year-old Paul.

There were also the Tsar's three brothers: Grand Duke Constantine Nicholaievitch and his wife Grand Duchess Alexandra Josifovna ('Aunt Sanny'); Grand Duke Nicholas Nicholaievitch (senior) and his wife Grand Duchess Alexandra Petrovna; and Grand Duke Michael Nicholaievitch, Viceroy of the Caucasus, and his wife Grand Duchess Olga Feodorovna. The Tsar had two surviving sisters. Olga was Queen of Württemberg; Marie spent long periods abroad but her daughters, Hélène Stroganoff and Princess Eugenie of Oldenburg, became Dagmar's close friends.

To the young princess from provincial Copenhagen it would be like stepping into a fairytale. Nothing she had seen before prepared her for the lifestyle of the Romanovs.

*

A gigantic firework display greeted Dagmar's arrival at Kronstadt, the island fortress which formed part of St Petersburg's naval defences, on the evening of 24th September. When they anchored for the night the princess was welcomed with the traditional Russian greeting of bread and salt on a silver salver.

The following morning was warm and sunny. Grand Duke Constan-tine Nicholaievitch sailed out to meet them and the officers and crew of the *Peder Skram* took leave of their King's daughter. Cheers and shouts of 'long live Princess Dagmar' from 350 officers and men echoed across the water and once more the band played 'In Denmark I Was Born ...' before the Danish vessel sailed away.

Twelve Russian men-of-war flying the Dannebrog (the Danish flag) formed a guard of honour as the Imperial yacht *Alexandria* approached. The Tsar and Tsarevitch greeted Dagmar warmly. Before leaving the Danish yacht she delighted the onlookers by shaking hands with one of the sailors.

As Dagmar and Freddie boarded the *Alexandria* cannons boomed, cheers rang out and the paddle steamers rushed forward whipping up the water into foam. Bands played the two national anthems and, as the officers lined up in salute, a steamer sailed past strewing flowers across the water. The Imperial yacht continued along the Gulf of Finland to the Tsar's summer estate of Peterhof, where Dagmar had her first sight of the imposing facade of the Grand Palace and its fountains. To superstitious Russians the princess' arrival on the 'Day of the Cross' – when St Andrew's Cross is reputed to have fallen from the sky – was a good omen.

Thousands of people had come to see her arrival. Russian flags decorated the Imperial gangway and a triumphal arch with the initials A & M (for Dagmar's Russian name, Marie) spanned the bridge. The crowds caught their first glimpse of their future Tsarevna as she stood on the deck of the *Alexandria*. A roar of approval went up as her tiny figure, wearing a white hooded cloak with a fur border, a dark hat and carrying a white parasol, was seen next to her giant fiancé. Maybe the romantic idea of the 'Sea King's Daughter' (as Tennyson called her sister), instead of yet another German princess, had caught the public imagination.

After being welcomed ashore Dagmar drove off in a carriage with the Empress and Grand Duchess Marie Alexandrovna, Sasha's young sister. The Tsar, Tsarevitch and Freddie (in Russian Colonel's uniform) followed on horseback, with the other Grand Dukes. Finally, came a line of carriages surrounded by a bodyguard of Caucasian Horseguards in picturesque uniforms.

They went first to The Cottage, a Gothic villa on the Peterhof estate, which the Tsar immediately presented to Dagmar as her private property. It remained so until 1917. She had little time to look round her new villa though, because as soon as lunch was over the procession set out again for Tsarskoe Selo.

After a service in the palace church there was a family dinner in the huge turquoise and white Catherine Palace, followed by the official welcome at Tsarskoe Selo town and another lavish firework display. It was late in the evening before Dagmar and Sasha left with the Emperor and Empress.

The glorious weather, which lasted for seven days, was remembered as 'Dagmar's week'. Her name had already been added to the toasts for the Imperial family and the 'Dagmar Waltz' was composed in her honour.

On 29th September Dagmar made her official entry into St Petersburg. The capital was in festive mood. Flags waved from the ships and houses lining the English Quay and troops marched up and down to the music of military bands. The excitement mounted as a rumour spread that the Imperial train had arrived.

The procession set off led by soldiers, footmen, hunters, Court entertainers in colourful costumes and the Master of the Royal Household on horseback. Among the Guards regiments and bands were Circassians with long pointed helmets and Cossacks in bright red coats with fur hats. Horses caprisoned in cloth of gold and led by liveried footmen pulled the open carriage in which Dagmar sat with the Empress, acknowledging the cheers as all the bells pealed. Dagmar wore the Russian national dress – a gold-embroidered blue sarafan with the traditional half-moon-shaped headdress, the Kokoshnik, in blue silk studded with diamonds. The Tsar and Tsarevitch followed, their carriage surrounded by a cavalcade of princes and noblemen. The procession was so long that it took one and a half hours to reach the Winter Palace.

After stopping at the Kazan Cathedral they drove along the Nevsky Prospekt as spectators strained to catch a glimpse of her. A 101-gun salute announced their arrival at the Winter Palace. Dagmar had invited the Danish sailors to see her pass by and later she arranged for them to be presented to the Tsarevitch.

The next morning, after a military parade in Winter Palace Square, Dagmar appeared on the balcony.

She spent the next few weeks at the Winter Palace and Tsarskoe Selo, learning the intricacies of Russian court ceremonial. The Danish princess who had once waited at her parents' table now ate off the finest porcelain and drank from gold cups. She was given her first lady-in-waiting, Countess Alexandra Apraxine (Tania) who, as Princess Obolensky, was still a loyal servant and trusted friend in 1919. Gradually, Princess Dagmar of Denmark was transformed into a Grand Duchess of Russia.

From the very first day Dagmar captured the hearts of the Russian people. 'Rarely has a foreign Princess been greeted with such enthusiasm … From the first moment she set foot on Russian soil, [she] succeeded in winning to herself all hearts. Her smile, the delightful way she had of bowing to the crowds …, laid immediately the foundations of … [her] popularity', wrote Princess Catherine Radziwill.[5] It was a popularity which, through all the troubles of the years to come, she was never to lose.

*

On a cold October morning Dagmar and the Empress were driven to the Fortress of SS Peter & Paul. An icy wind was blowing and the angel weather-vane blew backwards and forwards on top of the cathedral's soaring golden spire.

The church had been built by Peter the Great as a burial place for the Romanovs. Inside stood rows of identical white marble slabs with a name and a date in shiny brass. The two women entered by a side door and walked to a tomb covered in flowers which bore the name of Tsarevitch Nicholas. The princess laid a small wreath on the marble slab and knelt in silent prayer. After a few moments Empress Marie put her arms around the weeping girl, raised her up and helped her to the door. As they left, the Empress' look of longing towards her son's tomb was worth more than any words.

On 23rd October she made her last appearance as Princess Dagmar of Denmark, when the Danish community in Russia presented her with an enamel dish and matching silver salver. The combined weight of these pieces was 14 lbs. To Dagmar's delight, the bottom of the dish showed views of her Danish homes – Fredensborg, the Yellow Mansion and the Amalienborg – with the Danish and Russian flags.

The following day Dagmar was formally received into the Orthodox Church at a ceremony in the Winter Palace church. Brought up in the simplicity of the Lutheran faith she had 'no use for dogmas or for ritualistic niceties'.[6] Not for her the soul-searching of other princesses, the most important thing was to worship God rather than argue about how it was done. She embraced Orthodoxy wholeheartedly but without delving into the more mystical aspects of the religion. She was too worldly for that and her feet remained firmly on the ground.

Wearing a white satin dress with a long train and unadorned by any jewellery, she was sponsored by the Empress during the two-hour ceremony conducted by the Metropolitan, Mgr Isidore. During the service she had to abjure and curse the Lutheran faith, spitting three times to show her contempt. The Metropolitan annointed her on the forehead, cheek and chest before the Empress led her to kiss the icons. They then took Communion. Dagmar was also required to take the name of a saint in the Orthodox calendar and a patronymic. Princess Dagmar of Denmark now became by Imperial decree Her Imperial Highness the Grand Duchess Maria Feodorovna, although she was usually called Marie; the patronymic 'Feodorovna' ('Gift of God')[7] was a traditional one for foreign brides.

As Dagmar and Sasha walked back through the corridors of the palace, the sight of a painting of Nixa almost reduced her to tears but there was little time to give way to her emotions. In the White Hall members of the Imperial family were waiting to be presented to the new Grand Duchess, who now made her appearance in a blue velvet train edged with pearls, her simple white dress and a Kokoshnik studded with precious gems.

Her conversion was followed by a grand banquet and a ball. Balls and parties were a new experience for Dagmar and she found it exhilarating. King Christian was alarmed for her health and reports from his Ambassador that she was continuing to dance all night worried him further. On 18th October his fatherly concern spurred him to write and warn his daughter of the danger to both her health and looks if she continued to act in this way.

The marriage contract was signed on 13th October and ratified on 5th November. Dagmar would receive a morgengave of 50,000 roubles, a further annual payment of 40,000 roubles for personal expenses and the interest on a capital sum of 100,000 roubles. The contract also stipulated the income she would receive as a widow – 85,000 roubles a year (reduced to 42,000 roubles if she decided to live abroad), with a suitable residence and her court maintained by the new Emperor. Payments would cease altogether if she remarried. A dowry of 60,000 rigsdalers from King Christian was also mentioned but the Danish parliament refused to sanction it and no payment was made.

King Christian's financial situation had not really improved since the days in the Yellow Mansion because most of King Frederick VII's large fortune had been inherited by his wife Countess Danner. Unable to afford the journey to St Petersburg, King Christian and Queen Louise were represented by Freddie. The loss of the war precluded any payment for travelling expenses from the Danish government and the Tsar did not offer to help. Instead the bride's parents celebrated the wedding day with a gala dinner at Christiansborg Slot and attended the ball at the Casino Theatre.

To Dagmar's intense disappointment Alexandra was also unable to come as she was pregnant. With so many of her close relatives absent Dagmar hoped the Prince of Wales would attend but Queen Victoria raised objections. 'That Dagmar should wish to see her kind brother-in-law's face at so trying a time, I think perfectly natural', she told her son. 'I own I do *not* much like the idea … Your visit to St Petersburg (as … I told you when two years ago you wished to go to Dagmar's marriage with the other Cezarevitch) ought to be for *itself alone* … However, if you are still very desirous to go … I will not object …'[8]

The dazzling array of wedding presents overwhelmed Dagmar. From the Tsar there was a magnificent triple-row diamond necklace; from Sasha a diamond brooch; and from Alix and Bertie a cabochon sapphire brooch surrounded by diamonds with a hanging pearl drop. There was also a copy of the famous Dagmar Cross found in the tomb of Queen Dagmar. As was customary for a foreign princess, the Tsar presented Dagmar with a complete trousseau. Everything from fur coats and boots down to silk stockings, lace handkerchiefs and exquisite lingerie was stacked on tables in one of the vast halls of the Winter Palace.

The Russians were enchanted by her. 'Everywhere the same information reaches us from Russia that the day of the Germans is over', wrote a Danish observer, 'no-one has a chance of success who is on their side'.[9]

Despite the brilliant wedding preparations, Dagmar was sad. To her the rejoicing seemed like disrespect to Nixa's memory.

*

9th November was a clear, crisp morning. It had snowed heavily the night before and the sun shone brightly across a white world. Dagmar was woken at eight o'clock by a gun salute from the fortress of SS Peter & Paul, signalling the start of the festivities.

An Imperial wedding was governed by etiquette and tradition from first thing in the morning until the time the newlyweds were finally left alone and was an ordeal for any bride who was not born a Romanov Grand Duchess. According to custom Dagmar could not see her fiancé until they met to go to the church and her day therefore started in the Malachite Room of the Winter Palace. In this breathtaking room overlooking the river Neva, whose walls glittered with a precious green mineral from the Urals, polished until it shone like glass, were the Empress, her Mistress of the Robes and Ida Bille-Brahe.

The wedding dress (delivered by special courier from Paris a few days before) was of silver brocade, worn with a long court train of silver tissue, with clusters of diamonds along the edges and an ermine lining, made according to a style dictated by Catherine the Great. The formal ceremony of dressing the bride began in front of a dressing-table with a large silver-framed mirror which had belonged to Peter the Great's niece, the Empress Anna Ivanovna. The hairdresser arranged Dagmar's hair so that long side curls rested on her shoulders. Then came the jewels bequeathed by Catherine the Great to all Romanov brides. First the Tsarina placed on her head a diadem with a beautiful pink diamond in the centre, behind which was placed the Bride's Crown, six diamond arches rising from a diamond circlet, surmounted by a diamond cross and lined with crimson velvet. Attached to it was the bridal veil. Next came a diamond necklace, a triple-row bracelet and a pair of enormous drop ear-rings like cherries, which were so heavy they were attached to gold hoops and hung over the ears. Finally, after almost three hours, Dagmar stood up and the Empress' ladies draped a long, ermine-lined crimson mantle, with a deep border of ermine, round her shoulders. A short ermine-lined cape was placed over this and fastened with a large diamond clasp. The weight of these robes was tremendous and when the Tsar came to give Dagmar his blessing she could not move unaided.

A 21-gun salute sounded from the fortress as the procession set out for the Great Church of the Winter Palace led by the Tsar and Tsarina. The Empress Marie Alexandrovna, wearing a beautiful dress of burnished gold with four pages carrying her long crimson velvet train, blazed with diamonds. Behind them came the massive Tsarevitch in the blue and silver uniform of his Cossack regiment, leading his tiny bride in her silver gown, her pallor accentuated by the sparkling jewels. Next came the Prince of Wales with the Crown Princes of Denmark and Prussia, then the members of the Imperial family.

They were received by Mgr. Isidore and the clergy wearing gold vestments and jewelled mitres. As the unaccompanied singing of the Imperial choir rang out, the bridal pair kissed the gold cross and the Metropolitan's hand and were offered holy water from a large silver bowl. Then Sasha and Dagmar were led to the altar, which stood on a crimson-covered platform in the centre of the church.

Holding lighted candles, they stood before the Metropolitan while he intoned the service and clouds of incense enveloped them. The Crown Prince of Denmark, Grand Duke Vladimir, Grand Duke Alexis and Nicholas Maximilianovitch Romanovsky, 4th Duke of Leuchtenberg, took turns to hold golden crowns over the heads of the bridal pair, while the prayers of the Orthodox marriage service echoed round the church. Dagmar moved like a puppet under the weight of her robes, following the Metropolitan three times round the altar, hearing the prayers, the chanting of the choir, the voice of the Metropolitan droning on and on until, after an hour, it was over. Turning towards the Emperor and Empress the newly married couple made a deep reverence. Then, in the prayer for the Imperial family, Dagmar heard the deacon add for the first time: 'We pray for Monseigneur the Tsarevitch, the heir to the throne, the Orthodox Grand Duke Alexander Alexandrovitch and for his wife Madame the Orthodox Grand Duchess Maria Feodorovna'.[10] As a salute of 101 guns signalled the end of the ceremony they returned through the crowded halls of the palace.

More than five hundred guests sat down to the State Banquet in the Nicholas Hall, where the bridal couple sat at a large horseshoe-shaped table. Each guest was assigned a personal servant to hand them tall champagne glasses on gold plates. As salutes continued to thunder out the Grand Marshal proposed the toasts. The banquet was followed by the wedding ball in St George's Hall which began with the Polonaise, a stately processional walk. Dagmar partnered the Tsar, Sasha partnered the Tsarina. Dagmar was beginning to feel the strain and the long day was far from over.

It was late that evening before Sasha and Dagmar were able to leave. Escorted by Cossacks and accompanied by the Emperor and Empress, they drove off in a coach drawn by eight horses with golden harnesses. They were preceded by six gilt coaches carrying officials of the household and followed by five more carrying members of the Imperial family. In honour of the wedding the streets were specially illuminated for three nights.

When they reached the palace where they were to spend the night, Grand Duke and Grand Duchess Constantine offered them a silver platter of rye bread and salt signifying luck, plenty and happiness, before blessing them with a holy image. Dagmar was then led to the private apartments where the Empress and the other ladies helped her to undress.

Although the official part of the ceremonies was finished the newly-weds were still not free from the rules of the House of Romanov. Tradition dictated that every Romanov bridegroom must wear a 'wedding-night uniform' of a heavy silver dressing gown (which weighed almost sixteen pounds), silver slippers and a turban-like headdress. It was there-fore looking like 'an operatic Sultan in the grand finale', as one Grand Duke described himself[11], that Sasha made his appearance that night in the bridal chamber.

Although most sources state that Dagmar and Sasha spent the night at the Anitchkov Palace in St Petersburg, local historians say that in fact they went to a rococo villa two miles from Peterhof. Known locally as 'My Property', it was the privately-owned dacha of the Tsar and had been built by Stakenschneider in the reign of Nicholas I. Although Inger-Lise Klausen, in her translation from Sasha's diary, says they were at the Anitchkov, there is nothing in the entry, published below, to confirm it one way or the other:

I locked the door behind me', Sasha wrote. 'All the lights were turned off in her room … I walked into the dressing room, locked the door and reached for the handle on the bedroom door. It felt as if my heart was trying to escape from my body. Afterwards I closed both doors to the dressing room and walked over to Minny. She was already lying on the bed. It is impossible to describe the feelings that over-whelmed me as I pulled her towards me and embraced her. We embraced and kissed each other for a very long time, I then said my prayers, locked the door to the study, blew out the candles and lay down on the bed. I took took off my slippers and my silver dressing gown and felt my darling's body against my own …

'How I felt thereafter I do not wish to describe here.

'Afterwards we talked a lot. Both of us had many questions and many answers. Thus we spent our first night together – and we never slept![12]

*

The following days were busy ones for Dagmar. There was a visit to the SS Peter & Paul Cathedral to pray at the tombs of the Tsars, prayers in front of the Miraculous Icon of the Saviour and, the day after the wed-ding, a reception for the Diplomatic Corps. That evening they drove in state through the capital.

One morning Dagmar and Sasha went to the coffee house at No. 48

Nevsky Prospekt to meet his brother officers. She also had to accompany the Empress on courtesy calls to her new relatives, driving around St Petersburg in an open sledge, swathed in bearskin rugs to keep out the biting cold. Nevertheless, Dagmar suffered such a severe attack of bronchitis that further celebrations were postponed.

By 20th November she had recovered sufficiently to attend the gala performance at the opera with the élite of St Petersburg society. In white tulle with diamonds round her throat and roses in her hair, Dagmar looked radiant as she chatted to the Tsar, who seemed delighted with his daughter-in-law.

The festivities continued with a Court Ball for three thousand people, balls at the French Embassy and the Danish Legation and private theatricals at the Hermitage Theatre. At the British Ambassador's ball the guests looked on delightedly as the Prince of Wales, in full highland dress, partnered Dagmar. Finally, the Tsarevitch and his bride gave a grand ball at the Anitchkov.

Although most countries welcomed the marriage, in Germany it was seen differently. The Crown Princess, who had married for love, thought that Dagmar's happiness was being sacrificed on the altar of diplomatic necessity. 'A young life is thus being sold and sacrificed to the doctrines of the greater conventions',[13] she wrote to Queen Victoria.

Politically it was seen as an alliance which would be a bulwark against future Prussian expansion. Alexander II, a nephew of the King of Prussia, would always be strongly influenced by Germany; but what would the next Emperor, with a Danish wife whose family's hatred for Prussia was well-known, be like?

As Dagmar took her first steps as a member of the Romanov dynasty it remained to be seen how much influence this hatred would have on her husband.

CHAPTER 4

Early Married Life

'THEY ARE VERY DOMESTIC AND HAPPY
AND ATTACHED TO EACH OTHER'

Dagmar and Sasha's home was the Anitchkov Palace on the Nevsky Prospekt, by the Fontanka Canal. The three storey baroque palace, rebuilt by Carlo Rossi in 1817, was named after Colonel Anitchkov, the eighteenth-century commander of the Fontanka construction squad. To Dagmar's delight the palace had a small garden which became an important part of family life. In summer it gave them some privacy; in winter they built an ice hill and skated on the pond.

Imposing wrought iron gates marked the entrance to the palace, which had become the traditional home of the heir to the throne. Inside, an impressive staircase with a bright green carpet and green marble columns led from the entrance hall to the lavishly decorated state rooms. Massive crystal chandeliers were suspended from the high classical ceilings, Venetian glass torchères and Chinese vases stood everywhere and there was a profusion of flowers and plants. There were four drawing rooms, including Dagmar's music room furnished in red and gold and others with walls hung in gold or blue silk. There was also a ballroom, a Throne Room and a private chapel. In 1874 Sasha had some alterations made by the architect Monighetti. The 'Knights Hall' was decorated with large painted panels depicting medieval knights and a projecting vestibule was added to the courtyard entrance. Above it was Dagmar's Winter Garden, filled with palms, exquisite statues and two large stone frogs.

The private apartments on the top floor were cluttered with large plush Victorian furniture, gilt screens, potted palms, antimacassars and curtains looped back with large bows. Every available space was dotted with framed family photographs, knick-knacks and ornaments. The effect was homely and comfortable rather than elegant. A diplomat who saw the contents in 1917 described hideous Japanese screens, cheap pictures, stuffed monkeys under glass domes and antique statues mounted on pedestals covered with cheap plush. Although she could now order anything she wanted Dagmar liked practical furniture that was easily cleaned.

She was soon to learn that dirt and dust were an integral part of every Russian palace.

Her domesticity surprised the Russians. They were not used to a Grand Duchess who took special pride in the linen room, inspected the servants' quarters to make sure they were comfortable and insisted fresh air must circulate through the rooms. Dagmar disliked the hot-house atmosphere of the other Russian palaces. She was organised, methodical and resource-ful. That her household was considered to be very efficient by Russian standards was largely due to her training at the Yellow Mansion.[1]

The Empress selected the ladies of Dagmar's household. Her Mistress of the Robes was Princess Kurakin, who Dagmar looked upon almost as a second mother. Her ladies-in-waiting were Tania Apraxine (who later married Prince Vladimir Obolensky, the Head of the Tsarevitch's private household), Countess Elizabeth Vorontzov-Dashkov ('Lili'), and the two spinster Countesses Marie and Aglaia Kutuzov, descendants of the famous Field Marshal.

Dagmar's position was not easy at first. Many Russians considered betrothal to be as good as marriage and were scandalised when she married her dead fiancé's brother. It was even said in some quarters that she did so merely to keep her position as future Empress. That Dagmar overcame this prejudice was a tribute to her tact and diplomacy. Soon she was 'our Tsarevna', the idol of the Russian people.

Dagmar and Sasha had to work hard at their marriage until it event-ually became a success. She had been in love with Nixa, Sasha with Marie Mestchersky. Although fond of one another, both remembered what they had lost. They had very little in common. Sasha liked to spend his evenings quietly at home with his wife and he was the first Romanov since the seventeenth century to remain an entirely faithful husband. Dagmar loved social life, preferring parties and dancing to staying at home. Now, for the first time in her life, she could have as many pretty dresses as she wanted and it was a heady experience for a girl of just nineteen. She gave frequent lively balls. The invitations for one showed a picture of Sasha's little dog Moska and her own little dog Beauty. Her coquetry soon became well known but, although there was no shortage of handsome young officers to partner her and she naturally had her favourites, no breath of scandal touched her name.

Concerts, in which Sasha played the French horn or the tuba, and amateur theatricals, usually involving the participation of the Tsarevitch and his wife, were frequent entertainments at their palace. Dagmar tact-fully tried to improve Sasha's boorish manners but he remained awkward and tolerated social occasions just to please her. Nevertheless the Anitchkov soon rivalled the Court.

The Tsarina instructed Dagmar in Court etiquette and helped her avoid the many pitfalls. Perhaps the biggest change in her life was the rigid formality; it was impossible to go about informally among the people as she had done in Denmark. With her quick wits and sharp eyes she learned rapidly, soon feeling at ease in her new role and establishing herself as a favourite with society and her new relatives. As the Empress spent long periods abroad, Dagmar frequently found herself the leading lady at Court and it quickly became clear that she was eminently suited to the role. 'She had', wrote Sir Frederick Hamilton, 'a large measure of her [sister Alexandra's] subtle and indescribable charm of manner'.[2]

Dagmar never lost her foreign accent. Alexander Benois recalled her imperfect Russian spoken with a slight lisp, which he found charming but she found embarrassing. She wrote good society French and she and Sasha usually spoke to each other in that language, the language of the Court. Their letters to each other were written in French or Russian, sometimes passages in both languages appear in one letter. Sasha always called her Minny, or 'Manja', the Russian diminutive of Maria. They spoke Russian when they had guests, unless they were foreigners.

They settled into an easy domesticity. 'All the reports ... of [Sasha's] being so unhappy with Minny – and she having only married him to please her mother – are not true', the Crown Princess of Prussia reported. 'I think they are very domestic and happy and attached to each other and he makes a very good husband'. Queen Victoria agreed, ' ... but still I know neither wished to marry the other ...'[3] Despite their initial feelings after Nixa's death, by the end of 1866 Sasha was recording his happiness in his diary and his delight that his wife loved him with all her heart.

The only criticism levelled by Dr Plum, who had come with Dagmar from Denmark, was her total lack of initiative. 'In her present position she could do so much for Russia', he said.[4] Throughout these early months Dagmar's main concern was to try and influence the Russian Court to have North Schleswig returned to her father; to no avail.

The Tsar showed little inclination to initiate Sasha into the business of government. He became a Member of the State Council in 1866 and, two years later, a member of the Committee of Ministers. Dagmar was anxious to fill the gaps in her husband's education and encouraged him to study, observe and broaden his limited interests. At first reluctant, under her influence he studied literature, history and economic science. He was a conscientious student. One night when he was feeling unwell Dagmar ordered him to bed. He waited until she was asleep, then crept back to continue his studies.

As well as guidance and encouragement from his wife, Sasha was coached by a formidable figure. Constantine Pobedonostsev had given up the study of religion to take a degree in law. From 1861 he had taught Nixa and now, at the age of thirty-nine, he became Sasha's tutor. He soon became a regular visitor to the Anitchkov and his creed of 'Autocracy, Orthodoxy and Nationality' found a willing disciple in the Tsarevitch. A reactionary to his fingertips, Pobedonostsev encouraged him to believe that his father's reforms were a threat to the autocracy, a view in which Sasha needed very little prompting.

Although brought up in a more liberal court Dagmar had little interest in politics at this period. Pobedonostsev provided her with a grounding in history and social issues. At first he found her somewhat superficial but he changed his mind when he saw the beneficial effect she had on the Tsarevitch. She accepted Pobedonostsev's creed and it never occurred to her to question it.

There was only one significant way in which she strongly influenced her husband and that was in his anti-Prussianism. It was considered a strange prejudice in Russia – the Empress and many of the Grand Duchesses were from the small German courts and, technically, Sasha and Dagmar were both, by blood, mainly German. Alexander II had always been friendly to Prussia. Encouraged by his wife, the Tsarevitch now took the opposite line.

Bismarck had continued his policy of 'blood and iron'. In the summer of 1866 Prussia had declared war on Austria in a bid to seize complete control of Schleswig and Holstein and to establish supremacy in the German Confederation. When Austria was defeated all the small German states who had sided with her were annexed by Prussia and their rulers were dispossessed. Many of Dagmar's relatives found themselves without kingdom or personal fortune and her family's hatred of Prussia increased.

When the Tsar gave a dinner at the Winter Palace in honour of the King of Prussia's birthday, Dagmar, barely supressing her anger, was obliged to attend but she deliberately wore a dress in the red and white Danish colours. Later, she proudly told her father how, when the toast to the old King's health was proposed, she did not even have a sip.

In England, the Princess of Wales was also encouraging her husband to turn against Germany. The sisters were determined to make sure that, in the event of a war, their adopted countries would be fighting on the same side.

*

At the beginning of 1867 Dagmar began to keep a diary in a black leather book with the word 'Journal' picked out in gold on the spine. In it she recorded political events, observations and her daily round of tea, Mass, riding, cards and bedtime.

One of the events she recorded was her official presentation in Moscow. On 2nd May 1867 Sasha and Dagmar left by train with the Emperor for the old capital of Russia. After spending the night at the Petrovsky Palace outside the city Dagmar made her entry into the Kremlin by carriage the next day to the sound of pealing bells. The Emperor, on horseback, officially welcomed her before they attended a Te Deum in the Uspensky Sobor, the coronation church of the Tsars. This was followed by visits to the other cathedrals in the Kremlin's precincts. Later that evening they drove through cheering crowds to see the fireworks, which were spoilt by bad weather.

The next day, in a blue velvet dress embroidered with gold and loaded with diamonds to impress the Muscovites, Dagmar was presented to the aristocracy. Although she wanted to make a good impression, she was relieved when the ordeal was over. There was the usual round of receptions, balls and visits to institutions, including the Trinity-St Sergius Monastery, an important centre of the Orthodox Church about forty miles outside Moscow.

Soon afterwards they travelled to Denmark to celebrate the Silver Wedding of Dagmar's parents on 26th May. Dagmar's first homecoming after her marriage was a big event. Crowds turned out to see them drive through the city and later they appeared on the balcony of the Amalienborg. The whole family gathered for the occasion, including Dagmar's brother King George of Greece (still called Willie by the family), who had recently become betrothed to the Tsar's young niece Grand Duchess Olga Constantinovna.

Having consolidated his position in Greece, Willie's duty was to marry and ensure the succession but he needed a bride of the Orthodox faith. In the spring of 1867 he visited Russia in search of a wife. Grand Duchess Olga was only fifteen years old and still in the schoolroom but Willie spotted her peeping over the bannisters of Pavlovsk, where he was paying a call on her father Grand Duke Constantine Nicholaievitch and his wife Alexandra, Dagmar's 'Aunt Sanny'. Dagmar schemed to help her brother achieve this marriage which the Grand Duke initially opposed. Eventually Dagmar was able to inform her mother that there were no longer any objections. 'Where in the world have you, little rogue, ever learned to intrigue so well', King Christian asked her when he received the news, 'since you must have worked hard on your uncle and aunt, who were previously decidedly against a match of this kind!'[5]

Grand Duchess Olga arrived in Denmark with her family on 13th July to join the reunion of the Danish Royal family. This was also Sasha's first real experience of the more relaxed way of life at the Danish Court. He soon joined the others playing croquet, boating, walking or playing practical jokes. They were a very boisterous family and anyone trying to concentrate on anything more serious, even writing a letter, would instantly be teased and distracted by the others.

Leaving Dagmar with her parents Sasha continued to Paris where his father was attending the International Exhibition. Dagmar was happy to be back with her family and Sasha soon became distressed that she wrote him so few letters. By early June he was reproaching her for not writing every day. Then on 6th June, while the Tsar was driving in the Bois de Boulogne with Sasha, Vladimir and the French Emperor, a Polish man in the crowd fired two shots at him. The Imperial party were unhurt, although badly shaken. When the news reached Dagmar she was horrified. It was her first experience of such an attack and the sudden shock may have caused her to miscarry.

On 18th July *The Times* reported a statement from the Court at Copenhagen: 'The Princess Dagmar is unwell'.[6] It is possible that she suffered a miscarriage. On 3rd September the Crown Princess of Prussia, who was usually very well-informed, wrote to Queen Victoria: 'They say Marie of Flanders has had a mishap. I wonder if it is true? Dagmar has had one – and the Russians are much concerned at it'.[7] As the Countess of Flanders (whose husband Philip was the brother of Leopold II of Belgium) was certainly pregnant in August there is little doubt as to the nature of the mishap. Alternatively, the statement of 18th July may have been the first intimation that Dagmar was pregnant. As her duty was to ensure the succession, the miscarriage of her first child was naturally a cause of great concern to the Russian Court.

Sasha desperately wanted an heir and he recorded his feelings in his diary, preserved in the State Archives of the Russian Federation. On 8th August he prayed that he and Dagmar would have children, or at least could be sure that they would soon be starting a family, a strange concern for such a newly-married man unless there had been a problem.

By August Dagmar was sufficiently recovered to travel to Wiesbaden with Sasha, Queen Louise, Thyra and Willie. They were joined by Bertie and Alix, who was convalescing. In February, while awaiting the birth of her third child Princess Louise, Alix developed rheumatic fever and for a few weeks her life was in danger. Not until her parents were hurriedly summoned to London did Dagmar realise the seriousness of her sister's condition. Alix's recovery was slow and she was left with a permanent stiff leg.

Bertie soon became bored and went off to the races at Baden. Alexandra now used her ill-health as an excuse to refuse to meet the King and Queen of Prussia and encouraged Dagmar, who needed very little prompting anyway, to do the same. She was supported by Queen Louise, who immediately took Willie and Thyra off to Rumpenheim to attend the funeral of their grandfather, Landgrave William of Hesse-Cassel. Dagmar and Alix emphasised the intended insult by joining their mother.

Sasha and Dagmar travelled home via Berlin. It was her first visit to the city since the Schleswig-Holstein war. 'She was not well so I went to Berlin and spent the day with them', wrote the Crown Princess, who formed a very favourable impression of Dagmar. 'She certainly is a very attractive, charming and interesting little person. I never thought she would become so pretty. She seems quite happy and contented with her fat, good-natured husband who seems far more attentive and kind to her than one would have thought. I was pleased to see that she has not become grand – and does not give herself airs …'[8]

They returned to Russia for the marriage of Willie and Olga on 27th October. Dagmar was amused to see that, among the illuminated initials 'G & O' which decked the streets, there were some saying 'A & M' which had been used at her own marriage. When the sixteen-year-old Queen of Greece left for her new country her luggage contained a trunk full of dolls.

*

On 9th November 1867, her first wedding anniversary, Dagmar wrote to the Empress Marie in the Crimea, scarcely needing to tell her how happy she was that their greatest wish had been granted – she was in a happy condition. She hoped her mother-in-law was proud and looking forward to becoming a grandmother. Dagmar was expecting a child in the spring.

Yet it seems that there was still some doubt. In March 1868 Dagmar told Sasha that, after old Dr Schmidt had listened to the heartbeat, he was now sure she was pregnant. Although it was quite late in the pregnancy, she was relieved to have her suspicions confirmed.

Dagmar awaited her confinement at Tsarskoe Selo, the 'Tsar's Village', the Imperial family's summer residence fifteen miles south-west of St Petersburg. The Catherine Palace and the smaller yellow and white Alexander Palace (where rooms had been prepared on the garden side of the west wing for the Tsarevitch and his wife) stood only five hundred yards apart, each in its own park behind wrought-iron gates surmounted by a double-headed eagle and crown. The magnificent enfilade of State Rooms in the Catherine Palace included the Amber Room with priceless amber panels set into the walls and a Great Hall that surpassed the Galerie des Glaces at Versailles. Outside lay a dream world with lakes, hills, formal gardens, grottoes and Italian statues.

As the spring approached Dagmar prepared for motherhood. In March Sasha represented the Tsar at the christening of the Crown Princess of Prussia's son, Waldemar. 'Dagmar's husband gives very good accounts of her', Vicky told Queen Victoria.[9] 'I am glad Dagmar is going on well', the Queen replied. 'She will be kept so quiet that there will be no danger of her being confined too soon [as Alix was], but I fear it will be a very small child'.[10]

It was a difficult birth. Dagmar was asleep in her chintz-covered bedroom in the Alexander Palace when the pains began at four in the morning. At half-past seven, sick with pain, she was examined by the midwife while Sasha scribbled a note to his parents. The Emperor and Empress arrived at ten o'clock and were present throughout her ordeal, to Dagmar's obvious embarrassment and discomfort.

In her diary for 6th/18th May 1868 Dagmar described how Sasha remained with her throughout the protracted labour. Finally, still physically sick and by now screaming with pain, she went into the bedroom. With the Emperor and Sasha each holding one of her hands and the Empress also giving moral support, Dagmar eventually gave birth to a son at half-past two.

Dagmar embraced her husband and parents-in-law delightedly before the child was placed in her arms. All over the Russian Empire the birth was greeted with tremendous joy. Champagne toasts were drunk in clubs, theatres and private houses and a 300-gun salute was fired from the Fortress. 'Yesterday the Grand Duchess Marie H.I.H. the Cesarevna gave birth to a son, who has been named Nicholas', the American Minister cabled to Washington, 'the Grand Duchess deservedly popular; and the regular succession to the Imperial Throne will no doubt be secure'. An Imperial manifesto formally announced the birth the following day. 'We consider this gift to our Imperial House as a special blessing of the Almighty ...' ran the Tsar's words.[11] The ministers presented Dagmar and Sasha with the icon of the Madonna Fedorovskaya, her halo scattered with diamonds, mounted in a silver frame. The Tsar granted the customary amnesty; minor offenders were released and others had their sentences reduced.

The birth of their first child was a great joy and their choice of name surprised no-one. Although small compared with most recent Romanov babies he was a normal, healthy child and very much his mother's son. He was born on the day of Job in the Orthodox Calendar, considered unlucky by superstitious Russians. In later years Dagmar often remarked upon her son's exceptional fatalism.

At his christening on 1st June, which by Orthodox tradition his parents did not attend, Nicholas was immersed in the font and given a gold crucifix, a customary gift to all Romanov babies. Dagmar had made the christening gown herself from delicate cotton and lace. On a detachable bib at the front she embroidered a tiny double-headed eagle and

Imperial crown with the year 1868. All her children were christened in the gown, a new bib being made for each baby. It was brought out of Russia during the revolution and still has the bib on it made for the christening of Dagmar's youngest child Olga in 1882.[12]

In August Dagmar's parents arrived to see their new grandson. A few weeks later, after they had returned to the Anitchkov, she told Aunt Sanny that every day she prayed God would help her to give the little angel a good upbringing. Nicholas' rooms were directly below his mother's, much closer than if they had remained at Tsarskoe Selo. Dagmar added how pleased she was with the head nursemaid and the excellent wet-nurse.

They spent Christmas in Denmark. Alix and Bertie were there with their family and talk centred around Freddie's approaching marriage to the pious, plain but extremely rich Princess Louise of Sweden, only surviving child of King Carl XV. The Tsar had been against this marriage and, through Dagmar, he tried to promote a match with Queen Victoria's daughter Louise. Freddie preferred Princess Helena, whom he had become fond of when he was studying in England. The Queen vetoed a marriage with either of her daughters and promptly arranged Helena's marriage with Prince Christian of Schleswig-Holstein-Sonderburg-Augustenburg whose family had fought with the Germans in the war of 1864. Freddie married the Swedish princess (later called 'Aunt Swan' by her nephews and nieces because of her long neck) in Stockholm in July 1869 amid much rejoicing.

At the end of her diary for 1868 Dagmar pressed a pansy into the pages – according to Victorian tradition a sad declaration of love, a mixture of happiness and pain. For by now tensions were becoming apparent in her marriage and her diary also shows that she was unable to forget what might have been with Nixa.

Sasha was having trouble adjusting to his new position and all the public duties attached to it. On a trip to the Caucasus in 1869 relations between Sasha and Dagmar were increasingly strained. The presence of Dagmar's favourite brother-in-law Alexis, with whom she had a partic-ularly good rapport and was able to reminisce about Nixa, eased things. The enthusiasm everywhere gave her the courage to address the civic dignitaries in Russian. 5th August was an especially difficult day. Continuing their journey by steamer down the Volga they reached Khvolonshek. Despite the welcome laid on for them, Sasha refused point blank to leave the boat and insisted that the deputation come on board instead. After the presentation of bread and salt he returned to his cabin, leaving Dagmar to cope alone. The people implored her to go ashore which, saying nothing to Sasha, she did, obliging him to follow. Although he greeted the people cheerfully enough Dagmar's diary describes how she returned on board to find Sasha angry because she had stayed too long having tea with the people. He began to shout and throw things, to the extent that Dagmar became ashamed of his conduct in front of their entourage.

At Volsk, Sasha refused to do more than stand on the bridge before going back on board. Dagmar was disconsolate and upset by his behaviour. Later she sat with Alexis and they spoke lovingly about Nixa, until Dagmar could hardly restrain her tears.

Barely a month before they went to the Caucasus Dagmar's second child was born, on 7th June 1869. 'The Grand Duchess Marie Feodorovna, wife of the Czarewitch, gave birth today to a son', reported the Times, quoting a despatch sent from Russia. 'The son of the Czarewitch ... has received the name Alexander'.[13] He was a lusty baby and the Russians were delighted that the succession was well assured.

Alexander died when he was just eleven months old. 'Poor Dagmar', wrote Vicky. 'How much I feel for her, she lost her poor boy of "meningitis", the same as our darling child [Prince Sigismund]. Cecile Olga [Grand Duchess Michael] told me that the eldest was small and puny – and this 2nd one Alexander a splendid child and the special pride and delight of his parents, so it makes it all the more hard and cruel for them'.[14]

It was a bitter blow, even in an age of high infant mortality when most families could expect to lose at least one child. In a telegram thanking the Crown Princess of Prussia for her sympathy Sasha told her they were 'overwhelmed with sadness'. 'Poor young man', wrote Vicky, 'he has a kind heart and is very domestic and so good to his wife whom he is so fond of'.[15] The baby Grand Duke was buried with his ancestors in the Cathedral of SS Peter & Paul.

In her diary Dagmar described how Dr Gustav Ivanovitch Hirsch, Sasha's personal physician, seeing the baby's end was near, summoned the family. The Empress arrived at five o'clock. When the family had left, Sasha and Dagmar were alone with their little dead angel, which she found rather gruesome. Although Hirsch did not think he suffered, the young parents certainly did as they watched over their son for several hours, until, at half-past three, he died.

He was immediately placed in a lined coffin and they spent the night with what she described as the little corpse. Continuing her diary, Dagmar wrote of the terrible sacrifice of returning to God the precious life that he had given them only eleven months before.

It has been persistently stated that Alexander was the eldest son and that this 'lusty infant' was neglected by his nurse and the doctors, who contributed to the fall of the dynasty by allowing the puny Nicholas to become heir. Tempting as it is to believe that fate dealt such a mighty blow to the Romanovs the facts do not bear this out. The Grand Duke's tomb clearly states he was born on 26th May 1869 [OS] at Tsarskoe Selo and died at St Petersburg on 20th April [OS] 1870.[16] Although he was buried in the main cathedral, the catafalque was set up in the small side chapel of St Catherine, where the burial service was held. One hundred and twenty years later the remains of his brother Nicholas were laid to rest in this same chapel.

Just a month after Alexander's death Dagmar and Sasha had to return to the Caucasus for an official visit. She found it difficult to make the journey when they were in such deep mourning, but made the effort for Sasha's sake. It was even more difficult to leave Nicholas. He clung to her and cried, making it harder for Dagmar to tear herself away from her only surviving son. Again there were tensions apparent on the journey. On one occasion Sasha had just gone to sleep and deputed Dagmar to receive the delegations when they came on board. She decided to wake him because the Cossacks were keen to see their Ataman. Sasha did not seem to appreciate that this would probably be their only chance to see their chief. He was angry with Dagmar for some time afterwards. Yet, she wrote later, he knew that she was right.

Dagmar spent the unhappy summer of 1870 in Denmark, arriving with Nicky on 12th July for a stay of two months. She badly needed the support of her family and was overjoyed to see Alexandra again. Dagmar had particularly asked to have her old room over the Garden Room, with its view of the park towards Esrum Lake. She was in her element with her family and soon Sasha, who was on manuoevres, was complaining about her short, dispassionate, uninteresting letters. Exasperated, he told her that if she found it too boring to write to him she could stop. Sasha finally arrived in Denmark on 12th August, although the political situation in Europe was tense. France and Prussia were on the verge of war and the Tsar urged King Christian to remain neutral.

Their stay in Denmark was cut short by the Franco-Prussian war, which lasted six weeks and ended with the surrender of Napoleon III at Sedan. Dagmar was pro-French and she again influenced her husband. This put Sasha in direct conflict with his parents, especially his mother. The Te Deums held to celebrate the German victory disgusted Sasha and the gulf between him and his father widened.

The following January the King of Prussia was proclaimed Emperor William I of Germany and Bismarck became Chancellor. France's desire for revenge became a feature of European politics right up to 1914.

The Danes hoped that Russia and England would use their influence to ensure the return of the Duchies. In March 1871 Dagmar's father appealed for her help. 'If [the Tsar] would only strive ... to induce his uncle [William I] ... to give Danish Schleswig back to us, preferably with Flensborg; if this is impossible, we might at least have North Schleswig with the Island of Als and Sundevitt which are wholly Danish ... I beg my dear Minny with her warm Danish heart to speak to him ... as soon and as pressingly as possible ...'[17]

Experiencing the last uncomfortable months of pregnancy, it must have worried and hurt Dagmar to be forced to tell her father a month later that no specific answer had come from the Emperor. Finally, King Christian wrote to the Tsar urging him to have the Schleswig-Holstein question decided on an equal basis. There was no result.

Dagmar took Denmark's fortunes very much to heart and from the very first she endeavoured to promote Danish companies and business interests in Russia. She was able to 'give a little push to the processing of a Danish application to a Russian authority' and the royal link did nothing to hurt Danish business activities.[18] Among the companies she helped was the Danish Northern Telegraph Company, who in 1869 were granted a concession to send telegrams through Russia to their connecting cables in Europe.

On Easter Saturday, 9th May 1871, Dagmar's third son George was born at Tsarskoe Selo. She wrote to her mother that Georgie's mouth was small and he had blue eyes. Sasha gave her a cross of diamonds containing a Siberian precious stone. In the light it showed the Russian colours of red, white and blue. Yet all was not well with Georgie. He was weak and suffered from a severe respiratory problem. For a while the doctors despaired of his life. His health was never good and he was the cause of much future worry to Dagmar.

After the death of little Alexander homesickness became a frequent feature of Dagmar's letters to her parents and her thoughts turned increasingly to them and 'dear Bernstorff'. Leaving Denmark by train in 1872 Dagmar said she still could not believe that she had really gone. She always had the feeling that she was merely going on a journey and would soon return.

During the summer Sasha was frequently away on military manoeuvres and sometimes they did not see each other for weeks. He tried to persuade the Tsar to post him nearer to home so that he could visit his wife, whom he missed dreadfully. His letters are full of the longing to hold her, embrace her and be with her naked like Adam and Eve. Dagmar blushed when she read his sexual fantasies but she did not answer them.

On 12th December 1872 three-year-old Nicky appeared at his first official ceremony. He was very well-behaved, Dagmar told her mother, and looked very sweet in his uniform with tiny boots and bearskin. A week later he was seriously ill and Dagmar was alarmed that it might be typhoid. During the next difficult weeks her mother's letters were a constant comfort but it was the end of January before she was able to report that he had recovered. As Dagmar had more time to herself, she spent most of it with Nicky. They often walked in the woods because the fresh air was good for him.

Her alarm about typhoid had increased because in December 1871 the Prince of Wales contracted the disease and she received graphic details from Alix. As the tenth anniversary of the Prince Consort's death approached it seemed that the son would die of the same disease as his father, maybe even on the same date. On the fateful 14th December, against all odds, Bertie began to recover.

Russia's relations with England had been difficult since the end of the Crimean War. The Russians, spurred on by the old dream of capturing Constantinople from Turkey, moved forward across central Asia and the English newspapers warned of the menace to India as Russia disputed the Afghan frontier.

Dagmar worked hard to maintain good relations with her sister's adopted country. The family ties were strengthened by the betrothal of Queen Victoria's son Alfred, Duke of Edinburgh, to the Tsar's daughter Marie. Over the last few years Dagmar, Alix and Bertie's sister Alice (who had married Sasha's cousin Prince Louis of Hesse) had arranged regular family gatherings at the Hesse family seat of Heiligenberg. It was here that, towards the end of 1868, Alfred met Marie. She was not quite fifteen, short, plump and not particularly pretty but she had a huge dowry.

After a four-year wait (despite opposition from the Tsar, Tsarina and Queen Victoria) the betrothal was officially announced in 1873 and was seen as a sign of the Tsar's goodwill towards England. Although it was stressed it was a love match without political significance, there were fears in England that it was a political bargain over the Middle East.

In this climate of distrust, the Prince of Wales suggested a semi-official visit by the Tsarevitch and Tsarevna to smooth things over and stress the family ties between the two Royal houses. Dagmar hoped they would go to England, she told her mother on 16th February 1873, especially as it was a country that Sasha had never visited. She had not mentioned it to anybody, in case the answer was no. Later in the same letter Dagmar apologised to her mother for being stupidly bad-tempered and morose one evening during her last visit to Bernstorff, saying she had felt rather like a martyr or like Cinderella.

By March Dagmar was ill and spitting blood. It appears that she caught chicken pox but neglected to take care of herself, insisting on attending official functions during April. Queen Louise did not hear about it until September. Dr Hirsch then warned her that if Dagmar did not take sufficient care it could turn to pneumonia and he would not be able to save her life.

When it was announced that the visit to England would go ahead Dagmar was delighted. They would arrive in June 1873 and stay almost two months. She and Alix determined to make it the highlight of the Season and soon hit on a novel idea – they would dress exactly alike, day and evening. Soon their letters were full of dress patterns, materials, hats and trimmings.

Then the bombshell dropped. The Shah of Persia announced his intention of visiting St Petersburg, Berlin and London during May and June. Alix and Bertie were in despair. They would have to treat it as a full-scale State visit and the Shah would undoubtedly stay longer than the customary three days. Dagmar and Sasha would be eclipsed as society fought to entertain him, while Russia would be affronted at the slight. There was nothing they could do but make the best of it.

The Shah arrived in St Petersburg on 22nd May. The oriental potentate was charmed by Dagmar. During the military parade he asked her opinion of his horse. When she admired it, gallantly, he gave it to her.

*

In June the Imperial yacht sailed into Woolwich, where it was met by the Prince and Princess of Wales. The Princess and the Tsarevna were dressed identically, each in a white dress and a straw bonnet with cherries on it. Such a sight had never been seen before on a royal occasion. Dagmar stood waving on the quay with her sons Nicholas, five and Georgie, just two, behind her, before they set off on the drive to Marlborough House.

Dagmar and Alix were determined to enjoy every moment. Crowds gathered as they took a morning drive in Hyde Park wearing blue and white foulard dresses; in the evenings they caused a further sensation when they attended the great balls given by the leading society hostesses. Ballrooms became battlefields and lovely gowns became bedraggled as ladies climbed on chairs, tables, sofas and even pillars and potted palms to catch a glimpse of them. 'Young, lively and full of joie de vivre ... the sisters set each other off and became the centre of a glittering crowd wherever they went'.[19]

Sasha was happiest in the nursery of Marlborough House, where his sons were living with the Wales children. 'The poor Grand Duke *hates* Balls and was very unhappy at being dragged to so many, and point blank refuses to go to any more', wrote Princess Louise. 'I am so sorry for him. Minny ... seems to like going out as much as Alix does'.[20]

Dagmar was able to do things that would be impossible in Russia. In subdued dresses she and Alix visited the East End Houses of Refuge, where the stench and poverty were indescribable; and the London Hospital, one of Alix's favourite charities. Dagmar's eyes were opened to the plight of the poor and she was able to exercise considerable behind-the-scenes influence when she returned to Russia, where the poor suffered severe hardship in the bitterly cold winters.

The Shah arrived on 18th June. The Queen declined to come to London and the burden of entertaining him fell on the Prince and Princess of Wales. The people were agog at the sight of this tall oriental monarch, with his piercing black eyes and black moustache, who was rumoured to have three female Georgian slaves living with him in Buckingham Palace. He completely eclipsed the Russians. Society awaited the banquet at Marlborough House with bated breath.

The Shah arrived an hour late, sat down while the guests stood for Grace and dragged Dagmar and Alix down on either side of him. When he noticed their identical gowns he seemed to think it was a joke intended for his benefit. He thrust his fingers into the food, pulled good bits out of his mouth, replaced them and tossed rejected bits on the floor, using the tablecloth as a napkin. He lolled back in his chair with his arms around the Princess and the Tsarevna and belched. The strong spirits which he drank apparently had no effect.

At the Gala concert in the Albert Hall Dagmar and Alix wore white gowns and tiaras, while the Shah sat between them blazing with jewels. He embraced the chairback of each royal sister in turn, then both at once. Later, oblivious to the massive figure of the Tsarevitch at the back of the Royal Box, he sat with his arms round their bare shoulders and fed them with sweets, while they were rocked with hysterical laughter.

To the annoyance of the Russians, they found themselves practically ignored. The only person who did not seem to mind was Dagmar. All that mattered to her was that she was with her sister.

The Queen had ample opportunity to observe the Tsarevitch and his wife when they lunched at Windsor Castle. 'Minny [is] very simple and unaffected', she told Vicky, 'but she is not (excepting her eyes) pretty and she has not the distinguished face and appearance of dear Alix, though in manner they are much alike'.[21]

It was at the Great Windsor Review that Sasha and Dagmar had to give way publicly to the Shah for the first time but when a Highland Regiment, which had distinguished itself in the Crimean War, passed by, the Tsarevna tactfully clapped her hands enthusiastically.

To add to their humiliation *The Times* picked this particular day to reply to a scathing attack in the St Petersburg *Mir*, which accused England of fêting the Shah in order to show 'her spite against Russia rather than her friendship for Persia'. 'Such acrimonious rant as the comments of *The Mir* it has seldom been our lot to read', thundered *The Times*. 'Their Imperial Highnesses ... have borne a chief part in all these ceremonials. Is it to be supposed that they, too, have been aiding the moral conquest of the British tiger?'[22] Although Dagmar was not unduly bothered, Sasha felt his role as the guardian of Russian honour deeply. He soon grew edgy and impatient at what he felt to be slights inflicted on Russia.

At the end of June they were the Queen's guests at Windsor for three days. A big dinner was given in their honour, which may have gone some way towards easing Sasha's bruised feelings.

Their stay was brought to a conclusion when, after reviewing the fleet at Spithead, they went to the Isle of Wight for Cowes Week and visited Osborne House. The main social event at Cowes was a coveted invitation to a dance on board H.M.S. *Ariadne* in honour of the Imperial couple. Among the guests presented to Sasha and Dagmar that day was Lord Randolph Churchill. Lord Randolph was also introduced to Miss Jennie Jerome of New York and their subsequent marriage led to the birth of Sir Winston Churchill in 1874.

The next day Dagmar and Sasha left for Denmark.

*

Early in 1874 Dagmar was delighted to welcome her sister to Russia for Alfred and Marie's wedding on 23rd January. The magnificent Orthodox ceremony was followed, to the Tsar's displeasure, by a Church of England ceremony. On 4th February the Imperial family left for Moscow where, at the State Dinner in the Kremlin's St Vladimir Hall, Danish silver was used as a compliment to Dagmar's family.

Disquieting letters soon arrived from the new Duchess of Edinburgh. She disliked England and found it impossible to adapt to the more relaxed etiquette. Dagmar tried to smooth over the troubles by explaining to the incredulous Romanovs the differences between the Court of St Petersburg and the gloomy English Court. It was an attempt that was not entirely successful.

Two years later Queen Victoria became Empress of India. This not only gave England more prestige but, it was hoped, would make the Russians hesitate before making any further moves into Asia. The two Royal families continued their policy of mutual mistrust.

CHAPTER 5

The Cross and the Crescent

O n 6th April 1875 Dagmar's fourth child and eldest daughter, Xenia, was born at the Anitchkov. She inherited all her mother's charm, lively intelligence and an elfin beauty. Dagmar was thrilled by the birth of a daughter and wrote to tell Queen Louise that the new baby was delightful. She usually suffered from nausea during her pregnancies and Dr Hirsch advised her to eat raw ham in bed every morning. This time, Dagmar told her mother, she had felt particularly fat and awkward as well.

Dagmar had the final say in the upbringing of the children, who were raised almost spartanly, in the English manner which had been fashionable since Sasha's own childhood. They slept on camp beds, rose at six and took a cold bath, although occasionally they were allowed to take a warm bath in their mother's bathroom. Breakfast was usually porridge and black bread; mutton cutlets or roast beef with peas and baked potatoes were served for lunch; bread, butter and jam at tea-time. Cake was a special treat. Nicholas and George had a sitting-room, dining-room, play-room and bedroom, all simply furnished. The only trace of ostentation was an icon surrounded by pearls and precious stones. Sometimes they were taken to the 'Fairy Tale room', with its wonderful frescoes of Pushkin's characters on the walls, to be told stories.

They were probably among the least restricted and disciplined Romanov children. Dagmar taught them that family life was very important and, because of their parents' happy marriage, they were brought up in an atmosphere of love and security missing from most royal households. As they grew older they dined with their parents and these occasions frequently turned into battles as the children, in fits of laughter, pelted each other with bread. Sasha's aunt, Queen Olga of Württemberg, was appalled at his family's table manners.

In 1876 Dagmar engaged Alexandra Ollengren to educate Nicholas and George to the standard required to pass the Lycée entrance examination. She and her young son, Vladimir, lived at the Anitchkov and he became a fellow pupil of the young Grand Dukes. Their lessons followed the school curriculum for the next three years.

As Dagmar's official duties were few, she devoted much more time to her three eldest children. On a normal day Dagmar and Sasha saw the boys mid-morning to discuss their lessons and activities for the day. They loved to have rides on the train of her dress, although she always insisted that Vladimir Ollengren go first. At bed-time, she saw her sons for a shorter period. Occasionally they were allowed into her rooms while she dressed for dinner. She let them choose her gown and watch while the maid went through the daily ritual of brushing and arranging her hair, before winding ropes of perfectly-matched pearls around her neck. Nicholas adored his mother and envied the governess' son, whose mother was with him all the time.

The children were brought up to believe that the Emperor's word was law and his decision on any matter was final. Unfortunately this smothered both their individuality and independence of thought. Dagmar never forgot that, after her own rather weak children, the next heir was Sasha's brother Vladimir and his ambitious new German wife Princess Marie of Mecklenburg-Schwerin who, although she took the name of Grand Duchess Marie Pavlovna ('Miechen'), refused to renounce her Lutheran faith. Dagmar and Sasha disliked her obvious bias towards Germany and distrusted her friendship with Bismarck, for whom she was rumoured to be spying. Relations between the two women were seldom easy.

Sasha delighted in his young family. He liked nothing more than a good romp and insisted that they be brought up as normal healthy children. As they grew older he took pleasure in being with other children as well. He soon became Uncle Sasha to a whole tribe of nephews and nieces, delightedly leading them into mischief.

As his family grew, Sasha's relations with his own father became more distant. There were two main problems. Firstly, due to a complete difference in outlook between father and son, the Tsarevitch had no involvement with affairs of state. He was allowed to attend ministerial meetings but he disagreed with his father's policy and soon became the leader of a strong reactionary opposition party. A prominent member of this group was Pobedonostsev and, as Sasha grew more receptive to his ideas, it became obvious that once he came to the throne all reforms would stop.

As well as political opposition there was a second, more personal problem, which struck at the solidarity of the dynasty. The Emperor was infatuated with Princess Catherine Dolgoruky, a stunningly beautiful girl nearly thirty years his junior, and it was becoming obvious that this was no passing fancy.

Catherine's father Prince Michael Dolgoruky, a close friend of the

Emperor, had spent all his fortune on building and gambling. Just before he died, leaving colossal debts, he asked the Tsar to become the guardian of his children. The boys were sent to military academies and the two girls, Catherine and Marie, entered the exclusive Smolny Institute founded by Catherine the Great as a boarding school for the daughters of the nobility.

By 1862 it was noticed that the Emperor's calls at the Institute were becoming more frequent and that fifteen-year-old Catherine was always singled out for special attention. After Nixa's death the Tsar was unable to look to his wife for the comfort and support he needed and he turned more and more towards Catherine to fill the void. In 1865, when she was eighteen and had left the Smolny, he declared his love for her. For a year Catherine resisted his advances until she finally capitulated in the summer of 1866. 'From now onward', vowed the Emperor, 'I regard you as my wife before God'.[1]

In 1870, to Sasha's indignation, Catherine was appointed a lady-in-waiting to the Empress so that she could attend Court functions.

She bore the Tsar four children: George, in 1872; Olga, in 1873; Boris, who lived for only a few days, in 1876; and Catherine in 1878. All were given the rank and title of Prince or Princess Yourievsky. Catherine lived discreetly in a series of villas on the Imperial estates at Peterhof, Tsarskoe Selo and the Crimea. To Sasha it was an insult, not only to his mother but to the dignity of the throne, to know that his father's mistress was only two weeks older than Dagmar. Relations between father and son deteriorated still further and Sasha turned more and more towards the ideals of Pobedonostsev.

Dagmar never mentioned the Emperor's mistress in letters to her parents. She resented Catherine, who she felt had estranged the Tsar from his wife. She tried hard to avoid the princess and if they attended the same function, turned her head away. The Emperor noticed this and relations between them became strained. Dagmar frequently found herself ignored and was reduced to tears by his treatment.

The Tsarevitch and his wife soon became the leaders of the anti-Dolgoruky party. All through Dagmar's years as Tsarevna the Romanov family was divided and the animosity to Catherine flowed like an under-current beneath the surface. Ironically, Catherine cold-shouldered society, never let ambitious courtiers use her for their own ends and would probably have relinquished everything if only she could live in peace with the Tsar.

*

In 1876, prompted by atrocities against the Serbs living in Bosnia and Herzegovina and in Turkish-ruled Bulgaria, Prince Milan of Serbia declared war on Turkey. The Tsar made it clear that Serbia could not expect any support but he had not anticipated public opinion. After the proclamation of the German Empire many Russians embraced Pan-Slavism – liberation of the Slav races from foreign rule – with the aim of enlarging the Russian Empire to include the Slavs in European Turkey and the Balkans, forming a Slav Federation. It had long been Russia's dream to march on Constantinople and restore St Sophia's to the Orthodox faith. Soon the Russian Pan-Slavists were agitating for war.

The Imperial family was divided on the issue. The Tsar, who in the event of Serbia's defeat would have to stop Turkey from re-establishing her hold on the Balkans, was against going to war. The Empress wholeheartedly supported the Slavs, equipping a hospital train at her own expense, while Sasha called for active intervention and encouraged the élite Guards regiments to volunteer. Nearly eight thousand officers and five thousand men joined the Serbian army and the Tsar was powerless to stop them.

Dagmar was also an advocate of Pan-Slavism, although whether this was out of loyalty to her husband or to her hatred of Germany is not clear. Her first concern was how war would affect her family. Greece was the enemy of Turkey and stood to gain territorially if Turkey was defeated; England, who wanted Turkey as a barrier against Russian expansion in the Mediterranean, could not allow a Russian occupation of Constantinople, which would threaten the route to India. Despite the opposition of Bertie and Queen Victoria, who came down against Russia, Alix and Dagmar were determined to do something to help Greece. Willie hoped Dagmar would use her influence with the Tsar.

The Serbian army proved no match for the Turks and they blamed the Russians. The Tsar finally capitulated and in April 1877 he declared war.

Dagmar was delighted when the Tsar asked Greece to join the fight. She now saw her chance to put family connections to good use, but the mood was short-lived. Britain and France (who, with Russia, were Greece's guaranteeing powers) objected and, to Willie's disappointment, he was obliged to remain neutral.

Sasha was assigned to the command of the 40,000 strong Ruschuk Corps on the Danube, whose task was to cover the Russian troops' rear. Accompanied by nine-year-old Nicholas, Dagmar went to the station to say goodbye as Sasha, the Tsar, Vladimir and Sergei left for the front. Alexis was serving with the navy in the Danube. Sasha left his wife the gift of a black leather book with a note on the blotting paper inside: 'On the day of my departure for the Danube, to the army. Your faithful friend, Sasha. Tsarskoe Selo. May 21 1877. Au revoir!'[2]

Since she arrived in Russia Dagmar's self-confidence had grown enormously and, with hopes of helping her brother frustrated, she concentrated wholeheartedly on war work. Along with other noble ladies she trained as a nurse in one of the St Petersburg hospitals. The work was not easy for ladies used to a life of luxury; the soldiers were filthy and had little respect for anyone, including their officers. Military hospitals had changed little since the end of the Crimean war but Dagmar was willing, efficient and capable.

The Empress was President of the Red Cross but ill-health meant that Dagmar frequently deputised. She was soon forced to abandon her work in the wards to sort out the chaos in the hospitals and the voluntary relief organisations, who gave assistance to the soldiers in the field and their dependants at home. She attended nurses' training courses, organised a hospital train bearing her name and went to the station when the troops and nurses left for the front. She had never done any large-scale social work before but, despite inexperience, proved herself a first-class administrator.

Although Dagmar received long, detailed letters from Sasha, she missed him terribly. One night, it is said, the exhausted Tsarevitch returned to his quarters after a day in the field and saw the figure of a nurse illumin-ated in the dim light of his candle. Shocked at this impropriety, he was about to order her to leave when he realised it was his wife, who had travelled incognito to the front with one of the hospital units.

By June the Russian army had crossed the Danube and was heading for Constantinople. As the casualties mounted the Imperial family was not immune. On 24th October the Tsar's nephew, Duke Sergei of Leuchten-berg, was killed on the Lom. Things began to go wrong; the early enthusiasm of the people turned sour and they blamed the Imperial family. First Grand Duke Michael Nicholaievitch was forced to retreat and regroup after his supplies were cut off from the rear by mountain tribes-men; then at the sleepy little town of Plevna the Russian army was bogged down in a siege that lasted four months. The casualty lists were long, especially among the Guards. What should have been an easy victory over a relatively unimportant stronghold turned into a thorn in the Emperor's side. Dagmar was in regular contact with Willie and, when the Russians were defeated with heavy losses at the third main assault, she sent a secret wire telling him the offensive would not be continued. Willie immediately came to Russia's aid by moving his troops towards the frontier to draw off the Turkish army. Finally, on 10th December, Plevna surrendered and the Russian army advanced to the Shipka Pass, where they defeated the Turks in a surprise attack. The tide had turned.

On 23rd December the Tsar made a triumphal return to St Petersburg. The Turkish army had evaporated; the fortress of Kars had surrendered; Sofia, Philippololis and Adrianople had been taken and at the turn of the year the age-old dream seemed about to be realised – Constantinople lay within reach of the Russian army.

For the first time, Sasha and Dagmar were separated on 1st January. 'My dear sweetheart Minny', he wrote, 'this first chance I have to write to you on New Year's Day itself. I would like to embrace you in my thoughts and with my whole heart wish us both our old, sweet, dear happiness ... and preserve, O Lord, that happiness which we, thanks to your grace, have enjoyed for more than 11 years! ...'[3]

As the Russians swarmed across the Balkans, Turkey appealed to the Great Powers for help and Queen Victoria telegraphed immediately to the Tsar asking him to stop. England, anxious to prevent the growth of Russian influence, could not remain neutral if Constantinople was occupied by Russia and sent six warships into the Sea of Marmora to 'protect' the British subjects. England erupted in a wave of patriotism against Russian expansion. Dagmar railed against this anti-Russian hysteria and particularly blamed the Prince of Wales for his excessive bias towards Turkey. She felt unfairly blamed for the Prince's anti-Russian stance.

The Tsar quickly agreed to an armistice and, at the hastily concluded Peace of San Stefano in March, Russia gained a considerable increase in territory. A large Bulgarian state was created under Russian protection but England objected and started moving troops. Austria, seeing a threat to the balance of power, supported England. Faced with the threat of European war Alexander backed down and agreed to a congress in Berlin, with Bismarck as 'honest broker' to divide the spoils again.

At the peace negotiations in July 1878 Russia lost most of the territory recently gained and Greater Bulgaria was reduced to a small Bulgarian state. Russia acquired Ardaka, Kars, Batum and Southern Besserabia; Serbia, Montenegro and Roumania were freed from the Turkish yoke and confirmed as independent sovereign states. Thanks to the efforts of Disraeli, Greece was finally given Thessaly and a small piece of Epirus, although it took three years, after Dagmar became Empress and was able to exert her influence, before the convention was signed. Bosnia and Herzegovina were occupied by Austria and left to store up future trouble. Turkey, 'the sick man of Europe', was preserved.

The new peace terms provided no real answer to the Eastern Question and the Balkans remained a powder keg, with a fuse timed to explode in the summer of 1914.

*

Dagmar was a keen patron of the arts and seldom missed an art exhibition. A catalogue of one hundred of her paintings survives in the archives, almost a third of them purchased in Denmark. The collection included pictures of places in Denmark, her parents, other members of the Royal family and one of Nixa by Elizabeth Jerichau Bauman (who had painted Dagmar and Alix when they were children), a gift from Sasha in 1870. In 1867 she became head of the Society of Art Lovers in Moscow.

Under her encouragement Sasha also began to collect and, thanks to his art broker Bogoliubov, he acquired a number of Russian and Western European paintings which were displayed at the Anitchkov. Dagmar's Christmas present to him in 1875 was her portrait by Heinrich von Angeli. Sasha's collection of Russian decorative art later formed the nucleus of the Russian Museum in St Petersburg. They both patronised the Peterhof Imperial Lapidary Factory and ordered things both for their own needs and as gifts for relatives. Dagmar bought him many objets d'art and encouraged the family to do the same.

Literary works by both Russian and Danish writers also figured strongly in Dagmar's possessions and she kept a small book of autographs of famous musicians and composers. She often attended the literary soirées which were such a popular feature of society in the late 1870s. At one such evening Feodor Michailovitch Dostoevsky read a chapter from *The Brothers Karamazov*, in which he describes a woman's pain at the loss of her three-year-old son. As Dagmar listened, everybody noticed that she wept at the memory of her own little boy Alexander.

In 1880 at a literary evening at the Marble Palace, home of Grand Duke Constantine Constantinovitch (himself a poet and playwright who wrote under the name K.R.) Dagmar met Dostoevsky. A few months later she invited him to the Anitchkov where he was presented to the Tsarevitch. She last saw Dostoevsky at a charity evening at Countess Mengden's home in December 1880, a month before he died.

Dagmar's study at the Anitchkov, with its walls and furnishings of raspberry-coloured silk, played an important part in her daily activities. The walls were filled with paintings. Her desk was cluttered in the fashion of the day with family photographs and knick-knacks galore. In the centre was a letter file with the monogram 'MF', a sphinx with a clock and a small sledge bearing a water barrel with crystal ice, a popular ornament of the time. Here she wrote long letters to her family.

Dagmar never ceased to feel homesick for her parents and beloved Denmark. She looked forward to her mother's weekly letter, which arrived every Thursday and was full of all the latest events at home.

Occasionally she also received a letter from Thyra who, unlike her sisters, was not a prolific letter writer. Thyra had not had an easy time. In 1870, when she was seventeen, she fell in love with William Frimann Marcher, a Danish army officer and, it is said, became pregnant. To avoid a scandal Queen Louise took her to Rumpenheim and then to Athens, where rumour said a daughter was born around Christmas 1871. Marcher was forbidden to see the princess and hanged himself in January 1872 after an angry meeting with King Christian, leaving a letter for his brother-in-law which has been destroyed. A few weeks later Queen Louise told relatives that Thyra was ill.[4]

By 1877 Thyra was still without a husband and in January Dagmar told Queen Louise that Marie von Flotow's brother had hopes of marrying her. Although Dagmar thought it would be wonderful to have her sister living in Russia, she felt the prospective bridegroom was not really suitable. Although she would not object if her sister liked him, she would not actively support the idea.[5]

Nothing came of this and in December 1878 Thyra married Prince Ernst August, *de jure* King of Hanover, who on his father's death earlier that year took his British title, Duke of Cumberland. Ernst August's father was Queen Victoria's cousin the blind King George V of Hanover, who had lost both his kingdom and a large personal fortune when Hanover was annexed by Prussia in 1866. He and his family were bitterly anti-Prussian and never reconciled themselves to the loss of their realm.

Thyra and the remarkably plain Ernst August had first met in Rome in 1872 but political considerations stood in the way of a betrothal until the autumn of 1878. The marriage was seen by Bismarck as yet another manifestation of anti-Prussian feeling by the Danish Royal family and he retaliated by cancelling the promised plebiscite in the Danish parts of Schleswig. Dagmar never forgot how the shock of this decision hurt her family.

Dagmar did not attend the wedding. On 4th December 1878 she gave birth to another son, Michael, who she called 'Misha'. She tried to treat all her children the same and was against showing any bias. Nevertheless, she later admitted to King Christian that Misha could *almost* be her favourite. He was certainly Sasha's favourite son. 'The birth of children', the Tsarevitch told Pobedonostsev, 'is the most joyful moment in one's life, and it is impossible to describe it because it is a very special feeling, unlike any other'.[6]

*

In October 1879, on their way home from the Art and Industry Exhibition in Copenhagen, Sasha and Dagmar paid a courtesy visit to Berlin. The Tsar hoped to show by this visit that the family ties and friendship between the two countries had not been disturbed by Bismarck's alliance with Austria.

Dagmar, along with many other Russians, blamed Germany for the unfavourable peace terms. Large territorial gains had been made and

Russia had been cheated of them by Bismarck. She encouraged Sasha to be more anti-German than ever and he, sickened and disillusioned by the war, became one of the most outspoken opponents of his father's policies. Relations between father and son deteriorated to such an extent that a public reconciliation was staged.

At this point, as the Tsar's popularity faded in the aftermath of the war, the revolutionary movement, which had been dormant for some time, suddenly sprang into action. The new, highly-organised, 'Land and Liberty' movement split into two sections: the 'Black Partition', who were against terrorism; and the 'Nihilists', or 'People's Will', dedicated to the destruction of the old regime by violence.

It was the Executive Committee of the People's Will who formally condemned the Tsar to death.

CHAPTER 6

Reign of Terror

'THE GLORIES OF OUR BLOOD AND STATE
ARE SHADOWS, NOT SUBSTANTIAL THINGS;
THERE IS NO ARMOUR AGAINST FATE;
DEATH LAYS HIS ICY HAND ON KINGS'
— James Shirley (1596-1666)

There had been several attempts on the Tsar's life since 1866; in the autumn of 1879 there were three more as he returned from the Crimea. Three mines were laid on the railway but at the last moment the Tsar's route was changed. Although the Moscow bomb exploded, it only succeeded in blowing up the identical train carrying the Imperial luggage. 'Am I such a wild beast that they must hound me to death?', Alexander exclaimed.[1]

Then, in their most audacious exploit yet, the Nihilists infiltrated the Winter Palace itself.

That winter Stephen Khalturin found work as a carpenter in the palace and gradually smuggled sticks of dynamite into the basement in his tool-bag. The basement was under the guardroom which, in turn, lay under the Tsar's private dining-room.

By early 1880 the Empress was clearly dying and had returned to Russia from Cannes. On 17th February her brother Prince Alexander of Hesse and his son Prince Louis of Battenberg (father of Lord Mountbatten) were on their way to St Petersburg. After tea, Sasha left the Anitchkov to meet the two princes at the station and escort them to the Winter Palace where they would dine with the Emperor. Before leaving the palace that evening Khalturin lit a slow-burning fuse, timed to explode while the Imperial family were in the dining-room two floors above.

Prince Alexander's train was delayed and they were half an hour late when the Tsar greeted them at the Winter Palace. As the Emperor and his guests walked down the long corridor to the dining-room there was a loud explosion. Prince Alexander described how 'the flooring was forced upwards, the gaslights extinguished' and they were plunged into darkness. Dust and explosives filled the air and, in the confusion, someone

70

shouted that the huge chandelier had crashed down onto the table. The dining-room windows were shattered, the walls were crumbling in and through a hole in the floor the wrecked guardroom was visible.[2]

There were no casualties among the Imperial family but ten of the Finnish Guards had been killed and another forty-five were injured, many with severe burns.

Soon after six Dagmar arrived at the palace to find the corridor in darkness after the explosion. In her diary she expressed her horror, and her relief that the Emperor and his family had all been spared.

The following day, their morale shattered, the Imperial family attended a Thanksgiving Service. Badly shaken, they realised that if Prince Alexander's train had been on time the Nihilists would have killed them all. 'We are reliving the Terror', wrote Grand Duke Constantine Nicholaievitch, 'but with this difference: the Parisians during the revolution saw their enemies face to face. We neither see them nor do we know them'.[3] The Tsar still refused to grant a more liberal regime.

On 2nd March the Tsar's Silver Jubilee was celebrated with a Te Deum. Wearing a dress of cloth of gold trimmed with dark fur, Dagmar walked to the chapel followed by her ladies in crimson and gold. Despite the splendour of the occasion the atmosphere was tense. 'Heaps of people were there', wrote Lady Dufferin, the British Ambassador's wife, 'all very proud of their courage in coming'.[4]

Among her family, there was increasing concern for the Tsarevna's safety. Alix wrote immediately to Dagmar, expressing her concern that her beloved sister was not even safe in her own palace. Dagmar's parents were also extremely worried but King Christian could not help admiring his daughter's courage when she drove out unescorted in an open carriage, with only a lady-in-waiting, during the Jubilee celebrations.

Security was tightened and the Secret Police even spied on the Imperial family. Despite an outward appearance of courage Dagmar found the surveillance disturbing, so different from Denmark where no terrorists lay in wait for the Royal family. She trembled for the lives of her husband and children, aware that they were not even safe in their own palaces. Never again would she escape the shadow of fear – fear of the Nihilist assassins.

*

Long winters abroad had done little for the Empress' delicate health. She had not left her bed for several months and the Tsar refused to visit. He wanted nothing more than to spend quiet evenings with Catherine and their children and he moved them into the Winter Palace for greater security. The Imperial family were appalled and took it as *carte blanche* to do as they liked in their own private lives.

Dagmar's official duties now increased. She gave audiences, received the Ambassadors' wives and attended official dinners, as senior ranking lady entering on the arm of the Tsar. At Court she was the most popular member of the Imperial family, especially with the young boys of the Corps de Pages who appreciated her efforts to protect them when things went wrong. On one occasion, a page spilled hot soup on her bare shoulder during a state dinner. Horrified, he grabbed her napkin and began to rub her skin vigorously. Very quietly she asked him to stop and then, with a smile, put her finger to her lips as a signal to the other guests that they were not to let the Tsar know what had happened.

In the summer of 1880 Sasha moved his family to the Yelagin Palace on the island of the same name in the Neva delta. Yelagin Island was a popular place for fashionable society to watch the magnificent sunset over the Gulf of Finland and the palace became one of Dagmar's favourite summer homes. It was far enough outside the city to give them extra security but, being only half an hour's drive from the Winter Palace, close enough to allow them to visit Sasha's dying mother every day.

Huge mahogany doors opened onto an enfilade of state rooms decorated with a variety of different coloured marbles. Mirrors, crystal chandeliers and wall-lights gave a light and airy appearance. Even on the dullest day the gold and white north-facing dining-room, with huge mirrors reflecting the gardens, appeared bright and cheerful. French windows in the impressive Oval Salon led to a terrace but the main benefit for Dagmar's family was the palace's vast grounds. The large park ran down to the banks of the river. Swans and exotic birds filled the pond and centuries-old Oak trees gave the garden a very English appearance.

After the tension in St Petersburg Dagmar loved the peace and quiet of Yelagin and the cosy, comfortable palace. In a letter to Queen Louise, erroneously stated in Inger-Lise Klausen's biography to have been written from Gatchina, which is nowhere near the Neva, Dagmar said: 'I have a beautiful view of the Neva river's arm, which surrounds the island'. She went on to describe the flowers, the swallows and the 'masses of nightingales singing until long into the night'. Most of all it gave her family some freedom. 'The poor children ... are happy to be out of the city and enjoy this dearest place immensely'.[5] When Queen Olga of Greece arrived with her family the park proved ideal for the children's wild games. Dagmar's children always wore high leather boots outdoors and the Greeks pestered Queen Olga until she bought them some as well.

In May the Duchess of Edinburgh arrived at the Winter Palace to see her dying mother. As the Empress lay in the huge state bed she could hear Catherine's young children in the rooms above. The Duchess was shocked at her father's insensitivity and they had a serious row. Soon afterwards

Catherine left for Tsarskoe Selo and later that day the Tsar followed – he never saw his wife again.

The Empress died in her sleep during the night of 3rd June. The maid discovered her body the following morning. Later the Tsar said she died completely alone, without even a nurse in the room.

The funeral was hurried. Usually the services for a Tsarina lasted a month – in Marie Alexandrovna's case they were over in a week. During the procession to the SS Peter & Paul Cathedral there was a ferocious storm which nearly sent the coffin into the Neva. As the cortège passed along the banks of the river the atmosphere was tense. There were rumours of a Nihilist plot to blow up the bridge and the people watched the approach of the 'Herald of Death' – an imposing black-clad court official carrying a sword nearly as large as himself – with some alarm.

By now the tension in St Petersburg was immense. The Emperor, refusing to become a prisoner in his palace, was surrounded by a Cossack escort whenever he travelled and plain clothes police were everywhere. Every day a fresh attack on his life was expected. Although some of the Nihilists' minor accomplices were arrested, the core was still intact and continued to plan the assassination of the Tsar.

*

Forty-six days after the Empress' death the Emperor secretly married Catherine Dolgoruky. The indecent haste was said to be at Catherine's insistence, although the Tsar was equally anxious, saying that 'he could never be sure on any day that that day would not be his last on earth'.[6] He refused to wait either for the elapse of the customary year required by the Orthodox Church, or for his heir to return to St Petersburg. None of the Imperial family were told and even the palace servants were unaware of the ceremony. The marriage was to remain secret until a decent interval had elapsed since the Tsarina's death.

Sasha and Dagmar had been staying at the Villa Brevern in Hapsal on the Baltic, a place of which Dagmar was very fond. The children bathed and played on the sand, Dagmar rode and Sasha hunted wild duck. In July, leaving their children in the care of Princess Kurakin, they returned to St Petersburg for the service marking the fortieth day since the Empress' death.

Not until 21st July did the Tsar inform them of his marriage. He explained his concern to do his duty by Catherine and their children, to regularise their position and to ease her conscience. He asked them not to mention the wedding to anybody. Sasha and Dagmar were horrified.

The German Crown Princess did not hear about it until November. 'It is not to be made known until 2nd or 3rd December', she reported.

'... After the marriage ceremony the Emperor sent for Minny and the Cesarewitch and presented his wife to them and asked them to be kind to her ... What one must feel bitterly is the want of respect for the poor Empress's memory'.[7]

The rest of the Imperial family were stunned by the news. There were rumours that Catherine was to be crowned Empress. Dagmar threatened to leave for Denmark if they proved correct; the Tsar retaliated by giving orders that the Imperial yacht was to be 'unavailable'. If Catherine was crowned, Dagmar would be forced to yield precedence to her not only in the present Emperor's lifetime but, by the laws of the Imperial House, during the reign of her own husband as well. Such a possiblity was unthinkable.

In October, with Denmark out of bounds, Sasha and Dagmar accepted the Tsar's invitation to stay with him at his Crimean estate, Livadia. The Crimea was the favourite holiday resort of the Romanovs. Many of the Grand Dukes bought land there and by the end of the nineteenth century the Imperial estates covered half of the peninsula, their palaces dotted along the coastline between Yalta and Sevastopol. The railway only ran as far as Sevastopol. From there Livadia was reached by a four hour boat trip along the shores of the Black Sea, or by carriage, which took all day.

The scenery was spectacular. 'After climbing up and up for the last time we went through an old archway, then suddenly the whole of the Black Sea spread before our eyes', recalled Baroness de Stoeckl. 'It is the most beautiful and startling sight one can imagine'.[8]

On the boat from Sevastopol, Sasha and Dagmar were informed that Catherine was staying in the late Empress' quarters, not at her own villa near Yalta. 'Had I known [earlier] ... I could have ... taken another boat back to Hapsal', Dagmar said later. 'But here we were – trapped!' At Yalta the Emperor apologised because Catherine was not there to meet them. 'You have impressed me so seriously with the secrecy of the affair', replied Dagmar boldly, '... no-one in my entourage knows anything about it, and the presence of the Princess here would have created surprise and gossip'.[9]

The Tsar's wooden palace was dark and gloomy. Sasha and Dagmar occupied one wing and regularly joined the Emperor and his wife for meals, but relations between the two households were distant. On Sundays, the Tsar invited ministers and local dignitaries to lunch. On one Sunday Dagmar sat on the Tsar's right and acted as hostess; the following week she and Sasha went hunting or on an excursion into the mountains while Catherine occupied the place of honour.

Despite the warm weather Dagmar's manner was cold. She could not forget that the woman who now shared the Tsar's life had caused his estrangement from his wife. She remained proud and aloof and the princess wisely made no attempt to force her company on the Tsarevna. The Emperor insisted Catherine be treated with due deference and reprimanded Dagmar for her attitude. He also asked Sasha to take care of Catherine and the children in the event of his death.

Sasha, although outwardly courteous to his young stepmother, was unable to understand his father's obsession and was equally disapproving, feeling the insult to his mother's memory. He had not forgotten how kind the Empress had been to Dagmar, who had earned the Tsar's disapproval for her strong feelings against Germany.

Early in December they all returned to St Petersburg. A brief stop was made at Kolpino station where, at the Tsar's command, other members of the Imperial family were waiting. There was a short, formal ceremony of introduction but Catherine's reception was as icy as the weather. A few days later she was created Her Serene Highness Princess Yourievsky. The question in everyone's mind was, did the Emperor intend to have her crowned? They anxiously awaited the family dinner on 6th December at which an announcement was expected.

All the Imperial family, young and old, gathered in the dining-room that evening, the women making no secret of their disgust. Even the normally imperturbable Master of Ceremonies seemed embarrassed. As the Tsar entered briskly with a 'strikingly attractive' woman on his arm Dagmar lowered her eyes and several of the women turned their heads away.

All eyes were focused on Catherine as she sat in the Empress' chair. She was extremely nervous and frequently turned to the Tsar for encouragement but all her attempts to join in the conversation met with a polite silence. One of those present felt that the men would have melted a little if it had not been for their wives. They took their cue from Dagmar, who toyed with the food on her plate and maintained an icy reserve. When Catherine forgot herself and addressed the Tsar by his pet name, Dagmar shuddered. After dinner a governess brought in Catherine's three children. Dagmar's twelve-year-old son Nicholas was amused to discover that he had an uncle four years younger than himself.[10]

As news of the marriage spread across Russia the most incredible stories circulated and Catherine was accused of plotting the downfall of the autocracy. There were rumours that a palace revolution would place the Tsarevitch on the throne, or that he would be passed over altogether in favour of his eldest half-brother George Yourievsky (a fact that Sasha and Dagmar must have considered with some dismay). Superstitious peasants crossed themselves and remembered the old prophecy that instant death awaited any Romanov who married a Dolgoruky.

Sasha and Dagmar's attitude did nothing to check the gossip. Invitations to family dinners had to be accepted, their children played with their step-uncle and step-aunts, etiquette required calls to be exchanged – but every visit to the Winter Palace became an ordeal. They preferred to have nothing to do with Catherine except when they were forced to see her at Mass on Sunday.

Dagmar inflicted her own snub. After Mass the Imperial family filed past the Emperor as they left church. Normally Catherine tactfully stepped back, leaving the Tsar to greet his family alone; but one Sunday he kept her by his side. Dagmar was the first to approach the Emperor. 'Come, my dear, say how do you do to the Princess', he said. Dagmar gracefully curtseyed to her father-in-law and swept off, her proud head held high, without even a glance at Catherine.[11]

*

At the beginning of 1881 Dagmar was still feeling the Tsar's displeasure and he at first refused to partner her at the opening ball of the Season. Fortunately, at the very last moment, he was dissuaded from inflicting such a public humiliation on his daughter-in-law.

In her New Year's letter to her mother, Dagmar expressed her amazement that things had changed so quickly in a year. Now, only six months after the Empress Marie's death, the Emperor's new wife appeared in church with her eldest son and flaunted her children before the whole court.

The following week she alluded to the possibility of Catherine's coronation, saying she would no longer be surprised at anything that happened. Later that year Dagmar told her brother Willie that she had been absolutely convinced that Catherine would be crowned Empress.

The Emperor had become unpleasant to his family because of their animosity towards Catherine. On the Friday of the Great Easter Fast they assembled to ask forgiveness of one another, as was the custom. When Catherine approached, Dagmar extended her hand but did not kiss her and for this she was reproached by the Tsar. 'Sasha is a good son', he cried, 'but you – you have no heart!' Only the Tsarevitch escaped without a scathing remark from the Emperor that evening. The incident upset Dagmar and the following day the Tsar apologised.[12]

Catherine now had no hesitation in asserting herself and, shunned by the court and society, she soon found a champion. After the bomb at the Winter Palace, General Count Michael Loris-Melikov was appointed head of the Supreme Executive Committee, with the aims of rooting out sedition, destroying the terrorists and improving relations between the government and the people. Loris-Melikov demanded and was given absolute authority. He and Catherine tried to persuade the Tsar to introduce measures that would appease the terrorists. Under his virtual dictatorship (the 'dictatorship of the heart')[13] many of the more repressive measures were rescinded and conservatives were included in the Council of Ministers. Within ten weeks the political disturbances had stopped and Loris-Melikov relinquished his absolute powers, becoming Minister of the Interior.

In February Loris-Melikov presented the Tsar with a draft manifesto for the reform of the Council of State, paving the way for full franchise in the future. He had so far managed to remain friendly to Catherine and to retain the Tsarevitch's favour but, by the end of February, Sasha and Pobedonostsev (who had been appointed Procurator of the Holy Synod, effectively Minister of Religion) had grave misgivings, feeling Loris-Melikov had gone too far. Many people suspected that the Anitchkov Palace led the opposition. Rumours circulated that the Tsarevitch was under house arrest but Sasha wisely avoided any open opposition to his father.

On Saturday, 12th March, the manifesto was brought to the Winter Palace for the Tsar's signature. It was to be made public the following Monday.

A collision seemed inevitable.

*

All this time the People's Will had not been idle. Now reduced to a handful of dedicated conspirators, the Executive Committee, under the leadership of Andrei Zhelyabov and his lover Sophia Perovskaya, planned the most daring attempt yet on the Emperor's life.

They rented a front basement on the Maly Sadovaya, the Tsar's normal route to the Winter Palace and, under cover of running a cheese shop, began to dig a tunnel in which to detonate a mine. Four bomb throwers were also trained in case the mine failed to explode. Then Zhelyabov walked into a police trap. Although the cheese shop was searched the tunnel was not found. When the police realised Zhelyabov's true identity they were relieved, believing the terrorists incapable of acting without their leader.

They had reckoned without Sophia Perovskaya.

*

On Sunday, 13th March, Alexander II signed Loris-Melikov's manifesto before attending Mass with the Imperial family as usual.

Relations between Sasha, Dagmar and the Tsar were still strained but, despite this, the Emperor was reported to be in good spirits when he left to attend the parade at the Michael Riding School. Afterwards he called on his cousin Grand Duchess Catherine Michaelovna before returning to the Winter Palace, not along the Maly Sadovaya but down the road alongside the Catherine Canal.

Dagmar was at the Anitchkov when the first explosion occurred. She had planned to go ice-skating that afternoon and, thinking a gun salute was being fired at the parade, she thought no more of it. Soon afterwards there was a second explosion. As Dagmar and Sasha rushed downstairs an officer galloped into the courtyard, dismounted at speed and ran inside, shouting that a bomb had been thrown. Sasha called for a sledge and they raced to the Winter Palace, giving orders that Nicholas and Georgie were to follow.

By the time they arrived in Winter Palace Square thousands of people were kneeling bareheaded in the snow. 'Large drops of black blood' pointed the way up the marble staircase to the Emperor's study, where Grand Duke Michael Nicholaievitch stood at the door giving orders. The first confused reports said he had been killed. When his wife saw him alive she fainted.

From Grand Duke Michael, Sasha and Dagmar learnt what had happened. When the Tsar changed his route Sophia Perovskaya coolly gave a pre-arranged signal to the bomb throwers. As the Emperor's carriage clattered along the embankment a bomb exploded under the back axle, wounding some of the Cossack escort and killing a baker's boy in the crowd. Shaken and unhurt, Alexander alighted from his carriage but, instead of using another one to hurry back to the palace, he insisted on seeing his potential assassin and enquiring after the casualties.

While the Emperor stood talking there was a second explosion as Ivan Grinevitsky, standing unnoticed by the canal railing, calmly hurled his missile at Alexander's feet. When the smoke cleared the badly mangled body of the Emperor was seen lying among the other casualties in the blood-stained snow. 'To the palace, to die there', he muttered to Grand Duke Michael.[14]

As Sasha and Dagmar made their way through the crowd at the study door, an unforgettable sight met their eyes. Although the Emperor's face and body were intact, his legs were completely crushed right up to the knees. It took Dagmar a few moments to see that his right foot was just a bleeding mass with half a boot. Nothing remained of the left foot but the sole of his foot. A few days later Dagmar told Queen Louise that she was still haunted, day and night, by the image of the Emperor's disfigured body. It was so horrible, she continued, that she had never seen anything like it.

The room was already becoming crowded as members of the family

3. *Princesses Alexandra, Thyra and Dagmar with their pony, 1856.*
(The Amalienborg Museum, Copenhagen)

4. The children of Prince Christian and Princess Louise, 1858. Back: Alexandra and Frederick. Front: William, Thyra and Dagmar. Prince Waldemar was born that year.
(The Amalienborg Museum, Copenhagen)

5. The Yellow Mansion, Copenhagen. Home of Prince Christian and Princess Louise.
(Author's collection)

6. *Dagmar's favourite brother, the irrepressible Willie, tries to spoil his sister's photograph, 1862.*
(The Amalienborg Museum, Copenhagen)

7. *Dagmar and her dog Beauty. Beauty accompanied her to Russia and was eventually buried on the Children's Island at the Alexander Palace, Tsarskoe Selo.*
(Private collection)

8. *Dagmar and her first love, Tsarevitch Nicholas, at the time of their betrothal in 1864. The princess was devastated by his tragic death.*
(Private collection)

9. *Dagmar and Tsarevitch Alexander, 1866. Although at first reluctant to marry,
their union was one of the most successful dynastic matches in recent history.*
(Private collection)

10. *Dagmar on horseback in the Crimea.*
Sasha particularly asked his fiancée to send him a photograph of her
in a tight riding habit.
(Private collection)

11. *King Christian IX and Queen Louise, 1884. Dagmar's parents were too poor to attend her lavish wedding in St Petersburg.*
(The Amalienborg Museum, Copenhagen)

12. *The Russian Imperial family. Front, l to r: Alexander II, Dagmar with her son Nicholas, Empress Marie Alexandrovna. Back, l to r: Paul, Sergei, Marie, Alexis, Sasha and Vladimir.*
(Private collection)

13. *Tsarevitch Alexander with his parents, Alexander II and the Empress Marie Alexandrovna.*
(Private collection)

ДВОРЕЦЪ.
НА СОБСТВЕННОЙ ЕГО ВЕЛИЧЕСТВА
ДАЧѢ.

14. The Tsar's private dacha known as 'My Property',
where Dagmar and Sasha spent their wedding night.
(Private collection)

15. *The Anitchkov Palace on the Nevsky Prospekt. Dagmar's Winter Garden is over the main entrance.*
(Marion Wynn)

16. *Dagmar's Music Room in the Anitchkov. The Palace was her home until the revolution.*
(Charlotte Zeepvat)

17. The Cottage, Peterhof, photographed in 1991.
This charming house was Dagmar's private property.
(Author's collection)

18. The Winter Palace. The home of the Imperial family was also the setting for
the magnificent Court ceremonies.
(Author's collection)

Ея И. В. Государыня
Императрица Марія Ѳеодоровна
и Наслѣдникъ Цесаревичъ
Николай Александровичъ

19. *Dagmar and her eldest child, the future Nicholas II.*
Mother and son remained close until circumstances tore them apart in the revolution.
(Private collection)

20. Dagmar and Grand Duchess Xenia, 1875.
The birth of her eldest daughter was a special delight to the Tsarevna.
(Det Kongelige Bibliotek, Copenhagen)

21. *Devoted sisters. Dagmar and Alexandra were particularly close and looked forward
to their annual reunion in Denmark.*
(Private collection)

continued to arrive. Dagmar, still wearing her blue velvet skating costume and holding her ice-skates in her shaking hands, was stunned into disbelief. Sasha stood by the window and Nicholas, white as a sheet, clung to the arm of his cousin. At that moment Princess Yourievsky burst in. Almost hysterically she threw herself over the Emperor's body, kissing his hands and calling out his name.

The agony lasted for forty-five minutes. A primitive blood transfusion was considered but it was hopeless. A priest was summoned to administer the last rites and Dagmar sobbed aloud as Sasha and the princess held the dying man's head. None of those present were able to forget that terrible day. An eye-witness remembered Catherine's 'soul-tearing shrieks' echoing through the room.[15]

The Emperor died at 3.35 pm. The eighth attempt on his life had succeeded. As the family knelt in prayer the princess fainted and was carried from the room, her negligée drenched with blood. The Imperial standard was lowered to half-mast and the A.D.C. stepped onto the palace balcony to announce the Emperor's death.

Sasha strode out, giving orders that all his ministers were to meet him immediately at the Anitchkov. Dagmar followed, too stunned to notice the courtiers bowing and curtseying as she almost ran to keep pace with him. When they reached the waiting carriage they stood for a moment saluting the crowds before driving away, surrounded by a Cossack escort.

By the time they reached the Anitchkov Dagmar was in tears. The servants assembled in the hall and Ivan, the old valet who had been with Sasha since his boyhood, offered them bread and salt. Later that day the household swore allegiance to the new Tsar.

The following morning, as the doctors worked in a nearby room to restore Alexander II's mutilated body before the lying in state, there was a ceremonial reception for the new Emperor and Empress at the Winter Palace. 'It was a most painful ceremony', reported Lady Dufferin. The new sovereign appeared 'quite overcome' and Nicholas (now the Tsarevitch) cried all through the service. 'They say [the Empress] cried all the time, even in the carriage, driving along …'[16] All mourning was put aside, as ladies in full court dress and gentlemen in gala uniform greeted the Emperor and Empress with loud cheers.

Thirty-six years later, almost to the day, the dynasty would be swept away.

*

St Petersburg was a city of mourning and a city of fear. The mourning was most evident in the black sleighs on the frozen Neva, the black streamers on the tramcars and the black crepe shrouding the lamp posts.

The fear was everywhere. An English visitor described the city as 'reeking of dynamite – a nest of invisible assassins'.[17]

The new sovereign was in considerable danger. Alexander II had been murdered by his people, not as the result of a palace conspiracy; there were very real fears for the life of his successor, who held violently opposing political views. Loris-Melikov begged the Emperor not to expose himself to further danger and Sasha agreed to move his family to the top floor of the Winter Palace, where Dagmar's rooms looked out towards the Admiralty.

On Tuesday evening Alexander II's sons carried his open coffin in procession to the palace church, where it rested on a golden catafalque with gold curtains. Twice a day for seven successive days the family attended a service. This was something of an ordeal, as by custom the late Tsar's forehead had to be kissed and decay had already set in. The funeral services for a Tsar were interminable and it was only on the eighth day that a rather untidy procession passed through the crowded streets to the SS Peter & Paul Cathedral. For security reasons the date was altered. All along the six mile route, which had been kept a closely-guarded secret, there was the constant risk of a terrorist attack. There were rumours that bombs had been placed beneath the cathedral and torpedoes were embedded in the ice of the Neva. The family's nerves were strained to the limit.

In an echo of her father's words when he became King of Denmark, Dagmar lamented to her mother that their happiest time was over and their peace of mind had gone. She would never be certain about Sasha's safety any more.

When the Prince and Princess of Wales arrived the Empress was at Gatchina station to meet them. Dagmar needed all the comfort and support her sister could give. Alix found her 'looking thin and ill', constantly haunted by the memory of the Tsar's mangled body lying in his study in the Winter Palace.[18] Freddie also arrived for the funeral. Although they all stayed at the Anitchkov for security reasons, Alix spent as much time as she could with her sister and in the company of her close family Dagmar's state of mind gradually improved.

The final funeral service took place two weeks after the Emperor's death. Dressed in a long, black woollen dress, a Marie Stuart cap and a floor-length veil, Dagmar took her place as the four hour long service, 'the most moving of the Russian Orthodox rituals',[19] commenced amid the flicker of innumerable candles.

Before they left the Winter Palace the Emperor and Empress had seen Princess Yourievsky and her three children waiting to go to the cathedral. Dagmar and Catherine stood looking at each other for what seemed like an eternity. Then the Empress, instead of formally extending her hand to be kissed, embraced the distraught widow, for whom she now felt the utmost sympathy. Throughout all the services Princess Yourievsky was always the last to kiss the dead Tsar's forehead.

Immediately after the funeral Sasha and Dagmar moved back to the Anitchkov, where the Prince of Wales invested the Tsar with the Order of the Garter at a private ceremony attended by Embassy officials. 'We all marched into the ... Throne Room ...', wrote Lord Frederick Hamilton, 'the Prince of Wales leading the way, with five members of his staff carrying the insignia on ... narrow velvet cushions. We made, I thought, a very dignified and effective entrance. As we entered ... a perfectly audible feminine voice called out in English "Oh! My Dear! Do look at them. They look exactly like a row of wet-nurses carrying babies!" ... The Empress and Princess of Wales looked at one another for a moment and then exploded into laughter'. By this time the Tsar was trying hard to control himself. 'Never, I imagine, ... has the ... Garter been conferred amid such general hilarity ...'[20]

The foreign royalties, including Bertie, all left hastily as soon as the funeral was over but Freddie stayed on. Alix, encouraged by Dagmar, also pleaded to be allowed to stay another week. Although Queen Victoria initially objected, the sisters had their way. Freddie and Alix left on 7th April. Dagmar went to the station to say goodbye but was too distressed to write a letter for Freddie to give to their mother. 'The Empress was crying very much', recalled Lady Dufferin, 'and [I] felt very sorry for her'.[21]

*

Andrei Zhelyabov and Sophia Perovskaya were hanged, along with others involved in Alexander II's assassination. The Emperor refused all pleas for clemency.

Pobedonostsev opposed the publication of Alexander II's manifesto and did all he could to influence the new Tsar in this direction. Loris-Melikov and his more liberal supporters at first carried the day and the Emperor asked them to finalise a programme for reform. In the meantime, Pobedonostsev drafted a new manifesto which unequivocally supported the autocracy. After the Emperor and Empress had read it, Sasha declared that this new manifesto would be published, without any further consultation, on 11th May. The ministers only learnt of it while they were meeting to discuss the planned reforms. The Emperor and Empress were both wholly under the influence of Pobedonostsev. Alexander III would reign as an autocrat.

Loris-Melikov and the other liberal ministers of Alexander II promptly resigned and in their place were appointed the reactionaries favoured by the new Tsar.

Dagmar understood nothing of what had happened and was furious at the ministers' resignations, feeling that they had let the Emperor down. She could not understand their reaction to Pobedonostsev's manifesto, which she thought had been enthusiastically greeted in most of the country. Only a few people, led by Loris-Melikov and Abaza (the Minister of Finance) wanted more, she told Queen Louise.

Other inevitable changes followed. Terrorists were hunted down and imprisoned; newspapers, books and magazines were heavily censored; university studies were curtailed and student organisations suppressed. Civil liberties were suspended at will. Those who did not share the Tsar's belief in autocracy began the long trek to Siberia.

As Emperor Alexander III and Empress Marie Feodorovna began their reign this policy could best be summed up in three words: Orthodoxy, Autocracy and Nationality.

PART 3

EMPRESS OF RUSSIA
(1881-1894)

CHAPTER 7

The Citadel of Autocracy

'THE NEW EMPEROR IS A VERY STAY-AT-HOME KIND OF PERSON,
DEVOTED TO HIS WIFE AND CHILDREN'

When Sasha became Emperor, Dagmar was thirty-three. Young, lively and at ease in society, a fourteen-year apprenticeship had left her perfectly trained for the position in which she now found herself.

Only one cloud marred the horizon. The constrained, prison-like atmosphere in which they were forced to live had an effect on her nervous system. Wherever the Tsar went he was heavily guarded. Terrified that an attempt would be made on Sasha's life, Dagmar insisted on driving with him through the capital. Her courage did not falter. As she sat beside him bowing gracefully few guessed the strain hiding behind her smile; but the tension showed in her eyes.

If they visited a theatre, plain-clothes police hid in the audience; if the Tsar dined at an officers' mess, security men concealed themselves in the pantry; in a private house the building was searched from attic to cellar and police crouched in bathrooms or on stairways. The threat of assassination loomed large each time the Emperor and Empress appeared in public. Unspoken fear haunted every journey. Yet the security measures made the Tsar unpopular. He never moved freely among his subjects as his father had once done and the contact between monarch and people was destroyed.

Early in April 1881, for security reasons, Loris-Melikov persuaded the Emperor and Empress to move from St Petersburg to Gatchina, a magnificently isolated palace about thirty miles south-west of the capital. Dagmar preferred living in town but Gatchina was easier to guard. They arrived the day after Freddie and Alix's departure and at first the Empress did not like the large palace at all. Dagmar shed many tears when she left the cozy Anitchkov Palace, especially as Xenia and Michael were ill and had to be left behind for a few days, but Sasha was pleased to leave the capital after the trauma of the past few weeks. Dagmar still could not get used to thinking of Sasha as the Tsar but told her mother that she loved her new title of Empress and hoped to hold it until she died.

To her delight, Sasha insisted on living at the Anitchkov when they returned to the capital every year for the Season. To achieve this a whole street of houses behind the palace was taken over and an underground passage was dug all round, guarded every few yards. In future the Winter Palace would only be used for State occasions.

Gatchina had formerly belonged to Emperor Paul. From the outside it looked like a barracks with towers, battlements, high walls, octagonal towers and a moat. Imposing iron gates admitted, or excluded, visitors. Paul and his wife had created formal gardens; the terrace looked out across the large park, where islands in the huge lake became a favourite place to have tea. There were grottoes, summerhouses, a river and a boat-house. In the Tsarski Sad – the Tsar's private garden – there was a secret exit reached from behind the panelling of one of Gatchina's nine hundred rooms; other hidden staircases led to underground dungeons and another long tunnel led from the palace to the Silver Lake. In one of the towers was the bed from the palace where Paul was murdered and the children were told he haunted Gatchina. Present curators and workmen have heard the barking of Paul's ghostly dog.

The massive palace had to be hastily renovated and the workmen were still busy when the Emperor and Empress moved in. The State Apartments had been furnished with exquisite taste by Paul's wife, the first Empress Marie Feodorovna, and the galleries housed the great art collections – the Chesmi Gallery, whose magnificent tapestries commemorated the victory over the Turks in 1768; and the Chinese Gallery where the Imperial children played hide and seek behind the enormous vases of porcelain and jade. Like the other palaces it was pervaded by 'a quite special odour, a mixture of turpentine, Russian leather, cigarette smoke and scent'; like 'clean wood', recalled Grand Duke Cyril.[1]

Sasha left Paul's rooms untouched. Instead he chose a set of apartments on the first floor of the Arsenal block to the left of the main building, which had once been occupied by members of Paul's court. Old photographs at Gatchina show a series of small, gloomy, unostentatious rooms with not even space for Dagmar's grand piano. Sasha could lift his arm and touch the ceiling with ease. The sunlight barely penetrated into some of the rooms and at first Dagmar found the dark, stuffy atmosphere depressing. Yet once they had settled in, she told Queen Louise that living in the *entre sol* was much nicer than she had expected. The furnishings were in bad taste – poor quality furniture and pictures by second-rate artists; unframed family portraits; photographs, which the children cut out from magazines and pinned to the wall. The head chambermaid told one astounded visitor that the sovereigns had chosen these rooms 'because they can't find anything more ugly and uncomfortable'.[2] In this unpromising setting Dagmar tried to create the cozy atmosphere of her Danish childhood.

Although Nicholas and Xenia preferred St Petersburg, the youngest children were happiest at Gatchina. Their large, vaulted playroom, recalled Lady Randolph Churchill, was 'full of comfortable armchairs and writing-tables, games and toys. I even spied a swing'.[3] At one end was a stage. There was also a billiard table, an American mountain (a kind of slide on which the children careered down on wheeled trolleys), a gymnasium, railways, dolls' houses, a kitchen where they could cook and a fortress complete with soldiers. A British visitor after the revolution noticed the lingering sense of happiness in the room.

The Emperor's study was shabby. Sasha was not a man to indulge himself with luxuries and he resisted all Dagmar's efforts to have the room redecorated and properly furnished. A few old armchairs and a large desk cluttered with papers and family photographs served him very well. Only the Arab servant in oriental dress outside the door indicated that the occupant of this poorly furnished room was the Tsar of Russia.

The Empress' sitting-room was furnished in pale pink and silver, with armchairs, sofas and rocking chairs upholstered in velvet. Her gold-walled boudoir, full of potted palms, was copied from one of the rooms at the Alhambra. Here she drank caravan tea from a gold service and smoked thin Russian cigarettes. A large Carrara marble bath, surrounded by real plants and shrubs, filled her dressing room.

In 1882 a telephone line connected Gatchina with St Petersburg and there was also a semaphore system between Gatchina and the Winter Palace. Outside Gatchina's walls was a garrison town, home of the Blue Cuirassiers. The Emperor and Empress therefore lived almost in a state of siege guarded by ten thousand men. The roads were patrolled by cavalry riding one hundred yards apart; at night lanterns were strapped to the horses' heads. Outside the high walls the guardposts were constantly manned and no-one could enter without a pass. Plain clothes policemen even followed the Emperor on his walks, until he objected so strongly that they were forced to dive into the bushes when he approached. Sasha and Dagmar were anxious to shield their children from any unpleasantness and, as she explained to her mother, they were never allowed out alone. The private apartments were guarded by Cossacks chosen for their splendid physique. At night they stationed themselves outside the Imperial bedroom doors and paced silently up and down beneath the windows. General Tcherevin, the Chief of Police, lived at Gatchina for six months every year. He was very fond of Dagmar and amused her with the latest gossip from St Petersburg.

Dagmar still longed constantly for her parents and repeatedly told her mother of her wish that she could fly to see them. She was disappointed that they would have to cancel the annual visit to Denmark and pestered her parents to come to Russia. When agreeing, King Christian made it clear that his small Civil List could not cope with a large Russian entourage who would expect expensive presents.

The visit, which took place in the autumn of 1881, went some way to reassure the King and Queen about their daughter's safety, although they did not refrain from giving their son-in-law advice. While King Christian was in favour of granting a constitution to appease the revolutionaries, the Queen took the opposite line. Writing to Sasha on 27th June 1882 she urged immediate reforms backed by calming, influential and, above all, honest, reports in the newspapers.

The advice proferred by Dagmar's well-meaning parents fell on deaf ears. Sasha and Dagmar were both too much under the reactionary influence of Pobedonostsev. Soon after his accession, the Tsar received a letter from the Executive Committee of the People's Will offering him the choice of revolutionary violence or constitutional reform. He became more reactionary than ever and the task of hunting down the terrorists began in earnest. Having little confidence in the police, who had failed to prevent his father's assassination, Sasha allowed his brother Vladimir to form a society, The Holy Band, with the Empress as its patron. Conceived by Count Vorontzov-Dashkov, its aim was to protect the Imperial family and countermand the activities of the revolutionaries. It soon had more than seven hundred members, including many of great wealth and influence. Pobedonostsev, seeing the organisation's power as a possible threat to the autocracy, persuaded the Tsar to have it disbanded.

The revolutionaries were still active. In March 1882 a mineshaft was discovered underneath the Kremlin, where preparations for the coronation were underway. Eighty workmen were arrested. A plan of the Kremlin and a considerable amount of dynamite was found on forty more people. Stories circulated that the Tsar opened an Easter Egg and discovered a note saying, 'Christ is Risen! We shall also rise again!'; or he opened a family photograph album and was confronted by a photograph of his father's assassins. A mine was discovered on the railway a few moments before the Emperor and Empress were due to arrive and the Berlin police uncovered a plot to throw bombs when the Tsar next went to Denmark.

Sasha answered terror with terror. Terrorists were caught and imprisoned or exiled to Siberia. Those who escaped were forced to flee abroad, their revolutionary forces destroyed. Barricaded away in Gatchina or hidden behind a Cossack escort the Emperor was rarely seen and he was unfairly accused of cowardice. The closely-guarded fortress, isolated from the outside world, soon earned the name 'The Citadel of Autocracy'.[4]

*

'His Majesty's manner is as simple as his tastes', wrote Lady Randolph Churchill.[5] Certainly the accent was on simplicity at Gatchina. The Emperor rose at seven, washed in cold water and dressed in the costume of the Russian peasant, or Moujik – a long cotton blouse which hung below his belt and baggy trousers. He soon earned the nickname of the 'Moujik Tsar'. After making a pot of coffee he sat down at his desk and started work. Dagmar rose later and joined him for a simple breakfast, often rye bread and boiled eggs. Prince Vladimir Obolensky, head of the Tsar's personal household, discussed the day's arrangements before the Emperor received ministers and officials, who were usually invited to lunch.

The family dined at eight o'clock. The four course meal was served in strict order of precedence and the children had time for only a few mouthfuls before their parents finished and the plates were whisked away. Once Nicholas was so hungry that he ate the beeswax from his gold crucifix, in which was embedded a tiny relic of the True Cross. After dinner Sasha read aloud in Dagmar's small sitting room, before he went back to his study to work. If visitors were present, dinner became a more formal affair and afterwards the Emperor ordered the palace orchestra to entertain them, often playing the bassoon himself.

Dagmar tried to work off her tension by long walks or rides in the park. Superbly elegant on horseback, she was an accomplished horsewoman who adored horses. The Don Cossacks, expert riders themselves, long remembered her skill in handling a particularly difficult animal. She passed on this love to her children, who were taught to ride in Gatchina's large riding-school almost as soon as they could walk.

Dagmar also handled her small pony chaise expertly but Sasha did not share this enthusiasm. Once the horses reared as he climbed in. He immediately jumped out, turning a deaf ear to her entreaties and shouting, 'if you want to kill yourself you can do it alone'.[6]

The Empress personally supervised the stables. The official head, General Arthur Grunwald, was a kind old man but not really suitable for the post. Dagmar once asked him to buy a larger pair of horses for her pony carriage but, when she asked to see them, was somewhat dismayed when he replied, 'yes, I bought them, but I would advise Madam not to drive them!'[7]

Dagmar and Sasha were devoted to animals and their children had numerous pets. The Emperor tramped for miles through the woods with his two favourite setters, Spot and Juno. Dagmar liked small dogs such as pugs or Pekinese and she had one little pug who followed her around. They kept Colossi (used for hunting bears) and the silky Borzoi dogs that Dagmar adored. She also loved parrots. Her favourite grey parrot was later carved in jade by Fabergé.

Sasha and Dagmar both enjoyed angling. She stood for hours on the banks of Gatchina's lakes fishing for pike or carp. Sasha bought the estate of Zaretchie, forty miles from Gatchina, which had duck, Siberian geese and several lakes stocked with trout. Dagmar could often be found sitting on a specially constructed raft, with a line and hook baited with worms patiently waiting for a bite. The Grand Dukes particularly liked the goose and duck shoots at Zaretchie, when they spent a couple of weeks at the estate's simple country house.

Dagmar also enjoyed the autumn trips to the Imperial estates in Poland. There were two main hunting lodges – Bialowieza and Spala. Bialowieza was situated in the middle of a large, trackless forest with elk, buck, wild boar, stag and the last remaining herd of bison in Europe. The forest became Alexander II's private property in 1880 and, when he became Emperor, Sasha decided to build a new stone palace in place of his father's wooden lodge. Work continued throughout his reign.

Spala, near Warsaw, was an unpretentious lodge built by Sasha's father within a forest of pine and fir trees. Its forty rooms were small, cramped and so dark that lights had to be left on all day. The forest was smaller and more open, with a river and little pathways running into the woods. Spala boasted some magnificent red deer and the inside of the lodge was decorated with their antlers.

From 1890 the Master of the Imperial Hunt was a close friend of Dagmar, Prince Vladimir Anatolievitch Bariatinsky. When the hunting horn sounded at seven o'clock Sasha went out early with the men to stalk elk or red deer, often accompanied by his elder sons. Dagmar organised picnics, drives or her own shooting parties. Both she and Sasha were members of the Royal Copenhagen Shooting Society. Sasha had a special gun with square bullets for shooting bears, which is now kept at Gatchina. Like many women of her class and upbringing, Dagmar also enjoyed hunting.

'At 7.30 I drove with Beloselsky and Berg to my parforce hunt, in which we followed a large stag for quite some time, without, unfortunately, getting it ...' she wrote in her diary at Spala in 1888. 'It was heavenly in the forest; I rode the new brown [horse] which went excellently ... We ended the hunt here nearby so we rode home ... We were quite dazed and had a bit of cold food here at home at 2 o'clock. Then I rested for about an hour and at 4.30 drove out for the other hunt'.[8]

After dinner the Emperor and Empress went out onto the terrace with their guests and, by the light of torches, inspected the day's bag laid out on the grass below. The head keeper used his dagger to point out the beasts killed by the Tsar.

Another of Dagmar's greatest pleasures was painting. From shortly after her marriage she was coached by Alexis Petrovitch Bogoliubov, who remained her painting tutor for thirty years. In his memoirs, he noted the careful way in which his pupil worked and her 'well-developed feel for art'.[9] Dagmar painted in oils, watercolours or sepia and her life-sized portrait of a coachman was exhibited in a gallery.

The Empress became a keen photographer and exchanged pictures regularly with her relatives. Arranging the latest photos in their albums was another family hobby. Later, Professor Schnerl invited her to become editor of *Photographic World*, a popular European journal at the turn of the century. She was also asked to help with the production of an album, *The Photographic Art of Royal Persons*.

Dagmar was a confirmed smoker but did not want it known outside the family. Prince Christopher of Greece once spotted the Empress greeting visitors, cigarette hidden behind her back, oblivious to the clouds of smoke rising up behind.

Although in some ways they managed to recreate the lifestyle of an English country house there was no mistaking the rank of the occupants of Gatchina. There were thousands of servants in the palace and on the estate ranging from Russians, Greeks, Negroes and Finns to Circassians dressed in raspberry coloured jackets with white trousers. Dagmar had Abyssinian servants who wore black jackets trimmed with gold braid, baggy red trousers, yellow shoes and white turbans. Once when the Empress was away her servant, Mario, signed for a telegram. The post-master at Gatchina mistook the final 'o' for an 'a' and had the receipt framed, thinking the Empress had signed it personally.

The Emperor could not tolerate any signs of weakness, even in his children. The Empress, although more tolerant, not only had to conceal her own mistakes but also the lapses of the staff. When a coachman drank too much and fell asleep, so that only with difficulty were the horses pulled up, Dagmar's main concern was to treat the incident as a joke and prevent Sasha from hearing about it.

In the spring of 1882 they moved to the summer estate of Peterhof, on the Gulf of Finland, for the birth of Dagmar's last child. Aptly named 'the Russian Versailles', the Grand Palace had a water stairway leading to an ornamental lake and a long canal bordered by fountains which reached right down to the sea. Throughout the park there were formal French gardens with fountains and water cascades. Peter the Great's massive palace was only used for State functions. Numerous small villas were dotted around the estate – Monplaisir, The Hermitage, The Farm, Marly – but Sasha and Dagmar always used The Cottage, which had become Dagmar's private property on her first day in Russia.

It was built by Sasha's grandfather Nicholas I in 1826 for his wife, the Empress Alexandra Feodorovna, in whose honour the private part of the Imperial estate in which The Cottage stood was re-named The Alexandria Park. Adam Menelaws designed a pretty yellow and white neo-Gothic family home, with verandas, gables and balconies. The Alexandria motif, a wreath of white roses pierced with a sword, which was the special emblem of Nicholas and Alexandra, appeared everywhere. The rooms were small and the villa had an intimate, homely feel. Pretty wrought-iron porches stretched across the outside of the main bedroom, the drawing room and a small study. Glass doors opened on to the romantic wild park and the Naval Study right at the top of the house led out to a veranda, with marvellous views over the Baltic. Dagmar's drawing room had a clock with sixty-seven faces showing the time in all the different provinces of Russia. In her chintz-covered study was a shelf displaying her collection of distinctive blue and white Danish porcelain.

The Cottage always seemed to be full of Dagmar's relatives. Queen Olga of Greece often stayed with her parents at nearby Strelna and the winding corridors, stairways and balconies of The Cottage provided perfect places for all the children to play hide and seek on wet days. The Empress was a great favourite with her nephews and nieces and she treated the Greek children like her own, even giving little Princess Marie dresses and hats identical to Xenia's. A particular favourite was 'Greek Georgie', Willie and Olga's second son, who became a close friend of the Tsarevitch. The younger children were somewhat in awe of him. The admiration increased when a rumour circulated that fourteen-year-old Georgie had been having an affair with one of the Greek nursery maids. The fact that most of them had no idea what 'an affair' was did not diminish their excitement at the news. Another frequent vistor was the Duchess of Edinburgh. 'Here we ... enjoy life more simply by ... being out of doors from morning till night', the Duchess wrote to a friend.[10] At Peterhof everything was more relaxed. Dagmar drove out alone in a droshkey (a small open carriage), something she could never do in St Petersburg; the Emperor rose early and gathered mushrooms for breakfast.

The celebrations for the Empress' Name Day, Dagmar's Saint's Day of St Mary Magdalene (more important to Russians than a birthday), took place at Peterhof every year on 22nd July/3rd August. In the evening the park and fountains were illuminated by coloured lamps and the Imperial family were taken by boat to one of the islands. At the open-air theatre a distinguished audience in uniforms and evening dresses watched the Imperial Ballet perform on a floating stage in the middle of a lake. 'A more wonderful setting ... could hardly be imagined', recalled one of the dancers.[11]

*

On 13th June 1882 a salute of 101 guns announced the birth of Grand Duchess Olga Alexandrovna. Soon every city and town in the country was celebrating the first baby to be born to a reigning sovereign (born 'in the purple') since 1860.

Named after her godmother the Queen of Greece but called 'Baby' by Dagmar, Olga was plain and delicate. Alix advised her sister to engage an English nurse, so Olga was raised in one of Gatchina's vast tapestried saloons under the supervision of Elizabeth Franklin, 'Nana'.

Dagmar soon became very jealous of Nana. The increase in her official duties prevented the same amount of time being spent with Michael and Olga as had been possible with her elder children. Although devoted to them, this led to the development of a 'gulf' between Dagmar and her youngest child. Olga later wrote that her mother could never forget that she was Empress of Russia and found it hard to unbend and leave her dignity outside the nursery. To the young Grand Duchess it always appeared that, when she and Michael got into childhood scrapes, their father would laugh once they had been suitably punished; but they always dreaded news of the escapade reaching their mother, particularly visits to the soldiers' barracks, which were forbidden. Olga thought that Dagmar had an aversion to anything undignified or improper. She felt intimidated by her mother, whose manner suggested that she was not really interested in her little daughter's problems. Olga would never have dreamed of going to Dagmar for comfort or advice and she never felt at ease in her company. Dagmar was much closer to the elder children, although it is said that she was not a concerned mother at this time.

Nicholas, the Tsarevitch, was now fourteen and inherited the small stature of the Danish Royal family. Although he had considerable stamina and all his life was fond of physical exercise, there was no sign either of his father's enormous strength or his mother's vivacity. Completely overawed by his gigantic father he turned to his mother, consulting and confiding in her, while she acted as a buffer between him and Sasha.

The only one of the children who could be described as a typical Romanov was George. Tall, handsome and full of fun he was always getting into mischief and, because his mother had a great weakness for him due to his delicate health, getting away with it. Georgie shared the Danish Royal family's love of practical jokes and had a wonderful sense of humour. Generous, intelligent, charming and out-going like his mother, he was reputedly the cleverest of the children.

Nicky and Georgie shared the same bedroom, nannies and later the same tutors. After Mme Ollengren left they were educated in adjoining rooms, without companions of their own age. They followed the course of the Academy of the General Staff and, at the age of nine, Nicholas was given a Governor, General Gregory Danilovitch. The tutors, who included Pobedonostsev, were distinguished professors but Georgie's constant teasing of them reduced Nicholas to helpless laughter.

Their English teacher Charles Heath had formerly been tutor to Grand Dukes Sergei and Paul Alexandrovitch. Heath taught Nicholas and George to speak and write almost faultless English. From him they also learnt a love of sport, particularly shooting and fly-fishing. George's green parrot, Popka, detested Mr Heath and flew into a rage when he entered the room, imitating his English accent in a most outrageous manner. The unfortunate tutor finally refused to enter until the parrot had been removed. There were several French tutors. Monsieur Dupeyret was dismissed after an erotic scandal but, despite this, Nicholas became fluent in French and was reasonable in German and Danish.

George's favourite target was the geography teacher. Although he had never travelled much further than St Petersburg he described places and things with the confidence of someone who had actually been there. Afterwards George would ask all kinds of questions, until the tutor was finally forced to admit that he had never visited the place at all.

The tutors were not permitted to put questions to their pupils. Like all visitors, they arrived in formal dress with decorations. One of their young Greek cousins never forgot the sight of the American dentist treating Olga, 'his tailcoat carefully pinned back, his sleeves tucked over his wrists and an impressive row of orders glittering on his breast'.[12]

Xenia, now seven, inherited her mother's wonderful eyes. Dagmar told Queen Louise how much her daughter had grown and what a big girl she was becoming. She was also pleased that Xenia seemed to be clever at drawing, was seldom without a pencil and could accurately sketch small faces and figures.

Michael and Olga were kept very much in the background and became inseparable companions. He was usually called Misha by the family, although Olga had several nicknames for him and in later years startled guests by forgetting herself at official functions and calling him 'dear, darling Floppy'.[13] Jovial and popular with everybody, he was the only one who could be cheeky to the Emperor and get away with it.

One day Misha was sitting outside near the palace when the Emperor, coming out onto the terrace, tipped some water over him. Michael slipped quietly away but later he took his revenge. Seeing his father sitting on one of the seats, he filled a large watering can and emptied it over the Emperor's head. The Tsar took his punishment without a word.

Although the children grew up isolated from the rest of Russia the Emperor insisted that they have as normal a childhood as possible. In the winter they skated, went on sleigh rides, slid down the hill on a piece of board (a sport in which Dagmar often joined), sawed wood, worked in the garden and baked potatoes over an open fire. It was this latter activity which gained the playmates of Nicholas and George – the young Sheremetevs and Vorontzov-Dashkovs – the nickname of 'the potatoes'. Another playmate was Sasha's cousin Grand Duke Alexis Michaelovitch who was the same age as Xenia. The children particularly enjoyed watching the huge Emperor test the newly-frozen pond in the palace grounds. Treading carefully on the ice, until it gave way under his weight, Sasha landed up to his knees in water.

A favourite plaything of their Greek cousins was the miniature railway laid out in the park. It was presented to the Tsar's children by a renowned firm of railway contractors and came complete with stations, tunnels and bridges. Its engines and carriages were replicas of real locomotives and could reach speeds of four or five miles an hour.

Indoors, Sasha took great pride in demonstrating his enormous physical strength. Dagmar had forbidden this, so he always had one eye on the door as, to the children's delight, he effortlessly bent iron pokers, horseshoes and solid silver plates.

In the long summer evenings they piled into traditional Russian carriages with seats back-to-back, followed by the cook and the servants, and went on a picnic. A favourite place was a Finnish-style house in the park. The children helped with the cooking while the adults explored the neighbourhood.

Dagmar took tea at five o'clock and the children joined her after their walk. Sometimes it was a more formal occasion attended by ladies of St Petersburg society. Once, as her valet Stepanov regally carried in the tea tray, George stuck out his foot and tripped him up, sending china and cakes flying all around the room.

*

The Duke of Windsor once described Christmas at Sandringham as 'Dickens in a Cartier setting'.[14] This was equally true of Christmas at Gatchina.

For several weeks beforehand uproar reigned at the palace. Christmas trees were delivered, packages arrived, Nana baked plum puddings in the nursery kitchen and cases of merchandise were sent from the most exclusive shops so that the Imperial family could select their gifts. One year Xenia spotted an exquisite scent bottle from Cartier and gave it to her mother for Christmas. Because the children's gifts were paid for out of the Privy Purse, Xenia had no idea of the bottle's monetary value. Dagmar gave orders that in future the children were not to choose any presents from these St Petersburg establishments. Presents also had to be given to the thousands of people who served the Imperial family, from members of the household and government officials to domestic servants, soldiers and sailors.

All Russian Christmases were white. By Christmas Eve the palace was in turmoil and the excitement intense. As the afternoon grew darker the servants stood at the windows looking for the first star, which signalled the end of the six-week Christmas fast. After vespers the Emperor and Empress presided over a family dinner, which the children were usually too excited to eat, before walking towards the huge double doors where Cossacks stood on guard. In the darkened room the tension mounted until the Emperor rang a small handbell, the great doors were flung open and there was a stampede towards the banqueting hall.

Inside a 'magic kingdom' awaited them. There were six trees for the family and many more for other relatives and members of the household, all shimmering with candles and covered with silver and gold ornaments made by the most exclusive jewellers. Beside each tree was a small table covered with gifts. With a practical mother and a father who disliked ostentation, toys, books and even gardening tools were among the presents to their children. Olga's usual gift to her father was a pair of soft red slippers she had made herself.

Later Dagmar distributed gifts to the servants' children and the soldiers garrisoned at Gatchina. After tea the Empress and her family sang traditional Christmas songs. Three days later the Imperial children dismantled the trees, giving all the beautiful ornaments to the servants.

Despite the constant police surveillance and the tensions of the outside world the Imperial family was noted for its happy family life. 'The new Emperor is a very stay-at-home kind of person, devoted to his wife and children', the British Ambassador reported. 'There is still very little known about him, probably because there is very little to know'.[15]

CHAPTER 8

Coronation

'GOD SAVE THE TSAR,
MIGHTY AND POWERFUL,
LET HIM REIGN FOR OUR GLORY,
FOR THE CONFUSION OF OUR ENEMIES,
THE ORTHODOX TSAR,
GOD SAVE THE TSAR'
                – Russian Imperial Anthem

D agmar's first major occasion as Empress was the coronation, which to the Russian people symbolised the Emperor's God-given right to rule. The delay before Alexander III's anointing caused rumours that he was afraid of meeting a similar fate to his father. The real reason was probably the Empress' pregnancy. Finally, an Imperial decree published in January 1883 announced that the coronation would take place on 27th May that year.

In anticipation of the event, there was an especially glittering series of balls that Season. One of the most memorable was the costume ball given on 25th January by Grand Duke and Duchess Vladimir at their palace on St Petersburg's Palace Embankment. The ball emphasised the nationalistic direction of the new reign. Two hundred and fifty guests in old Russian dress were received by Vladimir, in a boyar's caftan of dark green velvet trimmed with sable, and Miechen in the gold-brocade costume of a boyarina. The Emperor and Empress were welcomed with bread and salt. Sasha, who disliked dressing up, wore the uniform of a general of the cavalry artillery. Dagmar was resplendent in the dress of a seventeenth-century Russian Tsarina – a gold brocade tunic and a mantle both studded with precious stones, and a brocade coat trimmed with sable and decorated with golden flowers. Her headdress was trimmed with sable and ornamented with more enormous jewels. After supper, the dancing continued until four in the morning.

The Tsars were crowned in Moscow and preparations were already underway. The Kremlin palaces and cathedrals were restored and the people whitewashed and painted their houses. The budget for the coronation was 2,715,704 roubles, of which some 50,000 roubles was allocated for gowns and other expenditure for the Empress, including the coronation gown made by Isanbard Chanseu of St Petersburg. This allocation was ten times that allowed for her successor in 1896.

Dagmar naturally wanted her family to be invited but, traditionally, no reigning monarch ever attended a Russian coronation. Despite King Christian's wish to share any danger his daughter faced (and to Queen Louise's disappointment), they had to be represented by Waldemar. The Duke and Duchess of Edinburgh, Sasha's sister, went on behalf of Queen Victoria and Queen Olga of Greece, by birth a Grand Duchess of Russia, also attended.

Towards the middle of May visitors poured in from all over Europe, the Guards arrived from St Petersburg and extra police and troops came from the provinces. There were very real fears for the safety of the Imperial couple and tension was in the air. A few weeks before the ceremony the Emperor and Empress went into retreat at the Trinity-St Sergius Monastery, before taking up residence at the Petrovsky Palace, a fantasy of red brick with Gothic windows and turrets situated on the main road into Moscow. From here, Napoleon had watched Moscow burn in 1812.

At the Petrovsky Palace the foreign diplomats presented their credentials. The letters of Mary Waddington, American wife of the French Ambassador Extraordinary, to her sisters give a vivid eye-witness account of the hectic period of festivities. The Waddingtons were so worried about the Nihilists that before they left Paris they appointed a guardian for their young son and left instructions regarding M. Waddington's Will.

On 22nd May excited crowds gathered early to watch the Tsar and Tsarina's entry into Moscow. The white, blue and red Russian flag fluttered from buildings; balconies were decorated with garlands and carpets; masts were draped with banners and greenery. Spectators crowded into buildings overlooking the route and, as an extra precaution, three rows of citizens formed a voluntary guard behind the troops lining the long processional route. Even a few spots of rain failed to dampen the enthusiasm of the crowd, many of whom had stood for hours waiting for the signal that the procession was setting out.

The spectators were rewarded with a magnificent cavalcade: Don Cossacks, Cossacks from the Urals, Dragoons, Cuirassiers, Asiatic tribes with exotic names in colourful oriental costumes, all clattering by on horses looking like a scene from the Arabian Nights. Special cheers of admiration greeted the Emir of Bokhara with an escort of princes from Turkestan; and a party of Buddhist Lamas in shining gold capes riding white ponies, contrasting sharply with the nobles of the Russian Empire wearing their strikingly simple black and gold uniforms.

Row upon row of colourfully dressed courtiers heralded the approach of the Emperor's procession – footmen in frock-coats with powdered wigs and tricorn hats; huge Arabs with gold jackets and billowing red trousers; the couriers, with hats sporting ostrich plumes; the Imperial Huntsmen in green with the falconers' feather in their tall caps; and the gentlemen-in-waiting and chamberlains.

A line of golden carriages followed, containing the Masters of Ceremonies, the Members of the State Council, the suites of the foreign royal guests and the Earl Marshal of the Court holding his wand of office. Bringing up the rear were the Chevalier Guards with their shining cuirasses and winged helmets.

The Emperor left the palace on a big white charger at exactly ten o'clock. He appeared a strikingly simple figure in a plain Russian infantry uniform and a sheepskin cap, contrasting sharply with the splendour surrounding him. His departure was signalled by the firing of a gun and the joyful pealing of all Moscow's church bells. 'As the time drew near one felt the anxiety of the Russians and when the first coup sounded, all of them in the Palace and in the street crossed themselves'.[1] Behind his massive frame rode the boyish figures of his sons Nicholas and George, the other Grand Dukes, the foreign princes in their colourful regimental uniforms, the army chiefs and the A.D.C.s.

The deafening roar which greeted the Emperor reached a new crescendo when the Empress' coach appeared. This superb golden vehicle, drawn by six white horses led by footmen, had been a gift from Frederick the Great to Empress Elizabeth in the eighteenth century. The Imperial double-headed eagle was depicted on its hand-painted panels, its wheels were golden and a large golden eagle with folded wings perched on each corner of the roof. On top was a crimson cushion holding a replica of the Imperial crown.

Dagmar wore a simple white and silver dress, a diamond diadem and a white veil spangled with silver. More diamonds glittered on her neck and the bodice of her dress. Although tears of emotion shone in her dark brown eyes, occasionally she looked anxious. 'It must have been an awful day for her', Mary Waddington wrote to one of her sisters, 'for she was so far behind the Emperor, and such masses of troops in between, that he might have been assassinated easily, she knowing nothing of it'.[2] Beside her sat eight-year-old Xenia, copying the way her mother bowed and waved.

The Empress was followed by more carriages carrying the Grand Duchesses, foreign princesses and ladies of the household. At the end of the long procession, which took an hour to pass, came the Emperor's Cossack escort and the Guards.

They passed through the Triumphal Gate and down the two mile long Tverskaya to the Iverskaya Chapel just outside Red Square. Waving aside the equerries, Sasha chivalrously helped his wife and daughter from their coach. Dagmar turned towards the crowd and waved before walking towards the chapel with Sasha and Xenia, her heavy train carried by pages. They were received on the steps by the Metropolitan and went inside for a few moments of silent prayer at the gilded shrine of the Icon of the Virgin of Iberia, one of the holiest in Russia. Then the procession set off again, stopping to receive deputations or to allow the clergy to pray for the success of the Tsar's reign.

Passing through Krasnaya Ploschad (Red Square), where Moscow's schoolchildren were assembled, they entered the Kremlin through the Spassky Gate to the strains of the National Anthem. When the cannon fired to announce the Emperor's safe arrival 'the effect was indescribable ... The extraordinary reaction showed what the tension had been'.[3]

After prayers in the three great cathedrals – the Uspensky Sobor, the Archangel Michael and the Annunciation – they ascended the Red Staircase to the old Kremlin palace, where they were offered bread and salt by the High Marshal of the Court. The long day had been very tiring and Dagmar was glad to reach the private apartments on the ground floor of the more modern Great Kremlin palace, which comprised a dining-room, drawing room, boudoir and study for the Tsarina; a bedroom, study and private reception room for the Tsar.

On the first floor were the State Apartments, a series of halls dedicated to Orders of the Russian Empire – St Vladimir, St Catherine, St Andrew, St Alexander and St George – all decorated with marble, granite, malachite and gold, lit by massive crystal chandeliers, with parquet floors of twenty rare kinds of wood. Here, the following day, Sasha would swear allegiance to the Imperial standard, while outside, Heralds in colourful uniforms proclaimed the forthcoming coronation at public places throughout the city.

Dagmar received the Ambassadors' wives. 'We talked easily enough', recalled Mme Waddington. 'I hadn't seen her for some years ... and I didn't find her changed'. The Empress spoke about Paris and dresses and asked what she had seen in Moscow. Dagmar gave no indication of being nervous the previous day and Mary Waddington had the impression of 'extraordinary self-control'. The Ambassadress asked what Grand Duchess Xenia thought of it all, to which Dagmar replied 'that she really didn't know – that she didn't speak but looked at everything ...' The Empress remarked that although the day of the coronation would be very long she was 'quite accustomed to getting up early', but when Mme Waddington spoke of the long service with no seats for the Diplomatic Corps, the

Empress was 'quite indifferent; evidently didn't think it was of the slightest consequence whether we were tired or not, and I don't suppose it is'.[4] She had already refused a request by Miechen (who had just recovered from a bad attack of measles) for a folding chair in the cathedral, saying that as *she* would have to stand all day the Imperial family must do the same.

After all the audiences Dagmar was thankful to escape to the suburban Alexandra Palace in the Neskuchny Garden, one of Moscow's few royal residences, where she could rest.

The Crown Jewels had been taken to Moscow by train. The Emperor's crown was made for Catherine the Great in 1762. It contained 5,000 diamonds and weighed over five pounds. On top was a diamond cross mounted on a 415-carat ruby, bought from a Chinese Emperor by Tsar Alexis in 1676. It replaced the Cap of Monomakh which had been used to crown the ancient Russian monarchs. The Empress was also crowned with the Tsar's crown to symbolise her association with him as co-ruler. Dagmar's own crown, a smaller version of the Imperial crown, was made by Duval in 1801 and covered in diamonds from India and Brazil. It was surmounted by a beautiful sapphire. In the golden sceptre (one end of which contained a huge ruby) sparkled the great 193-carat Orlov diamond, the fourth largest in the world, which had once formed the eye of a golden idol in India. The large solid gold orb was banded by diamonds and surmounted by a jewelled cross. The day before the coronation the Imperial regalia was transferred from the Armoury to the Hall of St Andrew in the Kremlin palace.

That evening all the Imperial family attended church before supper. Dagmar was able to sleep that night but Sasha tossed and turned. At seven o'clock they were woken by the cannons signalling the start of the ceremonies.

*

At ten o'clock on 27th May Dagmar appeared in the 200-foot long St George's Hall beside the Emperor. She looked magnificent. Her dress of heavy silver brocade woven with geometric patterns in silver thread was in Russian style with long hanging sleeves and a low neckline. A long train edged with ruched white satin ribbon was fastened to the waist and her hair was arranged so that long ringlets fell onto her shoulders. The only ornaments were a pearl necklace because, Dagmar told Queen Louise, she felt naked without any jewellery, and the red sash of the Order of St Catherine.

Sasha, in the dark green and gold uniform of the Preobrajensky Regiment, gave the impression that he would be glad when the day was over and seemed almost annoyed at all the pomp surrounding him. With a smile for everyone, Dagmar made the rounds of the guests as they all kissed her hand in the ceremony of baise-main. She loved society, meeting relatives and presiding over great ceremonial occasions but this time she admitted to feeling as if she were to be sacrificed.

Preceded by court pages in black and gold uniforms and dignitaries carrying the Imperial regalia on velvet cushions, the Emperor and Empress moved off through the halls of the Kremlin at the head of a stately file of gentlemen-in-waiting, chamberlains, ladies-in-waiting, court officials and the Imperial family. From the the door of the Holy Vestibule they stepped out on to the porch as the sun broke through the clouds. The crowds in the square cheered wildly and they stood for a moment, bowing.

As they slowly descended the Red Staircase, the Grenadier Guards in the picturesque uniforms of 1812 presented arms and the great bell in the Kremlin tolled once. 'The next moment the bells of sixteen hundred Moscow churches started their joyous pealing, and the opening bars of the National Anthem gave the signal to a chorus of five hundred singers'.[5] Thirty-two adjutants stood at the bottom, holding a large red and gold canopy topped with swaying plumes, under which the Emperor and Empress walked to the Uspensky Sobor along a specially constructed wooden path covered with a red carpet.

The Uspensky Sobor was built in Russian style by an Italian architect in 1479 and its five golden domes dominated the Kremlin skyline. In 1812 Napoleon had stabled his horses there but it had now been completely refurbished. The icons in its 52-foot high iconostasis (icon screen) had been painted by the best Russian artists, the walls and pillars were covered with frescoes on a gold background and a painting of the Last Judgement covered an entire wall. Two thrones now stood on a platform under a gold canopy embroidered with Imperial eagles, surrounded by a gold balustrade.

A fanfare of trumpets announced the arrival of the Emperor and Empress at the massive copper-plated cathedral doors. They were escorted inside by the three Metropolitans in jewelled mitres and ornate cloth of gold vestments. The Tsar's throne was the 'Persian Throne', studded with rubies, sapphires, emeralds and turquoises, given to Ivan the Terrible by the Shah of Persia. The Tsarina's carved and lacquered throne was the seventeenth-century Diamond Throne presented by Armenian merchants to Tsar Alexis in 1660. It was covered with jewels – emeralds, tourmalines, turquoises, pearls, 1,223 rubies and over 800 diamonds – giving the effect of a solid mass of sparkling gems.

The cathedral was filled almost to bursting point but the spectacle witnessed by those chosen few surpassed all expectations. The effect was dazzling. Icons blazed with gold, silver and thousands of precious stones; the air was heavy with incense. The light from thousands of candles and the beautiful unaccompanied singing of the choir made an impressive and memorable scene.

The ceremony proceeded according to almost Byzantine ritual. After Mass the Emperor donned the ermine-bordered Imperial mantle of cloth of gold and the chain of the Order of St Andrew. Then, receiving the crown from the Metropolitan, he placed it on his own head. Holding the sceptre in his right hand and the orb in his left, he sat on the throne as, outside, the cannon thundered. Dagmar now advanced, made a deep curtsey and knelt at Sasha's feet on a crimson velvet cushion placed there by Prince Waldemar. Her ladies put the collar of St Andrew and the heavy mantle of gold and ermine around her shoulders. Then Sasha gently touched her brow with his crown before placing the smaller crown on her head. 'At that moment the Empress raised her beautiful, expressive eyes towards his face', wrote an eye-witness, 'and one could see that between the two there had passed one of those fugitive minutes of intense emotion which occur but once in a human life ...'[6] One of the ladies secured the crown with some diamond-studded hairpins, which Dagmar later complained was rather unpleasant, as most of them went into the wrong place and hurt her head.

In a graceful movement the Empress stood up, then, instead of a formal peck on the cheek, she spontaneously flung her arms around the Emperor's neck. In one of the most moving moments of the ceremony the Imperial couple, oblivious to the congregation, embraced tenderly while the choir chanted a Te Deum.

The Emperor's titles were then proclaimed in all their medieval splendour: Alexander Alexandrovitch, Emperor and Autocrat of all the Russias, His Tsaric Majesty of Moscow, Kiev, Vladimir, Novgorod, Tsar of Kazan, Tsar of Astrakhan ... Then, as the guns fired a salute and the bells of Moscow pealed, the newly crowned Emperor and Empress received the homage of the Imperial family, including their sons Nicholas and George, both wearing uniform, and Xenia, in a short white dress and kokoshnik. Afterwards, in a clear strong voice, Sasha recited the ancient prayer of the Tsars of Russia asking for God's guidance.

Led by members of the clergy Sasha and Dagmar walked along a gold carpet to the Iconostasis where they were annointed and received the Sacrament. Then Alexander III entered the sanctuary for the only time in his life, to take Communion as an Orthodox priest. The Empress remained kneeling outside. The ceremony ended with a prayer for the long life of 'the Emperor Alexander Alexandrovitch and ... his consort, the Empress, Marie Feodorovna'.[7]

The combination of the heavy robes, the oppressive incense-laden air and the length of the ceremony, which had already lasted five hours, was beginning to take its toll. 'It must be no joke to carry five yards of ermine and some pounds of diamonds during several hours – while metallic popes drone and shuffle and wave candles and fling incense and bellow ...' wrote Everard Primrose.[8] As they stepped into the daylight, crowned and robed, they were greeted by the strains of the National Anthem, the pealing of the bells, the booming of the cannon and the cheering crowds. Even the sun shone down on the scene.

The procession, a 'wonderful ... mass of feathers, jewels, banners, bright helmets, and cuirasses, all glittering in the sun', moved slowly across the square to the sixteenth-century Cathedral of the Archangel Michael and the Cathedral of the Annunciation. Finally, the Emperor and Empress ascended the Red Staircase, bowed three times to the people and disappeared inside. At that moment 'a swarm of pigeons rose ... from the roofs of the Palace and began to circle overhead – a good omen in the eyes of the superstitious Muscovites'.[9]

One hundred and fifty-nine distinguished guests sat down to the coronation banquet in the Palace of Facets. This low, vaulted former Throne Room of the Tsars, had witnessed Ivan the Terrible celebrating the capture of Kazan in 1552 and Peter the Great's jubilation after his victory over the Swedes. Many more guests were seated in other halls of the Kremlin to enjoy a meal of clear beet borscht and potato soup, Piroshki, steamed sterlets, veal, aspic, roast chicken and game, asparagus, Gurev pudding and ice cream. The elaborate menu cards were printed in Old Slavonic.

The Emperor and Empress dined on a raised platform at the end of the room, under a golden canopy. All around the pillars of the room were large tables loaded with gold and silver plate. Each course was brought in by a Master of Ceremonies, preceded by a uniformed chamberlain and a Chevalier Guard with a drawn sword. The fish was so large that two men carried the massive silver salver. 'It really was a wonderful sight, exactly like some old medieval picture as they sat there in their robes and crowns in that old dark-vaulted room ... I certainly shall never see again a soup tureen guarded by soldiers with drawn swords'.[10] During the banquet the Grand Cup-bearer of the Court presented the Emperor with wine in a golden goblet, proclaiming loudly, 'His Majesty deigns to drink'. This was the signal for all foreign guests to leave the room, a tradition dating from the sixteenth-century fear of poison. The Foreign Ambassadors were admitted individually to toast the sovereigns' health.

Among the guests were descendants of a simple peasant, Ivan Susanin. He had been tortured and killed by Polish invaders in 1613 for refusing to reveal the hiding place of the newly-elected Tsar Michael Romanov, the first member of the dynasty. The story was used for Glinka's opera *A Life for the Tsar*, which was performed at the Coronation Gala at the Bolshoi Theatre a few days later.

After the banquet Sasha and Dagmar walked through the Kremlin's halls greeting their guests. That evening there were spectacular illuminations and fireworks.

The following day Dagmar, in a gold-embroidered blue velvet dress and magnificent sapphires, stood beside Sasha as delegations from all parts of the Empire presented them with gold and silver salvers and other valuable gifts.

Eight thousand guests attended the Coronation Ball. To the majestic music of Glinka's Polonaise, the Empress, wearing a pink velvet gown embroidered with silver, led the stately procession, 'the men all in uniform, with orders, and broad ribbons; and the women with their trains down the full length', their jewels glittering in the light.[11] That night, for the first time, the Kremlin's Great Bell Tower was illuminated by electricity.

For the next few days Dagmar was constantly on show, as balls banquets and receptions followed one another with alarming rapidity. Her feet were soon so swollen that she was barely able to walk. 'The Empress stands the great fatigue wonderfully', reported a British observer, 'but in slippers, as her feet now refuse to fit any properly sized shoe ...'[12] Many other ladies copied her and Moscow shoemakers were inundated with orders.

One of the highlights of the celebration was the colossal feast for the people of Moscow on 2nd June. By midday over two hundred thousand people were gathered on the Khodynka Meadow near the Petrovsky Palace, awaiting the arrival of the Imperial couple. On behalf of the Emperor everyone present received one pound of sweets, a cake, two pies and an enamel mug bearing the Imperial eagle and the Tsar's monogram. Beer flowed liberally, entertainment was provided and later in the evening there was a firework display.

On 6th June the Emperor and Empress attended the consecration of the recently-completed Cathedral of Christ the Saviour, which had been erected to celebrate the French retreat from Moscow in 1812. The French Ambassador's party tactfully absented themselves. This massive cathedral, destroyed by Stalin, has recently been rebuilt.

The three weeks of exhausting official festivities ended with a Gala Dinner in St George's Hall for five hundred people. Then, after the final military review, Sasha and Dagmar left for St Petersburg.

It was the greatest coronation Russia had ever seen, displaying all the pomp and splendour of the Romanov court. The fact that the ceremony passed off without incident was probably due to the terrorists' hope that the traditional manifesto might bow to the popular demands for constitutional reforms, coupled with the belief that an attempt on the Emperor's life at a time of national rejoicing would only harm their cause.

The coronation manifesto granted the usual amnesties and remission of fines but Sasha made no secret of how things would be in future. 'Do not believe the absurd and ridiculous rumours and stories about dividing the land, free gifts of land, and so on', he told the peasants who came to offer homage to their Little Father. 'These rumours are spread by your enemies. All property, including yours, must be inviolable'.[13]

'All seems to have gone off well at the coronation', wrote the Crown Princess of Germany, 'but I fear the state of Russia is not more reassuring notwithstanding! The Emperor does not seem to intend granting a constitution, and the people are sighing for the simplest form of liberty ...'[14]

CHAPTER 9

Scandinavian Idyll

'FINLAND'S BEST AND MOST FAITHFUL FRIEND'

The Emperor and Empress moved in a regular pattern between the Imperial residences. The New Year found them at the Anitchkov for the Season. During the early summer they moved to Peterhof and in August they attended the army manoeuvres at Krasnoe Selo. They then moved to Poland for the hunting, on to the Crimea or back to Gatchina after the autumn trip to Denmark. Sasha disliked change and the timetable was seldom altered. Dagmar hated being governed by the clock and punctuality was never her strong point, although she made an effort, not always successfully, to conform.

The time Dagmar loved most was the autumn stay in Denmark. She needed the complete relaxation, the freedom of being able to wander around without armed guards and the chance for her nerves to recover, especially after the strain of the coronation ceremonies. For her children, it was another world. In Denmark they could go into shops and do things they would never dream of in St Petersburg. It was a breath of fresh air in more senses than one. In later years Sasha always referred to the journey to Copenhagen as being 'out of prison'.

Their departure from Russia was like a military operation and for security reasons the date was never set until the last minute. Even Dagmar's parents seldom knew exactly when they would arrive. More than twenty railway trucks of luggage were transferred to Kronstadt for the three day voyage to Copenhagen. They were accompanied by over one hundred people, fifty camp beds, the children's pets and a cow to provide fresh milk, which Dagmar considered absolutely essential. At Toldboden Queen Louise, King Christian and Crown Prince Frederick, both in Russian General's uniform, formally welcomed them. A guard of honour was provided by officers of the Danish Royal Life Guards, whose uniform the Emperor wore as Honorary Colonel. The number of guardsmen on duty was always increased when the Tsar visited. From the harbour the royal party drove to the station and then went by train to Fredensborg for a private family holiday.

By 1883 King Christian and Queen Louise ('Apapa' and 'Amama') had a large family. Only Waldemar, a naval officer, was still unmarried. That autumn's reunion was the first time all the King and Queen's children had been together for many years.

Dagmar corresponded regularly with Alix and Willie, although she was sometimes tardy about answering his letters. Her relationship with Freddie had become more distant since his marriage to the pious Princess Louise. Freddie and Louise rarely attended the family gatherings, even though they lived at nearby Charlottenlund. This was partly because Dagmar and Alexandra considered Louise's family, the Bernadottes, to be upstarts and made little effort to be friendly. Louise fulfilled her dynastic duty admirably by giving her husband eight children to ensure the Danish succession.

Dagmar, Willie and Alix were often seen walking arm-in-arm through the streets, riding in cabs and calling on old friends. Dagmar was also fond of her sister-in-law Olga. The member of the family most often absent was Thyra, although Dagmar sometimes stayed with her in Austria. Every time a reunion was proposed Ernst August either would not or could not travel. It was difficult to persuade him to leave the excellent shooting and fishing at Gmunden and Dagmar put this down to his selfishness. In later years Thyra visited regularly with her three daughters but her husband was a rare guest. Bertie also avoided Denmark as much as possible. He maintained that there was only one place more boring than Fredensborg – and that was Bernstorff.

The King's brothers Prince William and Prince Hans of Glucksburg were sometimes present. If it was a small gathering they stayed at Bernsdorff. Even here they were short of space. Dagmar and Alix used the same drawing room; Nicholas and Georgie shared a bungalow in the rose garden. Eventually, with a total of thirty-six grandchildren and three hundred attendants, some of the gentlemen slept on sofas and a village of huts was constructed in the park to accommodate the servants and the Tsar's Cossack bodyguards. For larger gatherings they used Fredensborg. Sasha and Dagmar's suite, leading off the first floor gallery, consisted of three small, simply furnished rooms – a bedroom, a sitting room and a room for one of their entourage. There were no bathrooms. It was all a far cry from the Anitchkov and Gatchina.

In the company of her family Dagmar completely forgot her dignity. She joined the others when they stole apples from the orchard and hurled them through the attic windows to see who could smash the most lights; or acted as look-out while Sasha carved his crowned monogram on the tree trunks, a pastime forbidden to the King's grandchildren. Sasha was 'just like a schoolboy up to all kinds of pranks',[1] leading the children into mischief. 'The wild romps they had were simply indescribable ... The Queen of Denmark's furniture must be unusually strong – one sofa ... had to have the springs renewed', wrote an incredulous visitor.[2] All the family were fond of skating and if they came in winter they made up merry skating and tobogganing parties.

Sasha felt so at home, a rumour circulated that he intended to buy a property in Denmark. In 1885 his eyes fell on a house and land in beautiful surroundings next to the palace gardens, overlooking the village pond down Fredensborg's main street. The owner was reluctant to sell but changed his mind when the Tsar offered 25,000 kroner. Sasha's owner-ship of the house, situated on The Emperor's Road, was celebrated on 1st October 1889 with a large house-warming party. Here he could work on his state papers and perform physical fitness exercises in private. The house is still in existence.

Practical jokes were very much part of the family's way of life. Sasha, seeing the top-hatted figures of King Christian and King Oscar of Sweden, could not resist squirting water at them from a garden hose. At the sick bed of an old uncle, Prince Nicholas of Greece appeared with a joke candlestick protruding from his forehead like a unicorn's horn. Dagmar and Alix fled the room convulsed with laughter.

Breakfast and lunch were informal, without servants. The only formal meal was dinner, served in the huge marble-floored hall at six-thirty. After-wards they played Loo and other simple card games; or Dagmar, her mother and sisters performed eight handed piano arrangements. At nine o'clock there was supper of tea and traditional Danish open sandwiches. Sometimes, to the delight of the younger generation, King Christian and his sons amused them by turning somersaults over one of the sofas. Occasionally Dagmar and her sisters joined in, coping admirably with evening dresses and elaborate hairstyles. On moonlit nights a long procession of carriages left the palace in search of the ghost of King Valdemar Atterdag who was doomed to ride between Voordingborg and Gurre forever.

The Emperor and Empress were very popular in Copenhagen. The people appreciated the informal way they went shopping and sight-seeing. Once at the zoo Dagmar, wearing a cherry-trimmed straw hat held in place by elastic, stopped by the monkey cage. Unfortunately, one of the apes made a grab for the cherries and a tug-of-war ensued – the monkey holding the cherries, Dagmar holding the hat and Alix holding on to her sister. Suddenly the monkey let go and the hat flew back, landing with a snap on Dagmar's ear. To her distress, everyone was reduced to helpless laughter.

Together the family was a 'Tower of Babel', speaking seven different languages. Few people could believe that these gatherings were the inno-cent family holidays they seemed. 'If the Tsaritsa accelerated her yearly visit by forty-eight hours so as to find her brother, King George of the Hellenes, still at home, cypher telegrams flew to all corners of the globe raising the familiar spectre of the Eastern Question. If the future Edward VII made a detour to visit his father-in-law, then a new Anglo-Russian policy was in the making'.[3] The telegraph wires hummed constantly, keep-ing them in touch with their kingdoms. Bismarck dubbed Fredensborg 'Europe's Whispering Gallery', with Queen Louise constantly intriguing against him. King Christian's position as the grandfather of Europe ensured that the post of Minister at Copenhagen was highly prized and considered the last step before an Embassy. Although the Danish Royal family were known for their anti-German feeling all political discussions were forbidden.

'The daughters remain as unspoilt and as completely children of the house as when they were unmarried', wrote Queen Victoria. Nevertheless, royalty they remained. The celebrated hostess Roma Lister was among the guests at the British Legation's Ball in the autumn of 1883. 'When the royalties arrived the room seemed full of them'. She was particularly impressed with the Tsar of Russia, 'a very giant of a man' who towered over his wife and was very congenial.[4]

That autumn, the royalties lunched aboard the *Pembroke Castle* at the invitation of Mr Gladstone and Alfred Lord Tennyson, who was persuaded to read one of his poems. Afterwards Dagmar went over to congratulate him. 'Thank you, my dear', replied the short-sighted poet, mistaking the Empress of Russia for a maid of honour and patting her on the shoulder.[5]

Dagmar had always wanted to build a Russian Orthodox Church in Copenhagen. When Sasha came to the throne a grant of 300,000 roubles from the Russian government and a contribution of 70,000 roubles from the Tsar enabled her wish to become reality.

The St Alexander Nevsky Church was built on Copenhagen's Bredgade and crowned by three golden onion domes topped with golden crosses. The interior, approached by a marble staircase, was beautiful, with a magnificent iconostasis, marble mosaic floors and valuable carpets. The massive chandelier and the altar were gifts from Alexander III and an inscription on the altar confirms this fact. On 9th September 1883 the Emperor, Empress and their children attended the church's consecration with King Christian and Queen Louise and the King and Queen of Greece. Two days later a service was held there for the Tsar's Name Day. For many years the church served the staff of the Russian Legation and during her visits to Denmark Dagmar attended the church every Sunday, staying afterwards to chat to members of the congregation.

In 1890, construction began on a new station at Helsingør to replace the former building which was not considered suitable to welcome the Tsar. The new red-brick station was opened on 24th October 1891 and consisted of an enormous arrivals hall with a gallery and elegant coffered ceiling, a waiting room for first- and second-class passengers, and the Station Master's residence. At the top of the marble-clad stairs, flanked by two stone lions with the Danish coat-of-arms between their paws, were a pair of dark oak doors leading to the Royal Waiting Rooms.

An impressive salon for the entourage led to a larger room with gilded leather hangings, dark oak panels, a huge brass chandelier and an imitation fireplace with the Royal crown over it. On one side a door led to the King's Rooms with a view over the harbour square; on the other side, with a view over the Sound, were the Queen's Rooms. A staircase led straight outside so that the suite was entirely private. From here the Imperial family could arrive, or leave, from Copenhagen by train.

The Danish Royal family could seldom repress their feelings when they had to part and, with the danger in Russia looming larger, King Christian was in a state of constant anxiety about the possibility of his daughter's assassination. When the time came for Dagmar to leave she and Alix clung to each other for as long as they could, before the Empress finally tore herself away. As the Imperial yacht sailed out of Toldboden the King and Queen stood on the pier for over an hour, until they could see their daughter no longer.

*

A keen sailor, Dagmar looked forward with eager anticipation to their summer cruise along the coast of Finland on the Imperial yacht *Tsarevna*.

Finland had been annexed by Russia in 1809. The Finnish border was only about twenty-five miles from St Petersburg and the Tsar ruled as Grand Duke of Finland, a constitutional monarch. On his accession Alexander III confirmed the Fundamental Laws and promised to maintain Finland's privileges. The following year he spoke of his wish 'to ensure the happiness of my faithful Finnish people, of whose honest character I have particularly convinced myself in the visits to the country with my family, retaining at the same time in the most pleasant memory the feelings thus expressed to us'.[6] In 1885 he granted them the right to initiate legislation, with a Senate to conduct local affairs, while contact with the empire's administration was handled by a minister and State Secretary for Finnish Affairs. Nevertheless, Sasha had no liking for any form of constitution. He wanted nothing less than the total Russification of Finland, with the Russian language used in all Finnish institutions.

Dagmar first visited Finland in 1876, when she and Sasha

accompanied the Tsar and Tsarina to Helsinki. The people loved the informal way she went among them, spoke to the Swedish-speaking Finns in their own language and acted as interpreter for her parents-in-law and husband. Students followed her, singing the Danish Royal Anthem; girls presented flowers and recited poems. She won everybody's heart. Every summer afterwards they headed for a few weeks of relaxation in the Finnish archipelago.

The custom continued when Sasha came to the throne. Dagmar relaxed completely as they cruised in the Baltic or through the Finnish Skerries, an almost unbroken band of islands, rocks and tiny islets where they could fish, sail or picnic. Escorted by two torpedo boats and accompanied by an army of maids, footmen, valets and cooks, with those members of their suite who were their personal friends, they escaped from the fear of assassination and the cares of state. 'Since last Thursday we are on board the dear *Tsarevna*', wrote Dagmar, 'which gives me so much pleasure'.[7]

In 1884 the *Tsarevna* headed the Imperial squadron for the first time as the Tsar and his family cruised in the Finnish archipelago. When they went ashore they were welcomed by brass bands playing Finnish marching songs, including the Finnish National March, the 'Bjorneborganas March', a favourite of the Empress. Crowds rowed out to the Imperial yacht just to catch a glimpse of them. One young girl recorded in her diary how wonderful it was 'to see the enchanting Dagmar with my own eyes'. The following year her nine-year-old sister picked some flowers and they rowed out to the yacht. The Empress insisted that the little girl must come and present them herself. Nervously the child approached and Dagmar accepted the flowers with a smile. The little girl later said that when she kissed the Empress' hand it smelt 'so delicious'.[8]

Hapsal on the Estonian coast was one of their favourite places and the Empress Dagmar, as she was always called in Scandinavia, spoke to the inhabitants in Scandinavian. Another favourite was Kjallviken, a popular spot for relaxation near the little town of Ekenas. The fishermen were delighted when she visited their cottages and sat down for a chat. Nearby 'Dagmarkallan' (the 'Dagmar Spring') was named in her honour.

On 4th August 1885 the Emperor and Empress arrived at Vyborg, on the first stage of an official visit to Finland.[9] They were accompanied by their sons Nicholas and George, and the Emperor's brothers Alexis, Sergei and Paul. The previous year Sergei had married Princess Elizabeth of Hesse and by Rhine, and the beautiful Grand Duchess 'Ella' was also among the party.

After a formal greeting by the Governor General, Count Heiden and a visit to the Orthodox Cathedral, they drove through the crowded streets to the station. Finland had its own Imperial train consisting of six carriages – a saloon; a dining car; the Emperor's carriage upholstered in green; the Empress' carriage in blue, with a small compartment for the lady-in-waiting; a kitchen and a luggage wagon. Another carriage accommodated their entourage.

In this luxurious conveyance they travelled to Villmanstrand. A house had been put at their disposal, completely refurbished at the expense of the Finnish government, with satin hangings on the walls, paintings by Finnish artists and elegant furniture by Finnish craftsmen. Everything had been done for their comfort, a piano had even been installed for the Empress.

Their first engagement was a service at the Russian Orthodox Church, where they were offered bread and salt on a silver dish. Later the Tsar reviewed the Finnish troops at their camp outside the town, Dagmar and Ella travelling in a cabriolet drawn by white horses. The following day Dagmar watched proudly as Nicholas took part in the military parade. At the garrision of the reserve company the Tsar delighted onlookers by visiting the kitchens and eating a plate of pea soup and a slice of meat which he carved himself. The people turned out in force and they were loudly cheered.

At the Saima lake Dagmar was presented with a beautiful boat, the *Saima*, made from Karellian birch. The exterior was varnished in light yellow, Imperial crowns surmounted the flag poles and its interior had been expertly decorated by the women of Finland. Dagmar took a keen interest in sea rescue and the women asked permission to found a Finnish Society for Life Saving and name it after her. When the Imperial party left for Helsinki, Dagmar was presented with a bouquet of cornflowers with an inscription on the ribbon, 'Quickly fades the sweet beauty of a flower but eternal is the love of a people'. Her charm had captured all hearts.

Finland's capital was en fête. The harbour and all the boats were decorated with lights, buildings were illuminated and a triumphal arch bore the names Alexander III and Maria. The following morning, after a requiem for the Tsar's parents, there was a grand reception at the Imperial Palace (now the Presidential Palace), where the ladies of Helsinki presented the Empress with an elegant screen.

The fêtes and gala occasions continued for three days. One of the highlights was a performance of the student male voice choir, the *Muntre Musikanter*, at the Alexander University, of which the seventeen-year-old Tsarevitch was Chancellor. The following March, the Emperor was delighted when Dagmar invited the choir to St Petersburg to sing for his birthday. They also sang for the Empress' Name Day.

On the final evening there was a state dinner, followed by a ball at the

Governor General's residence. It was noticed that, while the Emperor did not dance at all, the Empress enthusiastically joined in most of the dancing. One of her partners gallantly said that he would never wear his pair of white gloves again.

The following day they left Finland after a triumphant six day visit. As the Imperial yacht sailed away to music, singing and cheers from the crowds, the Empress stood on deck waving.

In July 1889 they visited the island of Odenso, where a party was held on the grass. In a relaxed and happy atmosphere the Emperor acted as host and the Empress helped to fry the freshly-caught fish and prepare breakfast. Sometimes they used the Tender *Mareva* to penetrate deeper into the Skerries. This boat was so small that the officers slept with the crew in small cabins opening out of the saloon, which doubled as dining-room, drawing room and washroom. Sasha played cards, fished or took long walks. Dagmar painted and sketched, played board games or joined her husband fishing. 'The weather is beautiful and the air marvellous – so that everything conspires to make me happy and able to delight in the pleasures of yachting, which I adore!' the Empress wrote joyfully.[10] Far from the risk of terrorists the boat plied its way through the channels to the most remote places, where fishermen living in tiny hamlets were unaware of the identity of their visitors. When this idyllic time ended few returned with more regret than Dagmar.

She was very touched by the love of the Finnish people and emphasised her attachment to them by having several Finnish ladies-in-waiting. Sasha, however, was still determined to implement his policy of Russification.

In 1890 he set up a special commission to look into ways of limiting the Finnish Diet. He also wanted the postal system and the conscription laws of the Grand Duchy brought into line with those of Russia. The people bitterly resented the Tsar's central rule. All her life Dagmar showed concern for the rights of the Finnish people. She constantly intervened on their behalf and he was persuaded to restrain his policy out of consider-ation for her feelings. Many of the more restrictive measures did not come into force until the next reign. Many years later she described herself as 'Finland's best and most faithful friend'.[11]

Yet Sasha was keen to have a holiday home in Finland and shortly after he became Tsar a diplomat reported that the Emperor 'still was debating whether to buy Odenso'.[12]

Sasha had heard about the good salmon fishing in the Langinkoski rapids near Kotka, 150 miles east of Ekenas. In the summer of 1880 they anchored for the first time in the sheltered bay at the outlet of the Kymi River. This still bears the name of the Emperor's Harbour.[13] He and Dagmar soon fell in love with this beautiful place with swiftly foaming rapids and, in 1881, the Emperor said he would like to have a fishing lodge built on the banks of the river. Shortly afterwards the fishing rights were signed over to him and the Finnish architect Magnus Schjerfbeck set to work on the plans. In the summer of 1888 Sasha took two of his children to see how work was progressing and the following year the building was completed.

Langinkoski was presented to the Imperial couple by the State and the people of Finland. On 15th July 1889 Sasha and Dagmar gave a house-warming party. Among the guests were Queen Olga of Greece and the Duchess of Edinburgh. As they crossed the threshold a royal salute was fired and a little boy presented a bouquet to the Empress. Choirs and bands came from Helsinki and Vyborg and, at the banquet that evening, the Tsar proposed a toast to Finland and asked the band to play the 'Bjorneborganas March'. Later that night the Imperial family watched from the *Tsarevna* as bonfires were lit all along the coast.

The fishing lodge was small and very simple. Downstairs was a living room with furniture made by a local carpenter, two halls, a small room for the Empress and an even smaller room for the Emperor and a spacious kitchen. All the furnishings, porcelain and glassware were made by Scandinavian craftsmen. Upstairs the Emperor and Empress shared a bedroom with their two single beds placed one in front of the other. This floor also contained rooms for the children, five or six members of the suite and the Life Guards. The Emperor was forbidden to smoke his cigars indoors, Dagmar insisted he go outside onto the large veranda which ran down the length of the building.

The newspapers reported with some surprise that, although they brought their own staff, the Imperial couple led a very simple life. The Emperor chopped firewood with a locally-made axe. The Empress and her assistants peeled potatoes on the kitchen porch for the salmon soup she cooked for her family in a copper kettle on the kitchen stove. However, it was reported that she did not like to do the washing up. The amenities were very basic. There was no running water, the Emperor carried buckets from the river to the kitchen; no sewage disposal system and no electricity. There was a telephone – the number was Kotka 33. As the lodge was intended for short summer holidays, only two fireplaces were installed.

There was no railway connection between St Petersburg and Kotka, so every summer the Imperial yacht dropped anchor at the Emperor's Harbour. The Scandinavian-born Empress was especially popular. Dagmar and her daughters visited the Russian Orthodox Church at nearby Kotka and probably also worshipped in the small Orthodox Chapel near the fishing lodge. She frequently visited the local people and in the 1890s a cottage was built nearby for the Tsar's fishermen.

They made about ten visits to Langinkoski, the last one in July 1894, when the Tsar was already ill. Despite this he was reported to be in 'high spirits' and enjoyed some excellent fishing. In an unexpected speech at dinner he referred warmly to his wife and ordered her Standard to be hoisted. During the evening the band was asked to play the Bjornebor-ganas March no less than three times.

The following day Sasha and Dagmar left Langinkoski, never to return.

CHAPTER 10

Imperial Panoply

'COURT LIFE HAD TO RUN IN SPLENDOUR AND THERE MY MOTHER
PLAYED HER PART WITHOUT A SINGLE FALSE STEP'
– Grand Duchess Olga

On 18th May 1884 Dagmar's eldest son celebrated his sixteenth birthday and, according to the laws of the Imperial House, came of age. After Mass in the Winter Palace Chapel, the Empress watched proudly as Nicholas, wearing the uniform of the Cossack regiment, swore an oath of allegiance to his father. The following evening there was a banquet for eight hundred distinguished guests, members of foreign Royal families and the Imperial family.

The Empress was popular with her husband's family, always remaining accessible and encouraging them to call. 'She proved herself extremely tactful with her in-laws', recalled her daughter, 'which was no easy task'.[1] She of course had her favourites, especially Grand Duke George Michaelovitch and Grand Duke Constantine Constantinovitch. Constantine's sister Queen Olga of Greece remained one of Dagmar's closest friends throughout her life. The younger members of the family came to Dagmar for advice and, sometimes, protection from the Emperor's wrath. It was well-known that she could exert a subtle influence on his decisions.

Dagmar's rival as a leader of society was the haughty Miechen, who was liked by few members of the family. Staunch pro-German sympathies did nothing to endear her to the Empress. Grand Duke Vladimir envied his brother's power as Emperor and as the rivalry between Sasha and his brother Vladimir increased, so did that of their wives. In a court that was becoming more and more nationalistic, Miechen's refusal to convert to Orthodoxy did not help.

Alexander III kept the Imperial family firmly in place and, unless summoned, they had to request an audience. They were all expected to attend weddings, christenings and the Emperor's family dinners. The autocratic Tsar never let them forget they they owed him allegiance as subjects. 'Stop playing the Tsar', he told his brother Sergei when he overstepped the mark.[2]

117

Dagmar was an inveterate matchmaker and she was delighted when in June 1884 twenty-six-year-old Sergei married Princess Elizabeth ('Ella'), of Hesse and by Rhine, daughter of Grand Duke Louis IV. Ella's mother was Queen Victoria's daughter Princess Alice, who died in 1878. Dagmar and Alix had promoted the marriage against the wishes of Ella's grandmother, Queen Victoria. Sergei was a strict disciplinarian who expected to be obeyed. The Queen had been worried about Sergei's bad reputation, the effect of the cold Russian winters on Ella's health and the unstable state of the country. Ella refused to change her religion and did not convert to Orthodoxy until 1891.

In early November Sergei and Ella arrived at Gatchina for a stay of six weeks. Dagmar told her brother Willie how happy the newlyweds were and how much more animated Sergei had become. While Sergei performed his regimental duties Ella and Dagmar spent their afternoons painting and Dagmar's five-year-old son Misha sat drawing beside them. Ella was soon overwhelmed by the generosity and affection of the Emperor and Empress. She particularly appreciated the warm family atmosphere of Gatchina. Her letters to her grandmother were full of 'Minny's' kindness and she was especially fond of Nicholas and Xenia. To Ella's disappointment her own marriage was childless. It seems that by late November things had started to go wrong. Sergei no longer appeared happy and Dagmar could not understand why he had married. As she told Willie a few weeks later, nobody had forced him to do it. Nevertheless, there is as yet no evidence to substantiate the rumours that Sergei was homosexual. His niece later recalled that Sergei and Ella always shared the same bed.

Dagmar welcomed another sister-in-law when Prince Waldemar married. Waldemar had originally wanted to marry Countess Olga Toll, the daughter of the Russian Minister in Copenhagen but, as the Empress' brother, he could not marry a Russian subject. On 20th October 1885 he married Princess Marie of Orleans, daughter of the Duc de Chartres and niece of the Comte de Paris, pretender to the French throne. Marie was as staunchly anti-Prussian as the rest of her husband's family. She had never forgiven Prussia for defeating France in 1870.

Waldemar and Marie moved into the Yellow Mansion and while his naval duties took him away for long periods, she raised the five children born to them between 1887 and 1895. Marie was a talented painter, passionately fond of riding and fiercely patriotic. A Tricolour hung from ceiling to floor in her drawing room at Bernstorff. She was energetic, vivacious and had a tremendous sense of fun. One of the Prince of Wales' staff once opened the wrong door and found her dancing the Cancan.

Although Dagmar had no part in Waldemar's marriage, she arranged two other marriages which would have important consequences in the coming years. During the Russo-Turkish war the crafty Prince Nicholas of Montenegro had placed four of his daughters at the Russian Court in the care of the Empress Marie Alexandrovna, who arranged for them to be educated at the Smolny Institute. Montenegro was a small principality in the Balkans whose Slav population had put up a fierce resistance to the Turks. They were Orthodox in religion and, playing on that and on Alexander III's fervent nationalism, Prince Nicholas later obtained a yearly subsidy of £6,000 from Russia. Marija died in 1885 but in 1889 the prince's hope that the Empress would find husbands for his daughters materialised. To break the tradition of Romanov Grand Dukes seeking their brides at the small German Courts, Sasha and Dagmar arranged Militza's marriage to the Tsar's cousin Grand Duke Peter Nicholaievitch and Anastasia's to another Romanov cousin Prince George Romanovsky, Duke of Leuchtenberg. The remaining daughter, Elena, later became Queen of Italy. Militza and Anastasia ('Stana') became known as the 'Black Pearls' due to their origin, their jet black hair and their predilection for spiritualist charlatans. Superstitious, gullible and excitable they soon became prey to the hypnotisers, religious maniacs and healers who frequented the capital.

All these marriages prompted the Tsar to consider the ever-increasing numbers of Grand Ducal children. In 1797, when the Imperial family consisted of five people, the Emperor Paul had decreed that the title and income of a Grand Duke should always descend through the male line. By 1886 Russia was becoming overrun with Grand Dukes. Sasha therefore introduced a new statute limiting the rank of Grand Duke, which carried an allowance of £20,000 per year, Grand Duchess, with a dowry of £100,000, and the title of 'Imperial Highness', to the sovereign's children and grandchildren in the male line only. The next generation would be Princes and Princesses with the title of 'Highness' and a lump sum of £100,000 at birth. Great-great-grandchildren would be 'Serene Highness' and would be allowed to marry suitable non-royals with the Tsar's permission. In 1889 male members of the Imperial family were forbidden to marry anyone not already of the Orthodox religion and in 1893 a further law prohibited morganatic marriages.

There was a flood of indignant complaints from the Tsar's relatives, even his brother Vladimir did not support him. Sasha's uncle Grand Duke Constantine Nicholaievitch, whose family was the first to be affected, felt his children's position was being depreciated and his own lifestyle would be reduced. Many others felt the same. Dagmar needed all her skill and tact. Her own children's position was unaffected and their allowances remained intact until they came of age.

The drain on the Tsar's purse was still enormous. Alexander's income came from three main sources. Firstly, the Civil List of just under £1,200,000. Then interest from deposit accounts in German and English banks. Sasha kept £9,000,000 sterling, inherited from his father, in the Bank of England. This account was closed in 1900. Finally, there was income from the Tsar's private property. This included two rich gold mines and revenues from the Crown Appanages, consisting of millions of acres of vineyards, fruit gardens, cotton plantations, forests and orchards purchased by Catherine the Great to provide incomes for the Imperial family. There were also palaces filled with priceless art treasures and £16,000,000 in Crown Jewellery amassed over nearly 300 years, which the Emperor was unable to sell. The Emperor and Empress each received about £20,000 a year for the expenses of their Court and the Empress had her own Privy Purse and the interest from other capital sums.

This money also had to pay for the upkeep of the numerous Imperial palaces, including wages, food and uniforms for thousands of servants, who all received a present at Christmas and on the Tsar's Name Day. There were also the Imperial yachts, the Imperial trains, the five Imperial theatres, the Imperial Ballet and the pupils of the Imperial Ballet School. Individual petitions submitted to the Tsar's private chancery and appeals from hospitals, almshouses and orphanages were never turned away by Dagmar.

The Academy of Arts and the Academy of Sciences were officially financed by the government but Sasha found it hard to ignore their requests when they found difficulty in making ends meet. In architecture he favoured the revival of the old Muscovite styles of the sixteenth and seventeenth centuries. The Church of the Spilled Blood, which Sasha built on the site of his father's mortal wounding, was constructed in this style. He increased the funds available to the Academy of Fine Arts for purchases and sponsored art museums and schools in provincial towns. At his request Grand Duke Constantine Constantinovitch translated Hamlet into Russian.

He also patronised The Wanderers, a group of Moscow artists formed in 1870 to bring art directly to the people through travelling exhibitions. At one of these in 1889 the Imperial family bought twenty-seven canvasses. Dagmar ordered a copy of one of their early successes, 'The Rooks Have Arrived' by Savrasov, a painting of a Russian landscape in early spring. Sasha planned to house all his acquisitions under one roof in a new museum but he was still looking for a suitable site when he died. It was Nicholas II who purchased the Mikailovsky Palace in St Petersburg as a home for his father's collections. The Russian Museum of Emperor Alexander III opened in 1898.

The Empress' role was mainly ceremonial, both as a leader of society and of fashion. Dagmar performed these duties superbly. Her good humour, wit and vivacity were a perfect foil for Sasha's awkward, shambling, rather gruff manner.

She adored all the outward trappings of her position. Court dresses for official occasions were made by Mme Olga Bulbenkova. Other clothes came from Morin Blossier in Paris, Mme Brisac, or A.G. Gindus in St Petersburg. She patronised the Paris couture house of Charles Worth for over thirty years, spending thousands on dresses and giving Sasha unpleasant surprises when the bills arrived. Although she was scolded for extravagance, Sasha seemed unable to curb the spending. One beautiful sable cape, so dark it was almost black, cost £12,000.

The Empress' vast wardrobe and jewels were under the supervision of her lady's maid Marie von Flotow, who rose to a position of paramount influence. She was responsible for all the Empress' personal requirements and ensured that the bills were paid. Dagmar's jewels were among the most magnificent in the world. In 1873 London society was stunned by a necklace of huge diamonds, with a centre stone of 32 carats, and a string of graduated pearls, the largest as big as a cherry. In the evenings pink diamond stars or jewelled butterflies with diamond antennae were scattered down her gown. A moth of pearls and brilliants ornamented her hair. A necklace and tiara of emerald shamrocks with diamond dewdrops was teamed with a matching javelin of brilliants to catch up her skirt. Sasha gave her nine rows of perfect pearls held together by fleurs-de-lis. She also persuaded him to have the Crown Jewels moved from the Diamond Room of the Winter Palace to the Anitchkov, to save the trouble of applying to the State Treasurer when she wanted to wear them. They remained there throughout Sasha's reign.

Also kept at the Anitchkov was Dagmar's large collection of fans, a fashion accessory used to great effect by the sometimes coquettish Empress. From the time of her betrothal to Nixa in 1864, she received many of these graceful objects as souvenirs. Some commemorated family births or reunions and had the signatures of various relatives. Others recalled costume balls or visits to regions of the Empire. One was painted with pictures of Sasha and the children.

The Empress was attended by hundreds of ladies and the most distinguished wore her portrait framed in diamonds on their bodice. Some, like Tania Obolensky, Catherine Ozerova and Lili Vorontzov-Dashkov, were part of her intimate circle of friends. Lili shared the Empress' love of gossip and was always ready with juicy details of the latest scandal. Dagmar was equally always ready to listen.

The most important lady was the Mistress of the Robes. Princess Kurakin, who had held the post since Dagmar arrived in Russia, died in

November 1881. Dagmar's mother then recommended the remarkable Princess Hélene Kotchoubey, one of the last Grande Dames of the Russian Empire. It was a brilliant choice. With expert knowledge of the *Almanach de Gotha* and an ability to provide background information about people Dagmar was to meet, she proved invaluable. She died in 1888. Her successor, Countess Anna Stroganoff, was a stiff, prim, rather timid woman who allowed many of the old traditions to die. The male counterpart was Prince Ivan Galitzine, the Master of the Household.

At the head of the hierarchy was the Minister of the Imperial Court. The previous holder of this position, Count Adlerberg, had been abruptly dismissed in 1881, some said because the new Emperor could not forget that he had witnessed his father's marriage to Catherine Dolgoruky. He was replaced by Count Ilarian Vorontzov-Dashkov, husband of Lili. He organised court functions, administered the Imperial establishments, and handled the crown lands, the Imperial family's personal finances and the Tsar's private property. His sound common sense and tact were invaluable when his duties brought him into conflict with the Imperial family. He was assisted by Baron Fredericks.

Court life was extremely formal. Nothing was ever altered and many of the regulations had been issued during the reign of Catherine the Great. Courtiers backed away from the Imperial presence. Even in England Grand Duchess Marie Alexandrovna, the Duchess of Edinburgh, forced the head gardener to walk backwards for a considerable distance rather than allow him to turn his back on her. Although she had an innate sense of majesty, Dagmar's democratic upbringing made her more considerate. It also helped her to cope with unexpected situations. After a gala performance she asked to meet the American singer who had scored such a triumph. The young lady was duly coached on etiquette but when she saw the Empress all thought of protocol went out of her mind. She seized the Empress' hand and shook it, saying how pleased she was to meet her, much to Dagmar's amusement.

Under Alexander III the Court became more nationalistic. All the palace staff were required to be Russians. A new 'Russianised' army uniform was introduced, those with German names were removed from the government and high commands in the army and the German language was forbidden at Court. Sasha was the first Tsar since the seventeenth century to grow a beard.

He soon instituted drastic economies, reducing expenditure by two million pounds in the first year of his reign. Some colourful army uniforms were abolished, many of the servants were dismissed from the Winter Palace and much of the gold braid disappeared from the courtiers' uniforms. Table linen was no longer changed daily, soap and candles were used up and unnecessary lights were turned off. Sasha wore his old comfortable clothes until they were patched and threadbare and ordered his valet to darn them in the evenings. None of this economy rubbed off on Dagmar, who continued to dazzle the court with lovely gowns from Paris. French wines were replaced by Crimean vintages, unless the guests were foreign sovereigns or diplomats and, to the despair of the French chef, national dishes replaced expensive imported delicacies. The Emperor's frugality, combined with the fifty minutes allowed for meals, led courtiers to warn guests to eat something beforehand. The food at the Imperial table, wrote Count Witte, 'was sometimes such as to endanger the health'.[3]

Meetings with foreign monarchs were kept to a minimum. Some of these had their more amusing moments, such as Dagmar's dismay when the Shah of Persia asked if the Imperial children were all by the same mother!

In September 1884 the German and Austrian Emperors visited the Tsar in Poland. In the following August, Sasha and Dagmar travelled to Kremsier in Moravia to return the visit to Emperor Franz Joseph and Empress Elisabeth. The meeting had great political significance. Since 1881 Austria, Germany and Russia had been linked by 'The Three Emperors' League', renewed for three years in 1884. Germany and Austria then turned their dual alliance into a triple alliance by including Italy in 1882. The meeting in Kremsier was an attempt to lighten the mistrust between Russia and Austria.

They were met by the Emperor and Crown Prince Rudolf. Security was tight and, in contrast to the triumphant tour of Finland, the streets were empty and the windows overlooking the route were tightly shuttered. Rudolf wrote rather unkindly that the Russian Emperor 'has grown very fat', while the Empress looked 'old and worn by life'.[4]

The tension was relieved by the presence of the two Empresses, both superb horsewomen. Sasha had heard about Elisabeth's reckless driving. One day she took him out in her trap, drawn by fiery Hungarian ponies. He was soon visibly dismayed as they hurtled through the countryside, his weight nearly causing the frail vehicle to overturn. Finally, he grasped the reins and pulled the horses up so sharply that the trap nearly tipped up backwards.

During this visit a rare instance occurred of Sasha paying court to another woman. Franz Joseph had arranged for the Burg Theatre Company of Vienna to entertain his guests. As the champagne flowed the Tsar melted under the charms of Katherina Schratt and he promptly shocked the stiff Austrian Court by suggesting that the actresses be asked to supper. Later, to the alarm of his entourage, the Tsar disappeared.

It was afterwards discovered that he had gone to visit Frau Schratt, who dismissed his attentions so tactfully that the following morning an A.D.C. delivered one hundred roses and an emerald brooch from the Imperial suitor.

With the exception of the Danish Minister, the Emperor saw as little as possible of the foreign diplomats accredited to his Court and only invited them to the most formal balls and receptions.

Dagmar entertained throughout the year, either in the Grand Palace at Peterhof or at Gatchina. Often a special train brought more than a hundred and fifty people out to Gatchina for one of her informal parties. Sometimes she attended a party in the capital, not returning until dawn. On her birthday the children gave presents they had made themselves and in the evening there was always a grand ball.

Sasha had no liking for Court life but Dagmar was nevertheless determined to keep the splendour of the Season alive. Immediately after Christmas she began agitating to return to the Anitchkov until Sasha, unable to find any more convincing reasons to delay their departure, finally gave in.

*

At ten o'clock on every New Year's morning the Tsar, in uniform and the Tsarina, in Court dress and train, led the Imperial family through the Winter Palace to the church. Dagmar's niece remembered her wearing a tiara of sapphires 'so large that they resembled enormous eyes', with pearls and diamonds cascading from her throat to her waist.[5] Later there was a diplomatic reception in St George's Hall. On the Feast of Epiphany the Emperor took part in the ceremonial Blessing of the Waters, when the Metropolitan dipped his gold cross through a hole in the frozen Neva. These ceremonies marked the official beginning of the Season.

The most coveted invitations were for the Nicholas Ball at the Winter Palace. Elderly generals, statesmen, courtiers in black uniforms trimmed with gold lace, ambassadors, visiting oriental rulers and young Guards officers, whose elkskin breeches were so tight they required the assistance of two men to put them on, crowded into the enormous halls. The magnificent red-carpeted Jordan staircase was lined by Life Guards in scarlet tunics and Chevalier Guards in gleaming gold breastplates, with helmets surmounted by the Imperial eagle. Banks of flowers brought by train from the Crimea or Nice and palm trees from the Imperial hot-houses transformed the Nicholas Hall into a vast Winter Garden.

Under the expert direction of Princess Kotchoubey five maids helped the Empress to dress. 'It was an absolute beehive', recalled Grand Duchess

Olga, but the result was always superb as Dagmar emerged dressed in what the children called her 'Imperial panoply'.[6]

For this first ball of the Season Dagmar wore a white and silver brocade Court dress, open down the front to reveal a satin skirt studded with diamonds and richly embroidered with silver flowers. Across her bodice swept the blue ribbon of the Order of St Andrew and she also wore the Order's diamond Star. Long loose sleeves, which exposed elbow-length kid gloves, hung from the bodice's low-cut shoulders. On her head glittered a diamond diadem in the crescent shape of the traditional Russian kokoshnik with a huge pink diamond in the centre and a long lace veil. More enormous diamonds sparkled from her neck and wrists.

As she moved off to take her place with the other members of the family her long train was carried by two cadets from the Corps de Pages. The Emperor, who hated all this finery, wore the full-dress uniform of the Horse Guards and the Order of the Garter.

At precisely nine o'clock the huge doors of the Concert Hall opened. The Grand Master of Ceremonies struck the floor three times with his huge wand and announced, 'Their Imperial Majesties'. From the moment she made her entrance Dagmar was governed by etiquette, as she and Sasha led the Imperial family through the Nicholas Hall to the music of Glinka's Polonaise from *A Life For the Tsar*. Dagmar loved these balls. She knew everyone was watching and, as the stately file made its way through the palace, she looked marvellous.

After the Polonaise, the Emperor and Empress opened the ball with a waltz. She was passionately fond of dancing and always the centre of attention, partnered by a handsome young officer while Sasha stood on the sidelines frowning unhappily. Her favourite dance, the Polish Mazurka, was full of quick and sprightly steps which she performed gracefully and expertly. Over three thousand invitations were sent out and during the course of the evening all the society matrons and their daughters had to be presented to the Empress. Once there were so many that Dagmar complained she 'hardly ever got into the ballroom and finally only saw the Mazurka danced which lasted half an hour'. Even this had its lighter side. 'One poor lady lost her petticoat', she reported delightedly, 'which remained at our feet until … [someone] picked it up and hid it behind a pot of flowers. The unfortunate owner managed to hide herself in the crowd before anyone had discovered who she was'.[7]

Immediately after the mazurka supper was served. The guests crowded into adjoining rooms for soup, chicken, asparagus and fresh lobster. In the Heraldic Room the Empress' table was set with rare porcelain and her place setting was decorated with hyacinths and lilies of the valley, her favourite flower. At the 'Bal de Palmiers' the supper hall was turned into a tropical garden, with tables built around palm trees specially grown at Tsarskoe Selo. In 1885 the dresses and jewels glowed even more brilliantly, as some of the rooms in the Winter Palace were lit by electricity for the first time.

The Imperial family's departure at two o'clock signalled the end of the ball. Sometimes the Emperor decided that it had already gone on for far too long and began ordering the musicians to leave, one by one, until only a single drummer remained. If the dancing still continued Sasha began to turn off the lights, until Dagmar gave in and said with a smile, 'Well, I suppose the Emperor wants us all to go home'.[8]

During the next few weeks society lived in a frenzied whirl. Banquets, receptions, concerts, operas, ballets, midnight suppers, 'bal masques' and costume balls, when the Empress appeared in sixteenth-century Russian dress, followed each other in never-ending succession. Dagmar was in her element. 'Court life had to run in splendour', recalled Grand Duchess Olga, 'and there my mother played her part without a single false step'. Although the more staid members of the aristocracy criticised Dagmar's high spirits and love of dancing, these few disapproving voices went almost unheard. 'Of the long gallery of Tsarinas who have sat in state in the Kremlin or paced the Winter Palace', wrote a contemporary, 'Marie Feodorovna was, perhaps, the most brilliant'.[9]

All the Court Officials fell victim to the charm of the lively, flirtatious young Empress. Newly promoted officers had the honour of dancing with her but she always made these nervous young men feel at ease. Although the Empress liked to flirt and had an eye for a good-looking young man, there is no evidence that she was anything other than a faithful wife. From the 1890s, one of her favourites was her Cotillion partner, Vladimir Nicholaievitch Nicholaiev. An extremely handsome officer in the Chevalier Guards, Vladimir was the illegitimate son of Grand Duke Nicholas Nicholaievitch senior. If she wanted to further the career of a young officer who had caught her eye, she arranged for him to be invited to one of the Emperor's beer evenings, which Sasha preferred to the more formal Court entertainments. Here all the men had to play a musical instrument, the Emperor usually choosing the bassoon or the trombone.

She gave private, informal parties in the Anitchkov ballroom for her more intimate friends. The informality did not extend to supper, where the most distinguished guests ate from gold plate and everyone else from silver. At these lively gatherings, only the Viennese Waltz was banned as 'risqué' and dancing usually continued well into the small hours.

Among Dagmar's intimate friends was Sasha's cousin Princess Eugenie of Oldenburg. Eugenie, a granddaughter of Tsar Nicholas I, was the daughter of Grand Duchess Marie Nicholaievna and her first husband

Maximilian, 3rd Duke of Leuchtenberg. Early in 1868 Eugenie married Prince Alexander of Oldenburg, another Romanov descendant; her son Peter was born six months after Dagmar's son Nicholas. Eugenie was two years Dagmar's senior and they had much in common. She was a keen charity worker and was Chairwoman of the Artists' Encouragement Society.

Another of Grand Duchess Marie Nicholaievna's daughters was Hélène Sheremetev, whose father was the Grand Duchess's second husband Count Gregory Alexandrovitch Stroganoff. Hélène's head was reported to be filled with little else but gossip. In 1879, aged just eighteen, she married Vladimir Alexeievitch Sheremetev, a commander in H.I.M. Own Convoy. When Sasha became Tsar they did not hesitate to capitalise on their friend-ship with the Imperial couple and Sheremetev was soon universally known as 'the Anitchkov favourite'. In 1891 he was appointed a Major General of the Entourage. Most members of the Imperial family disliked them, as did the members of the Court. Sheremetev and his wife tried to live a grand lifestyle in their house on the fashionable English Quay, helped by subsidies from various relations. After he squandered all Hélène's money they were forced to let the house and live on an allowance paid by the Tsar and Princess Eugenie of Oldenburg, Hélène's half-sister. Sheremetev, who one member of the Court described as a 'dedicated scoundrel', then 'borrowed money and profiteered on the patronage of his own miserable men by the Empress'. When he died in 1893 Hélène married another officer, Gregory Nikititch Miklashevich.[10]

During the Season Dagmar was an avid theatregoer and was frequently seated in the Imperial box at the lovely blue and gold Maryinsky Theatre. 'We went to the opera for the first time last night', she wrote during the 1891 Season, 'and had the pleasure of hearing the brothers Reszke [Jean and Edouard de Reszke] in *Romeo and Juliet* and it was really quite ideal: first of all I adore this music and then they sang quite admirably'.[11]

One of Dagmar's greatest loves was ballet. The reign of Alexander III witnessed the premier of some of Tchaikovsky's greatest works, although *The Sleeping Beauty* was received 'coldly' at its dress rehearsal in 1890. *The Nutcracker*, first performed in December 1892 on the Tsarevitch's Name Day, only merited the comment 'very nice, Tchaikovsky', from Alexander III.[12] *Swan Lake* was first performed in 1877 but by the time it was was revived in January 1895 both Tchaikovsky and Alexander III were dead.

During her years in Russia Dagmar was fortunate to witness the flowering of the Russian Imperial Ballet under some of its greatest dancers, including Vaslav Nijinsky, Tamara Karsavina, Mathilde Kschessinska and

Anna Pavlova. At the Maryinsky, two evenings a week were devoted to ballet performances, which were unrivalled anywhere in Europe.

As society ate, drank and danced the Season away the Emperor and Empress were much in demand to attend the dinners, receptions and balls given every night by the Ambassadors and the aristocracy. Each hostess tried to outdo the other. The British Embassy only had sufficient gold plate for two people but it was always kept for the rare occasions when the Emperor and Empress dined.

Two smaller Imperial balls were given, one in the Concert Room of the Winter Palace and the other in the Hermitage, where supper was served in the picture gallery and the guests were surrounded by works of art.

Nothing was allowed to stand in the way of Dagmar's enjoyment. In January 1889, invitations for a particularly brilliant ball had been sent out when news of Crown Prince Rudolf's death arrived from Vienna. Court mourning required the cancellation of the ball. Then someone remembered a slight inflicted by the Austrian Court. Dagmar promptly re-issued invitations for a 'bal noir', at which all the ladies would wear black dresses and their jewels. Looking radiant in a gown of black velvet, the Empress enjoyed a form of polite revenge.

The last eight days before Lent were called 'Maslenitsa' (Butter Week). This was Carnival Week with masked figures and dancing bears in the streets, swings and huge ice-slides. Whole carnival towns with booths, puppet theatres and restaurants were erected and large quantities of thin little pancakes with butter, 'blinis', were eaten. One year the Emperor decided to eat blinis with the artists of the Maryinsky Theatre. At the end of the performance the Emperor and Empress came on stage. Dagmar put on an apron and sat at the head of a hastily improvised table filling the plates from a huge dish while Sasha chatted with the performers.

The Season ended on the last Sunday of Carnival with a final party at the Yelagin Palace. The 'Folle-Journée' (Mad Day) began with dancing in the afternoon, with interruptions for supper, dinner and the 'gulyanie', the promenade of carriages in the street. It was the last chance for Dagmar to enjoy herself. 'I ... let myself be carried away and took my full share in the dancing', she admitted joyfully.[13] At the stroke of midnight a supper of fish, vegetables and fruit was served and the Great Easter Fast began.

Lent was spent quietly at Gatchina. During this period of strict abstinence sugar and dairy produce were forbidden; the women put their jewels away; dancing and play-going were prohibited. Dagmar and Sasha took their children to the Palm Market in St Petersburg where toys, coloured paper flowers and brightly-coloured eggs were sold.

Dagmar was sustained by her faith, which was a sincere, wholehearted commitment accompanied by strong moral principles. Religion was not just a formality or an observance of time-honoured rites. Almost a third of every year was taken up by Holy Days, while the frequent Fast Days were observed by the Imperial family along with the humblest of their subjects. The climax of the Russian Orthodox calendar, more holy even than Christmas, was Easter – 'Veliky Post' (the Great Fast) and, whenever possible, the Emperor and Empress spent this most important festival in the capital.

On Easter Eve the Imperial family assembled in the Winter Palace church in full court dress, each holding a candle. All over Russia, people waited expectantly for the moment when the golden doors of the icon-ostasis were opened and the priest led them in procession round the outside of the church in search of the Saviour. The climax came when the priest, in a re-enactment of the discovery of the empty tomb, threw open the church doors and said to the congregation outside, 'Khristos Voskres!' (Christ is Risen!), to which they replied joyfully, 'Voistinu Voskrese' (Indeed He is risen). At midnight the church bells rang, public buildings were illuminated and in St Petersburg a salute was fired from the Fortress of SS Peter & Paul.

Afterwards the Imperial children rushed to enjoy all the things for-bidden during Lent, excitedly greeting everyone they met with three kisses of blessing, welcome and joy. In the Banqueting Hall was the thick round cylindrical Easter bread 'Kulich', topped with white icing and the symbol XB – Christ is Risen – and 'paskha', a rich, creamy dessert made in a pyramid-shaped mould.

On Easter Sunday Sasha and Dagmar distributed eggs of porcelain, malachite and jasper to the household and servants, the Emperor kissing all the men and the Empress all the ladies. The following day five thousand troops received Easter greetings from the Emperor and presented the Empress with a hard boiled egg, receiving in return an egg of painted porcelain.

Although Sasha liked to live modestly he also loved to give and his presents were always in true Imperial style. In 1882 the Emperor and Empress had been very impressed with the beautiful jewellery and other elegant objects displayed by the House of Fabergé at the Pan-Russian Exhibition in Moscow. Peter Carl Fabergé took over his father's jeweller's shop in St Petersburg in 1870 when he was twenty-four. He quickly caught the mood of refined elegance, producing objects of fantasy whose emphasis was more on the visual impression than on the value of the mate-rials – jewelled and enamelled cigarette cases, picture frames, bell-pushes and parasol handles; sprays of flowers in gold or enamel with diamond centres and nephrite leaves, set in rock crystal to simulate a vase of water;

tiny animals and birds with precious stones for eyes. In 1885 he was appointed Supplier to the Court and was asked to design an Easter egg as a surprise for the Empress. Eggs symbolising life and the Resurrection were a traditional Russian Easter gift and this was the beginning of Dagmar's collection of Fabergé Easter eggs.

From 1885 Dagmar received one of these masterpieces every Easter and, after her husband's death, Nicholas continued the tradition. Carl Fabergé always called personally to present the Tsar's egg, encased in a special velvet box. The first egg was similar to one in the Danish Royal Collection and opened to reveal a gold yolk, containing a golden chicken with cabochon ruby eyes. When she removed the hen from its red velvet cushion the delighted Empress found an exquisite model of the Imperial crown, accurate in every minute detail, and a tiny ruby Easter egg pendant. She was so pleased that the Emperor stipulated every egg must have a surprise.

The thirty eggs presented to Dagmar contained a variety of things, including pictures of institutions of which she was patron and a tiny gold model of Gatchina palace complete with flag. A folding screen showed the Imperial yachts *Tsarevna* and *Polar Star* and her Danish and Russian homes – Bernstorff, Alexander III's villa at Fredensborg, Fredensborg itself, The Amalienborg, Kronborg Castle, two views of The Cottage at Peterhof, and Gatchina.[14]

Over the years Fabergé's surprises grew more ambitious. '[The egg] is a true chef-d'oeuvre, in pink enamel', she told Alix in 1914, 'and inside a porte-chaise carried by two blackamoors with Empress Catherine in it wearing a little crown on her head. You wind it up and then the blackamoors walk: it is an unbelievably beautiful and superbly fine piece of work'. The eggs themselves were only four to six inches high. The lovely Winter Egg, made at a cost of 24,600 roubles, recently sold at auction for over three million pounds. It was no wonder that Dagmar called Fabergé 'an incomparable genius'.[15]

She often took the eggs with her when she moved from palace to palace. Soon her collection included Fabergé picture-frames, over a hundred hardstone animals, hardstone figures and a collection of miniature eggs which she kept in a showcase at Gatchina. These were traditionally worn on a long chain necklace at Easter. For the smaller Imperial balls the Empress even had a Fabergé kokoshnik of blue enamel and diamonds. Often she gave instructions for the design of an object and did not hesitate to say if she disapproved of Fabergé's drawings.

When she sent these beautiful objects as presents to her many relations Fabergé's fame spread to the Courts of Europe. Queen Louise once received a golden Easter egg, which opened to reveal a smaller egg studded with precious stones glittering in all the colours of the rainbow. Alexander III commissioned cigarette cases, clocks, desk-pieces and trays as official presents for the Court.

When the revolution came Fabergé, his workshops closed and his craftsmen scattered, escaped from Russia with the help of the British Embassy. He died in Lausanne in 1920. Twenty-two of the Easter eggs that delighted an Empress for thirty years are known to have survived, in private collections or museums, as an echo of a vanished past – 'the fatal fantasies of a doomed dynasty'.[16]

Society functions would never be as glittering again. Nothing, said Grand Duke Cyril, could compare with the 'brilliant occasions' of the reign of Alexander III.[17] It was a swan-song, as if Imperial Russia had one last fling before accelerating to its doom.

CHAPTER 11

Peace and Stability

'THE GUARDIAN ANGEL OF RUSSIA'

Sasha and Dagmar were very close throughout their married life. They were never separated for more than a few days and she naturally became her husband's confidante. Sasha discussed political affairs and confided his judgement of the ministers. She supported and encouraged him and if his opinion was too harsh she was sometimes able to modify his attitude. He was not always tactful and Dagmar occasionally took matters into her own hands. On the death of Count Peter Shouvaloff, a prominent statesman whom the Emperor had disliked, she immediately telegraphed their deep regrets. She knew everything that was going on. 'Why do you say you are afraid of intrigues?' she asked Sergei Witte many years later. 'There were intrigues against you in the time of my husband. Yet you remained his favourite Minister'. The French Ambassador was recalled against the Tsar's wishes. 'The offence is not to you but to us', she told his wife.[1]

Although not a clever woman in the intellectual sense, Dagmar was quick-witted, practical and knew how to handle people. Witte noted her generosity, loyalty and skill in diplomacy, although he thought she was not outstandingly intelligent. Polovtsov, Head of the State Chancery, provided summaries of the Council of State's deliberations to enable her to keep up to date with current affairs. Her political influence was carefully hidden and most contemporary observers were unaware of it.

Throughout her years in Russia, Dagmar subscribed to the newspapers *Dagens Nyheder*, *Nationaltidende* and *Flensborg Avis*, the latter to enable her to follow events in South Jutland. The newspapers were also sent to her if she was in Denmark. She took *Le Figaro* from France and the *Daily News* and *The Times* from England. Many Danish businesses continued to profit from the link with Russia. In 1884, King Christian asked his daughter to help Burmeister & Wain obtain a commission to supply an engine for a new ship in the Black Sea Fleet. Six months later, Dagmar told King Christian how delighted she was at the success of her mission. Their scheming had resulted in a Danish shipyard being given an order to build a gun boat and in the 1890s Burmeister & Wain built the new Imperial yacht *Standart*.

The Emperor was anxious that neutral Denmark should be well armed. Copenhagen's fortifications were strengthened to prevent the city falling into German or British hands, blocking Russia's exit to the Baltic. One of the forts was built with money collected by the women of Denmark under the patronage of 'Kejserinde Dagmar', although how much was contributed by the Danes and how much by the Empress personally is not known.

She was often accused of damaging Russia by promoting Danish interests but this was unfair. She was actively interested in Russia and promoted Russian businesses in Denmark. At the Scandinavian Industrial Exhibition in Copenhagen in 1888, eight of the large contingent of Russian exhibitors were appointed Purveyors to the Royal Danish Court, without going through the usual formalities.

With one sister in England and a brother in Greece it was natural that foreign affairs should especially interest Dagmar. Soon after Sasha's accession, the Foreign Office in London was warned that, under her influence, foreign policy would be more pro-Greek and the Prime Minister, Lord Salisbury, frequently expressed concern.

The marriage of Affie and Marie, which Dagmar and Alix had done so much to promote, had done little to ease the tension between Russia and England. In 1885 the two countries were close to war over Afghanistan, where the Russian advance to the south of the Sea of Aral had aroused English fears for the safety of India. A commission entrusted with the job of marking out the frontier between Russia and Afghanistan was suspended at Russia's request, whereupon the Russians advanced and defeated the Afghans at Pendjeh in March 1885.

England was outraged. Queen Victoria had appealed personally to the Tsar to prevent any conflict with the Afghans and, although the fact was not known at the time, the battle had taken place in direct infringement of his instructions. In England the reserves were called up and it seemed as if war was inevitable. Dagmar and her sister were horrified. Fortunately, Russia backed down and the frontier question was settled by arbitration.

In 1885 the southern Bulgars, still under Turkish rule since the war of 1878, declared their independence and were unified with the northern part of Bulgaria in direct defiance of the Treaty of Berlin. Northern Bulgaria was under the rule of the Tsar's cousin Prince Alexander of Battenberg ('Sandro'), who had been set up as sovereign prince in 1879 with the support of his uncle Tsar Alexander II. Unfortunately, Alexander III despised his cousin Sandro and did not give him the same support.

The action of the Bulgarians aroused Greek national aspirations. They began to demand their share of the territory that they felt should have been allotted to them at the Congress of Berlin. To Willie's horror, they were prepared to back their demands by action and seize what they wanted from the Turks. Willie appealed to the Prince of Wales. The Great Powers refused to help and insisted that Greece must give way. The Greeks replied by moving troops towards the Turkish frontier. In Russia, Dagmar wrote anxiously to her brother praying that the situation, which he was powerless to prevent, would not lead to war. The Tsar, she said, would do all he could to help Willie out of his difficulty.

By the end of April a naval blockade by the Great Powers and the possible bombardment of Athens were becoming daily more likely. When the diplomatic representatives were recalled, only those from France and Russia remained. The situation was diffused when the Greeks backed down and demobilized.

In Bulgaria, Sandro was not so lucky. The Bulgarian unification incensed the Tsar, who did all he could to discredit Sandro throughout Europe. Finally, in August 1886, Sandro was kidnapped from his palace in Sofia and forced to abdicate at gunpoint. He was then taken by boat to Russian Bessarabia. Although the Bulgarians demanded their prince back his return to Sofia was brief. Completely disillusioned, he confirmed his abdication and left the country.

The Bulgarian throne was then offered to Prince Waldemar of Denmark. Relations between Greece and Bulgaria were strained and there was almost certain to be a war between them sooner or later. Waldemar was the least ambitious member of Dagmar's family but the situation was best summed up by his wife: 'Nothing would induce me to go down there – ever!' Marie declared.[2] The choice fell on Prince Ferdinand of Coburg who kept his throne for thirty-one years.

The anti-Germanism that Dagmar had nurtured in Sasha also now bore fruit, helped by the fact that the family ties between the two courts were not as strong. In 1887 the Tsar refused to renew the Three Emperors' League. Bismarck, afraid Russia would turn towards France, offered a Reinsurance Treaty instead, giving Russia a 'certain amount of influence' in the Balkans. Russia pledged neutrality towards Germany unless the Germans invaded France but Germany would remain neutral towards Russia unless the Russians attacked Austria. Relations between them continued to be strained and anti-Germanism became the way to favour and promotion. As Russian foreign policy began to turn away from Germany, Dagmar used her powers of persuasion in favour of an alliance with France.

That November, a breakdown in the Imperial yacht forced Sasha and Dagmar to return home from Denmark by train. This entailed a courtesy call on the old German Emperor William I, then in his ninetieth year.

The Germany of 1887 was a far cry from the mass of small states that had existed in 1864. Fused with Prussian drive and militarism Berlin was now an Imperial capital and Germany was determined to become one of the Great Powers. The German Emperor gave a banquet but it was noticed that, throughout the visit, the Tsar was barely polite. His belligerent attitude caused Bismarck to think again. Perhaps when the war came they would have to fight on two fronts after all. Plans were immediately drawn up and these far-sighted preparations became part of the battle plan for 1914.

The old Emperor of Germany died in March 1888 and was succeeded by his son Frederick III (husband of Queen Victoria's daughter Vicky). He died of cancer after a reign of only three months. Broken-hearted Vicky then took the name of 'the Empress Frederick'. Dagmar viewed the accession of Vicky's son Kaiser William II with distaste. Her letters are full of sarcastic references to the Kaiser and his deeds. His militant regime was merely a more powerful manifestation of the Prussian state that had crushed Denmark when she was younger. To make matters worse, the new Empress, Augusta Victoria (Dona), was the daughter of the Duke of Augustenburg, who had set himself up with German help as Duke Frederick VIII of Schleswig-Holstein in 1864.

William had already tried to stir up trouble between the Tsar and the Prince of Wales. His comments, along with others accusing the Prince of trying to inflame Germany into declaring war on Russia, reached Bertie's ears through Dagmar's letters to Alix. Bertie's distrust of his nephew increased. When, within a month of his father's death, William proposed visits to Austria and Russia, the Tsar viewed the prospect with no more enthusiasm than his wife but they were both obliged to put on a brave face.

Dagmar kept herself abreast of the Kaiser's deeds through the newspaper *Holbaek Amts* (edited by Eugene Ibsen, a lecturer at Soro Academy). One of the newspaper's correspondents was the Danish Parliament's representative in Berlin and he provided Ibsen with information about the Kaiser's 'unstable and feverish activities'. Ibsen passed this information to the Russian Empress and to the Russian Ambassador in Paris.[3]

Things went reasonably well while the German Emperor ruled through Bismarck, whose policy was to remain friendly with Russia and maintain the status quo. Bismarck's thinking was undoubtedly conditioned by the knowledge that the Russian Empress had great influence over her husband and the wounds of Schleswig-Holstein cut deep. 'It is our belief', Prince Gorchakov had once written, 'that Germany will not forget that both in Russia and in England a Danish Princess has her foot on the steps of the throne'.[4]

*

The terrorists had remained largely dormant. Between 1884 and 1886 several dangerous organisations were routed out, leaving a feeling of complacency. Then, in 1887, there was an attempt on the Tsar's life.

Every year on 13th March the Imperial family travelled by train to the capital to attend the annual commemoration service for Alexander II in the SS Peter & Paul Cathedral. After the service they returned to the station in an open carriage along a route heavily guarded by police. March 1887 was no exception. As their train was about to leave, Sasha was informed that some students carrying crude bombs concealed in hollowed-out books had been arrested on one of St Petersburg's main streets. They had intended to hurl them at the carriage as the Imperial family passed. The Tsar remained silent and grimly boarded the train.

On the journey back to Gatchina he was lighthearted and talkative, joking with the children. Only when he and Dagmar were driving alone through Gatchina park did he tell her how narrowly they had escaped death. She was severely shaken and upset but Sasha steeled his nerves, saying he would do his duty whatever the cost.

Two days later a British diplomat reported that the Empress was still very nervous but the Tsar was in good spirits, he knew it was useless to try and avoid danger.

Among the five students tried and hanged for this attempt was Alexander Ilyich Ulyanov. His younger brother Vladimir was later known to the world simply as Lenin. Soon afterwards, the Tsar received another letter from the Executive Committee of the People's Will saying he had been condemned to death. Dagmar's nerves were shattered once again. Sasha took her and the children to Novorossisk on the Black Sea, far away from the oppressive atmosphere of Gatchina and St Petersburg.

Cut off from any liberal thought Alexander became increasingly unenlightened, suspicious, distrustful and obstinate. Pobedonostsev, nicknamed 'The Black Tsar' now spent half of every year at Gatchina in the dual role of advisor to the Emperor and tutor to the Tsarevitch. The Tsar was his own Prime Minister. There was no parliament and no elections. The State Council was purely an advisory body, ministers reported directly to him. He was not obliged to take their advice and could dismiss any of them at his pleasure. They were not permitted to resign. 'Shut up!' he bellowed at one unfortunate minister, shaking him by the collar, 'when I choose to kick you out you will hear of it in no uncertain terms!'[5]

Every day the Tsar worked through mountains of state papers, scrawling blunt comments, not always polite, in the margins. The country had become a police state and corruption was rife. The police controlled the internal passport system and a new police division, the Okhrana, was established. Their undercover agents intercepted letters, infiltrated organisations and collected evidence against those suspected of subversion. Nevertheless, capital punishment was only in force for crimes involving terrorism and assassination.

In the autumn of 1888 the Imperial family visited the Caucasus. The people were anxious to show their loyalty to the Tsar who, on this occasion, had brought his whole family. The journey took took them to Vlaadikavkaz, Batum, Tiflis and Baku. Everywhere deputations greeted them with bread and salt on ornate dishes and among the gifts they received were two horses for the Empress and items of Circassian traditional dress. On 25th October a gala dinner was held at Kutaisi for senior dignitaries and local officials. Dagmar was given a prominent part in all the ceremonies and treated as an honorary man, the highest favour the people could bestow. From the Caucasus they sailed to Sevastopol to join the Imperial train.

On 29th October the train was rattling across the Russian countryside on the return journey. Security was tight. The points were locked before they passed and the keys given to the Okhrana. Every bridge, every culvert and every level-crossing was guarded and the Tsar's destination was never announced in advance. To lessen the risk of an attempt by revolutionaries each of the eight carriages was painted in royal blue with the Imperial double-headed eagle embossed in gold on the side. Two identical trains were used on every journey, so the terrorists never knew which carried the Imperial family and which was the baggage train.

Inside it resembled a travelling palace. Inter-communicating carriages, unheard of in Europe at that time, housed bedrooms, bathrooms and drawing rooms all thickly carpeted and luxuriously upholstered, as well as a kitchen and a dispensary. Saloons were hung with pale blue brocade or pink damask. In the dining-room twenty people could sit at the long table, dine off silver plates and drink from silver goblets. Tartar servants in loose black shirts administered to every need. By decree the train's speed was regulated but on this occasion it appears that the Emperor had ordered the engineer to speed up.

At about eleven o'clock they approached Borki in the province of Kharkov. Sasha and Dagmar were sitting opposite each other in the dining-car at the front, Olga and Nana in the children's coach behind it. Suddenly the train gave a violent lurch. Then a second one. A few seconds later everything in the dining-car was thrown around. Dagmar instinctively closed her eyes. There was a mighty bang and several more jolts, followed by the sound of clanging iron as the coaches at the rear of the train crashed against those in front. Then silence.

Dagmar stood up and looked around. The walls of the carriage were pressed in. There was no roof over her head, part of it was hanging down like a partition between her and the section of the carriage where Sasha had been sitting. She emerged bruised and cut by flying glass, her beige silk travelling dress, a creation of Worth in Paris, spattered with blood and dirt. Her left hand had been trapped and was bruised, her right hand was bleeding heavily and she was black and blue all over.

The wheels of the dining-car had been ripped off and part of the train had rolled down the embankment, but there was no sign of her family. In a letter to Willie, Dagmar said it was the most terrifying moment she had ever experienced.[6]

Then Xenia appeared from behind the hanging roof. George and Michael had climbed up on top of what remained of the carriage and they called down to their mother. Last came Nicholas. All of them had cuts on their faces from the flying glass. Xenia and George had cut hands. Sasha's leg was badly trapped and it took several minutes to free him. His leg was coal-black from the thigh to the knee and he limped for several days afterwards. He is reputed to have joked that his ambitious brother Vladimir, who had always envied him the throne, would be disappointed that, as they had all survived, he would not be Tsar.

Dagmar finally managed to reassure Sasha that she was not badly injured and began to calm the children. Six-year-old Olga had been thrown clear and rolled down the embankment. Terrified, her one thought was to get away and when a footman picked her up she scratched his face. As she was reunited with her father, she was still screaming, 'now they'll come and kill us all!'[7] Later Dagmar recalled the moment of sheer relief when she saw that her husband and children were alive.

All around her Dagmar could hear the cries of the wounded. Summoning the uninjured members of the suite, she instructed them to help the Imperial doctor. Bonfires were hurriedly lit and the wounded and dying placed nearby to keep them warm. As the telegraph poles were damaged it was impossible to summon help quickly and, while Sasha pulled people from the wreckage, Dagmar worked tirelessly for over five hours in relentless drizzle, carrying water, murmuring words of comfort and tearing up strips of linen from her luggage to bandage the injured. 'Later I heard that my mother had been heroic', recalled Grand Duchess Olga, 'helping the doctor with a real nurse's zeal'.[8]

Eventually, a relief train arrived from Kharkov but the exhausted Emperor and Empress still refused to rest until all the wounded were comfortable and the bodies taken on board. Finally, they were persuaded that everything possible had been done and the train was driven to Lotsovoi station, where prayers were said by the local priest. Throughout the service tears streamed down the Emperor's cheeks, while the equally distressed Empress had her arm around Olga.

Twenty-one people, including Dagmar's faithful Cossack Sudurov, were killed and thirty-five were wounded. Sasha's favourite sheepdog Kamchatka was crushed. Dagmar's own little dog Tip was saved because she had forgotten to take him into lunch that day. Two days after the accident they visited the wounded in Kharkov hospital. One of Dagmar's servants had five broken ribs.

They finally returned to Gatchina on 2nd November. The entire Imperial family met them at the station and everyone attended the Te Deum. The Empress had her injured left hand in a sling. Even after massage, she was unable to move it several days later. Kamchatka was buried within sight of Sasha's window, the spot was marked by an obelisk.

The Commission of Enquiry found that the accident was caused by the excessive speed of a train that was too heavy, on rails that were too light and sleepers that were old. However, rumours persisted that a bomb had been smuggled aboard and the terrorists' ringleader died in the explosion. Some members of the Imperial family also inclined towards this view.

Although Dagmar had shown remarkable courage and presence of mind throughout the ordeal, the nervous shock took its toll. She was unable to get the incident out of her mind. Three weeks later she told her brother Willie that she was still dreaming about the crash. At least one writer has said she may have suffered a serious nervous breakdown.[9]

There is no doubt that the events at Borki increased the nervous tension of the Emperor and, especially, the Empress. Sasha became more moody and unsociable, shunning public functions to an unprecedented degree. He began to drink more heavily and the effects of terrorism, together with worry over his wife, took their toll on his own health. Dagmar, whose nerves had never recovered from the shock of seeing the mangled body of her father-in-law, now became prone to fits of nervous prostration. Even at the beginning of the following year one of her attendants described her as 'still noticeably nervous'.[10] Official entertaining was cut down even more.

Although Dagmar was now under intolerable strain she stood by her husband's decision to uphold the autocracy, never faltering and never trying to persuade him to make liberal concessions to appease the terrorists.

*

As well as her ceremonial role, Dagmar concentrated on charity work. Her involvement began during the St Petersburg cholera epidemic in the late 1870s when she visited the hospitals and spent time with the sick and dying patients. She even ventured into the districts which had been isolated by troops to prevent contagion spreading.

After the death of the Empress Marie Alexandrovna, Dagmar was appointed President of the Russian Red Cross Society. Its main purpose was to aid the sick and wounded in wartime but Dagmar also saw the need to train an adequate supply of nurses during peacetime. Permanent training centres were opened and hospitals maintained, where the training could be put to good use. Storage facilities ensured that the equipment needed for the large field hospitals was ready for any emergency.

The Empress' interest encouraged others. Donations flowed from the rich, who saw it as a passport to society. Prominent people gave their support and gradually many of the main provincial towns had their own branch. The Red Cross became a symbol of unselfish devotion to the Russian people, a symbol of which the Empress was very proud. Her decision that a case should receive benefit was final. When she heard that Henri Dunant, who founded the Red Cross in 1863, was living in poverty in a hospital she immediately arranged for him to receive a pension, which continued until his death in 1910.

She took an active interest in the Smolny Institute, founded by Catherine the Great to educate young ladies of the nobility. A portrait of Dagmar (to which the girls had to curtsey every day) hung in the main hall. Similar boarding schools, also known as Institutes, were under her care and by 1917 there was one of these state boarding schools in every main provincial town. Girls whose families could not afford the £80 a year fee were admitted free as nominees of the Emperor and Empress. Dagmar paid frequent visits, personally looking into all aspects of the girls' care and education.

She also devoted a great deal of attention to the 'Department of the Institutions of the Empress Marie', usually called simply the Department. It was founded by the wife of Emperor Paul, the first Empress Marie Feodorovna, to co-ordinate the activities of charities and educational establishments. Successive Empresses took over its patronage but none with more active enthusiasm than Dagmar.

She brought new life to the organisation, asserting her right of absolute control over its affairs. In matters of administration and finance her decision was final. In 1882 she appointed Constantine Constantinovitch Grot as Director of the Department and then used her influence to obtain him a seat on the Council of State. Grot was also Chief Marshal of the Imperial Court and Chairman of the Commission for Prison Reform. One of the most tireless workers for the Department was Baroness Rahden, who brought the Empress disturbing reports about the misery she had seen.

Dagmar opted for rapid reorganisation and expansion of the Department financed by voluntary contributions. She was aided by wealthy businessmen, who saw the way to nobility (Tchin) and the open doors of society, perhaps even Imperial favour, lay in becoming a public benefactor. As the money flowed in, Dagmar ignored their mostly dubious reputations, the only requirement being willingness and ability to pay. Under her patronage the resources of the Department showed a continuous growth.

Many institutions flourished under Dagmar's patronage – 27 Girls' Institutes (including the Smolny); 77 girls' schools such as the Maria Schools, which taught needlework and other useful skills to young girls who could not afford to be educated in a Gymnasium; 113 children's homes; 23 hospitals; The Imperial Alexander Lyceum; The Nicholas Children's Home at Gatchina; asylums for old people; orphanages; sanatoria; ambulance services; research laboratories; professional courses; 21 schools and orphanages for blind children; The Guardian Organisation (a benevolent society for the blind) and workshops for ex-servicemen. The Maryinsky Teachers Training Seminary, named after her, granted scholarships to promising students who could not afford to pay the fees. She was also a Trustee of the Women's Patriotic Society, the Life-Saving Society and the Society for the Protection of Animals. She visited the mental institutions to see that they were properly managed and paid for the education and care of a number of orphans from her own private purse. It was estimated that she spent only £5,000 of her yearly £20,000 personal allowance and the remainder was given to charity. In this way she helped 33,000 people in St Petersburg and 39,000 in Moscow every year.

She was greatly interested in the education of women. After Alexander II's reforms many privately-financed schools and professional courses were started, to train women for the new opportunities available. Dagmar's intervention saved many of these foundations when they were threatened with closure after he was assassinated. The Empress was not interested in political rights for women. When asked to intervene to save the women's University, she refused because she considered it a breeding-ground for revolutionaries. Her main concern was to educate women so they would be able to earn a decent living.

The Empress had a particular rapport with young people. It was usual for girls from the various Gymnasia, Grammar Schools and Institutes to be summoned to Gatchina to receive their medals from the Empress and stay for lunch. The young Maria Konyaeff recalled such an occasion when, in their smartest uniforms and on their best behaviour, she and her fellow pupils sat down to a formal luncheon attended by the Minister of Education and other notable dignitaries. Grand Duchess Xenia was also present, wearing a pink cotton dress trimmed with broderie anglaise, her hair tied back with a simple bow. Afterwards the Empress suggested a walk in the gardens and the girls were amazed to be told to help themselves to the sweets and fruit on the table as they went out.

Dagmar was a progressive, deeply interested in people, and she wanted to improve the lot of humanity. As head of more than 400 institutions her kindness and common sense in the areas of health and education relieved much distress for more than thirty years. Always moved by tales of suffering she donated freely, almost recklessly, to deserving cases, reducing her secretary, Feodor Adolfovitch de Oom, to despair.

Even when she travelled abroad Dagmar was always looking out for new advances in technology. In Copenhagen she and Alix heard about Dr Niels Finsen, the inventor of the cure for lupus, an ulcerous inflammation of the skin which he treated with ultra-violet rays. After visiting his clinic Dagmar arranged for the introduction of the treatment in Russia.

Alexander III believed that all the peoples of the Empire should observe Russian customs and the Orthodox religion. His most violent hatred was directed against the Jews. Persecution of the Jews was the most severe until the time of Hitler. One third must disappear, one third must emigrate and one third assimilate, declared Pobedonostsev. In 1882 the Minister of the Interior, Count Ignatiev, introduced new laws which forbade the Jews to live outside the Pale of Settlement and restricted their rights still further. Jews left Russia in their thousands. Many of those who stayed were converted to revolutionary ideas and there were frequent Pogroms, when the non-Jewish population were incited against the Jews, beating them up and destroying their property. Dagmar was a wholehearted supporter of anti-Semitism, fully agreeing with the Emperor's belief that the Jews were organising a plot to end the monarchy. She could never understand why the Prince of Wales befriended so many Jews, yet all her life her kindness was not denied to them. She also refused to allow religious differences to prevent Jews from aiding her charities. Jews who attained the 'Tchin' were freed from many restrictions and Dagmar was the only member of the Imperial family to be popular with them.

Her dislike of injustice was well-known. She often received appeals from people who had suffered at the hands of government officials, intervening personally to ensure they received redress or protection where possible.

Through her involvement with the various organisations she came into contact with people from all parts of the Empire, from whom she gained a first-hand knowledge of Russian affairs. Fittingly, Dagmar's personal emblem was the pelican, the symbol of maternal love. Her interest in education and national health was untiring and by the time her period of administration ended there was no part of Russia where the Department was not actively at work. She truly became 'the guardian angel of Russia'.[11]

CHAPTER 12

Faith and Hope

Dagmar treated her sons and daughters as children even after they had become adults. 'My dear little soul, my boy', she wrote to Nicholas in 1887, when he was a nineteen-year-old officer.[1] In this she followed the example of her parents. King Christian treated his sons and daughters as children although they were grown up with families of their own. The King of Greece was once severely reprimanded because he ordered horses for a drive without permission.

In 1887 Nicholas joined the élite Preobrajensky Guards under the command of his uncle Grand Duke Sergei. The Tsar had a very poor opinion of most of the army officers. Their superiors were instructed to make sure that they behaved, in order to avoid any corrupting moral influences on the Tsarevitch. It is therefore inconceivable that he would have entrusted Nicholas to Sergei's care if the latter was known to be a homosexual.

Dagmar was also concerned about bad influences. Whenever Nicholas was away from home, mother and son corresponded regularly, Dagmar mostly in French, Nicholas always in Russian. 'Never forget that everyone's eyes are turned on you now, waiting to see what your first *independent* steps in life will be. Always be polite and courteous with everybody, see that you get along with all your comrades without discrimination, although without too much familiarity or intimacy, and *never* listen to flatterers', she told him.[2]

Dagmar had the consolation of being able to pay Nicholas regular visits when he was at Krasnoe Selo, the military camp near St Petersburg where the Imperial Guard held their summer manoeuvres. The Empress maintained strong links with the army. She was Honorary Colonel-in-Chief of the Chevalier Guards and Colonel-in-Chief of the Blue Cuirassiers, based at Gatchina. Dagmar was also Chief of the Horseguard Regiment 'La Dame Blanche', the 'most respected military unit', whose white full-dress uniform with its scarlet cuffs, red and white belt and white braid galloon round the skirt suited her so well. Many other regiments bore her name and wore her monogram.[3] Alexander III took special pride and interest in the Russian Navy. From 1881 the Empress was Chief of the Garde Equipage (the Marine Guard), who served on the Imperial yachts. She always called them 'My Equipage'.

In the autumn of 1888 another link was forged between the Russian and Danish Royal families. For several years Sasha's brother Grand Duke Paul had spent the winters in Greece for the sake of his delicate health. He always appreciated the warm hospitality of the Greek Royal family and felt totally at home. Soon the inevitable happened and twenty-six-year-old Paul fell in love with Willie and Olga's eighteen-year-old daughter Alexandra.

Dagmar and Sasha had hoped for this outcome for many years. They were especially fond of Alexandra, who Dagmar always called 'Aline'. She was Willie's favourite daughter and they looked forward to welcoming her to Russia. Although delighted at the news of the betrothal Dagmar remarked to Willie how confusing it would be – their niece Aline would become their sister-in-law and Paul would be both Sasha's brother and his nephew.

The wedding in the Winter Palace church on 17th June 1889 provided Dagmar with another excuse for a reunion with Willie and Olga. The Empress, in a dress of heavy gold brocade, walked with her brother just in front of the bridal couple, who carried candles decorated with white ribbons and orange blossoms. Afterwards there was a large family gathering at Peterhof. When Paul and Aline's first child, Grand Duchess Marie Pavlovna, was born in April 1890 the Emperor and Empress were among the godparents.

Sasha's other brother Alexis, who succeeded his uncle Grand Duke Constantine Nicholaievitch as Grand Admiral of the Navy, remained unmarried. In the late 1860s he had fallen in love with one of his mother's maids of honour, Alexandra Vasilievna Zhukovskaya, who was eight years his senior. They may have even married secretly in Italy in 1869 or 1870 but the marriage was annulled by Alexis' father when he found out. Alexandra certainly gave birth to a son, born in Salzburg in 1871, who was named Alexis after his father and given the title of Count Belevsky-Joukovsky by Alexander III in 1884. In the 1880s society was diverted for years by Grand Duke Alexis' passion for Zina, the beautiful wife of the Duke of Leuchtenberg, with whom he conducted an open affair under the roof of her husband. Grand Duke Alexander Michaelovitch called them the 'ménage royal à trois'.[4]

In March 1890, the Imperial family attended the annual graduation performance of the Imperial Theatre Ballet School. That evening the

Tsarevitch met seventeen-year-old Mathilde Kschessinska, a small, viva-cious dancer with dark curly hair. The Tsar was determined to make a man of his son. At supper he encouraged Mathilde to sit beside Nicholas, who was immediately attracted to her. The friendship blossomed at Krasnoe Selo, where Mathilde was among the dancers chosen for the gala performance at the little theatre, but when Nicholas left camp that autumn he did not see her again for another year.

Dagmar and Sasha had decided to send Nicholas and Georgie on a nine-month long trip to India and Japan. Georgie would go as a naval cadet and Nicholas to complete his education by seeing something of the world. Dagmar hoped the warm sun and the sea air would improve Georgie's health, which had been causing concern for some time. They left Gatchina on 4th November 1890. Dagmar had never been separated from her sons for such a long time and she missed them terribly. 'You cannot imagine how sad and hard it is to be without you, my angel, and how dreadfully it hurts to think of this long separation', she wrote sadly.[5] They went first to Athens, where they were joined by their cousin Prince George of Greece ('Greek Georgie') and, by the time the warship arrived in Egypt, his ebullient spirits had rubbed off on Dagmar's sons and the voyage had become a pleasure-cruise.

To console herself for the absence of her sons Dagmar looked after Paul and Aline's baby daughter while the young parents were away. She had no sooner returned Marie to Aline than disturbing news arrived about her own son Georgie.

From Bombay, Nicholas telegraphed that his brother had to remain on board ship because of trouble with his leg. Although Georgie assured his parents that he was perfectly well, they were suddenly informed he had a fever and would have to return home. Dagmar was alarmed. 'You can't imagine in what anguish I have passed these last few days', she wrote. 'In spite of all the reasoning … I had to take things calmly, and to tell myself that it … is only this horrible malaria that will pass with a change of air …'[6] He had acute bronchitis and was sent back to Athens where he could be examined by one of the Imperial doctors. The Empress was distressed for Georgie, whose disappointment she felt deeply and for Nicholas, who was now deprived of his company.

In the heat of India, surrounded by English hospitality, Nicholas grew irritable and bored. Always with an eye on his conduct, Dagmar's letters contained constant reminders about the obligations of his position. 'You have to *set your personal comfort* aside, be doubly polite and amiable and, above all, never show you are bored. You will do this, won't you, my dear Nicky'.[7]

Despite her anxiety about her sons, the Season was now in full swing and Dagmar still had official duties. Archduke Franz Ferdinand, heir to the Austrian Empire since the suicide of Crown Prince Rudolf, was paying a visit to St Petersburg and had to be entertained. The Empress was kept extremely busy and told Nicholas that she did not even have time to paint. Her colours and paint brushes had all dried up and were hidden in a cupboard.

In April 1891 even more alarming news arrived from Japan. While Nicholas was riding in a rickshaw through Otsu, he was struck on the head by a fanatic wielding a sword. With blood streaming down his face he jumped out and ran along the street, pursued by the madman. His life was saved by the quick action of Greek Georgie, who knocked the man out with his cane.

The Empress received the news by telegram and immediately poured out her anguish. 'God be praised! No words can tell what dread and sorrowing tears we received that terrifying news with! ... You can well imagine what *agonies* we suffered ...'[8] The Tsar ordered his son to return home immediately.

Dagmar's anxiety was tempered by the joy of a reunion with Georgie. She was still unaware that he was suffering from tuberculosis and believed the doctor who said Georgie could be completely cured if he spent the next two winters in Algiers.

At the beginning of June, Dagmar and Xenia travelled to the Crimea, to meet Georgie's ship the *Korniloff*. Even now, when she was anxious to see her son, Dagmar still had to face the ordeal of an official reception, before a private reunion with Georgie in his cabin. At Yalta another yet official delegation awaited them, before they could drive to the Imperial estate of Livadia.

Sasha had constructed a small two-storeyed wooden villa near the old Livadia Palace, built in Moorish style with balconies and terraces against the wooded hills of Ai-Petri. The walls were overgrown with honeysuckle and vines. The rooms were 'dark, damp and unattractive'[9] and reflected his dislike of ostentation. Beautiful English style gardens dotted with statues and classical remains stretched in terraces down to the Black Sea. In the great park were orchards, olive groves and the vineyards of Massandra, which he bought from Princess Vorontzov in 1889. At Upper Massandra work was begun on a palace for the Tsarevitch.

Dagmar normally enjoyed the social life offered by holidays in the Crimea. The Youssoupovs, Bariatinskys and Vorontzovs all had villas nearby. When the Imperial family were in residence there were tennis parties, sailing and swimming in the sapphire blue sea, or picnics at Ereclic, the Empress Marie Alexandrovna's wooden palace on the mountainside. Free from the constraints of etiquette Dagmar could go shopping in Yalta. Alfresco dinners were served and afterwards the Empress and her guests danced the night away to the music of the Imperial orchestra or strolled on the terraces in the warm evening air.

This time it was different. There were no parties, instead they visited the caves at Massandra and went on excursions along the cliffs. 'The weather here ... is ideal, not too hot ... everything is in bloom; the white and yellow acacias and such a wealth of roses as I have never seen before in my life. The whole air is fragrant, and I am enjoying it all tremendously', she wrote to Nicholas.[10]

In late June they joined Sasha at Peterhof, before leaving on their annual cruise on the board the *Tsarevna*. Dagmar was pleased with Georgie's progress. The air in the Finnish Skerries did him good, his appetite improved and his temperature was nearly normal. Nevertheless, the doctors would not admit that he had tuberculosis and kept referring to his 'weak chest'. A change of air was recommended.

Dagmar and Georgie therefore left for Cannes. When the South of France did not bring the expected improvement the doctors decided to send him to the dry mountain air of Abbas Touman in the Caucasus. Dagmar made sure he was comfortable in a large villa before returning to the north filled with despair. From now on, Georgie was often in her thoughts and his health was a constant source of worry.

Nicholas returned home in August. Disinterested in affairs of state and given no encouragement by his father, who was reluctant to give him any responsibility, he settled into the easy-going life of a playboy. Although he still turned to his mother for advice, Dagmar was soon complaining that she hardly saw him.

He was appointed a member of the Finance Committee and president of the committee for constructing the Trans-Siberian Railway. At meetings of the State Council, Nicholas watched the clock impatiently. On the one occasion he dared to defy the Tsar, his father pelted him with bread pellets during dinner as a sign of displeasure.

He renewed his friendship with Mathilde Kschessinska, who was now living with her sister in a house on the English Prospekt. Mathilde soon became his mistress and they spent quiet, intimate evenings together. Dagmar was afraid that the affair would become too serious but Sasha seemed unconcerned. For Nicholas it was a time of happiness without any commitment and a way of postponing a confrontation with his parents. Although his affair with Mathilde continued, Nicholas was in love with a princess, but his chosen bride did not have his father's approval.

*

In September 1891 while the family were gathered at Fredensborg, news reached Willie and Olga that their twenty-one-year-old daughter Alexandra, whose marriage to Grand Duke Paul had been celebrated so lavishly two years before, was dying in childbirth. They left immediately for Russia.

Earlier that year Sergei had been appointed Governor General of Moscow. Paul and his wife were staying with Sergei and Ella at their country estate of Ilinskoe when Aline, seven months pregnant, became gravely ill as complications set in. The old midwife from the village could do nothing and by the time the doctors arrived the young Grand Duchess was in a coma. Six days after giving premature birth to a son she died without regaining consciousness. Her parents reached her bedside just in time. The newly-born Grand Duke Dimitri was forgotten in the tumult and was later found bundled in a heap of blankets. Small and feeble, no-one expected him to live.

When the news reached Denmark the family were devastated. The following day they left by train for the three-day journey back to Russia. This had the disadvantage of a few hours stop in Berlin, where the Kaiser, who was away, deputed his brother to act as host at an official dinner. The brothers and sister of the dead Grand Duchess had no choice but to attend. This example of the Kaiser's tact made Sasha and Dagmar angry and did nothing to improve their feelings for Germany. Aline was laid to rest in the Cathedral of SS Peter & Paul. In 1938 her body was brought back to Tatoi, where she now lies buried with the rest of the Greek Royal family.

In November the Emperor and Empress celebrated their silver wedding anniversary. To commemorate the event thirty-two members of the family presented them with a silver clock on an onyx base. At a cost of 18,585 roubles it was the largest commission given to Fabergé during the reign of Alexander III. Dagmar's father gave an elaborate porcelain vase with pictures of the Anitchkov and the Amalienborg on the sides. From their children, Dagmar received a brooch with the number '25' on it. Sasha was given a small gold screen with medallions of Nicholas, George, Xenia, Michael and Olga.

Dagmar and Sasha travelled from Denmark to the Crimea early in November on their new yacht the *Polar Star*. They were accompanied by King Christian and Queen Louise, the Princess of Wales with her daughters Victoria and Maud and Mlle L'Escaille. Alexandra's decision to celebrate her sister's Silver Wedding at Livadia, instead of returning to England in time for Bertie's fiftieth birthday, caused much comment about the state of the Wales' marriage. Great celebrations were planned at Livadia, including a magnificent firework display. All the old servants who had been in the Tsar and Tsarina's service since 1881 had assembled to congratulate them but the occasion was overshadowed by mourning for Aline.

The weather in the Crimea that autumn was unusually bad and cold. Seventy-four-year-old Queen Louise became ill, followed by almost everyone else. Georgie, who had travelled from the Caucasus where his health had improved, became unwell and Dagmar feared he would catch influenza. Then the Princess of Wales was informed that her son George had typhoid and she left immediately for home in a terrible state. Although Dagmar was delighted that her elderly parents were able to visit Russia, she was relieved to hear that they were back in Copenhagen and fully recovered.

Prince George of Wales also recovered but, in January 1892, his brother Eddie, Duke of Clarence & Avondale, collapsed with influenza, which turned to pneumonia. On 14th January he died, leaving Prince George heir to the throne of England after his father, and Eddie's fiancée Princess May of Teck without a bridegroom. The shock hit Dagmar very hard and Alix never recovered from the death of her first-born. Dagmar was reunited with her distraught sister in May, when the whole family gathered in Copenhagen to celebrate the Golden Wedding anniversary of King Christian and Queen Louise.

A third death followed soon afterwards. Grand Duke Constantine Nicholaievitch had suffered a stroke in 1889, followed by a second one which left him paralysed and unable to speak. On 25th January news came of his death at Pavlovsk. Dagmar was very close to his family, particularly his wife Aunt Sanny, who she frequently drove over to see while Sasha was out shooting at Gatchina. In a letter to her brother Willie, Dagmar said that she could not remember a worse year.

As well as a period of tragedy for Dagmar's family, the autumn and winter of 1891 was a time of famine and hardship for Russia. Millions starved, or were killed by the cholera epidemic which followed. The Red Cross collected funds to help the needy and provide medical aid and the Tsarevitch was appointed president of a committee for famine relief. Thousands of people were driven to seek work in the towns and the number of factory workers in the early 1890s increased to one and a half million.

In 1892 Alexander III appointed a brilliant new Minister of Finance, Sergei Yulevich Witte. He negotiated huge foreign loans to finance the construction of the Trans-Siberian Railway, which opened up the route to the Far East. Coal and iron ore were exploited, the engineering industry flourished and the textile industry thrived.

Some of these foreign loans came from France. After the Kaiser refused to renew the reinsurance treaty the Tsar, who had rebuffed French overtures, had second thoughts. He needed a counterbalance to Germany's immense military strength along his western frontier. The French sought revenge for the loss of Alsace-Lorraine in 1870 and were grateful when the Tsar responded to their advances.

In 1891 some French warships paid a ceremonial visit to Kronstadt and the Emperor stood bareheaded while the Marseillaise, previously banned in the Russian Empire, was played. When the Tsar and Tsarina visited the French Exhibition in Moscow he spotted the Marshal of the Court covering the statue of a nude woman with a curtain. 'Leave it alone', Sasha responded gallantly, 'I know that the costume she wears is one which the French most admire'.[11]

In 1893 Russia signed a secret military treaty with France; the following year they signed a full military alliance. Now Russia would not have to confront the mighty German army (or the combined forces of Germany and Austria) without an ally.

Europe was split into two opposing camps: the Triple Alliance of Germany, Austria and Italy on one side; France and Russia on the other. During Sasha's reign the Empire enjoyed a long period of peace but the battle-lines for 1914 were already being drawn. As Europe took sides, England would eventually have to choose between the leaders of the two camps, France and Germany. Dagmar prayed that she would choose France.

*

In 1892 Nicholas was twenty-four and his most important duty was to marry and ensure the continuation of the dynasty. Dagmar was already reviewing the contenders. Casting her eyes around Europe, she found a suitable, although surprising, candidate but for once she encountered Nicholas' implacable opposition.

Princess Hélene of Orleans was the twenty-year-old Roman Catholic daughter of the Comte de Paris, pretender to the French throne. The Romanovs and the Catholic Royal families had seldom intermarried because of religious difficulties but Dagmar thought a marriage would help to forge the alliance with France. Tall, dark-haired Hélene's brief romance with Prince Eddie of Wales had foundered because neither the Pope nor the Comte de Paris would permit her to renounce Catholicism. Dagmar was undeterred, despite her son's obvious lack of interest. 'Mama ... made a few illusions to Hélene ...', he noted in his diary. 'I myself want to go in one direction and it is evident that Mama wants me to choose the other ...'[12] Luckily, Hélene refused to convert to Orthodoxy.

Disappointed, Dagmar used her powers of persuasion in favour of her second choice. In 1883 Bismarck's plan to marry the fifteen-year-old

Tsarevitch to the liberal Empress Frederick's fourteen-year-old daughter Sophie had come to nothing. Nevertheless, Dagmar now suggested Sophie's younger sister Margaret. Nineteen-year-old 'Mossy' was a plain, bony girl and Nicholas refused to consider her, even in the face of his mother's arguments, declaring he would sooner enter a monastery. Prince Nicholas of Montenegro also hoped to secure the Tsarevitch as a husband for one of his younger daughters but this tentative proposal was rejected.

Nicholas had already fallen in love with another princess. 'My dream is some day to marry Alix H', he confided to his diary in 1891[13] but first he had to overcome the opposition of his parents.

Princess Alix ('Alicky') of Hesse and by Rhine, a younger sister of Grand Duchess Ella, was born in Darmstadt on 6th June 1872. Dagmar and Sasha were among her godparents. Nicholas had first met her when, as a twelve-year-old girl, she came to Russia for Ella's wedding. In 1889 they met again when seventeen-year-old Alicky stayed with Ella in St Petersburg. Alicky was beautiful with red-gold hair, pale skin and blue-grey eyes. Nicholas' attraction to her grew. He persuaded Dagmar to give a tea-dance, followed by a traditional Russian supper of blinis and caviar. When she left he pasted her photograph into his diary.

Dagmar and Sasha did not share their son's enthusiasm. The Empress thought Alicky was too shy, withdrawn and awkward to take her eventual place as Empress in the lively, immoral society of St Petersburg. Neither by upbringing nor temperament was she prepared for such an exalted position. When Alicky was six, diphtheria swept through the household at Darmstadt carrying off her mother Princess Alice, Grand Duchess of Hesse and Alicky's four-year-old sister Princess May. The double tragedy made Alicky serious and aloof. Queen Victoria stepped into the void. She frequently invited the children to England with their father Grand Duke Louis and received regular reports on their educational progress. Under her governess, Miss Jackson, Alicky acquired a fascination for politics which later was to prove fatal. Deeply religious, she had been confirmed into the Lutheran church at sixteen and grew up with the manners and morals of a typical upper-class Victorian Englishwoman.

All this was of no use in St Petersburg. The sophisticated society matrons said the princess lacked charm, was nervous and tongue-tied, danced clumsily and spoke poor French. She rarely smiled and her face and hands flushed red when she was agitated. Alicky suffered from sciatica and it was feared that like her great-aunt, the Empress Marie Alexandrovna, she would be unable to stand the Russian winters.

In the summer of 1890 Nicholas told his father he wished to marry Alicky. The Tsar was non-committal. Dagmar did not consider a princess of Hesse important enough for the Tsarevitch, she was hoping for a better catch. When Alicky visited her sister at Ilinskoe, Nicholas was forbidden to go there. Dagmar decided to ask Ella not to invite her to Russia again until Nicholas was safely married. She told Nicholas that his marriage was an affair of state which must override all personal inclination.

It soon became obvious that Ella was the chief matchmaker. In 1889 she had thrown Nicholas and Alicky together as much as possible and in letters to her grandmother she stressed the happy family life of the Emperor and Empress. Dagmar found an unlikely ally in Queen Victoria. 'It would not do on account of the religion', the Queen told Alicky's elder sister Princess Victoria of Battenberg, 'and I know moreover that Minny [the Empress] does not *wish* it'.[14]

The Kaiser's daughter, Princess Victoria Louise, believed that Dagmar (whom she described as the 'cleverest and the most single-minded of the Danish Princesses') ignored both the 'English descent and English education' of Alicky. She opposed the marriage deliberately because the German Emperor was in favour of it.[15]

In January 1893 Sasha and Dagmar sent Nicholas to the Berlin wedding of the Kaiser's sister Mossy and Prince Friedrich Carl of Hesse. Alicky would also be present. To Nicholas' surprise, his parents' attitude had now changed. He was given permission to find out about Alicky's feelings for him but he had no chance to speak to her alone.

Ella now acted as go-between. Although she knew that her sister was in love with Nicholas, Alicky had also said that it would be an insult to God to change her religion for a crown. Nevertheless, Ella and Sergei encouraged Nicholas to hope and even planned for him to meet Alicky at Coburg, where they were staying during the autumn of 1893. This fell through because Nicholas had just returned from Denmark and Sasha did not want him to travel again so quickly.

Instead, the Tsar and Tsarina invited Alicky to accompany Ella and Sergei to St Petersburg. They refused, saying that it would look as if Alicky was running after Nicholas. Dagmar then told Ella that Nicholas had been given so little hope, he could only expect to receive a refusal because he had not gone to Coburg. Ella replied that it was a shame, his last chance had been lost, adding how surprised she was at Dagmar's concern, as she knew the Empress was opposed to the marriage.

Dagmar was furious. Ella and Sergei had allowed Nicholas to regard the marriage almost as a settled matter but Alicky refused to change her religion. Sergei and Ella then put the blame on Sasha and Dagmar for not allowing Nicholas to go to Coburg to persuade Alicky himself.[16]

Finally, Alicky wrote to Nicholas saying that she could not change her religion. Although Nicholas was devastated, for once he showed his strength. He would marry Alicky or he would not marry at all.

*

The hoped-for improvement in Georgie's health never materialised and he now lived permanently in Abbas Touman. His plight distressed his mother. 'Life is really *too* sad for him', she wrote to Nicholas, 'it is wonderful with what fortitude he bears it, without a murmur of complaint'.[17] One of his cousins found Georgie sleeping under blankets with wide open windows in a temperature of ten degrees below zero. His only recreation was to sweep the snow from the flat rooftops. Nicholas occasionally visited him and they went sleighing, played skittles and had some lively dinners. Sometimes George was able to join his family in the Crimea, but most of the time he lived alone.

'It is so terribly hard to see one's *child* suffer and not to be able to relieve it!' Dagmar lamented.[18] Her one consolation was the annual journey to the Caucasus, which usually took place in late spring or early autumn. To the delight of the younger children they led a simple, relaxed, almost rustic life. They ate Caucasian food cooked and served by the locals, the one exception being Dagmar's favourite Danish cheese which usually revealed tiny mice hiding in its large holes. If the mice failed to appear Olga and Michael were bitterly disappointed.

Due to the proximity of the Turkish border, the Empress had special Caucasian armed bodyguards to protect her from robbers when she was out driving. Her favourite was Omar, a dashing, stalwart man with dark flashing eyes, who she loved to tease. 'Omar', she would say, 'when I look into your eyes I am sure you were once a robber yourself!' Omar always denied it, until one day he broke down and confessed it was true. Falling on his knees, he begged forgiveness. He was not only forgiven but made a member of her permanent bodyguard.[19]

The end of these visits came all too soon and Dagmar again had to leave Georgie behind. 'I am utterly miserable about it and grieved to the heart to part with him ...'[20]

In April 1893 Xenia celebrated her eighteenth birthday and began to figure strongly in the dynastic calculations of many of Europe's Royal families. Dagmar had come to rely on her companionship and discouraged any talk of marriage, protesting that Xenia was much too young. The truth was that she did not want to lose control over her. Nor did the Emperor want a foreign husband for his daughter. Luckily, Xenia fell in love with a Russian.

Grand Duke Alexander Michaelovitch ('Sandro'), a son of Grand Duke Michael Nicholaievitch the former Viceroy of the Caucasus, was one of the 'wild Caucasian' cousins who had been her elder brothers' playmates. Sandro served in the Russian navy, he and Xenia corresponded regularly and when he was home he had eyes for no-one else.

In January 1893 Sandro summoned his courage and asked the Emperor's consent to their betrothal. The Tsar listened kindly but made it plain that, although he had no objections in principle, the Empress did not wish her daughter to marry so young. He advised Sandro to raise the matter in a year's time. Disappointed, Xenia and Sandro resigned themselves to waiting.

By the following January Sandro was back in St Petersburg and Grand Duke Michael urged him to try again. Both men knew that the problem was the Empress, who hated to be contradicted or rushed. Sandro feared she would refuse his request in such a manner as to preclude any further discussion. Michael took matters into his own hands and set off to have lunch at the Anitchkov. He had been a close friend of Dagmar ever since his return from the Caucasus in 1884. He was also very fond of Xenia and hoped to bring about this marriage.

When Dagmar heard the purpose of Michael's visit she was annoyed. There had not even been chance to discuss it with Sasha in private. Finally she consented, writing to King Christian that she was comforted by the fact that Xenia would remain in Russia. Although Xenia was almost nineteen, the age at which the Empress herself had married, Dagmar said she wished her daughter had waited until she was older. The old King disagreed, he had tried to arrange Xenia and Sandro's betrothal some months earlier at Fredensborg.

Announcing the news in a letter to Aunt Sanny on 24th January 1894, the Empress wrote of her mixed feelings about giving Xenia away. Although Dagmar made the best of the situation, for months she refused to set a firm date for the wedding.

As preparations began, she little knew what tragedy the next twelve months would bring.

CHAPTER 13

Death of a Giant

'IT WAS LIKE SEEING A MAGNIFICENT BUILDING CRUMBLE'

In January 1894 Dagmar became anxious about her husband's health. The previous autumn Sasha had fever and bronchitis. At Fredensborg he felt too unwell to attend the banquet in honour of his Name Day. Influenza now weakened him further. He suffered from frequent headaches and insomnia and complained that his shoes did not fit. Nobody noticed his feet were swelling.

Dagmar summoned Professor Zakharine from Moscow. He found signs of nephritis, an inflammation of the kidneys, and for several days medical bulletins were issued. Although Xenia was making her debut that Season the Nicholas Ball was postponed for a fortnight.

His condition was not helped by his love of drink. In an age of heavy drinkers the Tsar was no exception but, once the doctor diagnosed kidney trouble, drinking was forbidden. Dagmar kept a stern eye on him to see that he obeyed the doctor's orders. Undeterred, Sasha had a special pair of boots made with a secret compartment for a flask. One of his closest companions, General Tcheverin, did the same. As soon as the Empress had left the room they played a game they called 'Necessity is the Mother of Invention'. The Tsar looked at Tcheverin and said, 'Necessity, Tcheverin?' 'Invention, Your Majesty', his companion replied. The hidden flasks came out and on the count of three they both took a swig.

Sasha recovered sufficiently to carry out his duties, although his sallow complexion was worrying. The doctor advised him to cut down his work-load. He was a month short of his forty-ninth birthday but the after-effects of Borki, the strain of his position and the constant fear of assassination had taken their toll. He looked and felt many years older and the doctors, deceived by his powerful frame, failed to see that he was very ill. Only Olga, out walking with her father, noticed that he seemed exhausted and could hardly keep up with her. Still, for the moment it seemed the crisis was over.

The alarm over Sasha's health made the Emperor and Empress look seriously to the future. That April there was to be a large gathering in

155

Coburg of what Queen Victoria called 'the Royal Mob' for the marriage of Alicky's brother Ernst Ludwig ('Ernie'), the new Grand Duke of Hesse, and Princess Victoria Melita ('Ducky'). Ducky was the daughter of Prince Alfred, who had now succeeded his uncle as Duke of Saxe-Coburg-Gotha, and Grand Duchess Marie Alexandrovna. It was decided that Nicholas would represent his parents and take the opportunity to speak to Alicky. She immediately wrote to Xenia, saying that she would not change her religion. Downhearted but undeterred, the Tsarevitch left for Coburg with Dagmar's advice to ask for Queen Victoria's help ringing in his ears.

The morning after his arrival Nicholas had a long talk with Alicky but, after two hours, was forced to admit defeat. The following morning Nicholas gave her a letter from Dagmar, a Lutheran princess who had happily converted to Orthodoxy, but still the situation was unresolved.

The royal relatives, including Ella, Miechen and the Kaiser, now joined the battle, which completely overshadowed the wedding. After Ella, who had voluntarily converted to Orthodoxy in 1891, convinced her sister that a change of religion was not so bad, Alicky gave in. Nicholas was ecstatic.

Dagmar received the news by telegram and when she attended church she was reported to be looking 'radiant'. Both Dagmar and Sasha were sad that they were not with Nicky. 'You can imagine what feelings of joy and with what gratitude to the Lord we learned of your betrothal', the Tsar wrote to his son. '... I cannot imagine you as a bridegroom. Not to be with you at such a time, not to embrace you, not to talk to you, to know nothing and to wait only for a letter with details ...'[1]

In a letter to her brother Willie, Dagmar wrote of their surprise that Alicky had agreed to change her religion and what a state Nicky had been in before he left for Coburg. It was strange, she said, to have two of her children betrothed at the same time.

She was genuinely delighted at her son's happiness and was now waiting impatiently to meet his fiancée. She received her first letter from Alicky, written on 21st April. The princess, who called her 'Darling Auntie', had been touched by Dagmar's letter. After saying how happy she was, Alicky referred to the struggle with her conscience and her hope that she would grow to love the Orthodox religion and make Nicholas a good wife. Dagmar instructed Nicholas that Alicky was not to call her Auntie but Mama or Motherdear, as she 'is already like a daughter to me'.[2] She sent Alicky an emerald bracelet and a jewel-encrusted Fabergé Easter egg. 'Ask her which stones she likes most', the Empress continued, 'sapphires or emeralds?'[3]

Two people were upset by the news. The first was Mathilde Kschessinska, who was devastated when Nicholas ended their affair. The other person was Queen Victoria. 'The more I think of sweet Alicky's marriage the more unhappy I am!' she wrote to Princess Victoria of Battenberg, Alicky's sister. '*Not* as to the personality, for I like him *very much* but on account of the country … and the awful insecurity to which that sweet child will be exposed'.[4] Her forebodings were to prove all too accurate.

*

With Nicholas hoping to be married in October or November, Dagmar took Xenia and Sandro to Abbas Touman. She found Georgie pale and worn out. Although he was delighted to see them, the happiness of both Nicholas and Xenia only highlighted Georgie's sad life in Dagmar's eyes.

They spent a month in the Caucasus trying to keep Georgie's spirits up but when the doctor's verdict came it was a bitter blow. 'Poor George!' the Empress wrote to Nicholas. 'He was so certain he would be at Xenia's wedding and remain till yours – just think how cruel the disappointment must have been for him!' Dagmar had hoped her son would be able to return with them but Georgie was weaker and 'had a premonition that he would never see St Petersburg again'.[5]

'God alone knows why he imposes this heavy cross upon us', wrote the despairing Empress, 'and we have to carry it with patience and resignation, saying to ourselves: "Thy will be done" – even if the heart breaks'.[6]

*

Dagmar was shocked by her husband's appearance when she joined him on board the *Tsarevna* in June. He had lost a considerable amount of weight and was badly in need of a rest and a change of air. 'I found him looking very poorly again and so very tired, just the same as when he left Gatchina. At Peterhof all this time he has been suffering from *insomnia* … I do hope this little cruise will be good for him'.[7]

Sasha arranged boat races for the younger children and enjoyed their stay at Langinkoski. Then Dagmar's hopes were dashed as it became evident that his health was deteriorating. A young doctor diagnosed that the Emperor was suffering from an acute case of nephritis which, in its advanced stage, was almost certainly fatal in those days. After consultation, the doctors informed the Empress.

Dagmar was shattered. They had all been enjoying the holiday: the fishing trips, expeditions, picnics and, in the evenings, their favourite card game of 'wolf'. Now she was told her husband was dying.

Whenever anything unpleasant occurred, her first reaction was always to disbelieve it and pretend that nothing had happened. She utterly rejected the doctors' verdict, gave orders that the Emperor, already upset by Xenia's approaching marriage, was not to be informed and hoped against hope that the situation would right itself.

They returned to Peterhof for Xenia's wedding on 6th August. As Dagmar walked through the rooms where the trousseau and the wedding presents were displayed, her emotions were a mixture of happiness for her daughter and the sadness of a mother: 'What shall we do in a few weeks when she leaves us? I don't dare to think – even now I can *hardly ever* see her *alone* – he [Sandro] never leaves her for one minute'.[8] Although Sandro's relations with the Emperor and Empress were rather strained, one of her ladies concluded that she was jealous at the thought of Xenia marrying.

Xenia's wedding was the last great occasion over which Dagmar presided as reigning Empress. All the splendour of the uniforms, the sumptuous Court dresses and the blazing jewels could not conceal the seriousness of the Emperor's illness. He looked old and tired, his clothes hung off him and his mighty frame sagged. Yet the Tsar of Russia was powerless against Romanov tradition. He could not even cancel the banquet. Nevertheless, he was happy and able to enter into the celebrations. 'Never again was I to see him like that', his younger daughter remembered.[9]

The review at Krasnoe Selo in August was Alexander III's farewell to his army and Dagmar followed on horseback as he reviewed the troops. It took over an hour for them to complete a circuit of the camp. Afterwards she stood on the Imperial dais with the Princess of Wales to watch the march past. It was a hot day and Sasha looked pale and tired as he took the salute. After lunch he fainted.

On 22nd August he carried out his last public engagement, the launching of the battleship *Admiral Seniavia*. Dagmar was by now seriously alarmed and insisted on summoning his physician, who diagnosed strain from overwork and advised him to travel south for a complete rest and change of air. Sasha disliked any change in his annual routine and was particularly fond of shooting. Their trip to Denmark was cancelled. Instead, they moved to Bialowieza, accompanied by Grand Duke Vladimir and other guests.

After a terrible two-hour drive through the dark forest they arrived at Sasha's new stone hunting lodge, set in a clearing surrounded by landscaped gardens. The hall and staircase were decorated with the heads of aurochs killed by the Tsar and the dining-room, which could seat 150 people, had antlers on the walls. The walls of one room were entirely covered by stamps.

The Tsar had also asked Georgie to come to Bialowieza. He was overjoyed when his son arrived, but George was so ill that Sasha spent the nights watching by his bedside.

Their stay was spoilt by bad weather, so in mid-September they moved to Spala. At first Sasha felt better, his spirits revived and he joined the daily shooting party. On 16th September Dagmar was able to tell her father that Sasha had been stalking for four hours that day and he fired four times. Unfortunately, she had to add that he did not kill anything. Although the forest was lovely and she was pleased that the fresh air was beneficial to him, soon he became restless, lost his appetite and ate alone in his study with Olga. Dagmar again summoned Professor Zakharine.

By now Sasha could not eat nor even finish a cigarette and his feet were so swollen he could not get his boots on. Dagmar begged him to see Doctor Leyden, the eminent Berlin specialist but Sasha refused because he was German. It took the combined efforts of Dagmar and Vladimir to change his mind.

The Tsar was examined by Doctor Leyden on 27th September in the presence of Professor Zakharine. Dagmar waited nervously in an adjoining room. When the doctor came out she swept foward anxiously and begged him not to hide anything. After the doctors had consulted, Professor Zakharine saw the Tsar alone and told him the truth. He had nephritis, there was no cure and little in the way of treatment, although they might be able to prolong his life for a few more months. There was a chance that a warmer climate might help.

Dagmar still refused to give up hope and immediately asked her brother Willie for the use of his villa 'Mon Repos' in Corfu. Elaborate preparations were made but the doctors advised a few days rest at Livadia first, to see what a warmer climate would do.

Their departure was delayed by the Empress' health. In times of great stress Dagmar had always suffered from nervous prostration and now, after the strain of the last few months, she retired to bed with lumbago. It was two days before she was able to dress. Even then they had some difficulty in transporting her to the train, which eventually left that evening for the Crimea.

They arrived in Sevastopol on 3rd October and Sasha reviewed the guard of honour before boarding the *Orel* for the four hour voyage. As the boat drew into Yalta harbour, the Imperial standard fluttering at its mast, the local dignitaries stood in the autumn sunshine speculating on the state of the Emperor's health.

He was now so unwell that Dagmar deputised. With her usual smile and a conviction she could hardly have felt, the Empress assured everyone that the Emperor was merely tired, he was really much better and she was sure a few weeks in the lovely Crimean climate would make him well again. Maybe she had managed to forget Sasha's premonition that he would never leave Livadia alive.

As Dagmar supported her husband down the gangplank it became obvious that he was indeed very ill. His face was pale, his frame was thin and he could only manage the saddest of smiles. After a few words with the Governor he climbed into his carriage and was driven speedily along the two mile route to Livadia through streets lined with palm trees and cypresses.

They settled into the small Maly Palace and at first were able to visit Massandra, Oreanda and other places in the vicinity. Dagmar's anxiety was eased by a reunion with Xenia and one afternoon they drove over to Sandro's estate of Ai-Todor for tea. The Tsar appeared more cheerful and was well enough to attend church. He often sat on the terrace overlooking Yalta harbour where a new warship was anchored. When he felt better, Sasha said, he would go and look over it.

Soon he grew restless again. Although Dagmar insisted he stick rigidly to the diet prescribed for him he complained that the mere sight of the food made him feel ill. Meals, which were served to the family alone as the Tsar was too weak to change from his red and blue striped jacket, military trousers and leather slippers, now became an ordeal for the Empress. Sometimes, when she was out of the room, he sent to the guard-room for a plate of rich cabbage soup and rye bread but the deviation from the strict diet showed in his deteriorating health. 'It was like seeing a magnificent building crumble', wrote his nephew.[10]

As his condition worsened prayers were said in churches throughout Russia and Dagmar again summoned Doctor Leyden. By mid-October Sasha was very feeble. There were five doctors at Livadia and the journey to Corfu was cancelled.

Sasha now spent most of his time in bed. He felt sick all the time and his feet were so swollen he was unable to walk. 'Every movement became an agony', recalled Grand Duchess Olga.[11] He was only slightly more comfortable sitting in his chair by the open window, from where he could see the terraced gardens stretching down to the sea. As it became obvious that he was failing, Nicholas' journey to Darmstadt was cancelled. Instead he was given permission to summon Alicky to Livadia.

Although the weather was warm and the air was balmy, a sense of fore-boding hung over the palace. Members of the family began to congregate. 'Thank God I've arrived in time to see you once more', Sasha's sister exclaimed tactlessly.[12] Aunt Sanny brought the saintly Father John of Kronstadt, who had a reputation as a healer and a miracle worker. The family went on foot to the church at Oreanda where he prayed for the Tsar. As more and more relations arrived Dagmar's family tried to carry on as normally as possible.

The doctors could do nothing. The Tsar was a difficult patient, he was suspicious of drugs and refused to take anything to relieve his pain.

During these trying days Dagmar, although nearly out of her mind with worry, displayed great fortitude and courage sustained by her faith and resignation to the will of God. Outwardly she remained calm, talking naturally to the family; those who saw her compose herself and wipe away the tears before entering the Emperor's room realised the full extent of her private agony. Sasha knew he was dying and, when Dagmar was not present, often spoke of events he would not live to see. Nicholas' wedding especially concerned him and he repeatedly emphasised that it should take place in the capital with all ceremony and not quietly at Livadia.

The Emperor still insisted on reading all the cabinet reports and Dagmar begged the ministers to show him only what was really essential. She later told a lady-in-waiting that only one minister was sympathetic. 'All the others were primarily interested in their personal influence, and consideration for the health and life of the Tsar was of secondary importance'.[13]

By now the Empress was almost at breaking point and the doctors were treating her as well as the Emperor. When she could leave Sasha long enough to get some fresh air she would be found sitting on a bench by the sea pouring out her heart to Queen Olga. Night and day Dagmar nursed her husband, struggling to keep back the tears and whispering comforting words to the dying man. She rarely slept but sat by his bed holding his hand. 'I have even before my death got to know an angel', Sasha said one day, tenderly kissing her hand. 'Poor dear Minny'.[14]

As the dreadful agony continued, Dagmar begged Alix and Bertie to come immediately. 'There are no better nurses in the world than the Queen of Denmark's daughters', Sasha had once told Bertie.[15] Fearing he would die before they arrived, the Emperor wrote a few words of farewell to Alexandra, commending Dagmar to her care. That day the usual service was held to commemorate the accident at Borki. The Emperor was growing more and more feeble and received Communion. None of the family dared to stray far from the palace.

In Denmark, Dagmar's parents still did not realise the seriousness of the situation. King Christian's Chamberlain thought that the Empress was sending only the most reassuring news to her parents but he noticed that the foreign newspapers wrote about Nicholas as if he were already Tsar.

Meanwhile, to Nicholas' delight, Alicky had arrived at Livadia. Sasha insisted on dressing in full uniform to receive the future Empress but the effort taxed him so much he could find the strength to do little more than wish her happiness and give his blessing to their betrothal.

It was during this final stage of the Emperor's illness that the future relationship between Dagmar and Alicky was established. Dagmar, distraught and exhausted, spent most of her time in the sick-room and was more concerned with nursing Sasha than with getting to know Nicholas' fiancée. Although she greeted the princess pleasantly enough, her mind was naturally on other things and to Alicky she appeared distant and formal. Dagmar was still very much the central figure as she received the doctors, heard their reports, made decisions and gave orders. Everyone, from members of the Imperial family down to the humblest servants, looked to the Empress, hardly daring to contemplate the magnitude of the disaster that was about to befall them. They found Alicky haughty and cold and were comforted by the knowledge that the Empress still exercised a strong influence over her son. When a paper had to be signed it was Dagmar who guided her husband's weak hand. The Tsarevitch and his fiancée were almost ignored.

This did not suit Alicky at all. Nicholas would soon be Tsar, he should be taking command. Although in a household stunned with grief and anxiety, she continually exhorted Nicholas to assert himself. Dagmar had always treated Nicholas as a child and it probably never occurred to her to consult him now. Equally, the family and the members of the entourage were aware that the Emperor did not have a very high opinion of the Tsarevitch. The first seeds of discord were sown.

On 31st October the Emperor's breathing became laboured and his heart rapidly weakened. 'The Emperor was coughing up blood and the doctors were extremely worried about the night', Sidonie L'Escaille reported to the Danish Court. '… The poor Empress prepared herself for the night. When she entered the room around midnight the Emperor suddenly complained he could not stay in bed, he could not breathe. Immediately the doctors were called in. For a few hours everything seemed to be calm, the Empress could sleep from 2 to 4. Then, the Emperor getting worse, his respiration more and more difficult, he sat in his arm chair'.[16] Several times Sasha asked Dagmar to see if the dawn was breaking. 'I feel the end approaching', he murmured. 'Be calm. I am quite calm'.[17]

At eight o'clock Sasha took coffee, then the Last Sacrament was administered and Father John heard his confession. The family came in and Sasha remembered that it was Ella's birthday. As a thick fog swirled outside the palace Dagmar sat with her arm around him, his head resting on her shoulder, hardly able to believe what was happening. As his breathing became more difficult oxygen was administered. 'During moments of lucidity he was able to … see his sister, kiss his children and brothers', Sidonie L'Escaille continued. The family knelt as Father John intoned the prayers for the dying. 'Then, without pain, at the very moment [Dr] Hirsch was presenting him with a glass of wine',[18] Sasha gave a big sigh and his head dropped onto Dagmar's breast. Alexander III was dead.

22. The Maly Palace, Livadia, in the Crimea.
The room where Sasha died is on the corner of the top floor, between the lattice-work.
Dagmar never visited the palace again after her husband's death.
(Private collection)

'Everything seemed hushed', recalled Grand Duchess Olga. 'Nobody sobbed. My mother still held him in her arms'. One by one they crossed the room to kiss the dead Tsar's forehead and embrace the Empress, before kissing Nicholas' hand. Dagmar sat stunned and motionless. Nobody dared intrude upon her grief. Father John flung open the doors and announced 'God has taken his servant to him'.[19] As members of the household filed in, Dagmar, now sobbing bitterly, was helped from the room.

The Tsar's death was a tremendous shock to the whole country. Nobody expected the powerfully-built Alexander III to die at the early age of forty-nine. Nicholas was crushed by the weight of the responsibility that had fallen upon him. 'What am I going to do', he wailed to Sandro. 'What is going to happen to you, to Xenia, to Alix, to mother, to all of Russia?' In his diary that evening he poured out his feelings. 'My God, my God, what a day. The Almighty has called to Him our adored, dear and deeply loved Papa ... I cannot believe it. Oh, God help us in these sad days! Poor dear Mamma!'[20]

*

At four o'clock that afternoon the Imperial family, courtiers, officers and servants gathered round an altar on the palace lawn where Father Yanishev, the late Emperor's confessor, administered the oath of allegiance to Tsar Nicholas II. Above them the Imperial standard fluttered at half-mast and they could hear the warships in Yalta harbour firing a mournful salute. Later that evening Dagmar was present at the first of the twice-daily services, this one held, as was customary, in the dead Emperor's bedroom.

The following morning, composed and dressed entirely in white, she joined Nicholas and Ella in the chapel where Alicky was received into the Orthodox Church as the Grand Duchess Alexandra Feodorovna.

To Dagmar's relief, Alix and Bertie arrived the next day. Hurrying across Europe, they received the news of the Tsar's death at Vienna. They found the Empress calm but the strain of nursing Sasha without rest had left her looking thin. She fell into Alix's arms weeping openly and the princess later described this first meeting with her newly-widowed sister as 'unspeakable agony'.[21] Throughout the ordeal of the days ahead Alix hardly left Dagmar's side, even sleeping in her bedroom.

Tributes to Alexander III were printed in newspapers around the world. Among the messages of condolence was one from Queen Victoria, to which Dagmar replied by telegram:

Your loving and deepest sympathy soothes my broken heart in my immense misfortune. I thank you with all my heart, my dearest aunt

and she signed herself,

your sincerely loving, despairing Minny.[22]

No arrangements had been made for the funeral. Nicholas, overwhelmed by his new responsibilities and overawed by his uncles, seemed reluctant to make any decisions. Dagmar, consumed with grief, was also unwilling, while apparently not encouraging anyone else to make them either. Bertie soon took charge and put an end to the bullying of Nicholas' uncles. For the next few days Sasha's embalmed body remained in the chapel at Livadia while officials in the Crimea and St Petersburg liaised over the arrangements. Twice a day Dagmar and her family attended services and kissed the dead Emperor's lips.

The other important question was the new Tsar's marriage. Nicholas needed Alicky's support and was unwilling to let her return to Darmstadt. The marriage had to take place before the six week Christmas fast, otherwise they would have to postpone it until January. Despite her late husband's wishes, Dagmar wanted the wedding to take place quietly at Livadia while Sasha's body was still there. Nicholas' uncles insisted that the Tsar's wedding could not possibly take place privately. They were supported by Bertie and Alix, who convinced Dagmar of the importance of the occasion.

For the next two weeks Dagmar moved as if in a dream. Five days after Sasha's death, heavily veiled and leaning on Nicholas' arm, she led a torch-light procession to the Byzantine Church on a nearby hill. The coffin, borne by Terek Cossacks and accompanied by the clergy and a military escort, was followed by members of the family while the bells tolled and a band played a hymn. As the torches flickered in the dark the moon suddenly broke through the clouds, highlighting the wooded hills of Livadia. When Dagmar and her children returned to the palace they broke down.

Two days later, brave and erect, she again followed her husband's coffin as it was carried to the jetty at Yalta by sailors from the Imperial yacht, along a path strewn with cypress sprays and laurel leaves. Dagmar could not help telling her mother how it reminded her of the beautiful weather in Nice when Nixa died. It took two and a half hours for the long procession, which included the Emperor's charger, without trappings, to reach Yalta harbour. 'The whole road was lined with thousands of weeping people who fell on their knees and crossed themselves reverently as their beloved Emperor was carried by them for the last time', recalled the Princess of Wales.[23] The coffin was placed on board the *Pamiat Merkuria*, the warship that Sasha had so wanted to look over. Accompanied by an escort from the Black Sea fleet and a final salute of cannons it sailed for Sevastopol where a train was waiting.

Dagmar had a further sadness to bear before the black-draped funeral train left for the north. The doctors had forbidden Georgie to accompany them to the cold of Moscow and St Petersburg. Now she had to say good-bye, as the *Orel* took him back to the Caucasus. Georgie was heir to the throne and could take no risks.

The following day was a particularly upsetting one as Dagmar sat beside Alix in the slowly-moving train. It was her twenty-eighth wedding anniversary. Sasha had chosen a bracelet, which he entrusted to his valet. The Princess of Wales now had the delicate task of giving Dagmar this last present.

All along the 1,400 mile journey soldiers lined the track, peasants knelt in prayer and at every major station the train stopped while a 'panikhida' was said for the repose of Alexander III's soul. 'At night ... [the train] would draw up at some wayside halt, and as it stood there, black and forbidding and surrounded by guards, people swarmed out of the countryside, and knelt for hours in the frost'.[24]

It took three days to reach Moscow, where snow was on the ground and the wind was biting. In a silence broken only by tolling bells and guns firing in salute, the coffin was borne through streets lined with thousands of sorrowing people. Ten times they stopped at churches along the route for a Litany to be sung on the steps before they finally reached the Archangel Cathedral in the Kremlin, where Alexander III lay in state for thirty-six hours. Still the interminable masses for the dead continued. One was repeated thirty-nine times.

The whole process had to be gone through again when the coffin was borne back to the station for the final journey to St Petersburg. Dagmar leaned heavily on her sister for comfort and support. 'I saw nothing of my mother in those days', recalled twelve-year-old Olga, 'she spent them with Aunt Alix and did not seem to want anyone else'.[25]

In St Petersburg the weather was cold and grey. The houses were draped in black and funeral arches lined the processional route. At the Nicholas Station the ladies entered black-draped carriages for the journey along the Nevsky Prospekt and across the frozen Neva to the Fortress. The men marched behind the hearse. Superstitious Russians crossed themselves as Alicky passed, saying, 'she has come to us behind a coffin'.[26]

The cortège took two hours to pass. The crowns and regalia of the Russian Empire, carried on red cushions, preceded the coffin, which was covered by a pall of gold brocade lined with ermine and borne on a funeral car drawn by eight horses caprisoned in black. Pages walked on either side carrying lighted torches. As they passed the Anitchkov, Nicholas was seen to wipe away his tears and Dagmar's feelings can scarcely be imagined. Within the cathedral, whose walls were covered with black cloth, the coffin rested inside an elaborate canopy of cloth of silver lined with ermine. By the light of thousands of tapers the Metropolitan conducted yet another Mass for the dead while Dagmar and the other ladies knelt by the bier.

For the widowed Empress the worst moment was her return to the Anitchkov. She was very weak and nearly fainted several times. Although Alix and Bertie were nearby, according to Grand Duke Constantine Constantinovitch Dagmar had a weak heart and was feeling the strain.

By now sixty-one royalties were assembled, including Dagmar's father, her brothers Willie and Waldemar and Prince George of Wales (now Duke of York). Queen Louise, whose health was failing, did not attend, although she felt Sasha's death deeply. The absence of her mother, who had been such a comfort and support when Nixa died, was a further great sorrow for Dagmar. She begged Queen Louise not to expose herself to the long journey in the winter cold and, on 6th November, wrote that she feared for her father's health as well, although she was glad of his presence.

Delegations arrived from all over Europe. Twice a day the men donned full uniform and the women black, high-necked dresses to attend the services. These were now becoming something of an ordeal as, according to Orthodox custom, they all had to kiss the Holy Picture in the dead Tsar's hands. 'It gave me quite a shock when I saw his dear face so close to mine when I stooped down', wrote the Duke of York, 'he looks so beautiful and peaceful, but of course his face has changed very much, it is a fortnight today'.[27]

Alexander III was interred on 19th November. During the four hour funeral service the Empress leaned on the arm of King Christian, her face hidden behind a thick black veil. 'The Requiem was commenced with a magnificent chant, at whose opening notes all the congregation fell on their knees and noiselessly lighted their tapers by passing one swiftly from hand to hand. When all rose ... the Cathedral was ... lighted through its whole extent, with an effect which baffles description. A thousand glimmering candles were reflected in the silver wreaths, the majestic brocade of the canopy, and the star-spangled breasts of the uniforms, producing a scene of such splendour as is seldom witnessed'.[28] France alone had sent five thousand wreaths.

When Dagmar bent over the coffin for the last time Alexandra's arm was around her. 'It was most affecting to see the Empress take a last farewell of her husband', wrote a lady-in-waiting. 'Over and over again she kissed his poor face and hands and then when she had torn herself away, she came back again to kiss him *once* more'.[29] The Duke of York was among the pall-bearers. 'We carried him and lowered him down into the vault ... and it was most impressive and sad, and I shall never forget it. Darling Aunt Minny was so brave and stood the whole time and never broke down once'.[30] When the Palace Grenadiers lowered the coffin and the bells tolled mournfully Dagmar, kneeling with Nicholas at the side of the open grave, was finally overcome by grief. Once again, Alix was there to comfort her.

After the service, Nicholas escorted his mother to a side door where her carriage was waiting. When she reached the Anitchkov she broke down and wept.

Nicholas returned for a last look at the tomb, which was just being closed, before leaving through the front door. As he stood on the steps the troops dipped their standards, cannon fired a salute and a band played 'God Save the Tsar'. Dagmar was now the Dowager Empress and the star-crossed reign of Nicholas II had begun.

PART 4

DOWAGER EMPRESS

(1894-1919)

CHAPTER 14

The Old Court and the New Court

'THE LAST MONARCH OF A STAR-CROSSED LINE;
ANOINTED EMPEROR BY RIGHT DIVINE,
FROM ARCTIC ICEFIELDS TO THE ARAL SEA
FROM WARSAW TO THE WALLS OF TARTARY'
'Epitaph' – Maurice Baring

Her husband's early death shattered Dagmar. Besides the personal loss, which she felt deeply, she was too young to be a Dowager. At almost forty-seven she had the youthful looks and stamina of a woman in her late thirties and it seemed cruel that this tragedy should happen so early in life. Everyone thought of her as young while Sasha was alive, now an even younger woman would take her place. However, as she was soon to remember, the position of Dowager Empress held many compensations.

After the funeral, the next ordeal was Nicholas' wedding on 26th November, Dagmar's birthday. Court mourning could be put aside, as no black could be worn in Russia on a birthday. Despite Dagmar's grief she soon became involved in questions of protocol as the merciless etiquette of the Imperial Court swung into action.

Alicky was staying with Ella and Sergei at their palace on the Nevsky Prospekt and usually joined Nicholas for dinner. There was little chance for intimacy between Alicky and Dagmar though, as the Empress took most of her meals with her sister. Dagmar and Nicholas spent the evening before his marriage together at the Anitchkov.

On the morning of the wedding Dagmar drove with Alicky down the Nevsky Prospekt to the Winter Palace. She received a warm ovation from the crowds. In the Malachite Room, where memories of 1866 flooded her mind, the Empress lifted the bride's crown and placed it on Alicky's head.

The royal guests who attended the funeral had stayed on. Dagmar, wearing a white Court dress with a long train carried by four chamberlains, a pearl necklace and a pearl and diamond tiara, leaned on her father's arm as they walked to the church. Although her red eyes betrayed the strain she was under, her grace as she acknowledged the sympathetic crowd far outshone the beautiful, although rather stiff and awkward, bride.

During the ceremony Dagmar wept openly while King Christian did his best to comfort her. His fatherly pats on her back rather upset the dignified Russian Master of Ceremonies. Although the wedding was magnificent, no-one could forget the sadness of the occasion. Afterwards Dagmar completely broke down, as she embraced her son tenderly and kissed her daughter-in-law, who had now become the Empress Alexandra Feodorovna.

As the Court was in mourning, there was no wedding banquet and no ball. Immediately after lunch Dagmar left for the Anitchkov to greet the newlyweds with bread and salt, as Grand Duke and Duchess Constantine had done on her own wedding day. Even the rooms she conducted them to held poignant memories – they were the ones Nicholas and George had shared as children. When Dagmar reached her private apartments she collapsed in a dead faint.

*

In the days after the wedding Dagmar was still struggling to cope with her grief. She poured out her heartache in a letter to Queen Victoria, who had sent some comforting books:

> Your sincere and warm sympathy deeply touched me and soothes my broken heart. You can really understand my feelings, because the Lord imposed the same dreadful loss on you, the greatest loss on earth, to lose the one who was everything for me, for I loved my dearest Angel above all else and I can't imagine how I will live without him. And my poor, beloved Nicky, apart from the irreplaceable loss of his deeply beloved father, has to carry the heavy lot on his young shoulders so early, this cuts me deeply to the heart. Thank God, he's so happy with his charming Alicky. She's his greatest comfort in his great misfortune and is certainly more and more loving and faithful in sharing everything with him.[1]

When the first shock had passed, Dagmar's natural buoyancy came to the fore and she found that life still had plenty to offer. She remained at the Anitchkov with Olga and Michael. Nicholas and Alicky occupied six small rooms, while they were waiting for their apartments at the Winter Palace and Tsarskoe Selo to be redecorated. Adjoining them were Xenia and Sandro. Dagmar remained very much the mistress of the household. She still had the invaluable support of Alix, who remained in Russia until the end of the year, much to the disapproval of Queen Victoria. Dagmar and her sister were happiest in each other's company. 'I can't tell you what comfort dearest Alix was and is still for me', Dagmar wrote to the Queen, 'such a support and help in this dreadful heartbreaking time'.[2] Although Alicky was not encouraged to call on her mother-in-law uninvited, she was sympathetic and treated Dagmar with respect.

Dagmar was pleased to have her son and daughter-in-law under her own roof. Answering Queen Louise's criticism that no-one had said anything about Alicky, Dagmar said how loving and sympathetic her daughter-in-law had been and how fond she was becoming of her. This initial sympathy between the two women was short-lived and soon, at first imperceptibly, a struggle began for influence over the Tsar.

The Dowager Empress' day began with breakfast at nine o'clock and she usually had guests to lunch. Nicky and Alicky took their meals with her but it was Dagmar who presided at the head of the table. While the Princess of Wales remained in Russia she spent the evenings with her sister, leaving Nicholas to spend some time with his bride. When the princess returned to England, Nicholas, concerned for his mother, often stayed to chat with her after dinner.

Alicky soon resented the way in which she detained him on the pretext of discussing family affairs. Although politeness was maintained – they called each other Motherdear and dearest Alix – the atmosphere soon became strained. The Tsar never questioned his mother's authority. If Alicky gave an audience she had to ask permission to use one of the State Rooms. Her maids took orders from members of the Dowager Empress' household. At the beginning of December Dagmar suggested that Nicholas take his bride to Tsarskoe Selo for five days' honeymoon. A few days later there is a telling entry in Nicholas' diary: 'Received a telegram from Mamma to say that we may remain another day'.[3] Alicky was annoyed at her mother-in-law's domination of Nicholas.

Although Dagmar considered returning to live in Denmark, she was bound to Russia by too many ties and could also be a great source of support and help to Nicholas. In the early months of 1895 she therefore steeled herself to return to Gatchina, where Sasha's rooms remained exactly as he had left them. Time and again she delayed her departure, dreading the return to a place with so many memories.

By Easter, Alicky was so cross with her mother-in-law that, when Nicholas asked her to pay half the cost of the Dowager Empress' Fabergé Easter egg, she refused. Nicholas intended it to be a joint gift but, significantly, payment for future eggs became the sole responsibility of the Tsar.

Dagmar's lifestyle remained exactly the same. Under the terms of her Marriage Contract, she had her widow's allowance of 85,000 roubles a year, which would be halved if she left Russia, plus various other payments. She had the Anitchkov Palace for life as well as Gatchina, where she lived during the spring and summer. The Alexandria Estate at

Peterhof remained her private property and she was quick to inform Nicholas of her requirements at The Cottage. 'I ... will take the rooms Baby [Olga] used to have so as to be side by side with adored Papa's study! ...' she wrote in the spring of 1895. 'I want the *old furniture* that used to be in Baby's *drawing-room*, put back, not forgetting the big sofa that made the corner so comfortable. I think they all can be found in the storeroom ...'[4] On his visits to Peterhof Nicholas used the newer Villa Alexandria near the sea, an old watch tower rebuilt and enlarged by his father and later extended by Nicholas as his own family grew.

Prince Nicholas Obolensky was appointed A.D.C. in charge of the Dowager Empress' household and Admiral Paul Zelenoy became comptroller of her Institutions. Prince Vladimir Bariatinsky, former Chief of the Imperial Hunt, was also attached to her household. The prince, four years older than Dagmar, was already a close friend.

Wherever Dagmar was in residence her flag flew above the palace and her guards presented arms. Her retainers obeyed every command and satisfied her every whim. She had exclusive use of the sumptuously appointed 4,100 ton Imperial yacht *Polar Star*, her own quarters on the Tsar's new yacht *Standart*, and a luxurious private train. Her clothes came from the best outfitters on the Nevsky Prospekt. She ordered tailored suits from Kitayev, near the Anitchkov Bridge, and boots and shoes from Henry Weis just along the road. Mme Olga Bulbenkova still made all the official Court dresses. Dagmar's right to do as she chose and spend as much as she wished was unchallenged. She developed a streak of selfishness and a determination to get her own way. In widowhood she really came into her own.

Her self-confidence was aided by the fact that the new Tsar was so shy and self-effacing. Nicholas had every intention of continuing the work that his father had been unable to complete. As he shakily took up the reins of government he was influenced by three groups of people: Pobedonostsev, his vigorous, powerfully-built uncles (all relatively young men) and, most important of all, his mother.

Dagmar now became indispensable. She had learnt a great deal from conversations with Ambassadors and ministers during Sasha's reign and was only too willing to help. The ministers remembered how her soothing influence had frequently softened his attitude and they respected her judgement. During the first ten years of Nicholas' reign they openly acknowledged her considerable influence on crucial appointments and they knew that a candidate she opposed would not be appointed. 'Her influence in both the State and society can hardly be underestimated', wrote the Kaiser's daughter Princess Victoria Louise.[5]

After the revolution she was accused of supporting her late husband's

23. *The main block of the vast Gatchina Palace. Easier to guard than the Anitchkov, it became known as 'The Citadel of Autocracy'.*
(David Downes, private collection)

24. *Yelagin Palace. One of Dagmar's favourite summer homes, where her children could play wild games in the garden.*
(Sue Woolmans)

25. *Langinkoski Imperial Fishing Lodge, Finland, from the south-west. Designed by the Finnish architect Magnus Schjerfbeck. A simple holiday home, where the Emperor fished and the Empress cooked salmon soup in the kitchen.*
(Photo: Ragnar Backström)

26. The Empress in Court dress. Although small in stature, Dagmar had an inborn sense of majesty.
(The Amalienborg Museum, Copenhagen)

27. *Tsaritsa Maria Feodorovna and Tsarevitch Nikolai Alexandrovitch* c.1889.
(Photo: Levitsky: The Royal Archives, © 1999, H.M. The Queen)

Prins · Hertuginde · Kronprins · Dronning · Keiserinde · Kong
Valdemar Thyra   Frederik   Alexandra Dagmar   Georg
                          1889.

28. *The children of King Christian and Queen Louise, 1889. l to r: Waldemar, Thyra, Frederick,*
Alexandra, Dagmar and George. Queen Louise is peeping out of the window above them.
(The Amalienborg Museum, Copenhagen)

29. Dagmar, Sasha and their children, 1880s.
Back, l to r: Michael, Dagmar, Nicholas, Xenia and George. Front: Sasha with Olga.
(Private collection)

30. *Tsarevitch Nicholas, Livadia, 1890. The Empress, worried about his playboy lifestyle, was urging him to find a wife.*
(Private collection)

31. One of Alexander III's last official functions, visiting the Guards at Krasnoe Selo, August 1894.
In the foreground: Queen Olga of Greece, Dagmar and Alix. In the background: Grand Duke Michael Nicholaievitch
and Count Vorontzov-Dashkov, the Minister of the Court.

(Private collection)

32. *Livadia, 1894. One of the last photographs of Alexander III. The group includes Grand Duchess Ella, Grand Dukes Alexis and Sergei Alexandrovitch (embracing), Dagmar (just behind the left-hand dog), Alexander III (centre) and Grand Duke Paul Alexandrovitch (to his right with the white cap).*

(Private collection)

33. *The room in the Maly Palace where Alexander III died. The cross marks the site of his chair.*
The palace was left untouched for many years but eventually destroyed by fire.
(Private collection)

34. *Alexander III's funeral procession passing through St Petersburg.*
(Det Livgardens Historiske Samling, Copenhagen)

35. *Dagmar (right) with Olga, Michael and George in the Caucasus, 1898.*
George died the following year.
(Det Kongelige Bibliotek, Copenhagen)

36. A family group, 1895.
l to r: Dagmar with Grand Duchess Olga Nicholaievna;
Grand Duchess Olga Alexandrovna; Empress Alexandra Feodorovna.
Back: Grand Duchess Xenia with Princess Irina Alexandrovna; Nicholas II.
(Det Kongelige Bibliotek, Copenhagen)

37. *Nicholas II and Alexandra with their children, 1904.*
l to r: Tatiana, Alexandra with Alexis, Nicholas and Olga. Front: Maria and Anastasia.
Although the family was now complete, the illness of Alexis
was a severe blow to the dynasty.

(Photo: Rotary. Author's collection)

38. *Xenia and Sandro with their family, c.1908/9. l to r: Nikita, Irina, Andrei, Dimitri, Grand Duchess Xenia holding Vassili, Feodor, Rostislav and Grand Duke Alexander. Xenia's strapping sons were in stark contrast to the haemophiliac Tsarevitch.*

(Photo: Boissonas & Eggler. Private collection)

39. *The Imperial yacht* Polar Star. *This luxurious yacht took the Empress to Denmark every year.*
(Collection of Senta Driver)

ministers when the new Tsar was trying to go in the opposite direction. She recognised Nicholas' weakness and knew that if she did not use her influence someone else would, like Sasha's old friend Prince Vladimir Mestchersky. He used his newspapers to blackmail ministers and obtained prominent court appointments for his homosexual lovers. Dagmar had always detested him and his influence on Nicholas was detrimental. 'How highly he values Mestchersky!' she wrote as late as 1911.[6]

In touch with society, aware of public opinion and extremely practical, she passed her knowledge on to Nicholas. Her shrewdness in matters of state was a surprise to Olga. 'She had never before taken the least interest … now she felt it was her duty',[7] the Grand Duchess recalled.

Those who hoped the accession of the new Tsar would herald a more liberal regime were therefore doomed to disappointment. Nicholas dismissed as 'senseless dreams' the hope that the Zemstvo representatives would be allowed to participate in internal government and declared he would reign as an autocrat.

Dagmar remained firmly in the forefront. 'I am sorry to have still to forward you *so many papers*', she wrote a few months later, 'but it is always like that in early summer just before the ministers go on leave; afterwards there will be a little less'.[8] She reprimanded Nicholas for walking alone down the Nevsky Prospekt. Although a cheering crowd gathered, Dagmar had not forgotten the mutilated body of Alexander II in the Winter Palace. Time and again Nicholas told his ministers, 'I must go and ask my Matoushka about this', or, when he wavered, they would respectfully suggest that perhaps His Majesty should consult his Matoushka.[9] Dagmar was never slow to speak out on behalf of her friends and frequently petitioned Nicholas on behalf of others. When Prince Nicholas Lopukin-Demidoff found himself in severe financial difficulties Dagmar asked her son to give him an interest-free loan of 1,000,000 roubles from the State Bank and cancel his large debt. For once Nicholas was firm and only agreed to cancel the debt.

Through charity work, she received first-hand information often denied to the Tsar. 'Her personality was magnetic and her zest for activity was incredible', recalled her daughter. 'She had her finger on every educational pulse in the empire. She would work her secretaries to shreds, but she did not spare herself. Even when bored in committee she never looked bored. Her manner and, above all, her tact conquered everybody'.[10]

In May Dagmar left for Abbas Touman. The distance lessened the tension between the two Empresses. 'I can only thank God that He has given you such a dear and sweet wife, who makes you so happy', Dagmar wrote to Nicholas. 'Next time I shall write to dear Alicky, whose last letter I enjoyed so much'.[11]

To Dagmar's relief, Georgie's health had improved. He was sad to have missed the weddings of Xenia and Nicholas and, although he was becoming accustomed to his solitary life, being away from his family made the grief for his father harder to bear. Never one to stand on ceremony, all Dagmar's attempts to persuade him to spend the summer in St Petersburg failed. They spent many happy days exploring the surrounding countryside before she returned to Russia in time for the birth of Xenia's first child.

On 15th July Xenia gave birth to a daughter, Irina who, as the granddaughter of a Tsar through the female line, held the rank of Princess. Dagmar always referred to Irina as her 'favourite granddaughter'. Alicky was also pregnant. While Dagmar was awaiting the birth of the child she confidently expected would be the heir to the throne, she took Georgie to Denmark.

It was her first visit since Sasha's death and standing in church next to his empty place was distressing. 'This incomparable sadness is with me *always* and *everywhere* and will remain for ever'. Georgie enjoyed himself with his relatives, who he had not seen for four years. Then, suddenly, his health deteriorated. 'Yesterday in the garden he expectorated some blood', Dagmar wrote anxiously, 'that frightened me again more than I can tell – the surprise of it was shocking, because he had been so well of late … I am quite desperate that this should have happened *here* …'[12] Georgie was forbidden to smoke and confined to bed until he was fit enough to return to the Caucasus.

When Nicholas became Emperor, George was proclaimed 'Grand Duke Tsarevitch' and Ataman of the Cossacks. The tragedy was, as the brother nearest in age to Nicholas and the most intelligent of Dagmar's children, he could have been of so much help to him in the early years of his reign. With George living in the Caucasus and Michael, ten years younger than Nicholas, barely out of the schoolroom, the Tsar was deprived of any support from his brothers. Rumours about George circulated widely in St Petersburg. It was said that he was secretly married to a lady from Abbas Touman and society, always avid for gossip, believed there was some genuine mystery surrounding the Grand Duke.

According to one source George was 'married' to a woman whose name is unknown and whom he rejected in 1893. A child is supposed to have been born from this union. The same source says that George then contracted a morganatic marriage in 1894 with a lady named Orkovska (or Orkanowska), who was born in 1873. From this marriage he had two sons and a daughter, who were given the surname of Romanovsky.[13] However unlikely this sounds, it would be nice to think that George had the consolation of some female company, if not a wife, in his lonely exile.

The birth of Alicky's child was now eagerly awaited and the Tsar and Tsarina moved to their new home, the Alexander Palace at Tsarskoe Selo. In Denmark, Dagmar was anxious for news. 'Do you think it will be at the end of October?' she enquired from Bernsdorff. 'I think it will not be before the beginning of November. The first time one never knows for sure; in Xenia's case I was right against the views of the entire medical faculty ...' Nevertheless, in October she hurried back to Gatchina.[14]

Her next concern was the choice of name. '[It] ... seems to be well chosen', she wrote carefully, 'though *Paul* for the *first* somehow frightens me a little; still, there is time to talk about that. It may be just a first impression ...' Confident that she could persuade Nicholas not to name his son after the murdered Emperor Paul, she continued, 'it is understood, isn't it, that you will let me know as soon as the first symptoms appear? I shall fly to you, my dear children'.[15]

The summons came on 3rd/15th November. It was a difficult labour and Dagmar waited anxiously for several hours. According to the wife of a British Embassy official, Nicholas had tears streaming down his face and the Dowager Empress was on her knees praying. Finally, a salute of 101 guns announced the birth of Grand Duchess Olga Nicholaievna a fair, fat baby weighing ten pounds.

The christening took place in the church of the Catherine Palace at Tsarskoe Selo on the young parents' first wedding anniversary, the Dowager Empress' forty-eighth birthday. Dagmar was one of the godmothers. None of them were too disappointed that the first child was a girl. The Empress was young and there was plenty of time to give Russia an heir.

*

Those who hoped or expected the Dowager Empress to retire into seclusion were to be disappointed. As the Court came out of mourning in January 1896 it was Dagmar who headed the Imperial procession on the arm of the Emperor, while Alicky followed with the senior Grand Duke. This was because of a law passed by Emperor Paul in 1797 which, unlike any other European monarchy, gave the Dowager Empress precedence over the Tsar's wife. She remained the first lady in the land. Few previous dowagers had been able to press the point, as they had either already died or had retired from public life in their widowhood. Only Emperor Paul's widow, the first Empress Marie Feodorovna, who was forty-two when he was murdered in a palace coup, was in a position to do so. Paul disliked his eldest son's wife and had passed the law so that his widow would always have precedence. Marie survived her husband for twenty-seven years.

Dagmar was only too pleased to return to public life, especially as it was quickly becoming apparent that the young Empress was either unable or unwilling to fulfill her social obligations.

A great deal has been written about the relationship between the two women and Dagmar's reluctance to help her daughter-in-law. Only a few letters from Alicky to Dagmar have survived. They apparently deal mainly with routine family matters, leaving little to base a judgement on. Dagmar was relatively young, certainly not a saint and she made no secret of the fact that she resented seeing a younger woman in her place. The contrast between them was never more apparent than on ceremonial occasions. Dagmar knew exactly what to say and do, always taking the trouble to know the background of the people to whom she was introduced. Her tact and warmth of manner enabled her to smooth over any awkward moments expertly. At dinner she was full of lively conversation, with a habit of dropping her voice occasionally to a deeper note. She made people feel at ease, as if meeting them had been her greatest pleasure.

Alicky stood stiff with nerves, thrusting her hand out while she stammered in her halting French. When married ladies were presented, Dagmar shook hands warmly and offered the older ladies a chair; Alicky kept all the ladies standing. At balls the contrast was marked – Dagmar cheerfully danced all night but Alicky always left early.

Dagmar had no intention of taking second place to this shy, awkward young woman. Nor was she above keeping Nicholas and Alicky waiting on ceremonial occasions, knowing that they could not leave until she was ready. Her ladies disliked the young Empress and were never slow to gossip. Although surprised and hurt to learn that Alicky disliked her prominence, Dagmar nevertheless liked to listen. She resented Alicky for taking away Nicholas and made no attempt to guide her through the minefield of protocol. By the time she emerged from the first shock of bereavement Dagmar's relations with Alicky were already strained and, because her daughter-in-law never asked her, she was unwilling to help. When Grand Duchess Vladimir attempted to guide Alicky she was immediately rebuffed. Members of Miechen's socially prominent court then became hostile to the young Empress and Alicky's mistakes were not forgiven.

The personality difference between Dagmar and Alicky was summed up by a lady-in-waiting: 'Without actually clashing', wrote Baroness Buxhoeveden, 'they seemed fundamentally unable … to understand one another'. Grand Duchess Olga felt 'they had tried to understand one another and failed. They were utterly different in character, habits and outlook'.[16]

One of the first sources of friction concerned the Crown Jewellery. When Nicholas suggested all the jewels be returned to the Winter Palace

Dagmar refused, saying that his father had left her the guardianship of them in his Will. Nicholas insisted, so she handed over a few heavy, old-fashioned pieces too heavy to wear. Alicky, who did not want the Court to see how offended she was, said that she did not care. Protocol required the Empress to wear the jewels on certain occasions and, to avoid a scandal, Dagmar gave in. She was finally allowed to keep seventy-seven items of Crown Jewellery at the Anitchkov.

She also refused to hand over patronage of the charities. The Department remained firmly in her hands. However, Dagmar was forced to yield on one point. Hearing that her mother-in-law wanted her own name to come first in the Orthodox liturgy, Alicky took the matter to the Holy Synod. They ruled that the Emperor and Empress' names should be coupled together before that of the Dowager Empress.

Although, like most women, Alicky smoked, she objected to her mother-in-law chain-smoking, a habit which increased after Sasha's death. Gossips said that Dagmar did it to annoy her daughter-in-law.

Dagmar dismissed most of the ladies who had come with Alicky from Darmstadt and chose new attendants. The Mistress of the Robes, Princess Marie Galitzine, was very brusque and even inspired awe in some of the Grand Dukes. When Dagmar selected Alicky's clothes the outcome was disastrous. 'She liked fussiness, trimming, and certain colours',[17] recalled her daughter, and always looked elegant. Unfortunately, these styles did not suit Alicky. Dagmar was upset when the gowns she ordered remained unworn.

The young Empress was considered a prude. She crossed the name of everyone who had been connected with a scandal from the invitation list for the first Court Ball. The result, to Dagmar's amusement, was that almost nobody attended. Nicholas tactfully decided that in future his mother should issue the invitations and the second ball was a resounding success.

Society poked fun at the 'provincial' young Empress and spoke of the 'old Court' and the 'new Court'. Gossips made the most of any slight friction but sided openly with Dagmar. She turned a blind eye to their love affairs, enjoyed any hint of gossip or scandal and played the leading role superbly. She remained as popular as ever.

*

In March 1896 Dagmar, Olga and Michael joined Georgie at La Turbie in the South of France. The Princess of Wales and her daughters Victoria and Maud were staying nearby.

One afternoon Dagmar accompanied Alix on a visit to Queen Victoria, who was on her spring holiday at The Grand Hotel in Cimiez. The Queen immediately noticed how young Dagmar looked, and how sad. 'She talked much of dear Alicky, and the baby', Victoria recorded in her Journal. The Queen mentioned her unhappiness that, since the death of the previous Foreign Minister, Giers, Russia had not been so friendly to England and asked Dagmar to speak to Nicholas about it. 'She said she would do so, and could not understand the coolness'.[18]

Georgie joined in few of the family's activities. He suffered another haemorrhage and Dagmar was once more worried about his health.

During Dagmar's stay she became involved in the construction of a new Russian Orthodox Cathedral in Nice. The archpriest, Sergei Lubimov, told her that the present church on the rue Longchamp was too small for the congregation and there was no room to enlarge it. She immediately decided to enlist the Tsar's support so that a new church could be built. A committee was formed under Prince George Romanovsky, 6th Duke of Leuchtenberg, and the architect's plans were approved. Unfortunately, the land acquired proved unsuitable and work was stopped.

In 1902 Dagmar again intervened. After Nixa's death in 1865 Alexander II bought the Villa Bermont, demolished it and built a chapel on the site of his son's bedroom. The estate passed in turn to Sasha and Nicholas. Dagmar now persuaded her son to allow the new church to be built in Bermont Park. The foundation stone was laid in April 1903 on the thirty-eighth anniversary of Nixa's death, in the presence of the Duchess of Coburg, Grand Duke Michael Nicholaievitch and his children Michael and Anastasia. The Russian Orthodox Cathedral of St Nicholas in Nice, which was decorated with mosaic icons of St Alexander Nevsky and St Mary Magdalene as a tribute to Alexander III and Marie Feodorovna, was consecrated in 1912.

It was generally believed that the Dowager Empress' involvement in 1896 was in memory of the time she spent in Nice with her dying fiancé. Now she was there with her seriously ill son but, much as she wanted to remain longer, duty called.

In May 1896, after nearly two months' absence, she returned to Russia for the coronation.

The ceremony was a great ordeal for Dagmar. On 26th May she led the Imperial procession down the Red Staircase and across the square to the cathedral. At this most trying moment she was glad of the support of her favourite brother-in-law Alexis, who understood her feelings so well, and her brother Freddie. Inside, she was conducted to the steps of the dais where three gold thrones stood. 'It was indeed a sad and moving sight to see her standing all alone ...' wrote Princess Victoria of Battenberg.[19] Dagmar later told her mother how pleased she was to have made the sacrifice and how a divine strength enabled her to get through the day.

Tuxen's painting of Nicholas' coronation conveys this perfectly. It shows the Dowager Empress bathed in an almost heavenly light against the darkness of the cathedral.

Dagmar took little part in the official festivities. She had given Xenia one of her ball gowns and, watching her daughter leave for the ball, Dagmar had the feeling that she was seeing herself as a young woman again, although she could barely stand the sound of the music coming from the hall above in the Kremlin. She told Queen Louise that she felt as if her grave was being violated. Although Dagmar shunned most of the celebrations, she crossed Mathilde Kschessinska's name from the list of dancers at the Gala performance, saying that the appearance of the Tsar's former mistress would be a scandal. Kschessinska had equally powerful backers. She went straight to Grand Duke Vladimir, who persuaded Nicholas to have her reinstated. Dagmar was furious.

On 30th May the traditional fête was held at Khodynka Meadow. By the early morning over 500,000 peasants were camped in the field singing, dancing and playing the balalaika. Soon the wagons arrived with the free food, beer and mugs which were to be distributed to everyone. Suddenly, at about six o'clock in the morning there was a stampede. As the people behind pushed forward, those in front fell into the military trenches which criss-crossed the field, or were trampled underfoot where they fell. In no time thousands of dead and wounded men, women and children were lying on the ground. Trenches were hastily covered with branches to hide the bodies; others were flung unceremoniously onto carts; more bodies were thrust under the pavilion where the Tsar was shortly to be received. The official estimate was 1,389 dead and 1,300 wounded. The true number was undoubtedly much higher.

Nicholas, misled about the magnitude of the disaster, decided the fête should continue. When Dagmar learned the full extent of the catastrophe she was appalled. She was determined that someone's head must fall and immediately demanded a commission of enquiry. She also insisted that all further festivities be cancelled, including the French Ambassador's ball that evening. Nicholas agreed but, once again, his uncles had their say. In a gesture of support for Sergei, the Governor General of Moscow, they persuaded Nicholas not to upset Russia's only European ally. The Tsar and Tsarina, both looking very upset, attended the ball, while the peasants murmured about their heartlessness.

Dagmar spent that evening at the hospitals, comforting the wounded and bereaved and seeing what practical help could be given. Many of them had been trapped under dead bodies until their faces turned blue, she told Queen Louise, and consequently had their chestbones pushed in and many other broken bones. During the next few days each of the wounded received a bottle of Madeira from her and she also attended services for the dead. The Dowager Empress was the only member of the Imperial family to visit the hospitals that day.

Nicholas initially agreed to an enquiry headed by Count Constantine Pahlen, former Minister of Justice to Alexander III and a protégé of Dagmar, but he revoked the mandate when Sergei threatened to resign. The question of responsibility divided the Imperial family. The Minister of the Court, Count Vorontzov-Dashkov, was in charge of the general arrangements for the coronation, Grand Duke Sergei was in charge of the arrangements in Moscow. Dagmar supported the Count whole-heartedly, declaring that she would not allow her friends to be harmed in the interests of any Grand Duke. She could not understand why the police were not at Khodynka Meadow all night and blamed Sergei. Alicky sided with Sergei, whose conduct was criticised by the family. The issue was never resolved. The Chief of Moscow Police was dismissed and in 1897 Count Vorontzov-Dashkov became Viceroy of the Caucasus. Baron Fredericks succeeded him as Minister of the Court. No action was taken against Sergei but Grand Duke Constantine Constantinovitch recorded the first outward signs of a veiled animosity between the two Empresses.

Although Nicholas paid for the funerals out of his own purse, the damage was done. The sovereigns were condemned as callous and insensitive and superstitious peasants viewed the disaster as a bad omen for the new reign.

*

In February 1897 the people of Crete rebelled against their Turkish overlords and demanded union with Greece. Willie sent a Greek force under the command of his second son 'Greek Georgie' to help them. The Great Powers would not permit the Ottoman Empire to be dismembered and sent an international force to Crete. The Greeks were ordered to withdraw their troops, they refused and the people clamoured for war. Dagmar feared that there would be a revolution if Willie tried to back down.

In April the Sultan of Turkey declared war on Greece. The ill-equipped Greeks, no match for the German-trained officers of the Turkish army, suffered defeat after defeat. Queen Victoria (whose granddaughter Sophie was married to Crown Prince Constantine of Greece) urged the Tsar to mediate and a ship stood by in case the Greek Royal family had to be evacuated. Dagmar blamed the Kaiser, who she referred to as the 'entrepreneur', for stirring up things which did not concern him just because he had fallen out with his sister Crown Princess Sophie and hated the King of Greece.

By the middle of May Athens lay open to the Turks and Willie was in regular contact with his sisters. Dagmar, panic-stricken, persuaded Nicholas to act. She was aided by the fact that the new Minister of Foreign Affairs, Count Michael Mouraviev, was an old friend, who had formerly been Russian Minister in Copenhagen. Nicholas had appointed him to the Foreign Ministry on his mother's advice. Alexandra wired that the British Government, on the orders of the Queen, would demand a cease-fire. Under the terms of the armistice which Turkey was forced to grant by the Great Powers, Greece had to withdraw her troops from Crete, leaving Turkish troops on Greek territory. Willie again appealed to his sisters for help.

Dagmar was worried about Nicholas' lack of experience and she immediately fired off a letter to him. '[Uncle Willie] telegraphed imploring that peace be made soon. As the Turks are continuing to send troops he fears that they will begin hostilities again as soon as the 15 days of the armistice have elapsed. In the name of Heaven be firm, the voice of Russia *must* make itself heard … You must insist that the Turkish troops be immediately withdrawn from Greek territory …' Mediation continued throughout the summer and Queen Olga left hastily for Russia to plead the Greek cause with the Tsar. When the peace treaty was signed in December Greece had to pay a four million pound indemnity. Dagmar was distressed. 'The Greeks will never be able to pay … Poor Uncle Willie sent me a desperate letter, for under the circumstances he sees no way out'.[20] Although Greece had to struggle to raise the money, with the help of European banks, the threat of a Turkish occupation of Athens had effectively been averted.

As anti-monarchist feeling rose in Greece the dynasty itself was threatened and Dagmar was frantic for the safety of her brother. Not until February 1898, after an assassination attempt against the King and his daughter Princess Marie ('Greek Minny') as they were driving in their carriage, did public opinion turn in Willie's favour.

On 10th June, in the middle of all this worry, Alicky's second child was born. It was another girl, who was christened Tatiana. Relations between the two Empresses had not improved. Dagmar believed that it was an Empress' duty always to be on show; Alicky avoided public life and made no effort to win popularity. Dagmar was concerned that Alicky shut herself away at Tsarskoe Selo and hardly saw anyone, not even members of the entourage. Once, when travelling in the Imperial train, she refused to open the curtains to acknowledge the crowds by the wayside. Dagmar was furious. 'If *she* was not there Nicky would be twice as popular', she said. 'She is a regular German. She thinks the Imperial family should be "above all that sort of thing". What does she mean? Above winning the people's affection? There's no need to go in for what I call vulgar ways of seeking popularity … How many times have I tried to make it plain to her. She won't understand; perhaps she hasn't it in her to understand. And yet, how often she complains of the public indifference to her'.[21]

In 1898 a new, and subsequently very influential, person joined Dagmar's household when Prince George Schervashidze became Chief Steward of the Dowager Empress' Court. The prince, born in 1847, came from an old Georgian family. He had held various administrative posts in Georgia during the reign of Alexander III and as Vice Governor of Tiflis had received the Emperor and Empress when they visited the province in 1888. Shortly after this visit he was appointed Governor of Tiflis.

Prince Schervashidze was a man of striking appearance, recalled his niece, with large dark eyes. He looked especially impressive in his Court uniform. In 1880 he had married a Baroness de Nicolay but because of his service with the Empress he was seldom home. The princess was often invited to lunch at Gatchina.

He was high in Dagmar's favour and even when scandal threatened she stood by him. On visits to Copenhagen, Prince Schervashidze enjoyed discovering his youth again. When the Danish newspapers printed a compromising story about the prince, a very pretty young maid of honour and an incident late at night the Empress leapt to his defence. The prince could not possibly have been with the young lady, she maintained, 'le Prince etait chez moi'.[22]

He was so highly regarded that he received the Grand Cross of the Order of the Dannebrog in 1900 and the Star of the Order, in diamonds, in 1910. As an even greater mark of favour he was given permission to travel overland to Denmark via Germany, as he was such a bad sailor. Dagmar's aversion to Germany was so strong that she refused to cross the narrow straits between Denmark and Germany in a boat flying the German flag. If she was forced to travel overland she sailed to Warnemunde in a Danish boat and boarded her own train, which stopped as little as possible on its way across Germany.

In July 1898 the Kaiser arrived in Russia for a state visit. Mutual hatred of him was probably the only point on which Dagmar and Alicky agreed. By the time William arrived with his wife Augusta, Dagmar had pointedly left for Bernstorff, where her mother was dying.

By the summer of 1898 Queen Louise had reached her eightieth year but, although almost stone deaf and confined to a wheelchair, she still presided over the household. Queen Victoria had once described her as false and intriguing, but she was neither. Her whole life had been devoted to the enhancement of the dynasty and the welfare of her family. In this she had undoubtedly been successful.

When the family gathered at Bernstorff that summer it was clear that Louise had not long to live. She spent her last weeks mainly out of doors, sitting in her beloved rose garden, while her daughters took it in turns to fetch her a drink or coax her to eat.

Louise remained mentally alert to the last. She asked for the newspapers to be read to her the night before she died. Her death on 29th September shattered King Christian. During the next few months his daughters arranged their lives so that one of them would always be with him.

Louise was laid to rest among the Danish Royal family in Roskilde Cathedral. For Dagmar, the death of the mother who had supported her through so many sad times was a great loss.

*

In June 1899 Olga would be seventeen and the Dowager Empress decided it was time for her debut. Olga, who was very much Sasha's child and had not inherited Dagmar's taste for society, dreaded the prospect. The gulf that Olga felt existed between them had never been bridged. Dagmar blamed Mrs Franklin, whom she felt had usurped the affection Olga should have given to her mother. She decided to appoint a lady-in-waiting and dismiss Nana.

The result was a terrible scene, with Olga threatening to run away. She appealed to Nicholas who, although he had given his mother complete control over Olga and Michael's upbringing, took his sister's side. Dagmar retaliated by cutting both the value and the number of her gifts to Mrs Franklin, who she called 'that odious woman'.[23] There was no lady-in-waiting and the gulf between mother and daughter widened. Olga's debut, however, was delayed by a tragic event.

During the spring Dagmar paid her usual visit to Georgie. His health was deteriorating and he now spent part of most winters in Algiers. The Grand Duke was studying the history of the Caucasus and had gathered an extensive library of books on the subject. He was also Honorary Chairman of the Astronomical Society and paid for the construction of Russia's first high altitude observatory, which was built on his Abbas Touman estate and named after him. He now found walking difficult because of his shortness of breath and, to Dagmar's dismay, had begun to ride out alone on a motor-cycle, although strictly forbidden to do so by the doctors. Dagmar tried to persuade him to return with her for the summer but, as usual, he refused and she left for Peterhof where, on 26th June, Alicky's third daughter Marie was born.

Two weeks later bad news arrived. Georgie had been out alone on his motor-cycle and some hours later, when he failed to return, his worried staff sent out a search party. By the time they found him it was too late.

A peasant woman had discovered him collapsed at the side of the road, blood oozing from his mouth as he struggled to breathe. She supported him in her arms until he died. He was just twenty-eight.

The news reached Nicholas by telegram and he had the difficult task of telling Dagmar. She broke down and wept. He had seldom been out of her thoughts for the last few years and his death came as a terrible shock. 'Thank you so [much] for kind sympathy in this terrible sudden bereavement', she telegraphed to Queen Victoria. 'My poor dearest son passed away quite alone[.] Am heartbroken'.[24]

The peasant woman who had found him, a member of the Malakani religious sect, was summoned to tell Dagmar about her son's last moments. She arrived at Peterhof in her flowing robes and the two women remained together for several hours. George's body was taken by warship to Batum and, once again, Dagmar's brother-in-law Alexis was there to lean on. He went with her to meet the body and bring it back for burial. Requiem masses were held in all the major towns along the route to St Petersburg.

Georgie's funeral on 26th July was a harrowing experience for everyone present. Dagmar stood dry-eyed throughout the service, holding Xenia's hand. When the coffin was lowered she could see the tombs of Sasha and her baby son Alexander only a few yards away and the ordeal of burying a second child was too much. She suddenly collapsed onto Xenia announcing, 'home, let's go home. I can't stand any more', and attempted to leave. As Nicholas took hold of her other arm she tried to push past the open tomb to get out. Xenia thought her mother was going to faint. A plank was quickly brought and, without stopping to throw flowers into the grave, she hurried out with Georgie's hat clutched to her breast.[25] Outside in the carriage she broke down completely, still clinging to the hat.

Court mourning for Georgie delayed Olga's debut and it was not until the summer of 1900 that Dagmar was able to give a large, lavish reception for her younger daughter.

Michael was now declared Heir, but not Tsarevitch. Although Nicholas had three lovely daughters they could not succeed to the throne, nor could the crown pass through them to their children. It was therefore imperative that Alicky give birth to a son. If Michael left no male heirs the crown would pass to Vladimir's family. The situation was not made any easier when Xenia produced three sons in quick succession (Andrei in 1897, Feodor in 1898 and Nikita in 1900), followed by three more in the first years of the new century. Dagmar must have frequently wished the crown could be passed to Xenia's strapping sons.

In October 1900 Nicholas contracted typhoid and it was feared he might die. Dagmar begged him to declare Michael Tsarevitch without delay and to let him rule as regent until his brother recovered. To Alicky, pregnant once more, this was like a slap in the face – a public acknowledgement of her failure. She insisted that if Nicholas died she should rule Russia on behalf of her unborn child. Witte, who was impressed by Michael, opposed her saying that they should immediately acknowledge Michael as Tsar. If the Empress then gave birth to a son he had no doubt that Michael would step down. Alicky suspected her mother-in-law and Witte of plotting to remove Nicholas from the throne so they could rule through Michael.

Nicholas recovered but his illness had accentuated the uncertain future of the dynasty. As the old century drew to a close everyone prayed that the child the Empress was carrying would be a boy.

CHAPTER 15

The First Cracks

'EVEN THE LOSS OF A DEAR PERSON IS BETTER
THAN THE DISGRACE OF A DIVORCE'

In the early 1900s the first cracks appeared in the solidarity of the
Romanov dynasty. The new century opened with the death of Queen
Victoria on 22nd January 1901. Dagmar's brother-in-law and sister
now became King Edward VII and Queen Alexandra. Their only surviving son George (who, following the precedent set by Dagmar and Sasha,
had married his dead brother's fiancée Princess May of Teck in 1893) was
created Prince of Wales that November. For Alicky, her grandmother's
death removed a guiding influence which her mother-in-law was unable,
or unwilling, to provide.

In the early years of the century the Dowager Empress' influence
reached its peak, before it slowly declined. As Alicky gained in confidence,
Dagmar began to complain that Nicholas avoided all opportunities for a
private meeting. Xenia was concerned and asked Nicholas to discuss
things with their mother more often. Dagmar seldom had the chance to
see her son alone, even at Peterhof where life was more relaxed and
informal. As the years passed, Alicky's influence became more and more
noticeable until she finally gained ascendancy after the birth of her son.
In the meantime, as the mother both of the Tsar and the heir to the throne,
Dagmar remained very much the matriarch.

Dagmar originally hoped that Xenia and Sandro would come to live in
Gatchina Palace. When Xenia refused an 'unpleasant conversation' took
place.[1] Xenia naturally wanted her own home, as her father had promised.
Dagmar was forced to give in and the former palace of Countess Vorontsov
on the Moika Embankment was purchased for Xenia and Sandro.

With Xenia busy producing children at regular intervals Dagmar did
not want to lose control of Olga. Although she made her debut in 1900,
Olga still hated society. She liked animals, long walks, music (she played
the violin) and was an extremely talented painter. She dreaded an empty
life of afternoon drives and evening balls but, most of all, she dreaded the
thought of marrying a prince who lived outside Russia.

In May 1901 St Petersburg society was stunned by an announcement that Grand Duchess Olga was betrothed to Prince Peter of Oldenburg ('Petya'). Olga was nineteen, her fiancé fourteen years older.

The Oldenburgs were among the German families who had come to Russia in the reign of Peter the Great and married into the Imperial family. Prince Peter's father, Prince Alexander, was a great-nephew of Tsar Nicholas I; his mother was Dagmar's old friend Princess Eugenie of Leuchtenberg, Nicholas I's granddaughter.

Dagmar broke the news to Nicholas in an undated letter from the Anitchkov. 'Children are children no more! I am sure you won't *believe* what has happened. Olga is engaged to *Petya* and *both* are very happy. I had to consent, but it was all done so quickly and unexpectedly that I still cannot believe it ...' and she signed herself 'your agitated Mama'.[2]

Nicholas thought it was a joke, until Prince Peter told him in person. Petya was a hypochondriac and a homosexual. He had no interest in women at all, preferring the company of his male friends in the clubs. He had nothing in common with his bride. No-one believed it was a love match and a story soon circulated that the marriage had been selfishly engineered by the Dowager Empress to enable Olga to remain at her beck and call. More likely she allowed herself to be talked into it by the ambitious Princess Eugenie, who had her eye on the Grand Duchess' wealth and position.

Olga believed she was tricked into accepting the prince's proposal. Arriving for a reception at the Vorontzovs', she was taken straight to a sitting-room where, as the door shut quickly behind her, she was surprised to see her cousin Prince Peter. Looking distinctly uncomfortable, he stammered through a proposal of marriage. Stunned, Olga barely had time to say anything before Countess Vorontzov ran in and offered her congratulations. That evening Olga went straight to Michael's rooms at the Anitchkov, where they both wept. Consoled by the knowledge that she would be able to remain in Russia, she did not resist.

The marriage was arranged for 9th August at Gatchina. Dagmar, having convinced herself that her daughter was happy, told King Christian in July that she dreaded the wedding. When the last child had left the home would be empty, yet Dagmar felt she ought to be pleased that the young people had found happiness.

Olga said afterwards that there was little rejoicing at her wedding, which was attended by only the immediate family. The newlyweds returned to the Oldenburg Palace. After crying herself to sleep the bride spent her wedding night alone. The bridegroom spent it at the gambling club, where he proceeded to gamble away his wife's fortune. The marriage was never consummated.

Shortly before Olga's marriage the eagerly-awaited birth of Alicky's fourth child had taken place at Peterhof on 18th June. It was another girl. They named her Anastasia, an old Russian name meaning 'Resurrection'. This time the sense of disappointment was palpable among all the members of the Imperial family. The Empress had felt so well during her pregnancy, unlike the other occasions that, as Grand Duke Constantine Constantinovitch wrote in his diary, they were all hoping this time it would be a son. 'Alix has again given birth to a daughter', Dagmar telegraphed to Xenia, who was in the Crimea.[3] No further comment was necessary.

Alicky, desperate to give her husband and country an heir, turned to mysticism and the fringe world of faith-healers, clairvoyants and miracle-workers. In a land where talk of miracles abounded and Holy Men, 'Starets', roamed the countryside, there had long been an interest in the occult among the upper levels of St Petersburg society. In darkened drawing-rooms spiritualism and table-turning were all the vogue as society, whose men gambled away their fortunes at the race track and staked everything on the turn of a single card, looked for novelty and excitement. Bored with the traditional rituals of Orthodoxy they turned increasingly towards the occult, where the line between superstition and religion was becoming increasingly fine. Two of the most prominent members of this mystical set were the Montenegrin Grand Duchesses – Militza, the wife of Grand Duke Peter Nicholaievitch and Anastasia ('Stana'), married to the Duke of Leuchtenberg, a distant cousin of the Tsar.

Dagmar had no time for the more mystical elements of Orthodoxy, she was too practical, level-headed and down-to-earth. However, Alicky's contemplative nature and zeal in discovering new Saints and collecting icons made her an easy prey. She had become very friendly with the Montenegrin sisters and threw herself wholeheartedly into the more Eastern aspects of Orthodoxy. Slighted (as she believed) by the Dowager Empress and disliked by society, she felt that Militza and Stana were the only members of the family to show her deference and respect.

It was the Montenegrin sisters who found Monsieur Philippe. Philippe Nizier-Vachot, a peasant from Savoy, practised faith-healing in Lyons and soon attracted a varied clientele. He was a small, rather unsightly man of about fifty with black hair and a black moustache but one of his great assets was his magnetism. The quiet authoritive tone of his voice soon convinced his clients that he had remarkable powers from God. In 1901 Militza and Stana presented him to the Empress during an official visit to France.

Philippe claimed not only to be able to foretell the sex of an unborn baby but also to be able to change the sex of a child in its mother's womb.

He was immediately invited to Russia. The Tsar and Tsarina became regular visitors to Grand Duke Peter's home Znamenka, near Peterhof, where they spent the evenings with Philippe. His smooth talk and persuasive manner soon convinced the Empress that he had been sent by God. When, in the spring of 1902, Alicky announced she was pregnant Philippe assured her the child would be a boy.

He soon began to influence the Emperor. Major decisions were deferred until Nicholas had consulted Philippe; it was said that the spirit of Alexander III was conjured up in a seance.

When Dagmar heard about this she was furious. Peter Rachkovsky, head of the Russian Secret Police in France, then informed her that Philippe was a charlatan, who had been prosecuted three times in France for unlicensed practising of medicine. Dagmar was appalled at the consequent discredit to the dynasty. Not wishing to be accused by her daughter-in-law of interfering, she asked Rachkovsky to inform Nicholas. Confronted with Rachkovsky's report the Tsar hesitated.

Dagmar decided to talk to Nicholas herself. He took absolutely no notice of his mother's warning – after all, he protested, the French police had not actually proved that Philippe did not possess occult powers. Perhaps preferring his mother's anger to his wife's hysteria Nicholas dismissed Rachkovsky. 'C'est un crime!' was Dagmar's only recorded comment.[4] The Tsar and Tsarina's visits to Philippe at Znamenka were kept secret, which only added fuel to the gossip and rumour when the news leaked out. When Dagmar found out she was extremely annoyed. Her displeasure extended to the Montenegrins.

In September 1902 the whole country awaited the birth of the Empress' child. The doctors were still not permitted to examine her. Finally, Alicky suffered what Xenia described to one of her mother's friends as 'a minor miscarriage – if it could be called a miscarriage at all – that is to say a tiny ovule came out!' The doctors then confirmed that Alicky was never pregnant, the symptoms were due to anaemia, and a bulletin was issued saying that a miscarriage had ended the Empress' hopes.[5] When Dagmar visited Alicky she took the opportunity to speak to Nicholas openly about her distrust of Philippe. There was no result.

Finally, in the wake of unwelcome publicity, the Tsar was forced to send Philippe back to France. Dagmar breathed a sigh of relief. For the first time Alicky's influence had prevailed over her own but, in the end, the Dowager Empress had won.

The Romanovs themselves added fuel to the dynastic crisis. After Michael the next heir was Grand Duke Vladimir, who resented the accession of his nephew Nicholas. Vladimir's sons Cyril, Boris and Andrei were still unmarried. Boris had already had liaisons with a number of unsuitable women. Andrei's mistress was the Tsar's former lover, the ballerina Mathilde Kschessinska, who consoled herself with Grand Duke Sergei Michaelovitch before meeting Andrei in 1900. In 1902 she gave birth to his son.

At the turn of the century the strict code which had formerly governed the marriages of the Imperial family began to crumble. They were forbidden to marry divorced persons or commoners and could not marry at all without the Tsar's consent. It was one thing for the church to permit divorce but quite another for the Tsar to sanction it. Dagmar, with her strong belief in the sanctity of marriage, was totally opposed. 'Even the loss of a dear person is better than the disgrace of a divorce', she wrote.[6] The few members of the family who dared to disobey Alexander III soon learnt what an autocrat was – but things were very different under his son.

In 1901 Dagmar was saddened and shocked almost beyond words to learn that Alicky's brother Ernie, the Grand Duke of Hesse, and his wife Victoria Melita, 'Ducky', were to divorce. 'It is simply awful', she wrote after a sleepless night. 'How dreadful to think of their future and that of the poor little child! {Their daughter, Princess Elizabeth} I am also *extremely* sorry for poor Alix, knowing well how dear Ernie is to her ...'[7] Alicky was sympathetic to the plight of her brother and sister-in-law who, she told Xenia, were simply unable to get on. But worse was to come.

For several years Victoria Melita had been in love with Grand Duke Cyril Vladimirovitch. Cyril returned her love but, because they were first cousins, their marriage was forbidden by the Orthodox Church. Queen Victoria then arranged Ducky's marriage to Ernie, one of her Lutheran first cousins, but when things went wrong she refused to allow them to divorce. The Queen's death removed the only obstacle and soon after-wards Ducky left her husband and daughter for Cyril. Nicholas refused to allow them to marry.

In 1903 Ducky's mother the Duchess of Coburg wrote to Dagmar and the Tsar asking permission for Cyril to marry her daughter in secret. The answer was no. Unless Cyril was prepared to give up his title and income for a life in exile he could only hope that the Tsar would relent.

Then came another blow. In 1902 Dagmar's brother-in-law Grand Duke Paul, a widower since his young wife Alexandra died in childbirth, secretly married Mme Olga Pistolkors, the divorced wife of one of Grand Duke Vladimir's aides. The ceremony took place at Livorno in Tuscany. Paul had given the Tsar his word that he would not marry Mme Pistolkors, born Olga Valerianovna Karnovitch, a thirty-six-year-old commoner with three children of her own. She and Paul already had a son, Vladimir, born in 1897.

Unsure of how to react to this *fait accompli*, Nicholas turned to

Dagmar. Her feelings left no room for doubt. 'Alas, he seems to have forgotten everything – his duty to his children, to his country, service, honour ... How could he go through with it after all he had been told by his brothers and by us all? ... And there is the *scandal*! I am simply ashamed ... and am not telling anybody, but of course it will come out only too soon ... such an act cannot remain unpunished and, into the bargain, marrying a divorced woman!'[8]

A divorced woman could not be received at Court. Paul and his morganatic wife were banished to Paris and in 1904 she was created Countess Hohenfelsen by the King of Bavaria. Although Paul was deprived of his revenues and army rank, he never omitted to put on his full-dress uniform and attend the service for the Tsar's Name Day in the Russian Orthodox Cathedral.

Dagmar felt very sad for the plight of his two children, twelve-year-old Marie and eleven-year-old Dimitri. Their father's estates were put in trust and they were sent to live with Sergei and Ella in Moscow.

Dagmar's youngest children, Olga and Michael, were also about to cause problems. Olga suffered her loveless marriage in silence, but the stress began to show when her hair fell out and she had to wear a wig. Dagmar still did not seem to realise that anything was wrong and told her father that she could only thank God for their happiness. When Olga and Petya had to go to Biarritz in 1903 for the sake of his health Dagmar was concerned, as she had grown quite fond of Olga's husband.

Michael followed the traditional path of a Russian Grand Duke into the army. He joined the Horse Guards Artillery and, in 1902, transferred to the Blue Cuirassiers, who were stationed at Gatchina. At a military review in 1903 Olga saw Michael talking to a tall, fair-haired young officer from his regiment. As their eyes met she knew it was love at first sight. The next day, when Misha obligingly invited them both to lunch, she discovered her love was returned.

Nicholas Kulikovsky, the son of Alexander Nikanorovitch Kulikovsky and Eudoxie Nicholaievna Kharina, was twenty-one. Although he came from a prominent military family he was a commoner. This did not worry Olga, who had no use for pomp or ceremony. She returned to St Petersburg and asked Petya for an immediate divorce. Convention decreed that the husband was always the guilty party and provided 'evidence' of his adultery. Petya refused to sully his family name but said that he might consider the matter again after an interval of several years.

Olga was seen more frequently at Gatchina, where she and Kulikovsky were often spotted driving around in an ordinary open cab. The affair was soon common knowledge around the garrison town and inevitably came to the attention of the regiment's Colonel-in-Chief, the Dowager Empress.

Dagmar was appalled that her younger daughter had compromised herself but she was more concerned that no hint of the affair should become public. The honour of the regiment was also at stake but if she had Kulikovsky banished the scandal would be immense. For the sake of appearances Prince Peter therefore appointed Kulikovsky as his A.D.C. and gave him rooms in their house at Sergievskaya Street, which became the scene of an extraordinary 'ménage à trois'. To Dagmar the fact that her younger daughter was living under the same roof as her husband and lover was distressing to say the least. Yet she found even this more palatable than a divorce.

Popular, athletic and handsome, twenty-four-year-old Michael was a more serious problem. Still heir to the throne and one of the richest young men in the world, he was extremely eligible. Dagmar knew that great care would have to be taken to find him a suitable wife. Miechen hoped he would marry her daughter Grand Duchess Helen. On the surface Helen was eminently suitable but Michael could not marry his first cousin. In fact Misha preferred another first cousin, Ducky's sister Princess Beatrice of Saxe-Coburg, 'Baby-Bee', the seventeen-year-old youngest daughter of the Duchess of Coburg. They met in 1902 and began to exchange passionate letters. Michael called her 'my own precious Sima'.[9] The same problem of consanguinity arose. Michael could not contract a marriage without the Tsar's consent and Nicholas forbade him to marry Beatrice.

In November 1903, with marriage ruled out, Michael was forced to tell Baby-Bee that they could never be any more than friends. Misha was upset and Baby-Bee became thin and ill. Her sisters accused Michael of dishonourable conduct and maintained that Beatrice never even thought of marriage. The Duchess of Coburg was annoyed with Dagmar. It was 1905 before the recriminations died down but by then Michael had met someone else.

Only in 1911 did the Emperor finally pass a law allowing the grandchildren of a sovereign who held the rank of prince or princess to marry Russian subjects of unequal rank, provided they came from a suitable background. Although the new law did not apply to the Grand Dukes, Dagmar commented that 'it was about time'.[10]

These squabblings weakened the dynasty and set the scene for the cataclysm to follow. Too many of them believed that 'Russia existed for the Romanovs, not the Romanovs for Russia'.[11]

*

Dagmar was never as close to her younger sister as she was to Alix and she saw little of Thyra and Ernst August. They lived at Gmunden, near the Salzkammergut mountains of Austria and also had a hunting lodge, as well as a small winter home at Penzing, near Vienna. Yet nothing could disguise the fact that this was the Court of Hanover in exile. Even when the reigning Duke of Brunswick died in 1884, leaving Ernst August as his heir, the Federal Council of the German Empire ignored Ernst's rights and appointed a Prussian prince as regent. Eventually, Germany restored Ernst August's confiscated estates, which eased their financial situation and enabled him to build a new castle. The price was a promise not to disturb the Empire's peace.

Illness and depression had also taken their toll on Thyra and in 1887 she had a nervous breakdown. In 1900 her daughter Marie Louise married Prince Max of Baden and the following year sixteen-year-old Prince Christian, the fifth of Thyra's six children, died suddenly of appendicitis. Soon afterwards, Thyra and Ernst August became grandparents.

Unfortunately, when the family gathered in Copenhagen in the spring of 1903 to celebrate King Christian's eighty-fifth birthday, the Kaiser decided to join them and ingratiate himself with the old monarch. Dagmar and Alix were annoyed that he was coming to spoil their party. Ernst August and Thyra immediately packed up and left. They had heard rumours that William was hoping to marry his eldest son to one of their daughters.

When King Christian celebrated the fortieth Jubilee of his reign that autumn, all his daughters were by his side.

Dagmar still took a great interest in Danish affairs. In February 1900 she was alarmed by a report that Denmark was to sell the Danish West Indies. She immediately wrote to her father, protesting that after 200 years it would be a crime and saying she hoped the report was false. Schleswig-Holstein also continued to rankle. After driving past Gottorp Castle with Alix the same year she told King Christian how unjust it was that the Duchy had been lost to Denmark and that he could not even pray at his parents' and brother's graves.

Although Dagmar made frequent trips to Denmark, she never stayed at the fishing lodge in Finland after Sasha's death. Nicholas paid one visit to Langinkoski in 1906. He and his family signed the visitors' book, little Anastasia managing only the single letter 'A'.

Nicholas did not share his mother's love for Finland and, despite Dagmar's protests, on the death of Count Heiden in 1898 he appointed General Nicholas Bobrikoff as Governor General, a man who could be relied upon to implement the policy of Russification. Dagmar was horrified. She considered him a liar and an evil genius but Nicholas was determined to carry through his father's plans.

In 1899 Nicholas issued a manifesto suspending Finland's rights and privileges. Both Dagmar and Witte protested. Five thousand people in

Finland signed a petition which was brought to St Petersburg by a delegation. The Tsar refused to receive them.

Dagmar watched with alarm as more and more repressive measures were introduced. She could only feel sorrow and concern. There were protests in Finland and an outcry all over Europe. Dagmar worried about the damage to Russia in the eyes of foreign powers. Hearing a rumour that Bobrikoff was about to introduce martial law giving him power to arrest, imprison or deport people without trial she fired off an angry letter from Denmark protesting against these 'flagrant injustices' and the campaign against Finland:

There, where things had always gone well, where the people were perfectly happy and contented, now everything is *broken* up, everything changed, disorder and hatred sown ... All that has been and is being done in Finland is based on *lies* and *deceit* and leads straight to *revolution* ... I implore you not to give your consent ... think of the number of poor innocent people who would have to suffer for this infernal plan! ... For God's sake do think it over again ... The only way out I can see is to recall him at once ... give his post to a man in your confidence, honest and sufficiently independent not to be afraid to tell you the truth ...[12]

Nicholas did not listen.

Bobrikoff brought in Russians to carry out his orders and occupy the higher government posts. The Constitution was suspended and terrorist attacks continued against Russian officials. Dagmar's opinion was vindicated the following year when the hated Bobrikoff was assassinated. By this time Finland was virtually at war with Russia.

Towards the end of 1902 Dagmar received the War Minister, General Alexis Kuropatkin. He shared the Emperor's hostility to Finland and was instrumental in the abolition of the separate Finnish troops. Dagmar had fought this policy for some time but finally had to admit defeat. 'She was polite ...' Kuropatkin wrote in his diary, 'asked many questions but the old heartiness is gone: she cannot excuse the abolition of the Finnish troops'. Three weeks later he recorded, 'The [Dowager] Empress ... talked for more than forty minutes about Finnish affairs. She was angry and excited ... I have not been able to recapture her goodwill ...'[13]

In 1905 she returned to the offensive over the appointment of the new Governor General. 'They are longing to have Count Armfeldt instead of Linden, whom everyone hates. Whereas Armfeldt is respected by everybody ... Another good choice would be Bjomberg, who is loved on all sides. Once the Finns have had their rights and privileges restored to them, they must be continued in the same spirit and promises must be kept; otherwise it will be *half-measures* again – and that is never any good'.[14] Not until the end of 1905 was the conscription law repealed and Finnish rights restored.

In 1910 further legislation was introduced which, although it brought no specific changes to Finland, the Finns considered a violation of the Fundamental Laws. Their autonomy had been violated for the second time and feelings against Russia mounted. The result of Nicholas' policy was the estrangement of the Finns from Russia. In 1917 Finland declared independence.

Dagmar once wrote, 'I love Finland just as I love all Russia' and she had always received a warm welcome there. Time and again she proved that she was still 'Finland's best and most faithful friend'.[15]

*

In May 1903 St Petersburg celebrated its bicentenary.

As part of the celebrations, a costume ball was held at the Winter Palace with the guests in seventeenth-century dress. The effect was stunning. Many of the guests wore costumes handed down from their ancestors and the array of priceless jewels was magnificent.

Although Dagmar and Michael did not attend the ball, it was repeated two days later for their benefit. Against her better judgement Dagmar lent Michael a priceless diamond clip (once the property of the Emperor Paul) to wear in his cap. It formed part of the Crown Jewels and because of its value and historic associations she hardly wore it. As the music of the old Russian national dances echoed through the marble halls and society danced the night away, the clip fell from Michael's cap and disappeared.

All that night the halls of the palace were searched but to no avail. Dagmar was in despair. A thorough search the following morning failed to reveal the whereabouts of the clip.

To the superstitious it was a bad omen – and, indeed, it was almost the last occasion on which the Winter Palace was seen in all the splendour of an Imperial ball.

*

Alicky's efforts to produce the longed-for son continued. In July 1903 the Imperial family attended the canonisation of the revered holy man, Seraphim, who was credited with a reputation for saintliness and miraculous powers of healing. Nicholas, spurred on by his wife, who wanted to invoke Seraphim's intercession, forced through the canonisation against the wishes of the Orthodox Church. A Bishop who protested was sent to Siberia.

Dagmar and other members of the family went on the exhausting journey to the monastery of Sarov. Over 300,000 pilgrims converged on the area and at one point the Tsar was hoisted shoulder-high. Nicholas was more than ever convinced of his people's loyalty.

That evening, after the canonisation ceremony, Alicky slipped out to bathe in the Sarovka River (whose waters were considered to have great powers of healing) and pray at the shrine. Within a few weeks she realised she was pregnant.

*

Even when Dagmar was abroad Ministers still came to see her, although she shared Nicholas' dislike of them, commenting that 'it's they who get in the way of everything'. With the exceptions of Pobedonostsev and Witte, Nicholas had replaced most of his father's ministers with men of his own choosing. The Minister of the Interior, I.N. Durnovo, resigned because Dagmar complained that he was reading her private correspondence. Her attitude 'made it impossible ... to remain in office', Durnovo told Witte.[16]

The peasants, suffering from a series of bad harvests and the falling price of wheat, began to agitate for more land. Soon they took to looting and burning the big estates and murdering the landowners. As the peasants became impoverished they flocked to the towns, while the conditions of the factory workers worsened. Anti-Semitism reached new heights as thousands of Jews were killed or wounded in the pogroms.

To the cry for better living conditions, a shorter working day and higher wages was soon added another cry – freedom of speech, freedom of assembly, freedom from autocracy and a constitutional government. Nicholas was determined not to concede one iota of his autocratic powers.

In July 1904, the harsh, unpopular Minister of the Interior, Vyacheslav Plehve, fell victim to an assassin's bomb. The revolutionary movement had stirred again.

*

By 1900 the revolutionaries had formed themselves into two parties: the Social Democrats (or Russian Marxists) and the Social Revolutionary Party (formerly Land and Liberty).

The Social Democrats were the more dominant party but in 1903 there was a serious split in their ranks. Matters came to a head over proposals for the party's organisation. George Plekhanov, who had dominated them for twenty years, wanted membership to be open to anyone; others wanted it restricted to a small, élite, dedicated professional body. When the vote was taken Plekhanov lost. He and his followers became the Mensheviks (minorityites), the others became the Bolsheviks (majorityites). The leader of the Bolsheviks was Vladimir Ilyich Ulyanov, more commonly known under the pseudonym of Lenin. By just two votes the Bolsheviks were born.

The following year saw the last great Court Ball. It was the swan-song of Imperial Russia. Never again would guests dance to the strains of a Court orchestra, or train-loads of flowers be brought up from the Crimea to adorn the Winter Palace.

In 1905 war abroad and revolution at home further weakened the dynasty. It set the Romanovs firmly on a collision course which would eventually lead to murder and, for Dagmar, the loss of home, country, possessions and many of her close relatives.

CHAPTER 16

A Short Victorious War

'LET US THANK GOD THAT THIS YEAR OF NIGHTMARES
IS COMING TO AN END'

On 6th February 1904 Japan, angered by Russia's penetration of Korea and Manchuria, launched a surprise attack on the Russian naval base at Port Arthur. In St Petersburg the Season came to an abrupt end.

For many years certain prominent Russians had favoured expansion in the Far East, but the biggest problem was Japan. In 1898 Russia obtained a ninety-nine-year lease on Port Arthur from the Chinese and began to build a strong naval base, giving Russia her first ice-free port on the Pacific. Witte was keen to export Russian goods to the Far East. As a first step, Russia obtained China's permission to extend the Trans-Siberian railway across north Manchuria and the railway was 'protected' by Russian troops. After the Boxer Rebellion in 1900 Russia occupied Manchuria but later recognised China's sovereignty. Alarmed, Japan tried to obtain compensation in Korea but failed. In 1902 Nicholas promised to evacuate Manchuria within eighteen months but in 1903 he suddenly called a halt to the withdrawal. Japan insisted that Russia honour the agreement with China. Russia refused and negotiations continued throughout 1903.

The Japanese would have been willing to let Russia control Manchuria if they could have a free hand in Korea but here the Imperial family was heavily involved. Nicholas had given two million roubles to Captain Alexander Bezobrazov, a friend of Sandro, who promised to bring Manchuria and Korea into the Russian Empire without bloodshed. Russia had obtained a Korean mining and timber concession in territory along the left bank of the Yalu river, which formed the border between Korea and Manchuria. Among the prominent investors in the undertaking, known as 'The Russian Timber Industry Stock Company in the Far East', were the Dowager Empress and the Tsar. Soon Bezobrazov's Russian troops infiltrated North Korea disguised as lumberjacks.

Admiral Eugene Alexeyev was appointed Viceroy of the Far East with absolute authority. His mandate was to increase Russian forces in the Far

East and ensure that Manchuria remained free of foreign influence. Russia now had control of both Manchuria and Korea. The Japanese demanded the withdrawal of the troops but Nicholas, encouraged by the Kaiser, refused all concessions. Dagmar urged him to negotiate. She had received repeated warnings that his policy could only lead to war with Japan. Witte opposed intervention and was 'promoted' to Chairman of the Committee of Ministers, in effect, retirement. There were many who thought a 'short victorious war' would divert attention from Russia's internal problems. On 3rd February 1904 Japan broke off diplomatic relations.

Three days later Japan began hostilities without any declaration of war. Port Arthur was taken completely unawares. 'Our poor sailors! God help them, but how terrible to be taken by surprise!'[1] Dagmar telegraphed to Xenia, who was in Cannes where her father-in-law Grand Duke Michael Nicholaievitch was recovering from a stroke.

In Russia it was taken for granted that the superior might of the Tsar's armies would crush the Japanese. The army would not even have to fight, ran the quip – they had merely to throw their caps at the Japanese to destroy them. On paper the Russian army was stronger but the Japanese had their army close by; the Russian men and supplies had to cross over 4,000 miles of territory, served only by the incomplete Trans-Siberian railway. Steamers had to be used to ferry them across Lake Baikal in Siberia. In the icy winter a light railway was built across the frozen surface. Added to this the two Russian commanders, Admiral Alexeyev in Port Arthur and General Kuropatkin, commander of the land forces, were at odds with each other.

England had signed a military alliance with Japan and Dagmar soon realised that she and Alix would be on opposite sides. Although England pledged strict neutrality, the Princess of Wales told a relative that Queen Alexandra supported the Japanese. Dagmar hoped the alliance would not lead to complications between Russia and England.

The Dowager Empress threw herself into war work. She received the Russian commanders before they left for the front and went to the Winter Palace to see many of her regiments depart. Work for the Red Cross took up a great deal of her time. Medical care had to be organised, hospital trains and field hospitals needed to be equipped and sent to the front. There were issues to be dealt with involving prisoners of war. She also worried about Sandro, and put pressure on Nicholas not to let him go to Port Arthur. Sandro remained in St Petersburg at the Ministry of Merchant Marine.

What followed was disastrous for Russia. Both on land and at sea the defeats were humiliating. The *Petropavlovsk* was sunk, with the loss of seven hundred men. Among the few survivors was Grand Duke Cyril. As the casualty lists grew longer Dagmar was depressed at the loss of life. The Russian fleet was blockaded at Port Arthur, giving the Japanese command of the sea – they soon occupied all of Korea. In a letter to her father on 5th September Dagmar prayed that God would make Russia victorious. The tension and worry, she said, were almost unbearable and she wondered how much longer the conflict would last.

In a last desperate gamble Nicholas sent the Russian Baltic Fleet to the Far East under the command of Admiral Rozhdestvensky. As the fleet sailed away Dagmar little knew how close it would come to bringing about war with England.

Sailing through the night, Admiral Rozhdestvensky opened fire on what he suspected were some small Japanese ships. It was a fleet of British trawlers. As one began to sink, Rozhdestvensky sailed off without even bothering to pick up survivors, leaving many dead and injured in the water. England screamed for vengeance. Dagmar's worst fears seemed about to be realised when, encouraged by King Edward who was anxious to maintain good relations with Russia, tempers cooled and the matter was finally referred to the international commission at The Hague. Russia was ordered to pay damages of £65,000.

Worse was to follow.

*

In the middle of the war one of Dagmar's most ardent prayers was answered. On 12th August the guns of the SS Peter & Paul Fortress fired a 300-gun salute to announce the birth of Tsarevitch Alexis, the first heir born to a reigning Tsar since the seventeenth century. At last the dynasty was secure. To Dagmar his birth was the first ray of sunshine in a long period of tragedy and sadness.

At the lavish christening on 24th August the Dowager Empress was the principal godmother; the godfathers included the whole of the Russian army. The Tsarevitch, who arrived in a gilded coach escorted by a troop of cavalry, was carried on a cushion of cloth of gold by the elderly Mistress of the Robes. She had a broad gold band over her shoulder to support the cushion and wore rubber-souled shoes to prevent her from slipping. The occasion was the first official appearance of Dagmar's three eldest granddaughters Irina, Olga and Tatiana, wearing short blue and silver Court dresses. Later Dagmar proudly invested Alexis with the Order of St Andrew, the highest distinction in the Russian Empire.

He was a handsome baby with grey-blue eyes, golden curls, pink skin and dimples when he smiled. Dagmar found him an 'adorable child ... so friendly'. She noticed his well-defined eyebrows and his vitality. 'Don't you think he's a beauty?' the Tsar asked a visitor proudly.[2]

Within a few weeks the jubilation turned to uneasiness and then to fear. In September Alexis haemorrhaged from his navel. Although the bleeding stopped, the suspicion remained. By early October the fears were confirmed. Dagmar was devastated to learn that her precious, long-awaited grandson, the heir to the 300-year-old Romanov dynasty, had haemophilia.

*

Haemophilia is a blood-clotting deficiency transmitted by the mother usually only to male members of the family. Although females are carriers they rarely suffer from the disease and never know until they have children if any of their sons will be affected. Any knock or bruise can produce painful swellings beneath the skin as the blood fails to clot and blood will continue to flow into the joints until the swelling is so hard that the haemorrhaging slows on its own account. Pressure can be applied to minor cuts to stop the bleeding but a nosebleed could be fatal. At the time of Alexis' birth there was no cure and two-thirds of haemophiliacs died before the age of eleven. A sufferer could die at any time, often in agonising pain, from only a minor bump or scratch.

Often called the 'Royal Disease' it had penetrated into Europe's Royal families through Queen Victoria. Of Victoria's sons only Leopold was afflicted but two of her daughters, Alice and Beatrice, were carriers. Princess Beatrice had two haemophiliac sons and her daughter, Queen Victoria Eugenie of Spain, also had two afflicted sons, one of whom was the heir.

Princess Alice was Alexis' maternal grandmother. Her son Friedrich ('Frittie') was thought to be a haemophiliac. He died from a haemorrhage after falling through an open window. Alice's daughter Irene, wife of Prince Henry of Prussia, had two haemophiliac sons, one of whom died shortly before Alexis' birth. It could therefore hardly have come as a surprise that Alicky proved to be a carrier. Dagmar's original opposition to the marriage may, in part, have been due to her uncertainty about this, although it is unlikely that the genetic pattern of the disease (already known in medical circles) was understood in the more sheltered atmosphere of Europe's Royal Courts.

Alicky was devastated. After four daughters, the discovery that this precious, long-awaited child had haemophilia and that she was responsible for passing on the defect was like a stab in the heart. The stress and anguish of Alexis' illness undermined her own health, leaving her prey to a string of psychosomatic illnesses. Nicholas became more fatalistic and frequently reminded people he had been born on the day of Job. Fearing the consequences for the dynasty if they admitted that Alexis was likely to die at any time, the Emperor and Empress told only their closest confidantes. Even Nicholas' sister Olga was not certain until 1912. Because they tried to carry on as if nothing was wrong, the Russian people never understood the expression of constant sadness on Alicky's face, nor the reason for her later dependence on Rasputin. The veil of secrecy was to be fatal.

Dagmar spent Christmas Eve at Tsarskoe Selo where her five-month-old grandson was the centre of attention. On Christmas Day, assisted by Misha and Sandro, Dagmar distributed gifts to the officers at Gatchina while Olga and Xenia took ornaments from the tree to give to the men as they left.

As Alicky drew her husband and children further and further into their own little world, Dagmar began to feel increasingly more isolated from Nicholas and his family. Her lively, sociable nature had nothing in common with the quiet, domestic, almost bourgeoise atmosphere created by her daughter-in-law and she saw them less frequently.

After the birth of her son, her position now secure, Alicky began to have more influence over her husband. Consequently Dagmar's influence decreased. Alexis' birth has been called 'the event which more than anything else determined the later course of Russian history'.[3]

*

The surrender of Port Arthur with a loss of 28,000 men started a howl of criticism of the government's management of the war. Unrest spread. A series of defeats had shattered the morale of the Russian army. The people, who had not understood why they were fighting anyway, began to agitate for a say in the running of the country.

Since Sasha's death, Dagmar had embraced some of the political values of the Russian aristocracy, particularly a dislike of bureaucracy and a desire for the freedom and influence exercised by the nobility in countries such as England. For many years she had deplored the curtailment of religious freedom and other rights as Nicholas pursued his father's policy of Russification.

After Plehve's assassination in July 1904 she therefore used her influence in favour of the liberal Prince Peter Sviatopolk-Mirsky, a moderate man whose appointment as Minister of the Interior would restore public confidence. The prince had fought in the Russo-Turkish war and been Director of the Department of Police at the Ministry of Interior. He was opposed to the authoritarian policies which had been continued after Alexander III's death, including excessive Russification. According to Count Paul Benckendorff, the Marshal of the Court, Nicholas intended to appoint General Wahl, who could be trusted to carry out his repressive policies. Benckendorff says that there was a scene, 'during which one [the Dowager Empress] almost threw oneself at his [the Tsar's] knees' begging him not to make this appointment and to choose someone who would make concessions. She said that if Nicholas did not agree, she would 'leave for Denmark, and then without me here let them twist your head around'.[4]

Dagmar knew and shared society's opposition to Plehve's policies, which she was convinced would lead to revolution. Sviatopolk-Mirsky's views were the exact opposite. 'One cannot absolutely change one's political colour just to give one's mother pleasure', Benckendorff commented. Sviatopolk-Mirsky was reluctant to accept the appointment. 'You must fulfill my son's wish; if you do, I will give you a kiss', Dagmar reputedly told the embarrassed prince.[5] Sviatopolk-Mirsky repealed some of his predecessor's more unpopular measures but when he proposed a programme of political reform Nicholas drove to Gatchina for a long talk with his mother. The proposed reforms remained only vague promises but the prince stayed in office because Nicholas refused to allow him to resign.

*

Although all Court functions had been cancelled because of the war, on the Feast of Epiphany, 6th/19th January 1905, the Blessing of the Waters took place as usual. After a service in the Winter Palace church Dagmar made her way to one of the rooms overlooking the river, while the clergy, singing anthems and carrying lighted tapers, led the Emperor and the Grand Dukes down the Jordan Staircase and out onto the frozen Neva. From the window Dagmar could clearly see the covered dais on the ice where the clergy stood, their jewelled mitres sparkling in the clear frosty light. After prayers the Metropolitan dipped the cross through a hole in the ice three times, as a salute sounded from the SS Peter & Paul Fortress. One after another the guns fired their blank shots. Suddenly one of the windows near Dagmar shattered under the impact of a live shell. For a moment confusion reigned. As she stood there, with splinters of glass all over her dress and shoes, Dagmar could see police and soldiers running everywhere and it was some moments before she knew that the Tsar was unhurt.

Nicholas believed that terrorists had infiltrated the fortress and placed live shells in some of the guns. The ministers and Court officials were thrown into a panic. Only Dagmar kept her head. Remaining outwardly calm she insisted on appearing in public to show that everything was normal. Three days later a spark ignited the revolution.

A strike at the Putilov metal works soon spread and thousands of disillusioned and dissatisfied workers roamed the streets. Then a rather unlikely leader appeared. Father George Gapon, a thirty-two-year-old priest, persuaded the people to follow him on a peaceful march to the Winter Palace, where he would present the Tsar with a petition stating their demands for a minumum wage and an eight hour day. Their 'Little Father' would hear them and deliver them from their oppressors. The day chosen was Sunday, 22nd January.

Marches were illegal, so Gapon informed the authorities. Although they were aware that he had contacts in the revolutionary movement they took no action. Then, belatedly, afraid of serious riots, the police report was taken to the Tsar. The police were in a panic. They had tried to arrest Gapon but were unable to find him.

On Saturday Nicholas asked his mother to leave for Gatchina immediately. Dagmar refused. She had stayed in the capital so far, showing herself in public and trying to behave normally; she would not run away now. Only when the Emperor gave her a positive command did she reluctantly consent – but not without first trying to convince him to face the crowd at the Winter Palace. His presence would calm them, they would present their petition and return peacefully to their homes. All her entreaties were in vain.

Dagmar spent Sunday with Nicholas and his family at Tsarskoe Selo. Meanwhile, five columns of marchers swept down St Petersburg's wide boulevards towards Winter Palace Square carrying icons, banners and portraits of the Emperor, singing hymns and 'God Save the Tsar'. At their head was Father Gapon. Extra police and troops had been drafted in but the march was peaceful. As they neared the Winter Palace their way was barred by cordons of police and troops. Still they pressed on, determined to see their Tsar, unaware that he was not even in the capital. Suddenly the soldiers opened fire straight into the crowd. Men, women and children fell to the ground, their blood staining the snow. The official number of dead was two hundred but unofficial estimates put the figure as high as a thousand. The Imperial family were stunned. Afraid of what might happen next Nicholas insisted that Dagmar remain overnight.

The day was soon known as 'Bloody Sunday'. No longer was the Tsar one with his people, their 'Little Father'. He was now 'Nicholas the Bloody'. It was the beginning of a year of terror.

*

By the end of January nearly half a million workers were on strike. Prince Sviatopolk-Mirsky was replaced by Alexander Bulygin, General Trepov was appointed Military Governor of St Petersburg and the city was put under martial law. An uneasy peace reigned. Nicholas spoke about 'conciliating action' and informed Grand Duke Sergei that a more liberal policy should be followed. Sergei, an unpopular reactionary, resigned his post as Governor General of Moscow. A few days later he was assassinated.

The bomb was thrown as his carriage was leaving the Kremlin. The explosion was so fierce that little remained of Sergei. One finger, a ring still on it, was later found on the roof of the Arsenal. Dagmar described his murder as 'dreadful'. She immediately sent a sympathetic telegram to his niece Marie, who had been under Sergei and Ella's guardianship since the morganatic marriage of her father Grand Duke Paul:

Think so much of you and dear Dimitri in your terrible loss of beloved Uncle Serge[.] God bless you both[.] Loving Kisses Gr. Aunt Minny.[6]

Few members of the Imperial family attended the funeral, the police could not guarantee their safety. Shortly afterwards the Dowager Empress, Grand Duke Vladimir and General Trepov all received letters telling them they had been 'condemned to death'.[6a]

Sergei's death changed Ella completely. Gradually she sold or gave away most of her possessions, even her wedding ring. In 1910, after her nephew Dimitri had joined the army and his sister Marie had married Prince William of Sweden, she built the convent of SS Martha & Mary in Moscow and became its Abbess. From that time, she devoted her life to the care of the sick and needy. Never again did she appear in St Petersburg's ball-rooms and at family weddings she left immediately after the service.

Still disaster followed disaster. In February the Russian army was routed at Mukden, with a loss of 90,000 men. Although in higher circles there was a lack of confidence in General Kuropatkin's conduct of the war, he was so popular with the people that his removal seemed unwise. Never-theless, after the defeat at Mukden he was replaced. Hearing a rumour that Grand Duke Nicholas Nicholaievitch was to be appointed, Dagmar begged the Tsar not to consider it. Although Dagmar wished Kuropatkin's successor the very best of luck, she had sympathy for the dismissed general, who had asked to remain with the army. In government circles it was felt that the Tsar must now take action quickly to save the country from the threat of revolution or imminent defeat by Japan. Those same people were convinced that the Dowager Empress was the only person who could convince her son that this was necessary.

Within a few hours of Sergei's death Baron Osten-Sacken, the Russian Ambassador in Berlin, was received by the Kaiser. Why anyone thought that William would have any influence over the Dowager Empress is unclear but the Ambassador nevertheless persuaded him to write to Dagmar and ask her to urge her son to act. William decided to increase his chances by writing almost identical twenty-two page letters to the Dowager Empress and to the Tsar.

After commenting on the 'terrible events' in Moscow, he proceeded to offer Dagmar his advice in the hope that she would back him up. The Tsar, he said in a 4,000-word letter, had forfeited the support of his people by not going to Moscow on the outbreak of war and by not receiving their petition at the Winter Palace. The only thing to do now was take personal command of his army and go to Moscow where, after praying at St Basil's, he should assemble the nobility and proclaim a *habeas corpus* act and the expansion of the State Council. Then, surrounded by the clergy with the symbols of the Orthodox Church, he should appear on a balcony of the Kremlin before his troops and summon them to battle with the Japanese. Both Nicholas and Dagmar, contemptuous of William's theatricals, merely replied that they were most interested to read his letter.

Russia's most humiliating defeat was still to come. In May, when the Russian and Japanese fleets met in the Straits of Tsushima, the Russian fleet was almost annihilated in less than forty-five minutes. Grand Duke Alexis, Grand Admiral of the Navy, resigned and went to live in Paris.

The defeat sparked off mutinies in the remaining ships of the Baltic and Black Sea fleets. At Odessa, sailors from the *Potemkin* locked up their officers or threw them overboard before hoisting the red flag and heading for Roumania. During the following months strikes and riots erupted all over the country and to Dagmar it seemed like the end of the world.

Dagmar's letters to King Christian were full of complaints about Russia's defeats, sympathy for the wounded and those whose relatives had been killed, hatred of the Japanese and despair about the internal situation of the country. She railed against the humiliation of having the revolutionary movement active in Russia during a time of war and deplored the Russians' lack of patriotism. The Japanese, she said, were patriots to a man which made it all the harder to bear. She fervently prayed for an end to the terrible war so that they would have peace again.

The war had prevented Dagmar from visiting Denmark for her father's birthday in April. As the months ticked by she still hoped to be able to visit him in the autumn, but admitted that the prospects did not look good.

After the disaster of Tsushima, President Roosevelt offered his services as mediator. Nicholas was convinced that his terms would be unacceptable to Japan and peace would therefore be impossible without making large concessions. At the conference in America Russia was represented by Witte, called out of retirement in his country's hour of need. To everyone's surprise, the Japanese gave in on almost every point. Although Russia was forced to leave Korea as a Japanese sphere of influence, surrender Port Arthur and evacuate Manchuria and the southern half of Sakhalin Island, there would be no disarmament and no indemnity. All the Imperial family were surprised by the suddenness of the agreement. A few days later Dagmar told Nicholas to 'cheer up and at least look as if he considered the peace a necessity'.[7] Nicholas put on a brave face and created Witte a Count.

In September a period of relative calm returned to Russia and Dagmar left for Copenhagen. Soon after her arrival, she received a letter from Miechen announcing Cyril's marriage to Ducky, the former Grand Duchess of Hesse.

They had married secretly abroad on 8th October 1905. As no Russian priest was willing to marry them in the face of the Tsar's ban, the ceremony was conducted by the Duchess of Coburg's Private Confessor. Cyril had returned from the Russo-Japanese war something of a hero as the only member of the Imperial family to be wounded in action when the *Petropavlovsk* hit a mine and sank. It was this brush with death, coupled with the birth of the Tsarevitch (pushing Cyril back in the line of succession), which prompted his decision.

Two days later a telegram announced Cyril's imminent return to Tsarskoe Selo. Dagmar was amazed at his audacity. 'How dare he present himself at your home after this action, *knowing perfectly* what awaited him and putting you in this painful position', she thundered to Nicholas. 'It is simply shameful ... Probably Aunt Miechen had the illusion that with *her* son one has to make an exception ...' Nicholas deprived Cyril of his army rank, title, privileges and income. He was ordered to leave Russia within forty-eight hours. Dagmar then received a letter from the Duchess of Coburg, indignant that Nicholas had removed the title of Grand Duke from the man who had married *her* daughter. 'What does Uncle Vladimir say?' Dagmar asked Nicholas.[8]

Vladimir resigned all his posts. He was furious with the Tsar for implying that Victoria Melita, a granddaughter of Tsar Alexander II and the daughter of a Russian Grand Duchess, was an unsuitable wife for his son. Although Nicholas at first stood firm he soon relented and, to mark the Tsarevitch's Name Day in October, he restored Cyril's title. Ducky converted to Orthodoxy just before the birth of their first child. In July 1907 Grand Duke Constantine Constantinovitch recorded in his diary that the Tsar had recognised the marriage and given Cyril's wife the title of Her Imperial Highness Grand Duchess Victoria Feodorovna.

After Dagmar's visit to England in the summer of 1873 political tensions between the two countries made it inadvisable for her to do so again, a situation that continued until the end of the century. Alix visited Russia mainly for urgent family reasons. Therefore, although the sisters corresponded regularly, their meetings usually took place during the family gatherings at Bernsdorff or Fredensborg.

When Dagmar arrived in the autumn of 1905 she also had the pleasure of seeing Thyra and Ernst August for the first time in two years. In October, after Alix had returned to England, Dagmar and Thyra moved to the Amalienborg. Every morning they walked round Copenhagen's shops or visited old friends. Unfortunately, the Duke of Cumberland became bored and declared that pressing business called for their immediate return to Gmunden. Dagmar found his conduct insufferable and she missed Thyra's company.

The Danish Court was becoming increasingly dull, although Dagmar and her sisters refused to admit it. The King was now eighty-seven and life in the Amalienborg continued as it had done for decades. The same tedious receptions, which taxed the ingenuity of foreigners to find a few words of suitable conversation. The same boring dinners with heavy food and the same simple card games played without stakes, the King and his daughters always playing together. The routine was so firmly established that the King's entourage admitted it was impossible to change. During this visit, however, something did happen to enliven the dreary routine – another of Dagmar's relatives was offered a crown.

In June 1905 Norway dissolved the Act of Union with Sweden, proclaimed independence and began to look for a King. Their choice fell on Dagmar's nephew, thirty-three-year-old Prince Charles of Denmark, son of Crown Prince Frederick. In 1896 Charles had married his cousin Princess Maud of Wales and they now had a two-year-old son, Alexander. King Edward VII, who hoped that at least one of his daughters would wear a crown, was anxious for them to accept. Charles and Maud were less enthusiastic but both possessed a strong sense of dynastic duty.

Not until the autumn did Sweden finally recognise Norway's inde-pendence. Even then Prince Charles, aware of the strong republican movement in Norway, insisted on a plebiscite. The result was over-whelmingly in his favour and on 18th November he was unanimously elected by the Norwegian parliament. 'The Norwegian question seems to be settled definitely', Dagmar wrote with a sigh of relief, 'and on Monday next a deputation is expected here to offer the throne of Norway to Charles. This time of indecision has also been very painful and annoying for Charles and Maud, but I think, since the decision has been taken, they are quite pleased though the parting is sure to be very sad. I will see them today; their baby is delightful'.[9]

Dagmar was present at the formal ceremony of acceptance in the throne room of the Amalienborg on 20th November. Charles took the Norwegian name of Haakon VII and his little son became Prince Olav (later King Olav V of Norway).

By October almost the whole of European Russia was in the grip of a paralysing general strike, as disillusioned soldiers drifted back to their homes. Nearly all the adult population of St Petersburg stopped work, demonstrators paraded in the streets waving red banners and revolutionary posters appeared. Central councils – 'Soviets' – were set up in St Petersburg and the workers elected delegates. Soon the demands for higher pay and shorter working hours turned into calls for a constitutional government, then into calls for a republic. The few tentative steps the Tsar had taken towards concessions in the summer had been too few and too late. The general strike was fast turning into revolution.

Dagmar was desperate for news. With postal and telegraph services disrupted she had to rely on reports in the Danish newspapers. The Russian government was paralysed and Nicholas was at Peterhof, only able to reach his capital by sea. Finally, Dagmar sent for the Russian Minister in Copenhagen. Alexander Izvolsky worked his way up the diplomatic ladder to become Russian Minister, a post greatly influenced by Dagmar. He helped his career by marrying Countess Marguerite Toll, daughter of a previous Minister, whose family she knew well. In 1906 Izvolsky became Minister of Foreign Affairs, an appointment he owed to the Dowager Empress.

Dagmar now sent Izvolsky to Russia with a letter. She backed Witte to the hilt and asked Nicholas to grant the country a constitution while there was still time. 'I am sure that the only man who can help you now and be useful is Witte, because he should be well-disposed *now* and besides he certainly is a man of genius, *energetic* and clear sighted'.[10] She also sent her son a personal message, strongly urging moderation. Although her letter arrived too late to influence the Tsar's decision her view was supported by Grand Duke Nicholas Nicholaievitch.

Count Witte urged Nicholas to give the country a constitution and a Duma. With troops patrolling the streets and General Trepov giving orders to relentlessly crush the strike, the streets became ominously quiet. Each side waited for the other to begin. Nicholas toyed with the idea of making Grand Duke Nicholas Nicholaievitch a military dictator but he said that, if this was forced on him, he would shoot himself in the Tsar's presence.

With a heavy heart Nicholas signed the manifesto. On 30th October Russia ceased to be an autocracy, becoming, in the words of the 1906 *Almanach de Gotha*, 'a semi-constitutional monarchy ruled by an autocrat', with Witte as Chairman of the Council of Ministers and Minister of the Interior. There would be an elected parliament with two houses – the State Duma and the State Council – and freedom of conscience, speech, assembly and association.

With the revolution at its height the situation was grave. Pogroms broke out, sailors mutinied at Kronstadt and there were reports of mutinous ships near Yalta. Dagmar had received no letters from Olga or Michael and was concerned about Xenia, who was in the Crimea. 'I have suffered so much and so intensely that I feel at least ten years older in this short time', she wrote. '… It is still hard for me to believe that all this has been happening in Russia … I am sorry for Witte, too. He has his measure of terrible difficulties, the more so as he did not expect them to be so great – it is essential for you to show him all your confidence now, and to let him act according to his programme …'[11]

Riots continued all over the country. In Moscow blood flowed in the streets, students and workers manned barricades and the Soviet proclaimed a provisional government. Dagmar could hardly believe what was happening. 'What a disgrace all these strikes are – what a ruin for one and all! No *patriotism* on one side, no *authority* on the other … God Almighty alone can lead us out of this chaos and save our country …'[12] The Guards were brought from St Petersburg to clear the streets with artillery and by the end of the year the strike in Moscow had ended.

Handicapped by bad communications Dagmar was unable to keep abreast of the situation properly and during December she made plans to return home for Christmas. Nicholas was horrified. It was impossible for her to travel without a military escort, which he was unable to provide. Nevertheless, Dagmar was upset when he begged her not to return.

It was the first Christmas she had spent in Denmark for many years. 'It is sad we had to be parted. I am delighted by your beautiful presents – the little Christmas Tree is really too attractive …' Passing on her good wishes for the New Year she added fervently, 'let us thank God that this year of nightmares is coming to an end and hope that with His help the new one will be a little brighter and give us peace at home and free our poor country from the clutches of the spirit of evil!'[13]

That Christmas was King Christian's last. On 29th January he received a ninety-year-old former actress, to whom he chatted for more than an hour. At lunch the King brushed aside all notions that he might feel tired and, to prove his point, danced a few steps round the room with his daughter. Then, declining help, he went into the adjoining room to fetch a cigar. When he returned, the cigar unlit, Dagmar noticed his sudden pallor and the beads of sweat on his forehead and immediately summoned the doctor. The King was still able to joke with Waldemar and when Dagmar asked if she should cancel dinner he would not hear of it.

She sat by the bed holding his hand until he fell asleep. Still uneasy, she left the room to scribble a note to Freddie. As Dagmar returned, King Christian gave two short sighs before he died.

'Thank God, I was *here* with him up to the last minute', she wrote later.

'I thank God for this happiness'.[14] Thyra returned immediately, followed by Alix, Xenia, Michael and Olga but the situation in Russia was still too serious for Nicholas to leave. Silent crowds gathered outside Roskilde Cathedral, where the new King Frederick VIII and his wife Queen Louise led the Royal family in mourning.

By the time Dagmar returned to Russia she had been away for nearly six months.

*

A few days before the state opening of the Duma, Dagmar was stunned to learn that Nicholas had dismissed Witte. He was replaced by Count Ivan Goremykin, a nonentity almost seventy years old. To show her disgust (and her support for Witte) she immediately invited the fallen minister to lunch.

The magnificent white and gold St George's Hall in the Winter Palace had seen many great functions but it had undoubtedly never witnessed anything like the cross-section of people who assembled on 10th May 1906. Down one side of the long room were ministers, courtiers, the nobility and the military, all in full-dress uniform. On the other side were the newly-elected representatives of the Duma in drab suits, shabby caftans, national costumes or loose blouses.

At one o'clock the Master of Ceremonies struck the floor with his wand of office and, preceded by pages bearing the Imperial regalia, the Imperial family entered the hall to the strains of the National Anthem. Although the men were resplendent in uniform and the ladies wore full Court dress most of them shared Sandro's view that 'deep mourning would have been more appropriate'.[15]

Away from her liberal Danish relatives Dagmar had second thoughts about the Duma and she had tried to find out whether Nicholas was justified in making concessions. Standing near the throne, in a white dress edged with Russian sable, she was 'extremely nervous and agitated', an eye-witness recalled. 'Her eyes were red, and she kept putting up her handkerchief as if to wipe away tears. She ... keenly observed the assembly, as if trying to read their countenances ... From time to time she turned to her chamberlain-in-waiting and asked him some questions evidently relating to the identity of the various deputies. The Socialist group attracted her ... particularly, and she watched it the whole time ... with something akin to anxiety in her lovely dark eyes ... Her countenance was perfectly dignified, and yet a whole tragedy lurked in her figure as it bent under the blessing of the Metropolitan'.[16] After the Te Deum, Nicholas, robed and crowned, read the inaugural speech from Peter the Great's silver throne. Only his trembling hands betrayed his feelings.

'... but how many indescribable emotions!' Dagmar wrote to Sidonie L'Escaille. 'I was crushed for several days afterwards. You are right to be surprised by the violent ... speeches ... in the ... Tauride Palace but one cannot expect anything else after the elections – the socialist democrats are *certainly* not the *real* representatives of the country ... Let's hope something good will come out of this, actually it does not look like it unfortunately'.[17]

Speaking to Vladimir Kokovtsov, the Minister of Finance, about the look of hatred on some of the men's faces, Dagmar wondered if it would be possible to collaborate with the Duma deputies. Kokovtsov feared that the Tsar would have to introduce a full parliamentary system or 'dissolve the Duma and prepare new electoral laws'. 'All this frightens me greatly', Dagmar admitted, 'and I ask myself if we would be able to protect ourselves from new revolutionary outbursts, if we have enough strength to suppress another revolt ... and if Goremykin is indeed the man to be of use at such a moment?'[18]

Her fears were justified. By the summer the situation was again critical. There were disorders all over the Empire, mutinies in the army and navy and fears that, once the harvest had been gathered, a peasant rising would follow. Nicholas was determined to dissolve the Duma.

On 8th July Goremykin was replaced by Peter Arkadyevich Stolypin, who also became Minister of the Interior. The following day troops bolted the doors of the Tauride Palace and posted notices announcing the dissolution of the Duma. The deputies were locked out.

The terrorist attacks continued and Stolypin only escaped death by a miracle when a bomb blew off the front of his house, injuring his children. Dagmar was outraged. 'There can be no peace or safety ... before these monsters are exterminated!', she wrote.[19]

Stolypin soon restored law and order. He gave the peasants the opportunity to withdraw from the communes and then increased the funds in the Peasant Bank, providing easy credit to enable them to buy land to farm and pass on to their children. To make more land available, the Tsar proposed that four million acres of Crown land in the Altai region of Siberia be sold off. Here he came up against opposition from Dagmar. These areas were the Emperor's personal property and were administered by His Majesty's Cabinet. She thought it would be a big mistake to give up even one kopek from these lands, which formed part of the Imperial appanages. 'It is a question of *principle*', she wrote, 'and *all the future* depends on it. The ignorance of the public is so great on this subject, that people know neither the origin nor the provenance of these lands and assets, the basis of the Emperor's private fortune, [which] can neither be touched nor discussed. They are of no concern to anyone other than the

Emperor. However, we must ensure that this is made clear to everyone'.[20] Despite her protest the Tsar had his way.

Dagmar supported Stolypin but when injustice came to her notice she was quick to act. When he tried to close some Polish schools on the pretext that the Catholic nuns who ran them were spreading anti-Russian propaganda, she demanded an explanation. Faced with her anger he backed down. Never one to bear a grudge she recognised the worth of a good man.

So successful were Stolypin's land reforms that the revolutionaries despaired. After 1906, when the strikes and disturbances abated under the country's new prosperity, the revolutionary movement almost ground to a halt. By 1911 even Lenin was despondent. 'I do not expect to live to see the revolution', he said many times during these years.[21]

CHAPTER 17

East, West, Home is Best

E very day the Dowager Empress scanned a large ornate list of the entertainments taking place in St Petersburg that evening. Although many of her social engagements were planned well in advance, she often decided to attend a party or theatre performance that day and expected to be accompanied by the reluctant Olga, who was given no choice in the matter.

Dagmar liked company and frequently held small, informal lunches at the Anitchkov. During the afternoon she visited hospitals or called on friends. In winter her sleigh was a familiar sight as it skimmed along the Nevsky Prospekt drawn by a pair of shiny black horses, with her Cossack bodyguards standing on the back. As she passed, swathed in furs to keep out the biting cold, gentlemen respectfully raised their fur caps.

One of the houses she frequently visited was the Youssoupov Palace on the Moika Canal, the home of her close friend Princess Zenaide Youssoupov. Zenaide was her father's sole heiress, and he was deeply disappointed when she married a Guards officer, Count Soumarokoff-Elston who, according to the custom of the time, then became Prince Youssoupov. They had two sons, Nicholas and Felix. The Youssoupovs were rumoured to be wealthier than the Romanovs. Some of their furniture had belonged to Marie Antoinette and one of the rock crystal chandeliers came from Mme de Pompadour's boudoir. Grand Duchess Olga always remembered their sumptuous palaces filled with over 5,000 paintings and objets d'art, where the tables were strewn with rock crystal bowls overflowing with uncut sapphires, emeralds and opals.

Dagmar often visited friends unexpectedly. When Prince Bariatinsky's son died she decided to call and express her sympathy. Finding the servants were at lunch she told the porter she could find her own way upstairs. The only person she met, an old serving lady, failed to recognise her. The family were surprised when the Dowager Empress suddenly appeared in their sitting room.

She greatly enjoyed the company of Princess Paskevitch. The Princess, whose husband disapproved of Alexander II's liaison with Catherine Dolgoruky, had closed her doors to the Romanovs with the exception of Dagmar. No other member of the Imperial family ever crossed the threshold of her large house on the Quai. When the revolution came, the Princess, eighty-one years old and almost blind, refused to leave the capital.

Alone among the Danish Royal family Dagmar was fond of reading and her library was full of the beautifully bound books she loved to collect. She read Taine's *Ancien Régime* and memoirs such as those of Countess Golovin and the former German Chancellor, Prince Chlodwig Hohenlohe, which she especially enjoyed. 'I can well understand William's [the Kaiser] rage and fury', she commented. 'It must be *too* annoying for him – how tactless and impertinent of the Prince to have them published – but for *me* very interesting and amusing'.[1] When Prince Andronnikov published his memoirs, in which he wittily discussed his enemies, Dagmar was among the many members of the Court who found his revelations highly entertaining.

Almost every day she received ministers, courtiers, provincial governors and other prominent men. Sometimes the visitors were more humble, like the courier who brought some melons and found when he arrived that they were rotten inside. Dagmar nevertheless granted him an audience, knowing how proud he would feel when he returned home and said he had spoken to the Dowager Empress.

She still had great influence over Court positions. When one of the Tsar's ministers tried to have his daughter appointed lady-in-waiting to the young Empress he ran up against the opposition of Dagmar, whose consent was necessary. For nearly a year she stubbornly refused to agree and finally consented only after Nicholas persisted. The Head of the Court Chancellery, Mossolov, was frequently asked to send an order or decoration to Gatchina for the Dowager Empress to award.

'Quite openly my mother enjoyed being the first lady in the Empire', recalled Olga.[2] She inspired devotion and dedication in her staff and, both at home and abroad, they all came to her with their problems.

To her children Dagmar was 'Motherdear', to her grandchildren she was 'Amama' but to the Russian people she was '*Matoushka* Tsaritza', 'Our *Matoushka*', or 'Our Empress Mother'.[3]

Dagmar's personal security was in the hands of the Combined Battalion of the Guard, formed by Alexander III in 1883. She was always on the move. As her private train rolled across Europe, there was an official welcome wherever it stopped. At her destination she was greeted by a member of a Royal family or the President of a republic, surrounded by ministers immaculately attired in frock coats and top hats. Her arrival always caused a stir, recalled a Russian diplomat. '[They] looked as if they had come from the North Pole. The Empress Dowager in an old-fashioned fur coat, the lady-in-waiting in a pre-historic coat, rushing about and looking for the Empress Dowager's dog, which had disappeared at the last moment – it was so typically Russian'.⁴

She travelled with a retinue of two hundred people. Servants, body-guards, maids, ladies-in-waiting all poured from the train as the fascinated crowd stood and stared. While Dagmar coped with the official welcome and was driven away, piles of luggage were unloaded and despatched to their destination. There were no tiresome problems about money. Her expenses were paid from funds deposited in banks all over Western Europe.

While abroad, the members of her suite lost no time in stocking up with cigarettes and other goods forbidden by Court regulations, which they then smuggled into Russia. The Minister of the Court, annoyed by this flagrant infringement, once had all the baggage searched and imposed fines – but he bargained without the Dowager Empress. Smiling, she graciously informed him that she would pay all the fines from her own personal account. As this account was his responsibility, he was forced to pay all the fines he had imposed!

Even the threat of terrorism was not a deterrent. In 1908 her armed escort challenged three men who attempted to enter her railway carriage. One of the men was arrested after shooting a soldier but his accomplices escaped. Dagmar still insisted on driving through St Petersburg with only a lady-in-waiting in attendance.

Her most frequent journeys abroad were to Denmark on the *Polar Star*. A religious service, accompanied by the yacht's own choir and military band, was held on board before the thirty-six to forty-four hour journey. Dagmar usually invited the officers to dinner and, in return, she was entertained in the wardroom. She remembered any special anniversaries, never omitted to visit the sick in the ship's infirmary and always gave the men a watch and some money when they left the Marine Guard.

Shortly after their father's funeral Dagmar and Alexandra heard that the widow of Legations Counsellor Bruun was selling his property at Strand-vejen, near Klampenborg. Approached by a small village road, 'Hvidøre' ('White Gravel') was a white Italian-style villa with a clock tower, loggia and caryatids. There were two acres of formal gardens full of roses, a kitchen garden with apples, pears and fruit trees and, across the road, another garden and a private beach, from which the property took its name. They asked their father's Adjutant, Rørdam, to make enquiries. The asking price, which the sisters felt was 'absurd', was 300,000 kroner. Rørdam offered 280,000 kroner in cash, which Bruun's lawyer could not resist; the Deed of Conveyance was dated 1st March 1906.[5]

Dagmar and Alix inspected the villa from cellar to attic and toured the gardener's house, the stables and the greenhouses. They discussed the possiblility of connecting the beach to the main gardens by a tunnel. Although permission would be needed it was unlikely to be refused to the King's sisters.

When they returned in September the alterations had begun. Alexandra went ashore from her yacht every day to buy things for the house and supervise the work. Dagmar was confined to bed for nine days with lumbago, something which would plague her for the rest of her life. By the time Alix left, Dagmar was up and about. 'We have been twice in our house at Hvidøre … The view is superb … a delightful garden, many flowers, a marvel. The house is not yet completely fitted out, we have chosen different fabrics for the rooms and I think that it will be quite charming and intimate'.[6] The furniture was ordered from Warings in London and Alix brought over a gardener and an interior decorator. The result resembled an English country house.

From the imposing white and gold hall a double staircase rose to the first floor. A large drawing room led into the study, where they each had their own desk and bookcases. Then came the Garden Room where they often took their meals; it was full of potted palms and trellis-work, with glass doors overlooking the sea. They each had their own drawing room. Electric lights were put in and five bathrooms were installed, all with hot and cold running water. Alix dismissed suggestions that they would freeze in early spring and late autumn; the fireplaces were replaced by electric heaters. One of the bedrooms was slightly larger than the other so they tossed a coin. Dagmar's was smaller but cozy, decorated in chintz and adorned with icons and sacred pictures; Alexandra's had a small balcony. With their usual thoroughness they ensured the housemaids' rooms were comfortable.

The effect was homely rather than palatial; a clutter of Danish porcelain, family photographs and the memorabilia with which they both liked to be surrounded. Willie bought them a large white and gold antique Bornholm clock which played a hymn tune every hour. To emphasise that Hvidøre was a home and not a palace they had 'East, West, home is best!' engraved over the billiard room fireplace and signed their names underneath. 'What is the use of my four hundred rooms [*sic*] at Gatchina, I never use more than two!' exclaimed Dagmar in a masterly piece of understatement.[7]

When they moved in on 9th September 1907 the guards at the main entrance presented arms and the Russian and British flags were hoisted. Visitors either liked the place or hated it. One described it as an 'enchanted spot' which she wished 'never to leave'; another said he 'had never seen a more ghastly property, there being no privacy ... those on the road could see straight into the windows, while access to the sea could be obtained only by crossing the road'.[8] Bertie found one visit quite enough. Squatting in front of an inadequate electric fire, still wearing his overcoat, he was distinctly unimpressed both with the house and their plans to alter it so that he could stay there. When someone suggested he climb the tower to see the view of Kronborg, he suddenly remembered urgent business in Copenhagen and ordered his car.

Dagmar and Alix were clearly delighted with 'our lovely place here'.[9] The Infanta Eulalia of Spain recorded their almost childish pleasure. She was shown their favourite chairs and their writing tables and the kitchen where Alix made the tea while Dagmar cut the bread and butter. They brought only two servants each and employed the Danish menservants, housemaids and cook who had served their father. Most of the thirty staff lived in the house and a further twelve were lodged in a wooden hut near the gardener's residence. It was all a far cry from Gatchina and Buckingham Palace.

They both loved flowers. Strolling arm-in-arm through the rose gardens, wearing identical straw boaters, they picked fruit from the trees, or walked along the beach collecting pieces of amber.

Only their closest friends and the family were invited. Freddie came from nearby Charlottenlund, Waldemar often cycled over for lunch or dinner accompanied by one of his sons and Willie always visited whenever he was in Denmark. A favourite guest was the Marquis Luis de Soveral, the Portuguese Ambassador to London, who could always be relied upon to keep the company entertained. Although the sisters shared the running costs Soveral made them laugh by declaring, 'The Empress orders and the Queen pays!'[10]

Dagmar always invited officers from the Royal Danish Life Guards to lunch on board the *Polar Star*, a custom which began during Sasha's lifetime. One year she presented Colonel Lemvigh with a large oil painting by Valentin Serov, showing Alexander III in the Guards' scarlet state uniform; they gave her a bronze statue of a guardsman in ceremonial dress. The Empress was very popular with the officers. Many of her letters to them are still preserved and she often visited the regiments in camp. In 1908 Dagmar commissioned a large silver punchbowl from Fabergé. On the lid was inscribed 'to the beloved Guard on the occasion of its 250th anniversary 1908'. She also became an honorary member of the Danish Guards Association, an organisation for ex-servicemen founded in 1885.[11] On the Guards' birthday in September, the band always played at Hvidøre.

After her sister had returned home Dagmar was lonely. She played the piano, or strolled down to the guardhouse to talk to the soldiers. On Sundays she dined with the King. Dagmar's visits to Denmark often lasted for as long as two months and, by November, Hvidøre was so cold she was obliged to move to the Amalienborg but it felt empty without her father. Sometimes her uncle Prince Hans of Glucksburg, the last survivor of King Christian's brothers and sisters, joined her for lunch or dinner. Afterwards they played bridge or went to the theatre with other members of the family. Xenia, Sandro and their children stayed at Hvidøre and often Dagmar brought her nephew Prince Christopher of Greece and her granddaughter Irina. Michael, Olga and the King and Queen of Norway were other frequent guests.

The purchase of Hvidøre was misunderstood by the English newspapers, who reported that the Tsar had bought a 'secret villa' in Denmark. He was planning to abdicate in favour of a regency under his brother Grand Duke Michael and retire there with his family.

*

Dagmar's attitude to divorce remained implacable. In 1907 Nicholas permitted his cousin Grand Duke Nicholas Nicholaievitch ('Nicholasha') to marry Anastasia of Montenegro. Stana was not only the divorced wife of the Tsar's cousin, the Duke of Leuchtenberg, but Nicholasha's sister-in-law. His brother Grand Duke Peter was married to Stana's sister Militza. Dagmar was shocked. She took some tranquillizing drops to calm herself down and poured out her surprise and displeasure at the unexpected news in a letter to the Tsar.

Misha was also causing more problems. In 1905 he fell in love with his sister Olga's thirty-year-old lady-in-waiting Alexandrina Kossikovsky ('Dina'). Dina was a commoner but, backed by her ambitious father, she wanted nothing less than marriage. In July 1906 Michael formally wrote to ask his brother's permission. Although Michael realised there was a possibility that he might have to be regent until his nephew was sixteen, he did not know that Alexis had haemophilia and might die at any time. If that happened, Michael, or his future children, would be called upon to succeed to the throne.

Michael had already spoken to Dagmar, who hoped the affair with Dina would run its course. Although Dagmar desperately desired her son's happiness she was torn between a mother's love and sorrow at his dereliction of duty. 'It is unbearable to see him in such distress!' she wrote to Nicholas. 'Whatever I say to him he explains away in his own way, and keeps on insisting he has no right to act otherwise. I try appealing to his sense of duty to his country, his obligations ... All he says is that that has nothing to do with the case'.[12]

Dagmar, at a loss what to do, suggested they look at the family laws. Nicholas was firm. He informed Michael that a morganatic marriage would mean removal from the army and banishment. Michael replied that, as his mother would not help, he would do what he wanted anyway. He refused to discuss the matter further. This upset Dagmar. She promptly dismissed Dina from her post and told her it would be best if she lived abroad.

Dagmar then took Michael off to Denmark. Realising that the only answer was to find him a suitable royal wife she and Alix put their heads together and soon found an acceptable candidate. On 24th September 1906 the Duke of Connaught was bewildered to read in the newspapers that his twenty-year-old daughter Princess Patricia ('Patsy') was betrothed to Grand Duke Michael Alexandrovitch. Later that day an embarrassed Buckingham Palace official was forced to issue a denial. The wishful thinking of the Queen and the Empress had been misinterpreted by a Russian Court official and picked up by a senior Reuters correspondent.

Bemused, Dagmar returned to Russia, saying nothing – but at least Dina was out of the way. Or so she thought. In the spring of 1907 the Dowager Empress was 'furious' when she was informed that Dina had returned to St Petersburg. The incredulous Imperial family then heard that Michael had found a country priest who was willing to conduct a secret marriage for a substantial payment. Dina was now forbidden to leave the capital and orders were given that if Michael left the country she must not be allowed to follow. There was a 'tempestuous scene', during which Dagmar forbade Michael to go to the capital to see Dina. He defied her, which left Dagmar 'terribly upset'. Although they were reconciled the next day, things soon became 'unbearable' again.[13]

Undeterred, Michael left for Sorrento with his sister Olga. Meanwhile, in defiance of the Tsar's orders, Dina took a train to Odessa, intending to go by sea to Naples and marry Michael in Italy. She was stopped by the Okhrana and taken back to the capital. Michael blamed his mother and Nicholas. He then proceeded to enjoy his holiday in Italy. When he joined Dagmar in Denmark she was surprised to find his mood had improved and he promised not to do anything against the Imperial laws. To Dagmar's relief it seemed that he had given up. Dina left for England, blaming the Dowager Empress all the way.

Michael soon forgot Dina and he was not interested in Patsy. In December 1907, in the Blue Cuirassiers' Riding School at Gatchina, he was introduced to the beautiful bride of a fellow officer. Her name was Natasha Wulfert.

Nathalie Sergeyevna Sheremetevskaya ('Natasha'), the daughter of a Moscow lawyer, was born in 1880. At the age of twenty-one she married

Sergei Mamantov and they had a daughter, 'Tata'. Soon bored, she divorced him to marry Lieutenant Vladimir Wulfert of the Blue Cuirassiers and went to live at Gatchina where his regiment was stationed. Now twenty-seven she was an extremely beautiful woman who quickly attracted a host of admirers but when she was presented to Grand Duke Michael, her husband's commander, her effect on him was electrifying.

Michael fell in love with Natasha on the spot and he soon became a frequent visitor to the Wulferts' apartment. Wulfert did not object and the three of them became a familier sight around Gatchina.

In August 1908 Dagmar took Michael to Denmark and Norway. She was still worried about Dina. Although letters between Michael and Dina were read by the Okhrana, he was also writing to Mme Wulfert and his seemingly innocent letters to her were ignored. While Dagmar remained at Hvidøre, Michael went to England with his Aunt Alix.

Dagmar dreaded Michael visiting England, in case Dina tried to spoil their plans to find him a suitable wife. Nicholas was also worried but, after speaking to her sister, Dagmar was able to reassure him. 'I had a talk with Aunt Alix about it and she promised they would never let him go out alone and that at any rate they would stay only three days in London and then go to Sandringham'.[14]

Dagmar and Alix had still not given up hope of marrying Michael to Princess Patricia of Connaught and when they set off for Sandringham Patsy was among the party. Despite Queen Alexandra's endeavours to throw them together, nothing happened and Michael returned to Russia a free man.

By the autumn, although Michael and Natasha were not yet lovers, they were clearly more than friends. The affair was now causing concern in the regiment, whose Colonel-in-Chief was the Dowager Empress. 'Les petits bleus de Sa Majeste' was the nickname given to the Blue Cuirassiers by the other Guards, as the Dowager Empress took a great interest in 'her' regiment. She attended their Church services, visited the hospital and often dropped in to the barracks.[15] However, because Wulfert had not made any formal complaint about the Grand Duke's attentions to his wife, the regimental commander could do nothing. As Michael and Natasha fell more deeply in love the situation soon became impossible.

The crisis came in June 1909. By now Wulfert found Michael's conduct intolerable. After a particularly violent scene, Natasha declined to share her husband's bed and took Tata off to Switzerland. When she refused to return, Wulfert promptly challenged Michael to a duel.

The matter then came to the ears of the Tsar and the Dowager Empress, who promptly showed her displeasure by cancelling her visits to the regiment. Within two days Michael was removed from the Blue Cuirassiers and sent to far-away Orel as Colonel of the Chernigov Hussars, a cavalry regiment. Wulfert was forced to resign from the regiment for misconduct. The duel did not take place.

News of the affair was now all round Gatchina and the scandal was immense. In August Dagmar took Michael to Denmark. She did not know that Natasha was staying at the exclusive Hotel d'Angleterre in the centre of Copenhagen and that Michael was slipping off to visit her at every available opportunity.

Michael had promised his brother that he would not meet Natasha in Orel, Gatchina, or his own estate Brasova. When Natasha returned to Russia in the autumn they therefore set up home together in Moscow, despite the efforts of Dagmar and Nicholas to keep them apart. Michael spent as much time with Natasha as his regimental duties would allow. In December 1909 Natasha discovered she was pregnant.

Michael was now concerned, as the baby would legally be Wulfert's child. In the spring of 1910 he asked his brother to speed up Natasha's divorce. He assured both Dagmar and Nicholas that there were no intentions of marriage.

On 6th August 1910 Natasha gave birth to Michael's son, George. She was still married and the child was legally George Vladimirovitch Wulfert. Although he was the grandson of a Tsar, George was a commoner and there were no godparents from the Imperial family. In November Natasha was finally divorced (the decree was backdated) and Wulfert relinquished paternity for a payment of 200,000 roubles. George's birth certificate was 'doctored' and Nicholas gave him the name of George Michaelovitch Brasov, but he was not given a title. Dagmar now urged Nicholas to take a more lenient line with his only surviving brother and, in May 1911, Nicholas granted Natasha the right to use the surname Brasova. He also agreed that she could stay at Michael's Brasova estate seventy miles from Orel, which he had inherited from Georgie in 1899.

At the end of 1911 Michael and Natasha went on holiday to Europe. All Russia's Embassies and Consulates were warned that the Grand Duke might try to marry his mistress abroad and was to be stopped. At about that time, despite his wish to remain quietly in Orel, Michael was appointed Colonel and Commander of the Chevalier Guards. When he took up his appointment in the new year he insisted that Natasha return with him to St Petersburg. Dagmar was also Colonel-in-Chief of this regiment and she refused to let him live at the Anitchkov. Michael moved to rooms at the regimental headquarters, although he was more often to be found in the apartment of his mistress and their son. Society ostracised Natasha. No-one in the regiment dared to risk offending the Dowager

Empress by receiving her, or even nodding to her in the street. When Michael visited his mother, he naturally came alone.

*

Dagmar was now spending more and more time away from Russia. In the summer of 1907 she joined Xenia and her family in Biarritz. After the Russo-Japanese war Sandro became commander of the new torpedo boat H.I.M.S. *Almaz*. Their children – Irina, Andrei, Feodor, Nikita, Dimitri and Rostislav – became an endless source of delight to their grandmother. By day they all toured the countryside in Sandro's Delauney-Belleville; in the evenings there were parties. Xenia and Sandro were delighted at the way Dagmar mixed with their friends and was ready to join in anything. 'I do not think even King Edward could have outdone my mother-in-law in willingness to participate in a bit of fun', wrote Sandro, who was devoted to her. 'Although I called her "mother" and was well aware of her age I considered her as my pal ... when it came to going out to a party ...'[16] They returned to Gatchina in time for the birth of Xenia's last child, Vassili, in July. By now Sandro had become infatuated with another woman and, incredibly, Xenia and the woman's husband also fell in love. Soon rumours of Xenia and Sandro's impending divorce were rife.

On her way home from Biarritz Dagmar paid her first visit to Cartier's establishment in Paris. Louis Cartier had heard of the Dowager Empress' love of jewels and he tried to tempt her by bringing out case after case of his most beautiful and expensive pieces. Other members of the Imperial family, including Xenia, had patronised Cartier for several years but Dagmar's only contact had been the cases sent to Gatchina every Christmas for her to select some gifts. Although on this first visit she purchased only two hard-stone figures of rabbits and two tie-pins, she was clearly impressed and was delighted to learn that Cartier's first exhibition in Russia was to be held that Christmas. Dagmar only made a few minor purchases and never became a great patron of Cartier to the extent of her sister-in-law Miechen, who remained his most influential client in St Petersburg. Nevertheless, she lost no time in recommending him to Nicholas and, soon afterwards, Cartier was appointed 'Official Purveyor to the Imperial Court'.

To Dagmar's distress relations between Russia and England had been close to breaking-point since the Russo-Japanese war. Antagonised by the Dogger Bank incident, disgusted by the repressions of the Russian autocracy and, after Bloody Sunday, considering Nicholas to be a blood-stained tyrant, the British made no secret of where their sympathies lay. Yet the complicated network of continental alliances also played its part. In 1904 England had become loosely allied to France in the Entente

Cordiale. Now, emerging from years of isolation, England also needed an Entente with Russia to counteract the Triple Alliance of Germany, Austria and Italy.

By 1906 the political climate was beginning to change and in the following spring Dagmar was at last able to visit England again after thirty-four years. 'I must ... tell you *how* happy I am to be back with dear Aunt Alix ...', she wrote exuberantly to Nicholas from Buckingham Palace. One morning they motored down to Windsor, where the crocuses were in bloom. Dagmar was particularly impressed by the castle. 'I have no words to describe *how magnificent* it all is ... Everything is so tastefully and artistically arranged – it makes one's mouth water to see all this magnificence!'[17]

In 1908 Dagmar was back again. She appreciated the freedom London offered her. The King usually left for his annual stay in Biarritz just after the Empress arrived, leaving Queen Alexandra to enjoy herself in her sister's company. They filled their days with excursions to hospitals, orphanages, The National Gallery or the Wallace Collection. Sometimes they walked in the gardens of Hampton Court so that Dagmar could admire the tulips, which always remained among her favourite flowers. In the evenings they attended a dinner or the theatre. They once kept guests at a state banquet waiting while they finished a particularly exciting game of billiards.

Despite massages she had frequent attacks of lumbago. Once, confined to bed at Buckingham Palace, she was feeling particularly low and Alix decided to cheer her up. Sending for their nephew Prince Christopher of Greece she dressed him up in a hideous tartan taffeta dress and feathered bonnet which had belonged to Queen Victoria, stuck a lace parasol in his hand and led him along the corridors. Throwing open the door of her sister's room she solemnly announced him as 'Her Majesty Queen Victoria'. When her nephew entered wearing this ridiculous attire Dagmar laughed so much that her condition deteriorated.

At Sandringham on another occasion she was being wheeled round the grounds in a bath chair when Prince Christopher chivalrously offered to relieve the nurse. After pushing the chair sedately for a few moments temptation overcame him. Coming to the top of a steep incline he gave the chair a hearty shove and sent it hurtling down the slope, only to start mounting the incline again on the other side. To the sound of the Empress' screams the chair then descended the slope backwards again. When he rescued her she was so terrified that she had quite forgotten her lumbago.

In 1907 an Anglo-Russian agreement was signed which formed the basis of a Triple Entente between Russia, France and England. To set the seal on this new alliance it was considered appropriate for King Edward and Queen Alexandra to visit Russia in June 1908. For security reasons they would not set foot on the mainland but anchor in Russian waters at Reval (now Tallin) on the Baltic Coast.

It was stressed both in England and abroad that the visit was a purely family affair and to emphasize this Dagmar was accompanied by her daughter Olga; Alix and Bertie by Princess Victoria ('Toria') and Nicholas and Alicky by their five children. There were also a host of ministers and politicians.

Hardly had the *Victoria and Albert* anchored when, in glorious sunshine, Dagmar, Olga, Nicholas, Alicky and their children stepped aboard from a pinnace. The young Grand Duchesses wore identical white broiderie anglaise dresses and picture hats. The King and the Tsar, each wearing the uniform of the other's army, greeted each other affectionately. Later Bertie, Alix and Toria returned the visit on board the *Standart* where, to the delight of the sailors, the King met them with the traditional greeting in Russian: 'Good morning, my children', to which they replied, 'God Save the King'. Caviar sandwiches were served, along with Kirsch which Sir Frederick Ponsonby thought tasted like boot polish.

At dinner that evening Nicholas, in flawless English, spoke of the close ties which united the two Royal families. Over the next two days, while Stolypin and Izvolsky had talks with the King and his advisers, these ties were reinforced as the Russian and English royalties exchanged visits. Dagmar spent most of her time with Alix.

One evening a choir of Estonians, Germans and Russians sang to entertain the party. Even this proved a security nightmare. Although they were to perform from a boat anchored nearby, the Russians still wanted to strip and search all the singers, including the ladies. The King's Private Secretary, afraid of the reaction in England, finally persuaded the Russians not to search the women. 'After dinner', he reported, 'the two monarchs ... stood on deck while a steamer full of some choral society came and sang weird Russian songs'.[18]

The question of precedence caused complications, as the English rule was to place the monarch's wife first, not the dowager. King Edward deftly avoided one difficult situation. Realising that by offering his arm to one Empress the other would be relegated to third place behind the Tsar and Queen Alexandra (and that their barely concealed hostility might then come to the surface) he acted quickly. Taking an Empress on each arm and telling them jokingly to keep in step, he led them both in to dinner.

On the last evening there was a lively dance on the deck of the *Standart*. The next morning the *Victoria and Albert* sailed for home. Decorations had been exchanged, Nicholas was created an Admiral of the

British Fleet and the King was made an Admiral of the Russian Navy.
One more step had been taken towards Dagmar's dream of an alliance.

*

In 1908, while Dagmar was staying at Buckingham Palace, the Balkans
threatened to explode again and Russia tottered on the brink of war.

In October, without warning, Austria annexed Bosnia and Herzegovina
which, although nominally still under Turkish suzerainty, had been under
Austrian administration since the Congress of Berlin in 1878. Serbia (who
had hoped to rule the two provinces as a South Slav State with the
backing of Russia) was furious. The question now was would Russia back
Serbia in a war against Austria, who had long been Russia's own rival in
the Balkans?

The Austrian Foreign Minister, Baron Aehrenthal, thought not. The
previous month he had come to a private agreement with the Russian
Foreign Minister, Izvolsky. Austria would support Russia's bid to have
the Bosphorus opened to Russian warships and provide an outlet to the
Mediterranean, in return for support for the annexation. He thought the
Tsar would be unwilling to risk another revolution by going to war and
he felt he could safely ignore his conditional promise to Izvolsky about
the Straits.

For six months the peace of Europe was threatened. 'One can only hope
that we shall not be dragged into a war', Dagmar wrote from London, 'it
is just what these "cochons" desire!'[19]

To the Tsar's embarrassment Emperor Franz Joseph sent him proof that
Alexander II had agreed to a future possible annexation of the two
provinces, a fact unknown to Nicholas. By early 1909 there were fears
that Austria would annexe the Serbian capital, Belgrade. Finally, informed
that Germany was ready to mobilize, Russia backed down. Hatred and
mistrust of Germany grew in the Tsar's mind and Dagmar encouraged it.
'The role Germany has played in this crisis is odious and disgusting. Here
we all agree about that and quite understand we had no choice in the
matter'.[20]

In Russia the cry went up for Izvolsky's resignation and Dagmar
supported Nicholas' refusal to let him go, believing his dismissal would
be classed as another triumph for Austria and Germany. 'The papers say
Izvolsky is going on a holiday. I hope you will not actually let him go, at
this moment it would be more than dangerous. Everybody here says so.
I am sending you a note sent to me by Benckendorff [the Russian Ambas-
sador] in which he says the same. I thought it would be good for you to
read the opinion of others on this great German intrigue which makes the
whole world indignant and with good reason'.[21]

When Nicholas visited the German Emperor at Potsdam, Dagmar was grudgingly forced to agree that such visits were a political necessity; but, after more than forty years, the wounds of Schleswig-Holstein had still not healed. The Kiel Canal now ran through territory that had once belonged to Denmark, although Freddie had managed to obtain more lenient treatment for the Danes living in the Duchies. When Dagmar heard that Empress Augusta had been appointed Colonel-in-Chief of Nixa's old regiment, the Grodno Hussars, it was too much. 'I could not sleep for two nights, I was so upset', she wrote. 'Uncle Nixi's splendid regiment and suddenly this foreign Empress butting in! It was too much for my feelings and I am very very sorry ... I hope never to see her in that uniform'.[22]

*

In the spring of 1909, Dagmar was delighted when Alix and Bertie asked her to join them on their spring cruise to the Mediterranean. The first stop was Malta where the King's brother, the Duke of Connaught, was High Commissioner. 'I liked Malta so much', Dagmar wrote to Nicholas, 'above all St Antonio [the Duke's residence]'. During their four-day unofficial stay they opened the new Connaught Hospital at Mdina and visited the cathedral.[23]

They sailed on to Catania, Mount Etna and Palermo, where Dagmar admired the groves of orange and lemon trees. At Baia King Victor Emmanuel III and Queen Elena of Italy came on board. Elena was one of the Montenegrin princesses who had been educated in Russia and knew Dagmar well. They also paid a poignant visit to the Duchess of Aosta at Castellammare. This was the same Hélene who Dagmar had wanted as a bride for Nicholas. 'She is terribly thin and feels very ill, poor thing', Dagmar told her son. 'She is always coughing, always feels cold, does not even find Naples warm enough'.[24] He was doubtless left wondering how she would have fared in the bitterly cold Russian winters.

They went up Mount Vesuvius, and also explored the ruined forum at Pompeii. To Dagmar's disappointment rough seas prevented them from landing at Capri. When Bertie returned to England, Alix and Dagmar travelled on to Corfu.

Holidays in Greece were always relaxed and easy-going. Corfu Palace was only used for official entertaining. Willie and Olga preferred their villa 'Mon Repos', where etiquette was almost non-existent. It had been built in 1832 by the British Governor but it had neither electricity nor heating. Water had to be heated on a stove and carried to the bathrooms. Dagmar and Alix spent most of their time outside taking tea under striped awnings and wandering among the orange trees, cypresses and magnolias which grew in abundance in the idyllic garden.

After spending two delightful weeks in the company of their favourite brother the holiday ended on 19th May, when the *Victoria and Albert* anchored opposite the Doge's Palace in Venice. They went shopping, sightseeing and took the obligatory ride in a gondola before returning to their respective homes.

*

A series of family deaths hit Dagmar very hard during these years.

In November 1908 her favourite brother-in-law Alexis died of pneumonia in Paris, where he had lived since his resignation from the navy after Tsushima. The Tsar permitted Cyril to return to Russia for his uncle's funeral.

It was just in time. Three months later Grand Duke Vladimir died suddenly at his St Petersburg palace after a cerebral haemorrhage. Shortly before his death, with her eye on her sons' future, Miechen had finally converted to Orthodoxy.

In December Dagmar learned with deep regret of the death of her old friend Grand Duke Michael Nicholaievitch in Cannes. Michael had never recovered from his wife's death after a heart attack in 1891, brought on, he believed, by the morganatic marriage and subsequent banishment of their son Michael. The Grand Duke had a stroke in 1903 which left him partially paralysed and he spent the rest of his life in a wheelchair. His body was brought back to Russia for burial in the Cathedral of SS Peter & Paul.

The death of Waldemar's wife Marie on 4th December 1909 at the early age of forty-four was a severe blow. Marie had literally burned herself out.

In the discreet language of the day, Prince Waldemar's 'dearest friend' was his nephew Prince George of Greece. As consolation, Marie threw herself into painting, sculpture, riding and even joined the Copenhagen Fire Brigade. She was especially active in European politics and in her hatred of Germany proved a valuable ally to Dagmar.

Waldemar and his elder sons were en route to the Far East when Marie became ill towards the end of November with a severe cold, which she refused to treat. Soon her face and eyes were swollen, she had a pain in the back and was coughing but when Dagmar visited her she was sitting at her writing desk and still refused to go to bed. Her face was a terrible colour and Dagmar thought her strangely apathetic.[25]

On Dagmar's birthday Marie sent her two youngest children, sixteen-year-old Viggo and fourteen-year-old Margrethe, with a present and an almost incoherent letter. Margrethe said her mother was talking nonsense but was still up and about. Dagmar wrote, imploring her to go to bed at once.

When Dagmar arrived the next afternoon Marie was sitting on the bed and did not recognise her. She thought it was the next morning and was determined to dress and go hunting. With much difficulty she was put back to bed. Dagmar never saw her conscious again, as during the final four days she slept continuously and could only take food through a tube in her neck. The sickness had attacked her brain. As Marie's condition deteriorated Dagmar sent telegrams to her family in France. Her brother Jean came quickly, her mother the Duchesse de Chartres arrived an hour before she died. Waldemar and his sons had started for home as soon as they heard of the seriousness of Marie's condition but they learnt of her death on the way.

During Waldemar's absence and Marie's illness Dagmar had been looking after Viggo and Margrethe. She took them for walks, or over to Sorgenfri to see Frederick and Knud, the sons of Crown Prince Christian. Now she felt great pity for the motherless children.

To her brother Willie, Dagmar described the funeral and the heart-rending moment when the coffin left the Yellow Mansion. All along the route people stood crying in the streets. Dagmar felt particularly sorry for her little niece Margrethe, who cried pitifully the whole way. Willie's son, 'Greek Georgie', had hurried to Denmark as soon as he heard the news and he stayed with the little ones the whole time. George, it seems, was not only a pillar of support to Waldemar but was also popular with his children.

An even more shattering loss, both for the family and the peace of Europe, occurred on 6th May 1910. The sixty-nine-year-old King Edward VII died at Buckingham Palace after an acute attack of bronchitis and a series of heart attacks. Dagmar hurried to London, where she found her sister distraught and confused.

Dagmar and Alix immediately left for the peace and quiet of Sandringham, where they remained virtually incommunicado for several days. Alix could not seem to understand what had happened. 'They took him away from me', was all she could say, over and over again.[26] With Alix in this state of mind Dagmar was able to be of valuable help but, unfortunately, she also stirred up trouble between her sister and the new Queen, Mary.

Since Sasha's death she had become used to the prestige and influence of a Dowager Empress and she could not (or would not) understand that in England things were very different. Alix was now expected to give way to the new Queen Consort but Dagmar, viewing things from her own experience, encouraged her sister to claim precedence. Luckily Queen Mary soon realised what had happened and tactfully gave way for the funeral. She then poured out her feelings to her ninety-year-old aunt the Dowager Duchess of Mecklenburg-Strelitz, born Princess Augusta of

Cambridge, Dagmar's cousin. 'I understand every word, expressed and *not*', Augusta replied, 'and have greatly *feared* what you so gently allude to! May that pernicious influence soon depart!'[27]

King Edward's funeral on 20th May was one of the last great gatherings of the old European order. Nine monarchs and an impressive array of princes followed King George V and the Duke of Connaught behind the coffin; four Queens, led by Queen Alexandra and the Dowager Empress, rode in closed carriages. In St George's Chapel Dagmar had to be prevented from throwing her wreath onto the coffin and jamming the machinery which would lower it into the Chancel Crypt.

'Today was the hardest day of all', Dagmar wrote to Nicholas. '... Poor Aunt Alix bore up wonderfully to the last ... But it is so unspeakably sad here now, his absence is so deeply felt everywhere'.[28] Dagmar stayed in England for three months to help her sister adjust and was always ready with support, comfort or advice. More practical, strong-willed and down-to-earth than Alix, her advice was often sought and it is unfortunate that it was not always wise.

Dagmar encouraged her sister to hang on to as much of the Crown Jewellery as possible, especially the diamond circlet worn at the Opening of Parliament, which should immediately have been handed over to Queen Mary. 'Oh! were I there instead of Minny!!' lamented Augusta, 'More I dare not say'.[29] Dagmar was trying to get Alix to take for herself the kind of power and position she had in Russia but the Dowager Queen remained oblivious.

Alix was also reluctant to move back to Marlborough House. By July Dagmar had persuaded her to go to Sandringham. She was anxious to return home but it was proving impossible to make any arrangements. 'Up to now poor Aunt Alix has refused to hear anything about it, and of course I couldn't leave her quite alone, but when Toria returns from Harrogate I intend to go home ... It is hard to believe so many months have gone by and I have remained here so long'.[30] It was August before she left (to the intense relief of Grand Duchess Augusta and Queen Mary) and by September she was at Hvidøre.

The following year Dagmar was back at Sandringham to be with her sister during the difficult period of the coronation. The Queen Dowager was seldom alone. With the same selfish streak that characterised Dagmar's behaviour towards Olga, Alix seemed determined that Toria would remain as her companion. Although Toria seemed inclined to tolerate it, Olga rebelled when Dagmar tried to treat her the same way.

Every year until 1914 Dagmar spent the spring in England and the autumn in Denmark with Alix. In 1911 they extended Hvidøre by purchasing the neighbouring Villa Sundsør for 28,000 kroner. This was partly to preserve their privacy, as it was rumoured that it would be turned into a restaurant. They built a charming Norwegian-style tea house in the grounds with a Viking ship for a weathervane. 'The Viking House' had only two rooms, one on each floor. Arranging furnishings and buying knick-knacks proved a welcome diversion for the widowed sisters.

Dagmar delayed her departure for as long as possible that year, moving to the Amalienborg in late November. When she finally left Denmark it was to face new problems. In St Petersburg, the name Rasputin was on everyone's lips.

CHAPTER 18

Rasputin

'THE NURSERY WAS THE CENTRE OF ALL RUSSIA'S TROUBLES'
– Sir Bernard Pares

To Dagmar's dismay, her daughter-in-law had become more anti-social than ever since Alexis' birth. Court life had almost ceased, as it seemed that Alicky only found the comfort and support she needed when she was with her family.

Alexis was a lively little boy, full of mischief. As he grew older two sailors were assigned to watch over him and prevent him from falling or injuring himself. Even Xenia's boisterous sons were discouraged from visiting for fear of Alexis being hurt. Nevertheless, there were frequent falls. When he was three he fell on his forehead, his face swelled up and his eyes almost closed. 'Poor boy, it is terrible', Dagmar wrote to Nicholas. 'I can imagine how frightened you were ... I hope it is all over now, and that his charming little face has not suffered'.[1]

Because Alicky felt responsible for passing on the disease to her son she spoilt and over-protected him. When he was ill she spent hours – some-times days – by his bedside. Afterwards she collapsed completely from nervous exhaustion, spending the days in her mauve boudoir and moving about in a wheelchair. She could never relax. As the worry took its toll on her health she became prone to all kinds of psychosomatic illnesses. Dagmar realised the nature of the problem but she also blamed Alicky's cold, draughty rooms and complained that she often caught cold herself when visiting the Alexander Palace. She was sympathetic to her son's worry over his wife's health. Travel, she advised, was the solution. 'What a sad life for my poor Nicky', Dagmar commented to her sister, as Nicholas took his wife off to yet another German health spa for a rest.[2]

With the family shut away at Tsarskoe Selo, Dagmar was disappointed to miss Alexis' first steps and his first words but she realised his signifi-cance to Alicky. 'The unfortunate little girls are moved into secondary importance', she commented in 1906.[3]

At first the Tsar and Tsarina clung to the hope that a miracle cure would be found but, as time passed, they had to accept that there *was* no cure.

234

As Alicky turned more and more to the fringe areas of Orthodoxy, Dagmar, who had breathed a sigh of relief when Philippe Nizier-Vachot was sent packing, became alarmed. Her concern was justified. When Alicky's prayers failed it occurred to her that, as she had been responsible for Alexis' sufferings, she needed a Holy Man to intercede for her, a man whose prayers would be answered.

Once again it was the Montenegrin Grand Duchesses who found him. In November 1905 Militza introduced Nicholas and Alexandra to Gregory Rasputin.

*

Gregory Efimovitch Rasputin was born on 10th/22nd January 1869[4] in Pokrovskoe, Western Siberia. As a young man he was a drunk and a lecher who seduced every girl he could but he also acquired a reputation for second sight, with the gift of prophecy. Like his father he became a waggoner. In the course of his journeys around the neighbourhood he visited the monastery of Verkhoturye, where he came under the influence of the Klysts, an illegal religious sect who believed that to drive out sin one must first be a sinner. Their meetings frequently ended in wild orgies. Rasputin stayed for four months and returned to his village seemingly a changed man. He gave up drink, abandoned his wild ways and began to hold forth on spiritual topics.

In Pokrovskoe he married a local girl. He took up farming but, after claiming to have seen a holy vision, went off on a pilgrimage to Mount Athos. He returned three years later with an aura of saintliness which made people murmur that he was a Man of God. He began to preach, knew long passages of the bible by heart and acquired a host of followers, mostly women. Soon he began to wander again. In 1903, armed with a letter of introduction from the Bishop of Kazan, Rasputin visited St Petersburg for the first time.

In the capital he impressed many influential churchmen with the sincerity of his faith. Among them were Bishop Theophanes, Confessor to Grand Duchess Militza, and Father John of Kronstadt. These churchmen saw in Rasputin a genuine Starets, a wandering Holy Man, and he soon gained an entrée into the salons of the nobility.

In the elegant drawing-rooms of St Petersburg the unkempt Siberian peasant with greasy hair, a stiff black beard, pungent odour and uncouth manners cut a strange figure but it was his magnetic eyes which impressed everyone as his most remarkable feature. Men and women alike found it hard to resist their almost hypnotic influence. Rasputin preached the doctrine of salvation he had learnt from the Klysts – to be purged of sin one had to have sinned. With the bored society women of the capital he was especially successful and they soon discovered that by committing adultery with him and purifying themselves at the same time repulsion and disgust could be thrilling sensations.

When Rasputin returned to the capital in 1905, Bishop Theophanes introduced him to Grand Duchess Militza. She, in turn, arranged the fateful meeting with the Tsar and Tsarina.

By 1907 Rasputin was a regular visitor to the Alexander Palace. He discussed religious matters, addressing the Tsar and Tsarina as '*Batiushka*' and '*Matoushka*', the Father and Mother of the Russian people. When Alexis suffered a haemorrhage, Rasputin stopped the flow of blood by praying at his bedside. The Tsarina was convinced that he had been sent by God to save her son.

Again and again this scene was repeated. As the doctors fussed and the distraught Empress passed on her air of despondency to Alexis, Rasputin's prayers instilled calm and peace into the little boy and the blood stopped flowing. To Alicky it seemed that the miracle had happened.

Disturbing rumours of Rasputin's womanising in Kazan soon reached the capital and caused many prominent churchmen to think again. The Montenegrin Grand Duchesses denounced their former protégé but Alicky refused to listen, believing the stories were fabricated. People began to wonder what went on when he was alone with the Empress. Lewd cartoons and scurrilous pamphlets were circulated and, now that censorship of the press had been abolished, stories about him were published freely.

Although Nicholas never mentioned Rasputin's visits in his letters to his mother, by 1911 Dagmar was thoroughly alarmed at the stories circulating in St Petersburg about his outrageous behaviour. He now moved confidently in society. People flocked to his apartment with petitions, knowing that his influence could ensure a favourable decision. His nearly illegible scrawl on a slip of paper could open almost any door. She was not the only member of the family to be concerned. The rumours had reached Ella's convent in Moscow. Although, as Grand Duchess Olga pointed out, neither Ella nor Dagmar knew all the details, it was the nature of the rumours which so distressed the Dowager Empress. She knew that what Rasputin did mattered less than what he was rumoured to have done. Dagmar had always upheld the prestige of the throne, now she had to watch while her daughter-in-law's name was dragged through the mud.

Dagmar refused to receive Rasputin. She considered him a fraud, who had talked his way round her gullible daughter-in-law and now, to her dismay, was beginning to meddle in affairs of state. He had already begun to control Church appointments and now the Empress was asking him to evaluate potential ministers. In an effort to silence attacks in the press

Alicky met him at the home of her confidante Anna Vyrubova at Tsarskoe Selo. The Dowager Empress soon found out that Alicky was meeting Rasputin secretly and she poured out her distress to Grand Duke Constantine Constantinovitch. She was upset that Rasputin told Alicky and the children to keep his visits a secret, a deception which Dagmar felt was bad for her grandchildren's upbringing.

Soon the church launched its own investigation. Two of the most prominent Bishops tried to warn the Empress about Rasputin but found themselves on the road to exile, Theophanes to the distant Crimea and Bishop Hermogene of Saratov to a remote monastery. The governess was dismissed when she protested about Rasputin's presence in the young Grand Duchess' bedrooms.

By early 1911 there was so much evidence against Rasputin that he went on a pilgrimage to the Holy Land. The initiative came from Stolypin who, alarmed at the results of his investigation, took his report straight to the Tsar. Although Nicholas did nothing he refused to overrule Stolypin's decision to banish Rasputin, even in the face of Alicky's hysterical protests. References to Rasputin increased in the newspapers and in the Duma there was talk of dark forces near the throne.

Stolypin had now earned the enmity of the Empress and he soon found himself the victim of a ministerial intrigue. A local government bill to establish Zemstvos (elected local government councils) in the six western provinces, which contained both Russian and Polish landlords, provided the excuse his enemies needed. When the bill was passed by the Duma, Nicholas authorised the members of the State Council to vote according to their consciences – against the government. The bill was rejected. Nicholas now had second thoughts about his involvement in the intrigue and promised to support a second reading of the bill in the State Council. Stolypin refused this compromise. He suspected the Tsar of engineering the move against him and he threatened to resign.

Dagmar supported Stolypin. She knew there was no-one to replace him. 'I feel sure that Stolypin will win for the present', she told the Minister of Finance, Vladimir Kokovtsov, 'but for a short time only; he will soon be removed, which would be a great pity both for the Tsar and for Russia … My poor son has so little luck with people … I see nothing comforting ahead'.[5]

Thanks to the combined efforts of the Dowager Empress, Sandro and Grand Duke Nicholas Michaelovitch, the Tsar eventually agreed to Stolypin's request that the Duma be suspended for three days while the law was passed by Decree. The Tsar never forgave Stolypin for forcing his hand and, although he remained in office, he lived in constant expectation of dismissal.

In September, Stolypin was assassinated in the Kiev Opera House in full view of the Tsar and his daughters Olga and Tatiana. The news reached the Dowager Empress at Hvidøre. 'I cannot say how distressed and indignant I am ...' she wrote. 'Is it true that my granddaughters saw that horror? How disgusting and revolting it is and just at a moment, too, when all was going well ... I ... regret so much that this scoundrel was not torn to pieces on the spot! ... One can say nothing good of the police whose choice fell upon such a swine as that revolutionary to act as informer and as guard to Stolypin. It exceeds all bounds and shows the stupidity of the people at the top'.⁶ Dagmar had accepted the official version of events – the assassin, Mordka Bogrov, informed the police of a plot against Stolypin's life and gained access to the Opera House on the pretext of identifying the assassins. He then shot him in the name of the revolution. However, rumours that Bogrov was in the pay of the government persist to this day.

Stolypin was succeeded as Minister of the Interior by A.A. Makarov and as President of the Council of Ministers by Vladimir Kokovtsov, who held the post for the next two years.

Rasputin had returned to the capital and, despite the efforts of the ministers and the police, the scandal grew worse. The police surveillance teams reported that he regularly picked up prostitutes. Sometimes he accosted women on the street or was seen to be drunk.

In February 1912 Kokovtsov, who was no supporter of Rasputin, told the Dowager Empress bluntly how ugly gossip about the intimate life of the Emperor and Empress was circulating in St Petersburg and damaging the throne. Dagmar wept. 'My poor daughter-in-law does not perceive that she is ruining the dynasty and herself. She sincerely believes in the holiness of an adventurer, and we are powerless to ward off the misfortune, which is sure to come'. Perhaps she remembered that, when she came to Russia as a bride, an old woman had predicted her son would reign over Russia and be on the way to obtaining wealth and honour but would be 'stricken by a moujik's hand'. She promised to speak to Nicholas but held out little hope of success. Alicky saw any attack on Rasputin as an attack on the health of Alexis.⁷

Everyone in the capital was talking about Rasputin and newspapers were confiscated merely for mentioning his name. Xenia had seen Alicky but she refused to listen to reason. Dagmar knew that something had to be done.

Nicholas had never spoken to Dagmar about Rasputin but on 26th February she went to the Alexander Palace determined to speak her mind. After tea she took her son aside and told him she had something of the greatest importance to say. As soon as the children had left, Dagmar voiced her fears for the dynasty, saying that the only way to avoid a scandal was to send 'a certain person' far away. Alicky defended Rasputin, saying they could not abandon such an exceptional man. Nicholas remained silent. To Dagmar's surprise, Alicky then thanked her for speaking out. Nothing changed and, not for the first time, Dagmar was forced to concede that Nicholas was dominated by his wife.

Nicholas had promised his mother that Rasputin would not accompany the family when they left for Livadia. A few weeks later Dagmar was astonished to read in the newspapers that he was in Yalta. At first she refused to believe it. Nicholas had given his word. She did not know that Rasputin had been smuggled aboard the Imperial train by Alicky. When Nicholas found out he threw him off and Rasputin made his own way to the Crimea, where he only stayed for a few days.

Dagmar's alarm was shared by other prominent people. Michael Rodzianko, the President of the Duma, was so worried as the clamour for an open debate in the Duma on the issue of Rasputin became louder and louder that he compiled his own dossier. Prince Felix Youssoupov then arranged for it to be seen by the Dowager Empress. Rodzianko had been given evidence that Rasputin was a member of the Klysts.

Dagmar was convinced that the only way to end the scandal was to rid the throne of Rasputin's presence once and for all. She read Rodzianko's report and remarked sadly, 'that her daughter-in-law appeared to lack political judgement of any kind'. But she held out little hope of his success. 'The Emperor ... is so pure of heart that he does not believe in evil'.[8]

Nicholas authorised Rodzianko to make a full investigation, even permitting him to use the evidence gathered by the Holy Synod. The following day he was ordered by the Empress to hand the papers back. He refused. When the report was finished Nicholas declined to read it.

Hectographed copies of letters purporting to be from the Empress and her daughters to Rasputin were passed around. The government was powerless as the letters were not in printed form and the public read them avidly. The Empress' alleged letters were written in Alicky's usual gushing, passionate style but the contents were widely open to misinterpretation and hardly likely to increase the prestige of the dynasty. They became the basis of the belief that the Empress and Rasputin were lovers.

Nicholas was powerless to stop either newspaper comment or debate in the Duma. The Tsar and Tsarina were so distanced from their people that neither understood the other – to Alicky Rasputin was a Holy Man who healed her son; to the people he was a drunken lecher from Siberia. The Empress could not understand the outcry when this saintly man prayed at her son's bedside; the people were indignant at this debauched man's reception at the palace. Nicholas could not send Rasputin away because, if Alexis died, 'in the eyes of the mother he would have been the murderer of his own son'.[9]

Meanwhile the police were trying to obtain the original letters written by Alicky and her daughters to Rasputin. Dagmar attached 'especial importance' to these, finding the letters written by her young granddaughters particularly disturbing as, although they were not improper, they contained what she considered rather inappropriate passages which were giving rise to disgusting comments in St Petersburg.[10] When the original letters were finally traced, Markarov, the Minister of the Interior, handed them over not to the Empress but to the Tsar. This sealed his fate and he was soon dismissed.

In the winter of 1911 Imperial Russia reached the critical point. By the autumn of 1912 Rasputin's position was unassailable.

*

In August 1912 Dagmar's yacht anchored at Pitkopas on the coast of Finland, where Nicholas and his family were cruising on the *Standart*. The squadron was decorated with flags in honour of the Name Day of the Dowager Empress and her granddaughter Marie. Dagmar gave an informal dance on board the *Polar Star* and later Marie and Anastasia performed a short French play. Although Dagmar seemed delighted, Anna Vyrubova felt that her manner towards the children was 'affectionate but a trifle distant'. She seemed to 'resent the fact that the first four children were girls, and there is little doubt that she felt bitterly the affliction of the heir'. After dinner Dagmar sat on the edge of Alexis' bed 'talking gaily and peeling an apple like any loving grandmother'.[11]

The *Polar Star* sailed on to Denmark and again the Dowager Empress' selfishness came to the fore. Dagmar insisted that Olga was well enough to accompany her, even though she had not fully recovered from a nervous breakdown earlier in the year. Only three months before, Dagmar had attended the funeral of her brother Freddie, who collapsed in the streets of Hamburg while staying there with his family. Now, at Hvidøre, she heard that her eight-year-old grandson Alexis was on the brink of death.

Nicholas and his family had travelled on to Bialowieza in Poland, where Alexis hit his leg as he jumped into a rowing-boat. After about a week the swelling disappeared and the family moved to Spala, where members of the Polish nobility had been invited to hunt with the Tsar. While out driving with his mother and Anna Vyrubova Alexis had a relapse. By the time they reached home he was almost unconscious.

Alexis had a severe haemorrhage on his left side, his temperature grew higher and higher but the blood continued to flow, filling the groin and lower abdomen. The specialists summoned were powerless to help. They could only hope that the bleeding would stop of its own accord.

For eleven days Alexis' screams filled the household as the Empress sat, day and night, by his bedside. Incredibly neither the guests staying at the lodge, nor the outside world, knew what was happening. In the evenings the Tsarina acted as hostess at the Tsar's receptions and was later seen rushing along a back corridor to the sickroom, holding up the train of her dress with a look of terror on her face.

One evening, as all hope faded, Alexis received the Holy Sacrament. The medical bulletin, still with no mention of the nature of his illness, was carefully worded so that the next one could announce the Tsarevitch's death. In desperation Alicky telegraphed to Rasputin in Siberia. 'God has seen your tears and heard your prayers', he replied. 'Do not grieve. The Little One will not die. Do not allow the doctors to bother him too much'.[12] Alicky immediately felt reassured and stopped worrying. The following day the bleeding stopped and Alexis began to recover.

Significantly, Rasputin's telegram was not mentioned in the letter Nicholas sent to Dagmar, nor did he mention haemophilia. Thanking his mother for her sympathetic letter, he merely says, 'on October 10th [OS] we decided to give him Holy Communion and his condition began to improve at once, temperature went down ... the pain almost disappeared and he fell quietly into a sound sleep for the first time'.[13] It was only later that she heard the full details. On her return from Denmark in December she found Alexis looking very thin, sitting in a wheelchair with his left leg curled up. The following autumn he was still having mud baths in the Crimea to straighten his leg.

Alicky was convinced that only Rasputin's intervention had saved her son's life and that without him Alexis would die. From now on Rasputin's enemies were God's enemies and therefore her own. His reputation outside the court was bringing discredit to the dynasty and this worried Dagmar. As Alicky fell more and more under Rasputin's influence relations between the Dowager Empress and her son and daughter-in-law grew increasingly distant. Letters between Dagmar and Nicholas became less frequent, her visits became more widely spread, her advice was less often sought and less often offered. Nicholas never ceased to love his mother but loyalty to his wife came first.

Dagmar never allowed herself to come between Nicholas and Alicky. She had formed a small circle of friends with whom she discussed politics freely but, tactfully, she refrained from interfering although there were several things about the government's conduct with which she disagreed.

In these crucial years before the revolution Dagmar, who could have given so much help if her son had only listened to her, absented herself more and more from Russia. Her retirement from politics was voluntary, there was no open breach. She knew Russia was heading for disaster but she also knew she could do nothing to prevent it.

CHAPTER 19

Swan-Song

'FOR THE PAST IS PAST AND NEVER WILL RETURN –
THE FUTURE WE KNOW NOT – AND ONLY THE PRESENT
CAN BE CALLED OUR OWN' – Marie Corelli

In October 1912, soon after Alexis' illness, both Dagmar and Nicholas were stunned to receive a letter from Michael announcing his marriage to Natasha Wulfert.

Michael and his mistress had been on holiday in Europe. While in Germany, according to a pre-arranged plan, they gave the Tsar's police agents the slip, crossed the border and were married in the Serbian Orthodox Church in Vienna. The marriage, although morganatic, was perfectly legal and the ambitious Natasha was now the sister-in-law of the Tsar. Only when George and Tata had been taken safely out of Russia did Michael write to his mother.

Dagmar was stunned. 'It is unbelievable', she wrote to Nicholas from Hvidøre. 'I can hardly understand what I am writing – it is so appalling in every way that it *nearly* kills me! I beg only this one thing of you: that it be kept *absolutely secret* to avoid *another scandal*! ... – otherwise I won't be able to show my face *anywhere* for the *shame and disgrace of it all*!'[1]

Dagmar had desperately wanted Michael to take a royal bride so that he and his children would remain in the order of succession. It was even said in some quarters that she wanted him to reign in place of the sickly Alexis. Michael would be co-regent with Alicky if Alexis succeeded while he was a minor, and Tsarevitch again if Alexis died. Now he was married to a twice-divorced commoner who, in Nicholas' eyes, was little more than a cunning adventuress. Although Michael gave Alexis' illness as his reason for marrying, this was not the case. The wedding had been planned for some time. To Nicholas, the blow came doubly hard. Not only had his brother placed his personal happiness above his duty but he was removed from the scene just before the Tercentenary of the dynasty, when he could have been a valuable source of support. 'He broke his word – his word of honour', Nicholas kept repeating. 'How in the midst of the boy's illness ... could they have done such a thing?'[2]

From Cannes, Michael wrote to his mother. 'I am ready to bear all the punishments and deprivations … the only thing which is very painful is the distress, which I have unintentionally caused you'.[3] He protested that he had only tried to act honourably by Natasha and begged Dagmar to give them her blessing.

Somehow Dagmar and Nicholas had to find a solution. Nicholas faced his brother with a stark choice: renounce his rights to the throne or divorce Natasha. Michael flatly refused to do either and matters had reached this impasse when Dagmar returned from Hvidøre.

Michael was banished abroad and prevented from administering his personal fortune. All his property was sequestered and he was placed under the guardianship of the Tsar as if he were a minor. He was also removed from the command of the Chevalier Guards and deprived of his right of regency. Michael asked Nicholas to make Natasha a Countess but the request was refused. Nicholas then told him that he could come home – without his wife. Having married without permission and presented the Tsar with a fait accompli, Michael naturally would not return to Russia if he could not bring Natasha. They remained in exile in Europe.

*

In 1913 the Romanov dynasty celebrated its Tercentenary. The red, white and blue Russian colours decked the streets of St Petersburg, buildings and monuments were lavishly decorated and portraits of all Russia's Romanov rulers hung from facades. The press published special Jubilee editions to mark the event. A set of postage stamps was issued showing all the monarchs of the House of Romanov and the new one rouble coin showed Nicholas II with his ancestor Tsar Michael in profile behind him. The Emperor gave large donations to charities and freed common thieves and murderers but there was no amnesty for political prisoners. The hope that the Tsar and his family would come out of their enforced seclusion also evaporated.

On Thursday, 6th March, a 21-gun salute from the Fortress of SS Peter & Paul heralded the beginning of the celebrations. Windows were crammed with people anxious for a good view as the procession set off, in brilliant sunshine under a cloudless sky, accompanied by a Cossack escort. The Tsar and Tsarevitch, both wearing uniforms, acknowledged the cheering crowds who mobbed their open carriage. Troops lined the Nevsky Prospekt from the Winter Palace to the Kazan Cathedral and military bands struck up the National Anthem as the Tsar's carriage passed. The people's cheers echoed again for the Dowager Empress, dressed all in white, who followed in a State Coach accompanied by the young Empress. The sight of Olga, Tatiana, Marie and Anastasia, wearing white dresses and large flower-trimmed picture hats, drew an especially warm response.

Inside the cathedral the other members of the Imperial family, the Diplomatic Corps, dignitaries from across the Empire and members of the nobility and the armed forces had already taken their places. The Patriarch of Antioch had come from Greece especially to conduct the service. Amongst all the splendour the figure of Grand Duchess Ella, in her simple nun's habit, stood out. Earlier there was an awkward moment when Rodzianko unceremoniously evicted Rasputin from the seats reserved for members of the Duma. As the Tsar and his family entered a murmer rose from the congregation at the sight of eight-year-old Alexis in the arms of a Cossack, still unable to walk after his illness at Spala. After three hundred years what did the future hold for this dynasty whose heir was a crippled child?

Delegations from all over Russia came to the Winter Palace in national costume to offer congratulations. Among the members of the Duma was a bearded farmer. He presented his congratulations to the Tsar but was then completely overawed by the opulence of the Winter Palace. When he was confronted by the Dowager Empress, standing erect and blazing with diamonds like a valuable icon, he was paralysed. Suddenly, thinking he was in church, he sank to his knees and began to cross himself, to the amusement of the younger members of the Imperial family.

That night the buildings in St Petersburg were illuminated with double-headed eagles, chains of coloured lights along the tramlines lit up the words 'God Save the Tsar' and spectacular fireworks filled the sky.

The following evening crowds gathered in the rain to see the Emperor and both Empresses on their way to the Maryinsky Theatre, which was filled to capacity for a gala performance of *A Life for the Tsar*. As the Emperor entered with his mother they were given a resounding ovation. During the performance, in which Kschessinska danced, Alicky was seen to leave the Imperial box in a state of distress. 'A little wave of resentment rippled over the theatre', wrote the British Ambassador's daughter.[4]

There was a succession of balls and parties. At a magnificent ball given at The Assembly Hall of the Nobility, Dagmar, in a dress of silver brocade, led the Polonaise on the arm of the Emperor. The splendour of this occasion was worthy of old Russia. Once again Alicky caused resentment by leaving early but the evening was notable for the first appearance in society of eighteen-year-old Grand Duchess Olga Nicholaievna, whose partner Prince Saltykov breached etiquette by forgetting to remove his hat during the Polonaise. The crowds were enormous and Dagmar stood for hours as an endless line of people filed past. Meriel Buchanan remembered her 'talking easily and animatedly in that quick rather husky voice, never missing a point, never forgetting a face or failing to say the right thing to the right person'.[5] Although the Tsar and Tsarina had returned to live at the Winter Palace for the first time since 1905, Nicholas refused to give any State Balls and Alicky did not even appear at many of the functions.

Shortly after the end of the festivities in St Petersburg, Dagmar received a terrible shock.

In the summer of 1912 Greece, Bulgaria, Serbia and Montenegro had formed a Balkan League with the object of dividing up Turkish-owned Macedonia. In October they declared war on Turkey. Within two weeks the allies defeated every Turkish army in Europe and the Turkish army collapsed. The Greeks, commanded by Dagmar's nephew Crown Prince Constantine, marched from victory to victory, crowned by the liberation of Salonika, capital of Macedonia, in November 1912 after four hundred years of Turkish rule. In the wake of the conquering army Willie tirelessly visited hospitals and inspected the troops.

On the afternoon of 18th March 1913 Willie and his A.D.C. took a walk through the streets of Salonika. They had just passed a rather squalid café when a raggedly dressed man standing outside pulled out a revolver and shot the King in the back. He died instantly from a bullet in his heart.

When the news reached Dagmar the following day she was devastated. Willie had been melancholy and care-worn when she saw him in Denmark the previous autumn but the success of the war had lifted his spirits tremendously. Now he was dead. By a strange coincidence he and Freddie both died in the streets of a foreign country and both were sixty-eight. Willie had been Dagmar's favourite brother. She was in a 'terrible state of mind', recalled Willie's daughter Marie ('Greek Minny'), who had married Grand Duke George Michaelovitch and now lived in Russia.[6]

Dagmar's health and state of mind had already suffered all winter because of worry over Michael. In March 1913 Xenia met him in Paris. He repeated that he was sorry for the distress caused to his mother but protested that he could not have acted otherwise.

Upset by her son's complaints that nobody wrote, Dagmar was desperate to see him. By June she was in London and Xenia and Sandro arranged for Michael to come to England.

They met at Marlborough House. 'Although our first meeting was rather disturbing and we *both* were rather shy at first ... I was happy to see that he has remained the same: just as nice and good and even kinder than ever', she told Nicholas. They talked things over quietly and sensibly and 'For the first time after all these dreadful worries *my heart felt relieved* and so, I think, did his'.[7]

That evening Michael returned with his wife and Natasha found out just how formidable Dagmar could be when she told her daughter-in-law 'a few home truths'.[8] She would never receive the previously divorced wives of officers from her regiments and would not receive Natasha again. Still barred from returning to Russia as husband and wife, Michael and Natasha made their home in England.

By July a second Balkan war was underway against Bulgaria. Dagmar watched the situation anxiously. 'I had a telegram from poor Aunt Olga', she wrote to Nicholas from Sandringham, 'imploring you to support the claim that *Kavalla be given to the Greeks*. I am very hopeful …'[9] As Greece and Serbia nearly doubled in size, few people doubted that Serbia's next move would be to free the Serbs living under the yoke of the Hapsburg Empire.

In September Dagmar and Alix went to Hvidøre as usual. After her sister left, Dagmar stayed on and was still there when she celebrated her sixty-sixth birthday in November. When the day of her departure arrived she was suffering from a heavy cold but insisted on leaving as planned.

As Dagmar left Denmark on 22nd December she little knew under what dramatic circumstances she would return.

*

Looking back across the chasm which separated the old world from the aftermath of war and revolution Dagmar and those who were lucky enough to escape remembered the Season of 1914 as especially brilliant. Rather as childhood is later seen as a time when the sun always seemed to be shining, the survivors looked back with nostalgia on the last winter of peace.

A glittering series of parties and dances were given but the social event of the Season was undoubtedly the ball given by the Dowager Empress for her granddaughters Olga and Tatiana. This was the first ball she had given for twenty years and the last ever held at the Anitchkov. The two girls danced until four-thirty in the morning.

Once again there were no Court Balls. At the Winter Palace reception the Emperor was accompanied by his mother. Dagmar was concerned that her granddaughters were not taking their rightful place in society. Olga had been given a coming-out dinner and ball at Livadia two years earlier and, in the winter of 1914, sixteen-year-old Tatiana came out. The girls were permitted to attend a small dance at Miechen's palace, where they were carefully chaperoned by the Dowager Empress.

During this glittering Season Dagmar attended many opera and ballet performances at the blue and gold Maryinsky Theatre. One of her favourite ballets was *Le Talisman*, in which Kschessinska danced a particularly difficult series of steps which always brought calls from the house for an encore. When members of the Imperial family were present the dancers were subject to strict rules of etiquette. Only when the Dowager Empress (who watched nearly every performance) nodded her consent did protocol allow Mathilde to repeat the solo.

Diaghilev's Ballets Russes had taken London by storm and Dagmar and Alix contributed greatly to the company's success by giving it their patronage. Dagmar followed the progress of *The Firebird*, *Petrushka* and the highly controversial *Rite of Spring* with interest and summoned Tamara Karsavina to the Imperial box at the Maryinsky Theatre, where she congratulated the ballerina on her triumph.

Dagmar did not attend the theatre for some time after Sasha's death. On her next appearance in the Imperial box she noticed that the dancers' skirts were considerably shorter. 'You ought to mention it one day to Vsevolojsky [Director of the Imperial Theatres]', she wrote to Nicholas, 'for it exceeds all limits of decency. I have often told him so and they changed it. But it seems when I stopped going to the theatre they quickly cut off a length again!'[10]

She took her place in the lower Imperial box to the left of the stage, sitting in a special high chair. In the interval a light supper was served in an anteroom for relations and a few distinguished guests. Porcelain and silverware were brought from the Anitchkov and the Empress poured the tea. Wine was available for those who wanted it.

During Dagmar's long absences abroad Miechen began to usurp the custom by arranging her own private tea table at the Maryinsky. Dagmar heard about this and decided to put Miechen in her place. On her next appearance at the theatre Dagmar arranged for the usual tea table but, when the interval arrived, it was found that Miechen had also ordered one. The Grand Duchess was acutely embarrassed. To lessen the discomfort, Dagmar treated the matter as a joke and suggested that they use each other's tables. The lesson had been learnt. Miechen never tried to rule the roost at the Maryinsky again.

On another evening one of the male dancers exceeded the bounds of decency. During a performance of *Giselle*, Nijinsky appeared on stage without the regulation trunks over his extremely brief costume. The Dowager Empress rose to her feet, glared icily at him and departed from the theatre, brushing aside obsequious officials on her way. After a blazing row Nijinsky resigned from the Imperial Ballet. The scandal diverted society for weeks.

*

In the middle of the 1914 Season Dagmar had a two-hour meeting at the Anitchkov with Nicholas. Among the subjects discussed was the future of Kokovtsov, who had been Chairman of the Council of Ministers since

Stolypin's murder. Nothing transpired during this interview to give the Dowager Empress any indication of what was to happen next.

On 13th February she was amazed to learn of Kokovtsov's dismissal. The elderly Count Ivan Goremykin became Chairman of the Council of Ministers and Peter Bark was appointed Minister of Finance. Kokovtsov's fall was a direct result of Rasputin's unfavourable report on him to Alicky. At the theatre that evening the Dowager Empress asked her son why he had dismissed Kokovtsov. 'Do you think I feel happy about it?' he replied.

Dagmar summoned Kokovtsov to the Anitchkov. 'You must understand my fears for the future', she said. 'My daughter-in-law does not like me; she thinks that I am jealous of her power. She does not perceive that my one aspiration is to see my son happy. Yet I see we are nearing some catastrophe, and the Tsar listens to no-one but flatterers ... Why do you not tell the Tsar everything you think and know ... if is not already too late'. Kokovtsov told her that the Tsar would neither listen nor believe him. The young Empress considered him her enemy.

Dagmar tried twice to talk to Nicholas but it was obvious that 'nothing would come of these conversations'.[11] Kokovtsov did not see Dagmar again until February 1917. Nevertheless, when he was created a Count, rumour ascribed it to the influence of the Dowager Empress.

Dagmar felt less and less welcome at Tsarskoe Selo and was always glad to return home from the cloying atmosphere of the Alexander Palace. When Nicholas visited the Anitchkov or Gatchina he seldom brought his wife. They were usually all together for Christmas. A copy of Fennimore Cooper's *The Pathfinder*, inscribed on the fly-leaf 'to Olga from Grandmother on Christmas tree at Gatchina, 1907' was preserved at Luton Hoo. Yet it was Xenia's sturdy sons who romped around Gatchina, walked with their grandmother in the park and, dressed in sailor suits, rowed her across the lake in a white-painted boat.

Alexis, of course, could never do any of these things. He was sheltered and protected, a burly sailor hovering over his every move to try and avert disaster. To compensate for his illness he was given expensive toys, including a small motor car from his grandmother, with which he was clearly delighted. When his parents took him to the Anitchkov in December 1913 Dagmar noted with pleasure that he was walking much easier. Alexis delightedly examined all the pictures, furniture and objets d'art, including her famous collection of Fabergé. He had never been there before.

Closeted at the Alexander Palace the four girls saw few people apart from each other, their close family, the servants and, occasionally, carefully selected children of Court officials. Dagmar was determined that they should see more of life and, from the end of 1906 to 1914, a regular feature of Sundays during the winter was a visit from her granddaughters.

After lunch at the Anitchkov they went to their Aunt Olga's house where, in the company of some of their Leuchtenberg cousins and other young people, there was dancing, games and tea.

During the annual summer stay at Peterhof they visited Dagmar at The Cottage nearly every morning. When cruising on the *Standart* or staying at Livadia the children wrote to their 'dear grandmother' for her birthday and Name Day. 'Grandmother birthday girl I send you many kisses. Tatiana', the Grand Duchess wrote on a postcard in 1903.[12] Alexis wrote about his lessons and in November 1913 Anastasia told her about a particularly lively ball at Livadia: 'We are having such a good and gay time here. On the seventh we had a ball and I danced a whole lot ... We had very many things for the cotillion, and I also got a lot ... We threw ... wreaths made from the flowers that grow here and the gentlemen caught them, and we were to dance a waltz with them, and afterwards there were fire crackers made of flowers; ... It was very gay'.[13]

Although they held their grandmother in some awe, Dagmar watched with pride as the two elder girls began to appear with their father on ceremonial occasions. Both were given the Colonelcy of a regiment – Olga the Hussars and Tatiana the Uhlans – and proudly wore their uniform as they rode side-saddle beside the Tsar at Krasnoe Selo. 'How delighted Olga and Tatiana must be to be able to review their regiments on horseback', Dagmar wrote from Sandringham in July 1913. 'I regret not to be able to be there and watch them do it'.[14]

Yet the Dowager Empress' two daughters having, by contemporary standards, made such unspectacular marriages (which at least kept them in Russia, where their mother wanted them), it seemed more than likely that one of Nicholas' pretty daughters would eventually wear a crown. Although Olga and Tatiana had their favourite young officers, they naturally became the focus for dynastic alliances.

King Peter of Serbia (whose daughter Helen was married to Prince Ivan Constantinovitch) hoped to forge a further link by marrying his son Crown Prince Alexander to one the Tsar's daughters. His plans were interrupted by the war. A marriage between Olga and the Prince of Wales was much favoured by Queen Alexandra (Olga was often teased about 'David' by her sisters) but, when they met at Cowes in 1909, David seemed more attracted to Tatiana. Other candidates included the eldest son of Tsar Ferdinand of Bulgaria and the Kaiser's son Adalbert. Not surprisingly, the Kaiser's advances were rebuffed due, it was widely believed in Germany, to the strong influence of the Dowager Empress.

More serious discussions concerned a marriage between Olga and Prince Carol of Roumania, eldest son of Crown Prince Ferdinand and Dagmar's niece Crown Princess Marie, but Olga and Carol were not interested in each other. Olga was determined not to leave Russia; Carol was more attracted to her fourteen-year-old sister Marie. When he asked for Marie's hand two years later the Tsar said she was too young. There were rumours that Olga and Grand Duke Dimitri were unofficially engaged but this came to nothing. In 1916 Grand Duke Boris, who was eighteen years Olga's senior, asked for her hand. He had already had many mistresses and Alicky was scandalised.

Dagmar's eldest and favourite grandchild had also reached the age of eighteen. Princess Irina was a dazzling beauty. Grand Duke Dimitri was madly in love with her but when, in 1913, Irina announced her intention of marrying Prince Felix Youssoupov, Dagmar viewed the prospect with some concern. 'She is not quite sure whether it would be a good thing', Xenia recorded in her diary.[15]

As the son of Dagmar's friend Princess Zenaide Youssoupov, Felix was heir to the largest private fortune in Russia, with more than forty estates all over the Empire. By the age of sixteen he found his disreputable elder brother's way of life more to his taste. Nicholas Youssoupov was twenty-one and had a mistress. One night they suggested a visit to the gypsies. To get round the problem of Felix's obligatory school uniform they dressed him as a woman. From then he led a double life, as a schoolboy by day and an elegant woman by night. Felix soon attracted the admiring attentions of Guards officers in fashionable St Petersburg restaurants and accepted invitations to intimate suppers in private dining-rooms. Once when the officers' amorous advances threatened a scandal he created a diversion by smashing a mirror with a bottle of champagne while he escaped. In a Paris theatre he noticed an elderly gentleman eyeing him persistently – it was King Edward VII. His potential career as a female cabaret singer was abruptly terminated when some friends of his mother recognised the family jewels he was wearing. The scandal had to be hushed up.

In 1908 Nicholas was killed in a duel by an avenging husband, leaving Felix as sole heir. He studied at Oxford, took opium and had a series of affairs. He was also 'an extremely active homosexual'.[16] There was gossip in St Petersburg that he and Grand Duke Dimitri were lovers. Now, under pressure from his family to marry and produce an heir, Felix decided he had found his ideal woman in Princess Irina.

Irina was very young and very innocent. She and her mother were ordering the trousseau and Felix was to meet them in Paris. Dagmar, worried about the disagreeable nature of the rumours concerning Felix, was determined to see him and decide the matter for herself.

Xenia did not believe the rumours. The more worldly Sandro, coming to the conclusion that there must be something in it, sent Count

Mordvinoff to meet Felix in Paris to ask him if the stories about his homo-sexuality were true. Felix explained that 'he had been [homosexual] once but was no longer'.[17] With Irina's father on the verge of cancelling the wedding Felix went straight to the hotel where they were staying and persuaded them to change their minds. Irina and her parents left for Denmark and preparations continued for the wedding. A few days later Felix received a telegram inviting him to join them in Copenhagen.

Aware that he now had to overcome the Dowager Empress' opposition he was consumed by awe and dread. She was 'certainly one of the most striking personalities of our time', Felix later wrote and was regarded almost with veneration by the younger generation. Dagmar had seen little of Felix when he was a child. His fate now rested in her hands.

During lunch with Xenia and Irina at the Amalienborg, Dagmar observed Felix keenly and he used all his considerable personal charm. Afterwards she took him to an adjoining room and, in the course of their conversation, was gradually influenced in his favour. 'Do not worry', she said kindly, 'I will do what I can for your happiness'.[18] She was as good as her word and the betrothal took place on 22nd December.

The wedding, on 22nd February 1914, took place in the chapel of the Anitchkov Palace, with the Dowager Empress as one of the bride's sponsors. Amongst the mountain of jewellery given to her was a diamond and pearl brooch from Dagmar. Irina, wearing a gown of white satin embroidered in silver with a long train, arrived in a coach drawn by four white horses and was led into the chapel by the Tsar. Her tiara, made by Cartier from solid rock crystal and diamonds, secured a lace veil which had been worn by her mother. After a champagne reception in the Winter Garden Felix and Irina left on the first stage of their wedding tour.

In spring, Dagmar left for London.

*

On Sunday, 28th June, the picturesque Bosnian capital of Sarajevo was en fête for the visit of the heir to the Austrian Empire, Archduke Franz Ferdinand and his morganatic wife Sophie, Duchess of Hohenberg. The Serbs bitterly resented Austrian rule but, at the Archduke's request, no soldiers guarded the route, even though it was Serbia's national day and trouble could be expected.

As the Archduke's convoy drove down the Appel Quay alongside the river, Franz Ferdinand's Austrian uniform was like a red rag to a bull. Beside him sat Sophie, in a white dress and hat. Suddenly a bomb hurtled through the air, bounced off their car and landed on the one behind, wounding one of the passengers. The Archduke's chauffeur accelerated and sped to the Town Hall. 'I come to Sarajevo on a visit and someone throws a bomb at me. This is outrageous!' Franz Ferdinand shouted as an official, blithely unaware of what had happened, began a speech of welcome.

Despite the risk of another attempt Franz Ferdinand and Sophie decided to visit the wounded adjutant in hospital. The Chief of Police was instructed to lead the convoy straight back down the Appel Quay. Unfortunately, nobody told the driver of the leading car and he turned off towards the old town as originally planned. The Archduke's chauffeur momentarily followed then, realising his mistake, began to reverse. At that moment two pistol shots rang out. Blood spurted from the Archduke's mouth and seconds later the Duchess slid to the floor. 'Sopherl, Sopherl, don't die. Stay alive for the children', muttered Franz Ferdinand as the car sped across the bridge to the Konak.

Within fifteen minutes the Archduke and his wife were both dead. In an adjoining room waiters were laying tables for the formal luncheon. 'It is nothing', Franz Ferdinand had muttered several times in his last conscious moments.[19]

The assassin was a nineteen-year-old Bosnian student named Gavrilo Princip. His action led to the downfall of three dynasties and the deaths of millions of people.

CHAPTER 20

The Iron Dice

'NOW THEY RING THE BELLS, BUT SOON THEY WILL
WRING THEIR HANDS' – Sir Robert Walpole

Dagmar spent the long hot summer of 1914 at Marlborough House. The London Season was in full-swing. Chaliapin was singing *Ivan the Terrible* and Diaghilev's Ballets Russes was causing a sensation. Dagmar and Alix were cheered as they drove down the course on Gold Cup Day at Ascot. Other members of the family were also in town. One morning Felix and Irina were woken by a commotion at their Knightsbridge flat. Downstairs Felix's Abyssinian servant, under strict instructions not to let anyone in, had tried to prevent the Dowager Empress and Queen Alexandra from entering. Words had failed and Dagmar was threatening the unfortunate man with her umbrella. The Sarajevo assassinations were on everyone's lips but there seemed no cause for anxiety. Dagmar and Alix decided to go to Sandringham at the beginning of August.

Belgrade was swarming with students vowing retribution against Austria for the annexation of Bosnia and Herzegovina and an enquiry established that the murders had been planned there with the help of Serbian officials. Austria, determined on revenge, was assured of aid by Germany if Russia entered a conflict and by the last week in July events were moving so swiftly that it seemed war was imminent. On 23rd July Serbia was presented with an ultimatum in terms so harsh they would be impossible to accept. A reply was to be given within forty-eight hours. When Serbia accepted all the points except one, Austria said this was unsatisfactory and declared war. The following day Austrian troops bombarded Belgrade and Serbia appealed to Russia for help. When the news reached London, Sandro left immediately. Dagmar laughed at his gloomy predictions, saying she was reliably informed that there was not going to be a European war.

Nicholas had already partially mobilized and, assured of the support of France, full mobilization followed on 31st July. Rasputin was isolated from the Tsar and Tsarina at this critical moment. On 27th June, while staying with his family in Siberia, he was stabbed in the stomach by a former prostitute who was acting as an agent for one of his enemies. For several weeks his life hung in the balance. Although Rasputin's terrific strength asserted itself he remained in bed throughout the summer. Nicholas, as protector of the Slavs, had no intention of suffering another humiliation and forcing the Serbs to back down. Rasputin could only send a string of urgent telegrams from Siberia. 'Let Papa not plan war', ran one, 'for with war will come the end of Russia and yourselves and you will lose to the last man'.[1]

On 29th July Alicky wrote to Dagmar from Peterhof sending greetings for her Name Day. She expressed her horror at the prospect of a European war, although she was pleased that England and France would naturally support Russia as allies and that Denmark and Belgium appeared to have mobilised their armies. She was wrong about England and Dagmar anxiously wondered what her sister's country would do.

Messages from Russia and the pleas of the Russian Ambassador, Count Alexander Benckendorff, soon persuaded Dagmar that she must go home without delay. When Grand Duchess George arrived, the Ambassador said that her only hope of returning to Russia was to travel with the Dowager Empress. At Marlborough House she found Dagmar anxious and crying, while the staff hastily packed for departure. Dagmar realised that it might be too late to cross Germany but was confident that the Kaiser would let her pass. The Grand Duchess decided to stay in England with her daughters.

The following day Austria, France and Germany mobilized and Germany declared war on Russia. Against this background Count Benckendorff, the Embassy staff and Court officials assembled in the waiting room of a London station as the Royal family said goodbye to the Empress. Dagmar and Alix parted emotionally. How many times they had done this before – but this time they had no idea when, or under what conditions, they would meet again.

At half-past five Dagmar arrived at Calais, where her private train was waiting. She had arranged to meet Xenia, but the Grand Duchess was not there. Worried, Dagmar pressed on towards Belgium, to cries of 'Vive la Russie' echoing along her route through France. At the border she finally met her daughter, whose retinue had lost their baggage. All over Europe, royalty and commoners alike were hurrying home before the frontiers closed. By the time Dagmar's train reached Berlin on 4th August the line to St Petersburg was closed. Despite Prince Schervashidze's certainty that the Kaiser would meet her at the station, only the Russian Ambassador in Berlin, Sverbaev, was waiting on the platform. He had to inform the Empress that she could go no further.

Determined not to appeal to the Kaiser for help, she sat in the train in the stifling heat surrounded by armed guards. Dagmar's hatred for Germany was well-known and, as word of her arrival spread, the Russian Imperial insignia on the train became a popular target for insult. Through the closed curtains she could hear the ribald songs and jibes of the crowd on the platform. What Dagmar did not know was that only the Kaiser's fear of international repercussions had prevented her internment. Hearing that the Youssoupovs had reached Berlin and were about to be arrested, she tried to send a message to them to join the train.

The situation quickly deteriorated. Crowds smashed the windows and tore down the curtains. When one of the retainers tried to go out for food the sentries thrust him roughly back. Seeing a group of stranded Russians huddled together on the platform Dagmar ordered her staff to bring them on board immediately.

After many hours of sitting in a hostile country, surrounded by jeering crowds and guarded like a prisoner, Count Mirbach, an official from the Ministry of Foreign Affairs, appeared. He told Dagmar that Russia had declared war on Germany (which, she informed him, was a lie) and gave her a choice: she could go back via England, Holland or Switzerland, or proceed directly to Denmark. Unhesitatingly she chose Denmark. After a two hour delay, and without being able to wait for the Youssoupovs, to Dagmar's intense relief the train finally pulled away from Germany towards Vamdrup.

Eleven years later her treatment at the hands of the Germans still rankled. The only good thing, she wrote to Xenia in 1925, was the train journey across Finland.

It was a nightmare journey. Besides her own large retinue the carriages were packed with stranded Russians who the Empress refused to leave behind. Soldiers with fixed bayonets guarded the locked doors and their slow progress was frequently halted to allow troop trains to pass. In this overcharged atmosphere it was with relief that Dagmar reached the Danish frontier, from where she telegraphed to Waldemar and Rørdam announcing her imminent arrival at Hvidøre.

At Klampenborg Station the Russian Minister, Baron Buxhoeveden, was waiting on the platform with Dagmar's nephew King Christian, his wife Queen Alexandrine and other members of the Royal family. As Dagmar stepped from the train she was reported to be very subdued. Although she was glad to be back at Hvidøre Dagmar had no intention of lingering. There were reports of insurrections in Finland and she had to get home. As she was making preparations, she heard that the Youssoupovs had arrived at the Hotel d'Angleterre after an eleventh-hour escape with the departing Russian Ambassador. Dagmar and Xenia, still upset after the shocking events in the German capital, immediately went to see them. Irina was ill but Dagmar decided they must return to Russia without delay.

The iron dice began to roll and soon the war engulfed Europe. Germany declared war on France and marched into Belgium. Dagmar waited anxiously to see what England would do. Then a jubilant telegram arrived from Alix saying that England was entering the fray. The following day Austria declared war on Russia; a week later Britain was at war with Austria. Taking the portraits of the Tsar and King George V from her writing table, Dagmar looked at them for a long time. 'My son and Alexandra's shake hands now!' she said delightedly.[2]

Although Denmark remained neutral, the Baltic Approaches were closed and Dagmar would not be able to visit her homeland during the war. The following morning, after inspecting the infantry and artillery regiments billeted at Hvidøre to man the coastal defences, she settled questions about the administration of the property. It was decided to evacuate the more valuable items to Christian IX's Palace at the Amalienborg and, in the event of communications with Russia being broken, Rørdam would meet the running expenses from Copenhagen's Handelsbank.

At six o'clock the following evening the Royal family assembled at Frihavnen, where the ferry was waiting. Dagmar was quieter than usual as she said goodbye. She had no idea when she would see them again. After a few final words on board, the bell rang and the ferry slowly glided away towards Malmo. Dagmar stood silently on deck and the emotion showed on her face as the shores of Denmark grew more distant – but she had no doubt where her duty lay.

From Malmo they went by train to Stockholm. The original idea had been to go by boat to Turku, in Finland, but this plan was changed. Instead they transferred to cars and drove north towards Karungi. At Torneo, close to the Polar Circle, they crossed the border and found the Finnish Imperial train waiting. The provision of this train had caused panic. The General Director of the Finnish Railway Board had received a secret message ordering him to transport the Dowager Empress home. The old Imperial train, unused and forgotten for nearly eighteen years, was hurriedly rolled out, uniforms were found for the personnel and, as it raced to Torneo, picking up bedding on the way, cleaners and maintenance men quickly carried out refurbishments. When the Empress saw the station master and his staff lined up along the platform she was visibly moved, remembering all the journeys she and Sasha had made through Finland.

Dagmar was concerned at the plight of the band of almost penniless refugees, some of whom had travelled with her from Berlin. She asked the railway board to give them free travel where possible. As delay followed delay, uneasiness set in and telegrams flew back and forth. While Dagmar and Xenia were having tea, a train arrived from Russia and, to their surprise, they saw familiar faces running towards them – Princess Victoria of Battenberg and her daughter Louise, who had been visiting Alicky. They just had time to exchange news through the open window before Victoria and Louise hurried across the footbridge into Sweden.

Their departure was repeatedly delayed. Finally, at two o'clock in the morning of 8th August, the train pulled away. The journey became a triumphal progress. All along the route Dagmar was greeted with ovations and flowers; choirs sang the Imperial hymn and, at her request, two songs banned by the government in St Petersburg. At Seinajoki the crowds were so great that Dagmar photographed them from her carriage window; in Tammerfors she was greeted with flags, garlands and more songs. It was her last journey through Finland and the last time the Finnish Imperial train was used for royalty. At the Russian frontier, she asked for assurances that transport would be provided for the refugees. They showed their gratitude by presenting her with bunches of Finnish wild flowers. On 9th August, after a nine day journey across Europe, Dagmar was reunited with Nicholas at Peterhof. Her arrival was a gala occasion, with the Tsar in naval uniform, a guard of honour of the Equipage de la Garde and a military band.

The news of her treatment in Germany aroused great indignation in Russia. 'The anti-German feeling has been immensely intensified by the treatment by the German authorities of the Dowager Empress ...' Reuters reported.[3]

Half a century after the Schleswig-Holstein war the opportunity for revenge had come. 'You cannot imagine', she told Rodzianko, 'what a satisfaction it is to me, after being compelled to disguise my true feelings for fifty years, to be free at last to tell everybody how I hate the Germans!'[4]

*

In St Petersburg the war was greeted with patriotic fervour. The people were confident of a speedy victory and officers openly debated whether to pack their full-dress uniforms for the Victory Parade in Berlin. At the Winter Palace Nicholas took an oath never to make peace while a single enemy soldier remained on Russian soil.

Dagmar moved to the Yelagin Palace with Xenia and her family. Now the country was at war she told Nicholas that Michael must come home. In fact he had already asked for permission to return with his family and, travelling via Norway, Sweden and Finland, was reunited with his mother at Yelagin on 24th August. He and Nicholas became close again. Michael was given command of the 'Savage Division' in Galicia and was later awarded the Order of St George for bravery.

Grand Duke Paul had also returned and was angling for a better title for his morganatic wife. Alicky was afraid Michael would do the same, therefore Natasha was never received by the Imperial family.

Olga became a nurse and Xenia supervised a large hospital for wounded and convalescent troops. To Dagmar's astonishment Alicky forgot her ills and enrolled on a nursing course with her daughters Olga and Tatiana, doing even the most menial jobs in the hospital at Tsarskoe Selo. Tatiana established a refugee committee and presided over its meetings at the Winter Palace, while her sister Olga received donations for the families of reservists. Other Imperial ladies were equally active.

Dagmar's family were fighting on opposite sides. Alix was an ally; Thyra was in the enemy camp. Her only surviving son Ernst August, who took over his father's Duchy of Brunswick, was married to the Kaiser's daughter Victoria Louise. Greece was neutral. Alicky's brother Ernie and sister Irene were in Germany; her eldest sister Victoria was in England, married to the First Sea Lord Prince Louis of Battenberg. Their cozy world of international family gatherings was no more. The only news they could get of their relatives in the opposing camp came through the neutral Courts of Scandinavia. Dagmar's nephew Prince Aage passed on news of the family in Denmark and reports on her beloved Hvidøre. He told her that the garden around the house had not been ruined but some cannon had been positioned in the beach garden. Mlle L'Escaille, now living in Denmark, often thought of her former pupil.

'It is becoming more difficult and painful to live here, so far from everything', Dagmar wrote to Grand Duke Nicholas Michaelovitch on 20th September. 'So much heartache and constant anguish come from knowing that people everywhere are struggling with their last bit of strength, and from expecting and learning the consequences. It's horrible to think that this is only the beginning'.[5]

Russia was in no state to withstand the strain of a protracted war. Vast distances and incomplete railways made mobilization difficult, reserves of rifles and ammunition were limited, field guns, heavy artillery and shells were in short supply. Only in manpower was Russia supreme. Over 1,400,000 men were mobilized and there were another 1,300,000 reserves. The Germans knew that their hopes of victory rested on crushing France before the 'Russian steamroller' could turn on them and within a month they were only thirty miles north of Paris.

A wave of anti-German hysteria swept over St Petersburg. Shops owned by Germans were looted and the Embassy was sacked. At the end of August the Tsar changed the German St Petersburg to the Slav Petrograd.

Nicholas' first impulse was to become Commander-in-Chief but, bowing to pressure, he appointed his tall imposing cousin Nicholasha, a career soldier, instead. There were two main commands, the north-west front against Germany and the south-west front against Austria-Hungary. As Cossacks raided East Prussia the Germans panicked and sent Hindenburg and Ludendorff to the eastern front with reinforcements. At the Battle of Tannenberg Russia suffered a resounding defeat. The Russian Second Army ceased to exist and General Samsonov shot himself in despair. Shortly afterwards the Russians were driven back to the frontier.

In November Dagmar returned to the Anitchkov. She worked tirelessly, receiving many people connected with the Red Cross. She soon realised that the Army Medical Corps was inadequate to cope with the casualties from large-scale military operations. Organisation and efficiency were sadly lacking and trucks of medical supplies were frequently sent to the wrong front. The wounded arrived in Moscow packed into goods trains, lying almost unclothed on the wooden floor, without food and with their wounds undressed. Transportation and medical supplies for even the most elementary first aid were lacking. Dagmar was horrified when she heard that the voluntary first aid organisations were forbidden to go to the front by the head of the Army Medical Department. She quickly sent a telegram to Nicholasha asking him to order that the Red Cross organisations be allowed through.

Hospital trains were improved and soon there were fifty, supplying the field hospitals with linen and medicines. Ambulances were equipped to bring casualties from the field hospitals to the waiting trains and Dressing Stations were sent to the front. Ten ambulances arrived from England and private cars were requisitioned. Countess Kleinmichael lent her villa for use as a hospital and the fishing lodge at Langinkoski in Finland was made available to the Red Cross as a convalescent home for wounded soldiers. Dagmar also visited the Danish hospital in Petrograd and sent money to Grand Duchess George in England, to fund beds for her hospital in Harrogate.

Eventually the Military Transport Service was completely reorganised under Prince Alexander of Oldenburg and Dagmar concentrated on raising money for the Red Cross. Here her personal popularity was a great asset. She also dealt with a constant stream of appeals from parents worried about missing sons, or war widows left in difficult financial circumstances. They all turned to her when they had exhausted the official channels and she helped them, both materially and with words of comfort and consolation. She founded charities for poor soldiers without resources; organised small groups of officers' wives to make bandages in the dining-room at the Anitchkov, often sitting down to help, and even knitted gloves for Nicholas to wear when he visited the front. She also went to bazaars selling the work of wounded soldiers. Although the theatres remained open, the only performances Dagmar attended now were concerts in aid of the war invalids.

Those who worked with her were full of admiration for her energy and organizing ability. 'She was vastly admired by the poor, and known wherever a helping hand was needed', wrote Princess Cantacuzene. She had a natural instinct for bringing consolation to people in distress, recalled Princess Bariatinsky. 'She could understand and enter into their feelings better than others'.[6] Dagmar was unceasing on behalf of her friends. 'I got a letter from old Countess Helen Shouvaloff … who lives at Cannes', she told Nicholas. '[She] begs me to tell you that if you have to send someone … to Italy or France she implores you to send her son Andrey as she is old and ill and would like to see him before she dies'.[7]

Dagmar was a tireless visitor to the hospitals, helping and encouraging the wounded and listening to their stories. Often she dropped in unannounced. An officer of the Chevalier Guards, lying severely wounded in the French hospital, was amazed when the Dowager Empress suddenly appeared with her lady-in-waiting and stayed chatting for nearly an hour. The hospital staff were mortified when they discovered that she had asked the way to his room without revealing her identity.

The Dowager Empress, said an English nurse, 'is a very charming but very slangy old lady'. The Kaiser 'was no favourite of hers'; she called him 'vulgar and detestable' and 'a silly ass!'[8] In 1915 Dagmar received the Report of the Danish Committee for Assistance to Russian Prisoners of War in Germany, after the Danes had inspected the prison camps. She was concerned about the Germans' treatment of prisoners of war and did not mince her words, calling them 'monsters' who acted like 'wild beasts'.[9]

Some of the Russians' prisoners were South Jutlanders from German-occupied Schleswig, who were fighting for Germany against their will. Through the Red Cross, Dagmar arranged for a Danish pastor to visit them and provided fur coats for forty of the men. On her initiative some of them were transferred to a camp near Moscow where they received many special favours. Years later one of these men visited her in Denmark and was amazed at how well informed she was about conditions in South Jutland.

In November, Turkey entered the war. Now supplies could only reach Russia through Vladivostok in the east or, during its ice-free months Archangel, 2,000 miles from the front. The western front had reached stalemate. By the end of the year the Russians had lost one quarter of their army. The men were inadequately clothed; many of them had no proper boots. Soldiers were forced to wait for their colleagues to die so that they could have their weapons and the Russian guns were rationed to three rounds a day.

The first Christmas of the war was a particularly lonely one for the sixty-seven-year-old Dowager Empress, with only Xenia for company. That Season there were no lively balls at the great palaces, only growing casualty lists and families mourning their dead as defeat followed defeat. The Imperial family was not immune. Prince Oleg, the talented young son of Grand Duke Constantine Constantinovitch, died in hospital from his wounds, the only Romanov to die in action. The army was coming to the end of its resources. Losses had been astronomical with many divisions losing half of their men. 'There were no balls, no music ...' wrote the British Ambassador's daughter, 'the men we danced with last year had lost their lives in East Prussia or were fighting in the Carpathians'.[10]

Dagmar followed the fortunes of the army closely, conscious that a series of defeats could spell disaster for the dynasty. 'May God help our forces in their terribly difficult task', she prayed.[11] At first she was not concerned unduly about the political situation but, as the war dragged on into the spring of 1915, a series of reversals forced Nicholas into a decision that would have serious consequences for them all.

*

By early 1915 Dagmar was under terrible strain because of all the suffering and carnage caused by the war. She had pains in her feet and legs and was too poorly even to attend church. She was also upset when Misha left without saying goodbye. 'How sad that is. I can't even believe it', she wrote in her diary. 'Not one of my brothers and sisters would have done that to our angel parents'.[12]

On 21st March Princess Irina gave birth to a daughter, Dagmar's first great-grandchild. She was named Irina after her mother, but always called Bébé. The christening took place in the Youssoupov chapel with the Dowager Empress as godmother and the Tsar as godfather. The priest performed the ceremony very badly and poor little Irina swallowed a lot of water. 'I was terribly frightened', Dagmar wrote.[13]

Throughout the early part of the war Dagmar was able to correspond freely with Alix and sometimes pass on privileged intelligence. 'Aunt Alix wires to say they know for certain that the Germans intend to attack Warsaw this week and she hopes we are aware of it', Dagmar told Nicholas in February, adding, 'her information has usually been correct. God grant that they do not succeed'.[14] Many of their letters were carried by Hans Niels Andersen founder of the East-Asiatic Company, Denmark's largest trading empire, who was well-known to all the Danish Royal family.

Dagmar's influence had often gained concessions for his companies and Andersen's name is frequently mentioned in her diaries and correspondence. Erik Scavenius, Denmark's Foreign Minister, went so far as to describe Andersen as 'the old agent and debtor of the Court and especially of the Dowager Empress'.[15]

In March the Russians captured Przemysl and headed towards Vienna. In Petrograd the streets were thronged with people cheering and singing. Soon the rejoicing turned to despair as Lemberg and Przemysl were lost again. Many of the Tsar's subjects came under enemy occupation and refugees fled before the German advance. As the Russians retreated, all their western fortresses, all of Poland and part of Lithuania were lost, together with three million men. As refugees flooded in from Poland, Dagmar worked hard to provide them with food and necessities. In Russia there was anger, disillusionment and bitterness. Crowds gathered in Red Square shouting insults at the Imperial family. They demanded that the 'German' Tsarina be sent to a convent and the Tsar abdicate in favour of Nicholasha. Anger turned against all Germans and spy mania reached fever pitch. In the wake of the retreats the incompetent War Minister Sukhomlinov was replaced by General Polivanov. Alicky now turned her attention to Nicholasha. She wrote letter after letter to Nicholas at the front, urging his dismissal. Alicky hated Nicholasha because he was popular with the soldiers, his majestic stature overshadowed the Tsar and, most of all, because of his opposition to Rasputin.

Rasputin's standing had been low when he returned to Petrograd in the autumn of 1914 making no secret of his anti-war sympathies. Then, early in January 1915, Anna Vyrubova was seriously injured in a train crash and seemed unlikely to live. Rasputin was summoned to the bedside and rallied her with a superhuman effort. As he predicted, Anna was crippled but she survived. Later that year Alexis suffered a nosebleed on the Imperial train during a visit to the front. By the time they reached Tsarskoe Selo the haemorrhage was so bad that there was little hope. Again Rasputin's appearance at the child's bedside stopped the bleeding. His position was once more assured.

In July 1915 King Christian X sent Hans Niels Andersen to Tsarskoe Selo with an offer to act as mediator. He made several trips between London, Berlin and Petrograd and in July saw the Dowager Empress. 'At last I can hear again about everything and everybody', Dagmar wrote.[16] Andersen told her they should have concluded peace. Although she refused to hear of it, she never grew tired of praising 'clever Andersen'. Andersen also told her he had spent two hours on the French border with the Kaiser and heard his speeches. 'He [William] even dared to send me greetings!' she recorded incredulously. 'Merciless beast!'[17] Nicholas turned down King Christian's offer of mediation. Andersen left Copenhagen two days later, carrying a letter to Prince Waldemar from Dagmar.

By 10th August the Dowager Empress was again ill. 'Felt bad. Quite weak. Thought I was dying. Thought of my beloved mother', she wrote in her diary. She just wanted to cry. A letter from Alix restored her spirits but the bad news from the front continued to make her depressed.[18]

Soon Nicholas had taken the fatal decision to become Commander-in-Chief of the army, believing it would strengthen morale. Dagmar was horrified. By taking personal command Nicholas would associate himself with all the defeats of his army. On 21st August she had a visit from the Marshal of the Court, Count Paul Benckendorff, brother of the Russian Ambassador in London. 'We are exasperated because of the horrible news from the front', she wrote in her diary, 'but most of all: the "evil spirit Gregory" has returned and Alicky wishes that Nicky would take the High Command instead of Nicholas. She is mad if she really wants that! ...'[19]

Dagmar resolved to speak to Nicholas at once. Her diary entry for 25th August 1915:

Youssoupov was here and told me the dreadful things that are being talked about in town. Nicky himself came over with all four little girls. He himself said he wanted to take over the High Command instead of Nicholas. I was in such a fright that I nearly had a stroke. I told him my opinion and insisted that it would be a major mistake! I pleaded with him not to do this. Especially now, when our situation at the front is so precarious. I added that if he were to do this, everyone would see it as an order from Rasputin. I think this made an impression on him because he blushed deeply. He does not understand how dangerous it is and what misfortune it may bring upon us and the whole country.[20]

'For over two hours', says Anna Vyrubova, 'a painful scene was enacted in the Empress Dowager's gardens' as she tried to convince him that his place was in the capital; if things went wrong he would have to take the responsibility; and his decision could only lead to disaster. She begged him to reconsider and did everything she could to persuade him not to go. Although visibly shaken the Tsar maintained his resolve, insisting 'it was his duty, to save Russia'.[21] The Tsar later said that it had been more difficult to tell his mother than to tell his ministers.

'Everything is terrible at the front and at home', Dagmar's diary continued. 'I have spoken about everything with Schervashidze. It is a critical moment from whichever way you look at it'.[22] Other influential people shared her views. Prince Alexander of Oldenburg predicted the most terrible consequences. He and Princess Zenaide Youssoupov begged Dagmar to use her influence. Grand Duke Paul 'passed on to me everything he had told Nicky about the intended changeover ... Paul is of the same opinion as the rest of us', Dagmar continued.[23] Some members of the cabinet even took the unheard-of step of threatening to resign. Over the next few months Alicky had them all removed from office.

On 31st August the Dowager Empress descended upon the Alexander Palace. '3.45. With Xenia to Tsarskoe Selo to try my luck', she wrote. 'Nicky was at Kronstadt and didn't get back until seven. Drank tea with Alicky, who spoke about everything except what exercises me the most. I did have a chance to speak to Nicky, but without result'.[24]

Alek [Oldenburg] brought Dimitri Pavlovitch 'in the hope that this might help', Dagmar wrote on 2nd September. 'We walked in the garden and he told me his impressions of Nicholasha and how dangerous it would be to replace him, since everyone has such great trust in him ... A deadly situation'.[25]

The following day Nicky and Alicky came to lunch. 'She was with me for the first time after a year's break', Dagmar recorded. 'I again asked Nicky to leave the Commander-in-Chief in his post but unfortunately all my words were in vain. Alicky was in splendid spirits – how badly this sits in my head. Nicky said goodbye'.[26]

Later that day Miechen called at Yelagin, where she found the Dowager Empress 'désespérée' over her son's decision. 'It is quite disastrous', she told Miechen. The Grand Duchess stayed so long that she was thirty-five minutes late for dinner at her palace – an event unprecedented for a Romanov.[27]

The following day the Tsar left for Stavka (headquarters), now transferred to Moghilev, five hundred miles from the capital. Behind him he left uneasiness.

On 5th September came more bad news. Prince Vladimir Orlov, the Chief of the Tsar's Private Secretariat, was dismissed for speaking out against Rasputin and the Empress. 'This is madness', Dagmar wrote. 'To remove so loyal and devoted a friend as this. Incredible. So few friends and even these are thrown out'.[28]

'I can't understand why she [Alicky] is so imperious', Dagmar continued the following day. 'Even such a wonderful person as Orlov is removed because he got in her way. It's completely mad to force Nicky to isolate himself so completely and to dismiss those few devoted people who had remained'.[29] When Grand Duke Andrei visited Yelagin, he found Dagmar 'shaken' by recent events. She believed that Nicholasha's removal 'would lead directly to the downfall of her son', who was inadequately prepared to lead the army.[30] She acutely saw the danger to the throne if Russia was defeated. Worse still, by absenting himself from Petrograd Nicholas would leave the government in the hands of Alicky.

Later that day she received a telegram from Alicky informing her that Nicholasha would be relinquishing the High Command. 'May God be merciful to us', Dagmar commented. Only Grand Duke Cyril disagreed. 'Cyril thinks it is for the best', Dagmar noted in her diary on 9th September.[31] Nicholasha was packed off to the Caucasus.

The Dowager Empress, aware that for once she had failed, said she was reminded of the end of Emperor Paul's reign – but she also knew where to lay the blame for this latest disaster. Nicholas seemed content to be dominated by his wife. 'None of this is his [Nicholas'] wish, but her distorted views', Dagmar wrote the following day.[32] 'Where are we going, where are we going?' she asked Grand Duke Andrei. 'This is not Nicky ... he is gentle and honest and good – it is all her'.[33]

On 15th September Alicky brought Olga and Tatiana to have tea with their grandmother. Dagmar recorded her impressions of her daughter-in-law: 'What a tiring and curious person she is. She was in an unusually good mood and talked of indifferent matters, as if we were all doing splendidly'.[34]

Twelve days after Nicholas left for the front the Duma was prorogued. No regency council was appointed and, as Dagmar had foreseen, things went from bad to disastrous as the Empress took command. Beside her stood Rasputin.

From now on Alicky's hectoring, almost hysterical letters to her husband were full of 'Our Friend's' ideas on everything from taxes to food supplies. Soon she was nagging Nicholas incessantly to dismiss this or that minister who was opposed to Rasputin, the autocracy, or both. In their place were appointed nonentities favoured by Rasputin. In a space of just thirteen months, twelve ministers were replaced in what became known as 'Ministerial Leapfrog'. The Empress and Rasputin then turned their attention to the military situation. Alicky faithfully transmitted his instructions but, when things failed to improve, the outcry against 'Niemka' ('the German woman') grew louder.

Early in 1916 the senile Goremykin was replaced by Boris Sturmer, another incompetent reactionary favoured by Rasputin. From now on the ministers reported direct to the Empress and the cabinet had ceased to function.

*

In October 1915 Dagmar spent two weeks in Kiev, living on her train and visiting the hospitals, including the main military hospital where her daughter Olga was working as a nurse.

Olga, who was well aware of Dagmar's feelings about divorce, now had to tell her that she had decided to ask Nicholas for an annulment, in order to marry Colonel Kulikovsky. She and Petya had led separate lives for many years and Olga, who was now thirty-four, wanted to have children while she could.

To her surprise, Dagmar was sympathetic and calmly said that she understood. Perhaps it was guilt at having pushed her daughter into such a disastrous marriage; perhaps, sensing the storm that was to come, she felt that Olga deserved some happiness. There is no doubt she resented the fact that Kulikovsky was a commoner but, for the moment, said little.

When she returned from Kiev, Dagmar suffered from stomach trouble and at times was in considerable pain. She moved to the Yelagin Palace and discussed politics with her friends. 'I regret your Mama has returned to town', Alicky told Nicholas. '[I] fear one will fill her poor ears with unkind gossip'.[35] Soon Alicky accused Prince Schervashidze of turning her mother-in-law against her. Dagmar was becoming increasingly pre-occupied with the internal situation, realising that the course Nicholas was steering would lead to disaster. 'It is impossible to govern a large nation without the support of enlightened people and against public opinion', she said, repeatedly urging moderation. 'Had her advice been heeded', wrote the British Ambassador, 'Russia might have been spared much suffering'.[36]

The new year of 1916 found Dagmar lonely, unwell and unable to visit the hospitals. In March Polivanov was dismissed after a series of insistent, hectoring letters from Alicky. Seriously alarmed, statesmen and politicians begged the Dowager Empress to use her influence to break the power of the young Empress and Rasputin. Dagmar had tried before to open Nicholas' eyes. Now she hesitated. 'It's not want of courage or inclination that keeps her back', Miechen told the French Ambassador. 'It's better that she shouldn't. She's too outspoken and impetuous. The moment she begins to lecture her son, her feelings run away with her; she sometimes says the exact opposite of what she should; she annoys and humiliates him. Then he stands on his dignity and reminds his mother that he is the Emperor. They leave each other in a rage'.[37]

Nevertheless she resolved to have one last try. No-one knows for sure what took place at that painful interview but Prince Youssoupov later said that the Dowager Empress gave her son an ultimatum: 'Either me or Rasputin' – unless Rasputin was dismissed she would leave Petrograd. When Nicholas refused to dismiss Rasputin she knew the situation was hopeless: Russia was ruled by a 'shady character' and a daughter-in-law whom she had long considered to be 'mentally unbalanced'.[38]

The realisation that she had lost and Alicky had won was a bitter blow. Sadly Dagmar returned to the Anitchkov, where she made a momentous decision – she would join Olga in Kiev, where the atmosphere was more to her liking.

There have since been rumours that she was involved in one of the plots to depose her son in favour of a regency. Prince Nicholas Romanov does not feel she could have been involved in any such thing and has never heard of a serious quarrel between the Dowager Empress and the Tsar.[39] Their published letters show no evidence of such a breach.

Whatever happened her departure was sudden. She was anxious to leave within a few days. On 11th May Alicky and her daughters had tea at the Anitchkov, without Alexis, who was once again unable to walk.

On Sunday, 14th May she boarded her train. Although it seems her stay was only intended to be temporary it was a decision that probably saved her life. 'It's much better Motherdear stays … at Kiev', wrote Alicky, 'where the climate is milder and she can live as she wishes and *hears less gossip*'.[40] As Dagmar left Petrograd she did not know that she had also left the Anitchkov for ever.

CHAPTER 21

Revolution

'WOE TO THE COUNTRY WHERE ONLY THE SLAVE AND THE LIAR
ARE CLOSE TO THE THRONE' – Pushkin

Kiev, 'The Mother of Russian Cities', was a city of green trees and golden domes 1,550 miles south of Petrograd. Here in 988 St Vladimir began the conversion of his country to Christianity and had the whole population of Kiev baptised in the River Dneiper. At the end of the tenth century, when Kiev was already twice the size of London, the first stone church in Russia was constructed and dedicated. In 1888 Dagmar and her family attended the celebrations commemorating the 900th anniversary of the introduction of Christianity to Russia.

By May 1916 Kiev had grown into a modern city. After an enthusiastic welcome at the station Dagmar settled into the Baroque-style Maryinsky Palace on the right bank of the River Dnieper. With her were Prince Sergei Dolgoruky, Prince George Schervashidze and, as ladies-in-waiting, Countess Olga Heyden and Countess Zinaide Mengden. 'Zina' Mengden had joined the household in January 1912. She remained a devoted servant and friend for the remainder of Dagmar's life.

'I came here on Tuesday, straight into Summer, everything in bloom, all very beautiful and what is more, calm and peaceful', Dagmar wrote to Nicholas. The following day was his birthday. 'I ... wish you all that the loving heart of a mother can wish to a beloved son ... I am sending you a modest little present ... not very beautiful, but Fabergé had nothing else ...; all his workmen have gone to the war'.[1]

Kiev was nearer the front line. The Dowager Empress became actively involved in the work of the Red Cross, visited the hospitals and infirmaries, and organised special courses and schools to enable the wounded to take up a trade when they were discharged. Dagmar was very popular in Kiev, particularly for the way in which she always paid special attention to the maimed, disabled and blind soldiers. The administration work of the Red Cross was still handled by Prince Alexander of Oldenburg, Olga's father-in-law, who was responsible for ensuring that much-needed supplies and equipment reached the hospitals.

When not out visiting hospitals, she went for drives down the chestnut tree lined Kreshchatik, or called on old friends but she disliked her car being followed by plainclothes policemen. The Governor of Kiev, Count Alexis Ignatiev, and a police official were forced to follow a long way behind, so that they would not be seen. Dagmar soon became so at home that she developed a habit of referring to the city as if she owned it.

Sandro was also in Kiev, as Supreme Commander of the Russian Air Force. His duties frequently took him to Moghilev and Petrograd. On Sundays he came to lunch, sometimes accompanied by Olga if she was able to leave her nursing duties at the main military hospital, and they all discussed the events of the past week. 'We presented a pathetic group', he recalled. 'There we were, mother, sister and brother-in-law of the Emperor … willing to do everything he could ask of us … cognizant of the approaching upheaval, and yet wholly incapable of opening his eyes!'[2]

Dagmar had many other visitors, including Queen Olga of Greece, Grand Duke Andrei, Xenia, who came for a fortnight in July, and Michael. His marriage had upset Olga. As a result, Michael and his sister, so close in childhood, had become estranged. Now Olga, who desperately wanted to marry Colonel Kulikovsky, found herself in a similar position. Michael's visit cleared the air and, to Dagmar's relief and joy, Michael and Olga were reconciled. The previous October Nicholas had allowed Michael to regain control of his assets. Although this gave Dagmar added pleasure, relations between the brothers had become strained.

Michael suffered from poor health. Gastric ulcers had plagued him for years and the condition was exacerbated by his service in the army, where he was unable to follow his normal strict diet. Despite this, Michael had recently been appointed Commander of the 2nd Cavalry Corps. He saw it as further proof of the intention of the Tsar (and particularly the Tsarina) to keep him away from Natasha as much as possible. Michael wanted an appointment at Stavka and was lobbying his brother to obtain it. Natasha was incensed by their treatment of Michael and her anger included the Dowager Empress, who she blamed for the hostile attitude which she encountered almost everywhere. One day in June 1916 Natasha called unexpectedly at her hospital in Kiev, which she funded in Michael's name, only to find that her portrait had been removed from the entrance hall. The hospital authorities were expecting a visit from the Dowager Empress and could not afford to upset her by having Natasha's picture on show. During the summer of 1916 Natasha repeatedly urged Michael to 'have it out' with his mother and ask her to write to Nicholas about it. 'Any open conversation, even a quarrel, will be better than the silence you've been keeping', she added.[3]

*40. Hvidøre — the villa bought by Dagmar and Alexandra
after their father's death in 1906.*
(Collection of Senta Driver)

41. Hvidøre — The Drawing Room. The effect was homely and comfortable.
(Collection of Senta Driver)

42. Dagmar's bedroom at Hvidøre. The Empress died in this room.
(Collection of Senta Driver)

*43. The Viking House at Hvidøre. Furnishing the tea house provided a welcome
diversion for the widowed sisters in 1911.*
(Collection of Senta Driver)

44. Alexandra Feodorovna and Alexis. Alicky's reliance on Rasputin to heal her son was to have incalculable consequences for all the Romanovs.
(Private collection)

45. *Fredensborg. Early 1900s. Among those present are, l to r: Prince Louise of Schaumburg-Lippe, Crown Prince Frederick, Queen Alexandra, King George of Greece, King Christian IX, Princess Thyra of Denmark, Dagmar, Prince Hans of Glucksburg, Grand Duchess Olga. Empress Alexandra Feodorovna, Princess Victoria of Wales, Nicholas II, Edward VII and Princess Maud of Wales. Front: Prince Christian and Princess Marie-Louise of Schaumburg-Lippe, Grand Duchesses Tatiana, Olga and Marie Nicholaievna.*

(Ballerup Egnsmuseum, Denmark)

46. *Grand Duke Vladimir and his family. l to r: Boris, Cyril, Marie Pavlovna, Vladimir,*
Andrei and Helen. Marie Pavlovna never forgot that her sons were close in line for the throne.
(Private collection)

47. *The Fabergé Silver Punch Bowl. This magnificent punch bowl was a gift from the Dowager Empress to the Royal Danish Lifeguards on their 250th anniversary in 1908.*
(Det Livgardens Historiske Samling, Copenhagen)

48. *Dagmar and Alexandra playing billiards at Hvidøre.*
They once kept guests waiting while they finished an exciting game.
(Det Livgardens Historisk Samling, Copenhagen)

49. Dagmar on the veranda at Hvidøre.
(Det Livgardens Historiske Samling, Copenhagen)

50. Dagmar and her son Nicholas II. Although Nicholas never lost his love for his mother, his first loyalty was to his wife.
(Private collection)

51. The Maryinsky Palace, Kiev. Dagmar stayed here from May 1916 until she was forced to leave when the revolution reached Kiev in March 1917.
(Author's collection)

*52. Ai-Todor,
the Crimean
estate of Xenia
and Sandro.
The revolution
was slow to
reach the
Crimea and at
first
it seemed
that nothing
had changed.*
(Photographed
in 1916.
Jacques Ferrand)

*53. Djulber. The Crimean palace of Grand Duke Peter Nicholaievitch was like
something from the Arabian Nights.*
(Private collection)

54. Harax. The English-style home of Grand Duke George Michaelovitch was Dagmar's last refuge in Russia.
(Author's collection)

55. Waiting for H.M.S. Marlborough to set sail, Dagmar looks towards the Crimea for the last time, 11th April 1919.
(Private collection)

56. *Dagmar, Waldemar and Thyra photographed in Denmark in the 1920s.*
(Det Kongelige Bibliotek, Copenhagen)

57. *Christian IX's Palace at the Amalienborg. Dagmar returned to her father's old palace in Copenhagen in her exile. It is now the home of H.M. Queen Margrethe.*
(Author's collection)

58. *Dagmar as an old lady.*
(Det Kongelige Bibliotek, Copenhagen)

59. *The Dowager Empress' funeral procession in the streets of Roskilde.*
(Det Livgardens Historiske Samling, Copenhagen)

60. *Dagmar's tomb in the private crypt in Roskilde Cathedral.*
The icons came from her bedroom at Hvidøre.
(Photo: Flemming G. Rasmussen, Photographer at Roskilde Museum)

61. *The tomb of Nicholas II and his family in the SS Peter & Paul Cathedral, St Petersburg. Photographed three days after the funeral in July 1998.*
(Author's collection)

Below:
62. *The hand-written sign outside the chapel containing the Tsar's tomb says simply:* 'FORGIVE US'.
(Author's collection)

A constant worry to Dagmar was the lack of regular tidings from England, although Alix was still able to get some important news through. 'I have just had a telegram from Aunt Alix who wires in despair that they had lost six battleships', Dagmar wrote to Nicholas as the Battle of Jutland raged. 'But I do *hope* the German losses are even *heavier*'.[4]

Even though she was away from the capital the Dowager Empress was still an important person and foreign visitors called on her in Kiev. She still had some influence over the Tsar, who frequently consulted her about army and navy appointments, as well as Court matters. Count Pahlen was deprived of his rank as Marshal of the Court after the censors intercepted a letter in which he condemned military censorship. Dagmar immediately wrote to Alicky about the matter and the Count's rank was restored.

In June the revitalised Russian army gained a great victory on the Austrian front. Roumania (now ruled by King Ferdinand and Dagmar's English-born niece Queen Marie, a daughter of the Duchess of Coburg), entered the war on the side of the allies but was soon defeated. The Royal family fled to Jassy and the Germans triumphantly entered Bucharest. The eastern front now ran from the Baltic to the Black Sea.

In July Sazonov, the Foreign Minister, was dismissed. His replacement was none other than the incompetent Sturmer, who remained as Prime Minister. Alicky then urged Nicholas to dismiss the Minister of the Interior. To this key post, which controlled the Empire's police, the Tsar was cajoled into appointing Alexander Protopopov, Vice President of the Duma, another nonentity favoured by Rasputin. Dagmar made no secret of her feelings.

Now all the key posts in the government were occupied by Rasputin's nominees and even reports of his drunken orgies in public places could not destroy Alicky's faith in him. 'Remember that I need neither the Emperor nor yourself', he told her; 'if you abandon me you will lose your son and your crown within six months'.[5]

*

On 14th September 1916 there was a big lunch to celebrate the 50th anniversary of Dagmar's arrival in Russia. Members of the family, deputations from Kiev's municipal authorities and delegations from all corners of the Empire came to offer their congratulations. Nicholas awarded her a decoration with the figure '50' picked out in diamonds and there was a gala concert. Dagmar attended it with Sandro but the performance went on for such a long time that the sixty-eight-year-old Dowager Empress began to nod off in the Imperial box.

On 11th November Nicholas and Alexis arrived. When their train pulled in to Kiev Station the Tsar's overjoyed mother was waiting to meet them, with her brother-in-law Grand Duke Paul, Sandro, Miechen, the District Governor and the Mayor. Although the streets were dark and foggy as they drove back to the palace nothing could dampen Dagmar's spirits. She was delighted at this intimacy, without the presence of her daughter-in-law. 'Mama was very kind and charming', Nicholas told Alicky. 'In the evenings … we had long talks'. The antipathy between his mother and his wife worried Nicholas and he did not mention that, during the first of these talks, Dagmar demanded the dismissal of Sturmer and the removal of Rasputin. There are no records of what was said but it is unlikely that Dagmar would have launched a direct attack against her daughter-in-law; she knew Nicholas would never listen to any criticism of his wife. Alicky was upset that her mother-in-law listened to gossip. 'When you see poor Motherdear', she wrote, 'you must rather sharply tell her how pained you are, that she listens to slander and does not stop it, as it makes mischief and others would be delighted, I am sure, to put her against me …'[6]

The days passed quickly in a haze of activity. After dinner mother and son spent cozy evenings together and were able to re-establish their former close relationship. Yet Dagmar noticed a worrying change in Nicholas. He was abnormally quiet and his face was pale and drawn.

On the second day Paul and Miechen came to tea. The Grand Duchess presented Dagmar with an icon signed by nearly all the members of the Imperial family to commemorate the 50th anniversary of her wedding. As Nicholas' train pulled away Dagmar had no way of knowing that next time she met him it would be under vastly different circumstances, or that she would never see Alexis again.

*

Olga's marriage to Prince Peter of Oldenburg was annulled that autumn and on 17th November she married Colonel Nicholas Kulikovsky. Although Dagmar had said little when Olga originally raised the subject, she was afraid of public opinion. For once, she was united with Alicky in her feelings. The Tsar, however, shared Olga's view that it was better if they married quietly now while people were occupied with the war. The day before the ceremony, Dagmar decided to attend after all – provided she was not followed. Count Ignatiev instucted the plainclothes police that they were not to come anywhere near the church.

All the way to the lovely old Kiev Vasily Church on Tryokhsviyatitel Street Dagmar suffered from acute anxiety. Inside, only a handful of people were present and, when the formidable figure of the Dowager Empress entered, the priest was nearly frightened out of his wits. Despite the falling snow outside, when he was introduced to her, beads of perspiration ran down his face.

Instead of the heavy silver dress and Romanov jewels the bride wore a simple dress, a wreath of orange blossom and a veil. Afterwards they all went back to Olga's hospital for supper and some of them got tipsy on homemade wine. Dagmar's departure at eight o'clock was the signal for a lively dance to begin. Later that evening Olga and her husband left for a honeymoon in Kursk.

For Dagmar, by now resigned to the marriage, it was a very emotional occasion. 'I am so very glad I was able to attend', she wrote, adding 'may God give her every happiness'.[7] Later she told Xenia that she would never have been able to forgive herself if she had stayed away. Despite this, she never referred to Colonel Kulikovsky by his Christian name.

*

In the wake of Nicholas' visit Dagmar was distressed. Once again she had failed to make him see that the influence of Alicky and Rasputin was endangering the dynasty. According to Prince Youssoupov, she wrote to her son 'begging him to send Rasputin away and to forbid the Tsarina to interfere in affairs of state'. Nicholas told his wife and she broke off relations with the family. The Tsar and Tsarina sent no Christmas presents to the Grand Dukes or their families that year. Alicky was particularly wary of her mother-in-law. 'Should Motherdear write, remember the Michaels are behind her', [Sandro and his brothers, sons of the late Grand Duke Michael Nicholaievitch] she wrote. 'Thank God she is not here, but kind people find means of writing and doing harm'.[8]

Dagmar had a very high regard for Sandro's brother Grand Duke Nicholas Michaelovitch but, when he came to see her, she was dreadfully upset. At her insistence, he wrote to the Tsar warning him about Alicky's influence in government affairs. 'I have hesitated for a long time before telling you the truth', he said, 'but have now decided to do so on the persuasion of your mother and sisters'.[9] The response from Alicky was a hysterical outburst. Many other members of the family voiced their concern but to Dagmar's dismay Nicholas ignored them all.

Eighty people came to lunch on Dagmar's sixty-ninth birthday. Among them was Grand Duke Paul, who brought his morganatic wife, now created Princess Paley. Despite the festive occasion the tension beneath the surface could be felt. The next day Paul was warned that the situation was serious and, now that the Dowager Empress had failed, the family were counting on him to speak to the Tsar.

The internal situation had deteriorated. Prices were soaring, at the end of October all Petrograd's factories went on strike and two regiments of

the garrison, summoned to suppress the strikers, fired on the police. Officers took extended leave and were seen nightly in the theatres, indifferent to the war. There were desertions at the front and mutinies among
the troops. Thousands of lives had been lost taking territory which, a few
weeks later, was lost again and in the Duma the government was attacked
from all sides. German spy mania reached a new pitch. Sturmer and the
Empress were hated by the people, who believed that a pro-German
faction in the palace was betraying Russia's secrets. Hatred against the
'German woman' increased. Rasputin was widely believed to be a German spy and he and the Empress were rumoured to be trying to bring
about a separate peace with Germany. In contrast, Dagmar's patriotism
was never questioned during her fifty years in Russia.

On his return from Kiev, with Dagmar's insistent pleas ringing in his
ears, Nicholas dismissed the hated Sturmer and replaced him with Alexander Trepov, a conservative monarchist and enemy of Rasputin. Trepov
asked for the Tsar's promise that Protopopov's dismissal would follow but,
influenced by the hysterical pleas of his wife, Nicholas broke his word and
Protopopov stayed.

Two members of the Imperial family made a last bid to rid the throne
of Rasputin's influence. Grand Duke Paul had tea at Tsarskoe Selo and,
after warning about the harm Rasputin was doing, asked Nicholas to
grant a constitution without delay. The Tsar refused and the Empress
vehemently defended Rasputin.

Soon afterwards Ella came from her convent in Moscow. The Empress
cut the conversation short and the next morning the Grand Duchess was
asked to leave. Ella had been the Imperial family's last hope. She had failed
and it was left to Prince Felix Youssoupov to supply the alternative.

*

In 1916 it was reported that the British government, worried about
German influence on the Imperial family, had asked the Danish Royal
family to intervene. It was proposed to send Prince Waldemar to Russia
to see the Dowager Empress. By this time, of course, Dagmar had little
political influence over her son and certainly none over her daughter-in-
law. Whatever they hoped to achieve, the plan was abandoned because of
Denmark's neutrality in the war.

By the autumn the German government was encouraging revolution
as a means of getting Russia out of the war. The Kaiser, afraid that
revolution would spread to Germany, sent Alicky's brother, Grand Duke
Ernst Ludwig of Hesse, to initiate peace moves without the knowledge of
the High Command.

Despite the war Ernie, a general in the German army, had been in regular contact with his sister but to travel on such a mission was extremely dangerous for him. With anti-German hysteria at its height, Alicky's decision to see her brother could only be seen as treason. The visit was a closely-guarded secret. Details only leaked out many years later when the trip took on a wholly unexpected significance in the Anastasia court cases.

Travelling incognito in civilian clothes, Ernie arrived at Tsarskoe Selo by way of Haparanda, on the Finnish/Russian frontier. Several people, including members of the Kaiser's family, later confirmed the visit, although it has always been denied by the Hesse family.

In 1987 some entries purporting to be from the 1916 diary of the Dowager Empress were used by Anthony Summers and Tom Mangold in their book *The File on the Tsar*. The entries had been given to them by a researcher working on a related project. 'GDE has arrived unannounced!' said the entry, in English, for 15th November 1916. 'I suspect A knew! I am told not even the P.M. is to know. A is behind this, and [here it continued in Danish and the content was not noted] ... E paid his respects. *No* mention of this dangerous adventure'. 'What foolishness E proposes, how foolish', the alleged diary entry says on 16th November. 'We must not accept these ridiculous proposals!'[10]

As the sudden appearance of the Dowager Empress at Tsarskoe Selo would have aroused comment, the phrase 'E paid his respects' suggests that Ernie travelled to Kiev, another somewhat risky undertaking in wartime. Nevertheless, the 1916 diary entries are unauthenticated. The diary is missing and is not in the State Archives of the Russian Federation where the researcher claimed to have seen it in 1984. It surfaced briefly in 1925 before disappearing again. Unless a copy was taken, the mystery remains.

Other witnesses place the Grand Duke's visit in February. Nicholas and Alexis left for the front on 7th November and did not return until about 31st December. There were no letters between Nicholas and Alicky from 25th November to 17th December, as she was visiting Stavka. It would therefore have been perfectly possible for Ernie to have visited Alicky, but not Nicholas, at Tsarskoe Selo around 15th November.

Dagmar's reaction to any German peace proposals was always a categorical rejection and the diary entries, if genuine, are perfectly in accordance with her feelings. She once called the Kaiser 'a false person' and 'an unprincipled beast'[11] and she fully backed Nicholas' vow never to make a separate peace.

In December 1916 the Kaiser put out a more open peace offer. 'It is always the same thing', Dagmar said. '[William] wants to act as a peace-maker, throwing all the responsibility on us if we do not accept. I do hope nobody will let himself be duped'.[12] Later that month the German Chancellor made a formal peace offer to all the allies. It was rejected.

*

One evening during the last days of December, Prince Dolgoruky received a telephone call from Count Ignatiev. When he returned to the Dowager Empress the prince brought some startling news. Rasputin had disappeared and was believed dead. Zina Mengden recalled that everyone breathed a sigh of relief.

On New Year's Day 1917 Sandro brought some even more startling news. Rasputin had been murdered by a group of conspirators who included her nephew Grand Duke Dimitri, Prince Felix Youssoupov and the right-wing Duma member Vladimir Purishkevich. Dagmar reacted, as she usually did when she heard something alarming, by jumping up and crying, 'No! No!' in a tone half surprised and half exclamatory.

Rasputin had been lured to a specially prepared basement room in the Moika Palace, the magnificent Youssoupov mansion in Petrograd, on the pretext of meeting Princess Irina (who was, in fact, in the Crimea). Felix plied him with poisoned cakes and wine, while the others played a gramophone upstairs to simulate a party. When, after almost two and a half hours, the poison failed to work Felix, almost prostrate with nerves, went upstairs for a gun and shot Rasputin in the back. Yet still he was not dead. Minutes later he opened his eyes, crawled up the stairs and escaped into the courtyard where Purishkevich shot him again. His body was wrapped in a curtain and thrown through a hole in the frozen Neva. The corpse was discovered two days later. Although the cause of death was established as the bullet wounds there were traces of water in his lungs, indicating that Rasputin may have died by drowning. All sorts of rumours were circulating in Petrograd. The Danish Minister's wife heard that four women were present in the palace on the night of the crime.

Dagmar was horrified that members of the Imperial family had stooped to such lengths. As a Christian she disliked the idea of murder but she was glad Rasputin was dead and hoped that Alicky's power would also decline. Sandro summed up her reaction as, 'the Lord be praised for taking away Rasputin, but we were in for a much greater trouble'.[13]

Whatever their misguided motives, the law said the murderers must be punished and it was obvious that Alicky would be crying out for vengeance. Sandro hurried to Petrograd to see the Tsar. The Allied Ambassadors now wanted Dagmar to return to the capital, as the Tsar 'still fears her a little (not very much)'.[14] Others also hoped the Dowager Empress would use her influence. 'Surely Grandmother [Dagmar] will come in an endeavour to do something for you', wrote Mme Rodzianko guardedly to

Zenaide Youssoupov. 'He [the Tsar] is completely browbeaten and incapable of doing anything, while she [the Empress] and her agent – the equally mad P [Protopopov] – are ruining us all'.[15] Felix was exiled to his estate near Kursk and Dimitri was sent to the Persian front. The other conspirators went free. The Imperial family then presented a joint letter to the Tsar asking for leniency. Nicholas replied icily that murder is murder and it was not only Dimitri who was implicated.

Dagmar (accompanied by Irina who hurried from the Crimea) left for Kursk to support the Youssoupovs. She had already received a despairing letter from Grand Duke Paul, who was not even given a chance to say goodbye to Dimitri. Now, on her return to Kiev, she received a visit from Paul's daughter, the younger Grand Duchess Marie Pavlovna. She had always been fond of Paul's children and received her niece warmly. However, there was little she could do, and Marie left with the feeling that she would not interfere. Nevertheless, Dagmar telegraphed to Nicholas demanding that the investigation into Dimitri's part in the murder be closed. A reply soon followed: 'Prosecution will be immediately stopped. Embrace you. Nicky'.[16] Rasputin's murderers were never put on trial.

Dagmar followed this with a tactful letter, expressing her worry and distress that she had been unable to help during the last trying months. Then she came to the subject uppermost in her mind: 'One should search in oneself and forgive ... I am sure you are aware yourself how deeply you have offended all the family by your brusque reply, throwing at their heads a dreadful and entirely unjustified accusation. I hope also ... that you will alleviate the fate of Dimitri Pavlovitch by not leaving him in Persia where the climate is so dreadful ... [he had tuberculosis] It is not like you with your kind heart to behave in this way; it upsets me very much'.[17]

Contrary to the expectations of Dagmar (and almost everyone else), the news of Rasputin's death did not cause a palace revolution, nor did the Empress have a breakdown. The main telephone at Tsarskoe Selo was in her sitting room and a wooden staircase now connected this room to a balcony outside the Tsar's audience chamber. Here, lying on a couch, she could listen while he talked to his ministers.

Although observers reported that the Tsar's reaction to Rasputin's death was relief, Nicholas does seem to have suffered a nervous collapse. Ministers and Ambassadors were shocked by the change in his appearance. Rumours circulated that the Empress was giving him drugs – Tibetan herbs, reported the French Ambassador – and stories to this effect had been circulating for some time at the Dowager Empress' court. Nicholas certainly showed signs of mental and physical exhaustion, remaining secluded in his private apartments at Tsarskoe Selo, avoiding decisions and giving the French Ambassador the impression that he was overwhelmed by events and was resigned to disaster.

Sandro returned from his six-day stay in Petrograd and gave Dagmar a full report on the situation. He had no doubt that revolution would come sooner, rather than later if Alicky continued to intervene in government affairs. Sandro pleaded with her to withdraw from politics but Alicky refused to listen. When he launched into an angry tirade Nicholas showed him the door. Early in the new year Trepov resigned and the old, ineffectual Prince Nicholas Golitsyn replaced him as Prime Minister. He had been deputy chairman of one of Alicky's charitable committees. As ministers came and went with alarming rapidity the Imperial government began to crumble. Yet Protopopov stayed – the Empress refused to hear any talk of his dismissal.

When Dagmar and Olga heard Sandro's account of his interview with the Tsarina they shivered. The only explanation for Alicky's behaviour, Dagmar told Xenia, was that she must be crazy. She prayed that God would help 'poor Nicky' escape his wife's dangerous influence.

Next Dagmar heard that all the ministers had resigned and that Mouravel, a 'wolf in sheep's clothing' who she called 'evil' and 'a liar' and who she had repeatedly warned Nicholas not to trust, was the ringleader. Instead of remembering his mother's advice Nicholas continued to listen to Alicky, who only favoured people who flattered her.[18]

Desperate and utterly crushed, Dagmar told Xenia that she could see no future other than being flung into the abyss ...

Dagmar had no intention of returning to live in Petrograd. In Kiev she was away from all the intrigues and avoided the gossip her close relations with Prince Schervashidze would cause in the capital. He had been in her service for nearly twenty years but just how close their relationship had ever been is not yet clear.

Nevertheless, Dagmar was worried about the current state of affairs. On 19th January 1917 she noted her concern in her diary, again adding her wish that Nicholas would stop following his wife's disastrous counsel. She now received few letters from Nicholas. Sandro and Felix hoped that, once the Tsar went back to the front, they and the Dowager Empress could descend upon Petrograd. There they would have Protopopov and Shcheglovaty (Chairman of the State Council) arrested and demand that Alicky and her confidante Anna Vyrubova be sent to the Crimea. Only by this course of action, Felix felt, could disaster be avoided.

Xenia had returned to Petrograd but correspondence with her mother was tampered with by the secret police. Dagmar was concerned about German activity in Danish waters and worried that they would destroy Hvidøre out of malice. She was frightened for her old homeland, she told

Xenia in January, but could now do no more than sit quietly in Kiev and await events. Misha, she said, agreed with her.

The Imperial family, the ministers and even the Allied Ambassadors were unanimous in the opinion that, unless the Empress withdrew altogether from government affairs and the Tsar appointed a ministry acceptable to the Duma, revolution was inevitable. Many of them stated their concern in personal interviews or letters to the Tsar. Others went to see the Dowager Empress to ask her advice. One of the signatories to the Imperial family's joint letter to the Tsar, the liberal Grand Duke Nicholas Michaelovitch, was exiled to his estate for spreading insulting stories about the Empress. On his way into exile he went to see Dagmar in Kiev. Writing to Xenia, Dagmar could only wonder how Alicky had such power over Nicholas and concluded she must use hypnosis.

Misha, complaining of lack of influence over the Tsar, begged Rodzianko to tell Nicholas that the Empress must be removed from public affairs. Again, Nicholas rejected the advice. On his way back to the front to take up a new appointment as Inspector General of Cavalry, Michael spent the day with his mother. Dagmar had now decided to remain in the calm and peace of Kiev and not become involved in any unpleasantness. She had heard nothing, she told Xenia, since Misha and Sandro left. A small camp church had been erected in the Maryinsky Palace to enable her to prepare for Communion without going to the Governor's palace twice a day. Although Dagmar felt at peace with herself, she admitted to Xenia that her heart harboured such terrible feelings.

In the Imperial Yacht Club the Grand Dukes were discussing plots and counter-plots. The dethronement of the Tsar and the establishment of a regency was very much on the minds of the Imperial family, who, after all, had the most to lose if there was a revolution. Their only point of disagreement was about who should be regent. Some of them drafted a petition to the Dowager Empress asking her to make her views known.

They were all united in their condemnation of the Empress. 'Alexandra Feodorovna must be banished', said Dagmar. 'I don't know how but it must be done. Otherwise she might go completely mad. Let her enter a convent or just disappear'. Miechen finished a conversation with Rodzianko by saying that the Empress 'must be annihilated'.[19] Soon afterwards Cyril and Andrei were ordered to leave Petrograd. Miechen followed.

On the morning of 7th March Nicholas wavered and agreed to go to the Duma the following day to announce the appointment of a respons- ible ministry. Later in the day he changed his mind. That night he returned to Stavka.

'I believe that God will have pity on Russia', wrote Dagmar.[20] Rasputin's murder had come too late. The dynasty was incapable of reforming and the country was ripe for revolution.

*

The winter of 1917 was bitter in Petrograd. In temperatures of 35-40 degrees below zero the railways, essential for bringing food to the cities and supplies to the front, froze to a standstill as the boilers burst; factories closed through lack of fuel; flour, wood and coal disappeared and a shortage of food in the capital pushed prices up to an exorbitant level. Rumours of bread rationing provoked panic buying and women queued outside the bakeries for hours in the snow, cold, hungry and disillusioned.

On Thursday, 8th March, there were disturbances in the capital. Bakeries were looted and columns of protesting workers marched through the streets. The following day there were more demonstrations. By Saturday, 10th March, over 200,000 workers were on strike, marching defiantly through Petrograd with red banners chanting, 'Down with the Government! Down with Protopopov! Down with the war!' The Cossacks failed to use their whips to break up the mob. The Tsar was urged to return and appoint a ministry acceptable to the Duma. Nicholas, five hundred miles from Petrograd and unaware of the seriousness of the situation, refused and ordered the streets to be cleared.

On Sunday morning troops were sent to break up the crowd and there was shooting on the streets of Petrograd. Two hundred people were killed and many others were wounded. Nicholas ordered the Duma to be prorogued but Rodzianko ignored the order. An Executive Committee of the Duma under Rodzianko remained in the Tauride Palace but in another room. A Soviet of Soldiers' and Workers' Deputies was meeting in the left wing of the palace. The Vice-Chairman was thirty-six-year-old Alexander Kerensky. Rodzianko pleaded with the Tsar to appoint a responsible ministry. Instead, Nicholas sent General Ivanov to Petrograd with reinforcements to quash the uprising by force.

Monday, 12th March, was the decisive day. The Imperial Guard, the Preobrajensky, Semonovksy and Ismailovsky Guards who, although they now comprised factory workers and raw conscripts, were still considered the élite regiments of the Tsar's army, fraternised with the mob. By night-fall over 66,000 soldiers had mutinied and joined the revolution. Rodzianko's power was waning rapidly. Later that day the Duma and the Soviet reached a compromise and a Provisional Government was formed with Prince George Lvov as Prime Minister and Alexander Kerensky as Minister of Justice. The Tsar's ministers, including the hated Protopopov, gave themselves up to the protection of the Duma.

In Kiev there had been no newspapers or telegraph communication with Petrograd for three days. 'Where is my eldest son?' Dagmar telegraphed to the Ministry of Foreign Affairs on 12th March.[21] In her diary she gave full vent to her worry and distress. 'No news at all from Petersburg, very distressing', she wrote the following day. 'Ignachev [Count Ignatiev, Governor of Kiev] came to lunch; he has heard nothing either. The Duma closed, why? People say that it is definitely her [Alicky's] work again, a terrible error at a moment like this! Must be mad, unbelievable to assume such a responsibility ...'[22]

As the revolution spread to the Baltic Fleet, Kronstadt and Moscow, the worried and despairing Dowager Empress heard rumours of the street disturbances in Petrograd from trusted friends but any news she did receive was out of date and there was no way of knowing the seriousness of the situation. It was understood that the Tsar was on his way back to Tsarskoe Selo but Dagmar still had no idea of his whereabouts. 'The Empress, Olga and myself ran out of words', wrote Sandro. 'We glared at each other in silence'.[23]

Nicholas' train had left for Tsarskoe Selo early on the morning of 13th March. En route he heard of the collapse of the Imperial government and the passing of power to the Duma. A hundred miles south of Petrograd he was informed that revolutionary soldiers were blocking the line ahead and he could go no further. He doubled back to Pskov, headquarters of General Rusky's Northern Army, where he heard the latest news. Ivanov's regiments had reached Tsarskoe Selo, where they were met by revolutionary soldiers and discreetly melted away; Grand Duke Cyril had marched to the Tauride Palace at the head of his regiment of the Guard Equipage to pledge allegiance to the Duma. He was the first Romanov to break his oath of allegiance to the Tsar. Nicholas at last agreed to appoint an acceptable ministry but it was too late. Petrograd had passed into the hands of the revolutionaries.

'Nothing from St Petersburg, horrible situation ...' Dagmar wrote in her diary on 14th March. 'Saw Fogel [Sandro's A.D.C.], who told me what he knew. Riots in all the streets, all after the Duma was closed; for this we can thank her stupidity and hunger to rule in Nicky's absence; it is incomprehensible to assume such a responsibility. They were fighting in the street; the army that was called in refused to shoot at the people. So the police shot at them; many killed! Rodzianko has put himself at the head of a new government ... All the previous ministers were dismissed, arrested ...'[24]

'No news from St Petersburg. Not right at all', Dagmar continued on 15th March. 'Then Figi Leuchtenberg came to express her sympathy for everything that is happening. Very nice ... Finally got a telegram from

Micha [*sic*], who is with Xenia in St Petersburg ... Heard that there was a mutiny in Kronstadt, they killed that dear Admiral Viren; infamous! in addition to many others, we don't know who ... They say that my poor Nicky is in Pskov. Can only speak and think about this horror. Got a telegram from Xenia, who says no one knows where Nicky is; dreadful what they are going through! May the Lord help us'.[25] That night, restless and agitated, Dagmar was unable to sleep.

She was not prepared for what happened next.

Nicholas, isolated in his train at Pskov, was told that it was too late now for concessions. Unwilling to plunge his country into civil war, he took the course urged upon him by the Duma, the Soviet and his generals. On 15th March, Nicholas II abdicated in favour of Alexis, with Michael as regent. Then Dr Fedorov pointed out that Alexis' illness was incurable. He would in all likelihood be separated from his family and sent to live with Michael and his unsuitable wife. Nicholas changed his mind. Later that day he abdicated for himself and Alexis, leaving the throne to Michael.

The following day Michael, aware only that he was to be regent, attended a meeting of the ministers at Princess Putiatin's house in Petrograd, where he was informed he was to be Tsar. After several hours of discussion, Michael, advised that anti-monarchist feeling was high and that his safety could not be guaranteed, issued a manifesto stating that he would not accept authority until invited to do so by an elected Constituent Assembly.

The 304-year-old Romanov dynasty had fallen.

*

At nine o'clock in the morning of 16th March Sandro brought Dagmar the news that Nicholas had abdicated in favour of Michael. It hit her 'like a thunderbolt', recalled Olga. She was 'in a terrible state'. Although the Dowager Empress quickly recovered her composure, she still could not understand Nicholas' reasons for abdicating. She repeatedly called it 'the greatest humiliation of her life'.[26] 'Am completely disconsolate!!', she wrote in her diary. 'To think that I should live to witness such horror ... I am in despair over everything'.[27]

At eight o'clock that evening Dagmar and Sandro left Kiev to meet Nicholas in Moghilev, where he had gone to say goodbye to the army. She left accompanied by full honours, although she was unable to use her own train, which was in Petrograd. There was a Cossack escort to the station and, in the Imperial waiting room, still resplendent with silk wall-hangings and red carpet, Count Ignatiev was waiting for her departure.

At midday, after another sleepless night, Dagmar arrived at Moghilev in a snowstorm. Nicholas was waiting on the platform. Zina Mengden took the only photographs of their reunion – the train standing by a snow-covered platform. She could not bring herself to photograph the fallen Tsar.

At some stage during this momentous day Dagmar received the further shock that Michael had refused the throne. Her published diary entries make no mention of it:

Beloved Nicky met me at the station. A sad meeting! We drove together to his house, where we immediately ate lunch with everyone ... Then my poor Nicky told me all the horrible things that had happened in the two days ... He is splendidly calm, collected and magnificent in this awful, humiliating position. It was as if I had been hit on the head and do not comprehend it![28]

When Sandro was summoned he found Dagmar 'sobbing aloud', all trace of her habitual self-control gone. Nicholas 'stood motionless, looking at his feet and, of course, smoking'. The Tsar was calm but pale and 'criticized ... Misha for refusing to accept the throne and for leaving Russia without a ruler'.[29]

Xenia was told later that, when asked why he had abdicated and whether he would ever return to the crown, Nicholas replied, 'what could I do when Nicholasha and General Alexeyev asked me to resign for the country's sake? No, I will never return'. Dagmar telegraphed to Xenia that she was 'happy to be with him in this gravest moment' and described the weather as 'also desperate'.[30] She could not forget that Alicky's influence was responsible for the circumstances of this meeting. After dinner on Dagmar's train, 'poor Nicky opened his poor, bleeding heart and we wept together'.[31]

Dagmar's three day visit was extremely painful. At church on Sunday the Emperor and his mother were named in the prayers but, for the first time in 304 years, mention of the family was omitted. At lunch Count Fredericks (the Minister of the Court) and Prince Alexander of Oldenburg told Dagmar that she must persuade Nicholas to go abroad at once, despite the fact that his children were ill with measles at Tsarskoe Selo. A meeting was then called, at which General Alexeyev, Sandro and his brother Grand Duke Sergei Michaelovitch were present. 'Nicky ... said that no answer had arrived yet from Petersburg if it was safe. The answer could not come until tomorrow. Nicky himself was unbelievably calm; how much he must suffer beyond all description!'[32]

Afterwards, as they drove through the streets, she could not bear to look at the red flags intermingled with the bunting. As their car passed, people knelt and schoolgirls pushed forward begging for souvenirs from their former sovereign. Late at night, in a pathetic gesture of defiance, Dagmar had all the lights put on in her train.

The following day Sir John Hanbury-Williams (Chief of the British Military Mission) was summoned to Dagmar's train. She was very distressed that the Tsar's abdication had been insisted upon and asked him to thank his colleagues for their sympathy. He had already asked his government about the possibility of the Tsar going to England and was confident of the other Allied Chiefs' support. Dagmar, who was worried about the sea voyage during war-time, intimated that she would prefer them to go to neutral Denmark. Nicholas' refusal to go anywhere without his family worried her, because it presented grave difficulties. She also thanked him for helping to maintain morale in the army. The most urgent concern, she told him, was to co-operate with the Emperor to 'paralyse the harmful forces ... active ... in the army and fleet'.[33] Reporting to the King, Sir John added that the Dowager Empress was 'marvellously plucky and sensible, in fact wonderful with all the troubles she has to bear, and alone'.[34]

The Provisional Government had given Nicholas permission to join his family. He had rejected all suggestions of escape and all offers of help or protection from the Allies. On 21st March, he and Dagmar lunched together before a deputation came to escort him to Tsarskoe Selo. He tried to comfort her by saying they would meet soon but she cried almost continuously as he covered her face with kisses and strode across the platform with the few members of his suite permitted to accompany him home. As his train slowly pulled away Dagmar could see him framed in the window, waving, with an expression of infinite sadness on his face. Her eyes overflowing with tears, she made the sign of the Cross as the train slowly disappeared. When it was out of sight she broke down completely.

'One of the most awful days in my life!', she wrote, 'when I was separated from my beloved Nicky! ... An awful, sorrowful parting!! May God hold his hands over him ...'[35] In a telegram to Alix, she described this final parting as 'heartcrushing'.[36]

Mother and son were never to meet again.

*

The harsh reality of the revolution was brought home to Dagmar the moment her train arrived back in Kiev. Civilians wearing red armbands stood on the platform, there was no reception committee, no Cossack escort and the train did not even stop near the waiting room. After climbing over an untidy roll of red carpet, Dagmar and Zina Mengden entered a carriage and drove to the palace preceded by a car full of civilians sporting red cockades. Zina noticed that the Imperial crowns had been removed from the carriage doors. At the Maryinsky Palace there was no Imperial standard flying from the flagpole and the guard of honour had been replaced by ill-dressed, untidy soldiers who did not even present arms as they passed. Inside the hall, Count Ignatiev received Dagmar in civilian clothes. Grand Duchess Olga was hastily summoned to pacify her mother, who she had never seen in such a state. Dagmar's anger and misery almost boiled over, she was unable to sit still and kept pacing up and down the room, totally unable to accept the reality of the situation. 'She understood nothing of what had happened', Olga recalled. 'She blamed poor Alicky for ... everything'.[37]

Several days after her return from Moghilev, Dagmar told Xenia that she was still unable to recover from all the awful experiences, especially parting with Nicholas and seeing him leave as a prisoner on his own train. She never believed they would be treated like this in Russia and was so angry she was even unable to cry. A few days later, wishing she were dead and buried, she called the revolutionaries the 'abominables'.

On 20th March the Petrograd Soviet had called for the arrest of all the members of the former Imperial family. A few days later more than one hundred deputies of the Petrograd Soviet protested that 'Nicholas the Bloody', the Tsarevitch, the Empress and the Dowager Empress were still free. They demanded that 'the most resolute steps' be taken to imprison all the Romanovs.[38]

In Kiev the public mood was still joyful. Dagmar and her family watched as massive demonstrations, with red flags and the 'Marseillaise' playing, were held in honour of the people's newly-acquired freedom. A Ukranian National Assembly, the National Rada, met and preached independence for the Ukraine and promised to fight the Bolsheviks. Then, gradually, the mood of the people turned ugly. The police were abolished. Prisoners, released by the mob, roamed the streets and the public cheered them like heroes. Obscene graffiti about the Emperor and Empress appeared on walls and the Imperial double-headed eagle was torn from buildings. Overnight the Dowager Empress and her relatives became 'Romanovs, the enemies of the Revolution and the Russian people'. Dagmar could not understand the people's change of attitude. 'My unfortunate Nicky may have made some mistakes', she murmured, 'but to say that he is an enemy of his people. Ah, never ...'[39]

Although Dagmar telegraphed repeatedly to Tsarskoe Selo she never received an answer and was certain her telegrams had been stopped. She was sure that Nicholas, who was proud and stubborn, would never understand what he had done. In despair she told Xenia of her fears for the family at the Alexander Palace. She could not even help nurse her sick grandchildren and only hoped they could leave there as soon as possible.

By the end of March the British Royal family were seriously worried about the stability of the Provisional Government and Sir George

Buchanan was instructed to enquire about the Dowager Empress. He was able to assure London that she was in good health, perfectly safe and there was no need for anxiety, although she was not permitted to receive letters and had no news of her sister. He was waiting for permission to forward two letters from Alexandra and added that there was no point in the Queen telegraphing.

The Danish Government was also concerned. After consultations with King Christian X, on 22nd March the Danish Minister in Petrograd was instructed to report on the possibilities of the Imperial family going abroad. It is likely that they had decided to give them asylum in Denmark or, at the very least, to help them get to western Europe. It is also possible that an approach was made by the Provisional Government, who were considering both England and Denmark as places of asylum.

The Danish government concentrated their attention on Dagmar and they were fortunate to have two very remarkable men at hand – Erik Scavenius, the Foreign Minister, and his cousin Harald Scavenius, Denmark's Minister to Petrograd since 1912. Harald was a 'fiery' character whose methods were sometimes unusual. Once he went into the street and saved a man from lynching by the mob. Grand Duchess George described him as the man 'who showed the greatest courage in the whole of that terrible time'.[40]

Immediately after the Tsar's abdication Harald telegraphed to Kiev for news of the Dowager Empress. On 17th March the reply came that she was well and not in any danger. A few days later the Tsar and Tsarina were arrested and Harald received assurances from the Provisional Government that the same fate would not befall Dagmar. After all, they could hardly accuse her of trying to make a separate peace with Germany. He also asked permission to maintain contact with the Dowager Empress and requested that any letters from the Danish Royal family would be delivered to her promptly and unread. This request, although approved by the Provisional Government, was refused by the Petrograd Soviet.

Although the Department and her presidency of the Red Cross had been taken away immediately after the revolution, Dagmar persisted in visiting the hospitals as usual, much to her family's distress. Then one day the gates of Kiev's main hospital remained firmly closed and the head surgeon, supported by his entire staff, rudely informed her that she was not required. Shaken, the sixty-nine-year-old Dowager Empress returned home.

Sandro had already tried to persuade her to go to the Crimea but Dagmar firmly refused; she would rather go back to Petrograd to be with Nicholas. Besides, it was impossible for her to leave quickly. She was still convinced that deep down the people's loyalty to the Tsar remained unchanged and she received many touching letters. The incident at the hospital opened her eyes. Kiev had become dangerous. There was no guarantee that they would not be turned out of the palace and murdered by the mob. Dagmar finally yielded.

She had not been to the Crimea since Sasha's death twenty-two years before. Writing to Queen Olga of Greece, who was in Petrograd, Dagmar said that although it was very beautiful, she could not bear the thought of being there without Sasha and not living in their own lovely house. Still, there was consolation in being with Xenia and her family, but …

The Kiev Council had made it plain that the Dowager Empress was now 'unwelcome' in the city. Influential friends therefore appealed to Alexander Kerensky who, as Minister of Justice in the Provisional Government, was responsible for the safety of all the Imperial family. At the beginning of April Dagmar and her family were ordered to leave immediately for the Crimea.

On 5th April she invited all the officers on duty to lunch to say good-bye. Later that day she went to church. Many of those present provided touching proof of their devotion.

Although prayers for the Dowager Empress were still being said in the city's churches, the Romanovs were to find that leaving Kiev was easier said than done.

CHAPTER 22

The Ex-Empress Marie

'HER MAJESTY IS LONGING TO BE AT HOME AGAIN AND SURROUNDED
BY A SYMPATHETIC ATMOSPHERE' — Harald Scavenius

On 5th April, in the dead of night, several small groups of people made their way through the bitterly cold streets of Kiev to a deserted siding outside the city, where they quietly boarded a train. They included Dagmar, accompanied by Prince Dolgoruky, Zina Mengden and two Cossack bodyguards; Sandro with his A.D.C. General Fogel; Colonel Kulikovsky, Grand Duchess Olga and some servants. The Petrograd Soviet was still calling for the arrest of all the Romanovs and the local communists would never have let them leave openly. Sandro had somehow organised the train and, to avoid suspicion from colleagues at the hospital, Olga had not even put a coat over her nurse's uniform. The devoted Prince Schervashidze was not with them; he was returning to Petrograd to sort out the Dowager Empress' business affairs.

Their journey took four days. Confusion reigned everywhere. At each stop swarms of refugees attempted to come on board but were repelled by a small unit of loyal sappers, who guarded the doors of every coach with fixed bayonets.

At Sevastopol the train stopped outside the town and the Imperial party transferred to cars provided by the Military Aviation School, who had served under Sandro. As they left the train, the Romanovs were aware of the hatred on the faces of a band of local sailors standing nearby.

They drove to Ai-Todor, Sandro's estate twelve miles from Yalta, which he had inherited from his mother. Set in 175 acres of parkland with woods, vineyards and gardens running down to the sea, Ai-Todor consisted of several buildings. There was the 'old house' where Xenia and Sandro lived, and which had remained unaltered since his childhood, a smaller building where Feodor and Nikita lived which was connected to the main house by a passage and, nearby, a larger stone house where Sandro's other sons had their apartments. Dagmar had last visited the estate shortly after Xenia's marriage when Sasha was so ill. She admired Sandro's garden full of flowers and the way the park had been replanted but would never have lived in the Crimea again out of choice. It brought back too many sad memories.

Xenia had tried to obtain permission to visit Nicholas before she left Petrograd but it was refused. Sad and depressed, she and her three eldest sons joined her younger children at Ai-Todor shortly after Dagmar's arrival. Other members of the family were at their estates nearby. Irina, Felix and his parents were at Koreiz, Nicholasha was at Tchair and his brother Peter was at Djulber. It was hard to believe there had been any change. The Crimea was peaceful, the Tartar regiments were still loyal to the Imperial family and some officers provided a voluntary guard. 'Those few weeks ... were almost too good to be true', recalled Olga. 'It was Spring and the park rioted in blossom. Somehow there was hope'.[1]

Dagmar was now cut off from her relatives in Denmark and England. Immediately after the revolution the British Ambassador Sir George Buchanan and the Danish Minister Harald Scavenius requested permission to stay in telegraphic contact with the Dowager Empress via the Russian Foreign Ministry. The Soviet forbade this, fearing a counter-revolution by the Romanovs. The only contact would be through the official, censored, channels. To get round this all telegrams to, or on behalf of, Dagmar were sent through the Youssoupovs at Koreiz.

Letters sent via the Danish Foreign Ministry or the Legation were returned, including five from Prince Waldemar. The Provisional Government asked Scavenius not to send correspondence out of Russia for the Romanovs. Several people had offered to carry letters secretly to Ai-Todor but Scavenius did not think it right to involve the servants.

Queen Alexandra had received some letters. Her letters to Dagmar, although received and read by the Provisional Government, were not delivered. Some of the Queen's language was so vehement that the Foreign Office finally asked her not to send even the simplest messages of sympathy, which could be misconstrued as political interference and make things very awkward. Dagmar's loyal friends, like Princess Cantacuzene, continued to smuggle her correspondence to Petrograd but Buchanan was unable to forward anything. Kerensky was afraid of the extremists.

Xenia had not dared to tell her mother this but when Felix returned to Petrograd in May the Grand Duchess gave him a letter to Buchanan, asking him to have one more try to obtain permission. None of them realised that they were in a very difficult and dangerous position. Dagmar was furious at what she saw as the British Embassy's refusal to help. Sir George finally arranged for the Queen to telegraph a message which Felix delivered verbally, in the hope that this would calm Dagmar.

Felix also tried to retrieve their valuables from Petrograd, or hide them until better times. Many of the Youssoupov treasures were concealed in the Moika Palace or their Moscow house under Felix's supervision. Kiki, Dagmar's maid, had brought some of her jewellery when they left the Anitchkov. Felix learnt that the remainder had been confiscated but he managed to cut Dagmar's favourite portrait of Sasha from its frame. In September, eighty-four cases of valuables from the Anitchkov were taken to Moscow.

On 2nd April all Court property, including the palaces and private estates, was transferred to the State and Feodor Golovin was appointed Commissioner for the Ministry of the Court. Dagmar's stud-groom Bennett, who had been with her for thirty-seven years, a French servant and two Italian servants, were told to leave the Anitchkov. The following day they were informed that they could remain at the palace and their wages would be paid. When Bennett left Russia in November 1917 he was given, in lieu of notice, 'the sum agreed upon in the original contract with the Empress Marie'.[2] The Anitchkov was given to the Food Ministry, many of Dagmar's old servants were thrown into prison and the church at Gatchina was robbed. Armin von Reyner, Dagmar's former adminis-trator at Gatchina, ensured that all her valuables and objets d'art were safely packed away.

If the Romanovs were unprepared for the revolution the revolutionaries were even more so. At the beginning of 1917 Lenin was sitting gloomily in Switzerland. When news of the revolution reached him he was desper-ate to return to Russia but any such journey was fraught with danger of arrest. The Germans, anxious to knock Russia out of the war, came to the rescue and transported Lenin and his followers on the so-called 'sealed train' through Germany. Lenin arrived at Petrograd's Finland station on 16th April and was soon hammering home his slogan – 'Peace, Land, All Power to the Soviet' – from Bolshevik headquarters, once the mansion of Mathilde Kschessinska.

Although life seemed to go on as usual in the Crimea, there was one very fundamental change – the Romanovs now ceased to receive their income from the Imperial appanages.

Dagmar's previous state income of 300,000 roubles had been altered in 1906. Since then, money for her food, servants, carriages and travel-ling expenses had been sent to Prince Schervashidze, who forwarded receipts to the Ministry of the Court. This now stopped. Dagmar had no private fortune or income of her own, so Prince Schervashidze asked the Provisional Government for 30,000 roubles for the journey to Kiev and another 30,000 roubles for living expenses at Ai-Todor.

On 2nd April, Dagmar's secretary Prince Dolgoruky wrote to Golovin in an urgent attempt to obtain the payments due, together with some money from capital. He asked Golovin to continue to provide money from the personal account of Grand Duke Michael for the expenses of Abbas Touman Palace. He indicated that the Dowager Empress' personal capital was 500,000 roubles. In addition, there was 245,300 special capital (dividends from estates), capital from money given to her since she arrived in Russia, money inherited from the widow of Emperor Paul (presumably allocated to the Department) and money from Michael's property which she spent in memory of Georgie. The Dowager Empress' State income of 209,000 roubles, paid in three instalments, was kept separately and used for Court expenses. Total income was 235,000 roubles.

Expenses amounted to 225,000 roubles, of which 50,000 went towards gifts, clothes (40,600 roubles) and personal expenses; the remainder on such things as pensions, charities and salaries. When, as usual, the expenses exceeded her allowance, she met the difference from one of the other sources, or even from personal capital. Her secretary estimated the future deficit as some 30,000-40,000 roubles.

In July, Golovin arranged for payment of the overdue May instalment of the State allowance (69,666 roubles), salaries for the servants and reimbursement of the travelling expenses for 'her various journeys to and from Kiev' and the journey to Ai-Todor. He found that, as the widow of a former Emperor, her financial position was unaffected by the abdication. She was entitled to 200,000 roubles a year for Court expenses during her lifetime; if she left Russia the sum would be halved. On 14th July Golovin agreed that the Dowager Empress would not have sufficient money if the Provisional Government stopped making payments.[3] He also told Count Benckendorff that the 'jewels, works of art and other possessions which belonged to her personally would be restored to her'. Prince Schervashidze would agree the settlement.[4]

All the family now began to take stock of their financial situation and make economies. Xenia and Sandro sent most of their servants away, as they could not afford to keep them.

At first Dagmar and her family were left in peace. The Romanovs were allowed to visit each other and go on excursions. Some of the party distributed leaflets, 'Forward, for Tsar and Holy Russia' in Yalta. Dagmar found it impossible to enjoy the lovely Crimean scenery under the changed conditions and she did not visit Nicholas' new palace at Livadia, which he had built on the site of Alexander II's old palace in 1911. (The Maly Palace, where Sasha died, was still standing.) Xenia noted in her diary on 15th May that her mother did not sleep well and her health, although generally bad, changed daily. They drank tea together, walked in the park and discussed the chaotic situation and the day's events. The revolutionaries, Xenia said, were 'svinehunde'.[5]

Scavenius tried to get Kerensky's permission to visit Dagmar but the Foreign Office in Copenhagen told him that he must not leave his post. He then asked if a Red Cross delegate could go but this came to nothing. Prince Waldemar sent a letter to the Provisional Government via the Danish Foreign Ministry. Although the contents are not known, it was probably a request for her to leave Russia.

The revolution now reached the Crimea. Soviets were established at Yalta and Sevastopol to take control of the area and these rival Soviets both claimed jurisdiction over the Romanovs.

Just before dawn on a May morning, some dirty, unshaven sailors from the Sevastopol Soviet arrived at Ai-Todor with a search warrant. Sandro was woken by the cold barrel of a revolver against his head. Heavily armed, the sailors demanded the keys and ransacked the property for anti-revolutionary propaganda, machine guns, ammunition and a secret telegraph.

At half-past five, an officer entered Dagmar's room and told her he had been sent by the government to conduct a search. At first she did not understand, as she was not involved in any counter-revolutionary propaganda. In a letter to Queen Olga of Greece she described how a sentry was placed by the bed and she was ordered to get up.[6] When she refused unless he left the room a horrible old woman was sent to watch her. Dagmar, by now boiling with rage, had barely time to throw a dressing gown over her nightclothes and sit behind a screen. She was not even allowed to use the chamber pot.

Soon the room was full of rude, dirty sailors who stared at her and walked around with their caps on their heads. Dagmar's clothes were strewn across the floor, the curtains were torn down, the carpet ripped up and broken pieces of furniture were scattered about. When they pulled the bedclothes off to search the mattress she was so angry that only Sandro's intervention prevented her from being taken away. The officer sat at her desk and gathered up all her letters, along with anything else that had writing on it, put them into a large bag and took them away in the hope of finding compromising documents.

They even took her Danish bible. This was a particularly treasured possession and contained an inscription written by Queen Louise when her daughter left for Russia. Although Dagmar yelled and abused the sailors, her words had no effect.

For three hours Dagmar sat behind the screen in the freezing cold while the search continued. When they had finished ransacking the bedroom they moved to her drawing room while Dagmar fumed with anger and indignation. They were all under arrest. Not until twelve o'clock were the occupants of Ai-Todor permitted to leave their own rooms and have a cup of coffee, but they were not allowed to leave the house. The shock to Dagmar was great and she said that she would never be able to forgive them for this barbaric treatment. She summed it all up to Queen Olga in one word – 'nice!'

Although her diaries, photographs and letters were taken, along with a ruby ring which Sandro had given Xenia on the birth of one of her sons, they left Dagmar's jewel box, which was standing on the table. Similar searches also took place at Tchair and Djulber.

Sandro lodged a formal complaint but there was little the Provisional Government could do, they had no control over events in the distant Crimea. On 1st June a commission, headed by the President of the Sevastopol Naval Court Martial, was sent to interview them. All the Romanovs were called in to answer questions from the general and the other judges, who sat round a large table like a tribunal. For Dagmar, this was another unpleasant, humiliating experience. She had written a short statement, in order to avoid speaking as much as possible and the presence of Sandro gave her, she felt, a measure of dignity.

Nevertheless, with a soldier on one side of her and a sailor on the other, Dagmar sat exasperated, shaking with anger, while the statement was read. Then the questions began. After enduring this farcical situation for half an hour Dagmar was allowed to leave. She was told to sign her state-ment 'the *Ex*-Empress Marie'. Saying nothing, she defiantly signed 'the widow of Emperor Alexander III'.[7]

It has always been stated, particularly by Grand Duke Alexander, that Dagmar's bible was only returned to her in the 1920s. However, in her letter to Queen Olga of Greece describing the house search and the enquiry, quoted by Inger-Lise Klausen, Dagmar clearly says: 'It wasn't until yesterday that my Danish bible was brought to me, for which I was greatly pleased, as you can imagine. But all my letters and the remaining things the brutes have kept …'[8]

Among the letters was one to Prince Waldemar, from whom she had not heard since February. It was begun on 4th/17th May, continued on 7th/20th and still unfinished when it was seized: 'My heart is bursting with desperation', she told him. 'Only the Lord can help us begin to endure this misfortune, which has hit us like a bolt from the blue … Poor Nicky … I could never have imagined that they would throw us out, and that we should be reduced to living as exiles in our own land'.[9]

Dagmar reminded him that since the previous year she had felt some-thing would happen. Nevertheless, she was unprepared for the magnitude of the disaster. Only the presence of her grandchildren, particularly Irina who brought her two-year-old daughter over every day, seemed to give her comfort and inject some life into their existence. She had even become used to having Olga's husband in the family circle, especially as the couple were so happy together.

The Dowager Empress also told her brother she was extremely annoyed at Swedish newspaper reports that she had joined the side of the revolutionaries and could only hope that none of her relatives believed such outrageous rubbish.

Waldemar was able to keep in contact with other Romanovs in the Crimea by telegraph and at the end of May he received a report from Scavenius: 'Her Majesty is in good health and maintains a surprising calm. However, it would be foolish to deny that events have made a severe impression on her and, in particular, that the lack of knowledge as to the Tsar's fate has heavily affected Her Majesty's frame of mind. To be completely without news from Denmark or England is also depressing. The Empress often talks about Your Royal Highness and about Denmark and I believe that Her Majesty is longing to be at home again and surrounded by a sympathetic atmosphere'.[10]

The atmosphere at Ai-Todor was becoming anything but sympathetic. The Provisional Government's Special Commissar now moved in with twenty heavily-armed Soviet sailors. Sentries patrolled the entrance and the Romanovs were subjected to petty humiliations. If they wanted to go for a drive they had to say so in advance, otherwise the doorkeeper refused to let them out. The guards' slovenly attitude – hat on, cigarette in mouth, newspaper in hand – when talking to her, upset Dagmar, who often felt like spitting on them. She shared the general sense of shock felt by the aristocracy at the rudeness and hostility the formerly respectful Russian people now showed towards the ruling classes. Her only comfort was to sit down by the sea. When Xenia received a letter from her Aunt Alix in England, Dagmar was so upset she could not read it.

Soon they were confined to the limits of the estate. No letters could be sent or received without permission, no excursions were permitted and visitors were restricted to Felix, Irina and Dr Malama, Nicholasha's doctor, who helped keep them in touch with their relatives on the neighbouring estates. At meals an interpreter was often present in case they spoke in a foreign language. Dagmar maintained her dignity and the sight of her small, majestic figure walking in the park caused many of these rough men to salute.

The restrictions did not apply to Olga who, married to a commoner, was not considered a Romanov by the guards. Despite her remarks in the letter to Waldemar, Dagmar could not bring herself to accept her new son-in-law on equal terms and pointedly excluded him from the family councils. In fact the Romanovs were beginning to get on each others' nerves. Olga and her husband therefore went to live in another house on the estate, taking with them all Dagmar and Xenia's jewels concealed in cocoa tins which, at the first sign of trouble, they hid in the rocks by the sea.

In June Princess Irina Dolgoruky, the wife of Dagmar's secretary, died suddenly and Dagmar was permitted to attend the funeral at Koreiz. After the service everyone set out on foot for the cemetery a mile away. The Hon. Albert ('Bertie') Stopford, 'The Scarlet Pimpernel of the Revolution', who worked for the British Embassy (and also probably the Secret Intelligence Service)[11] recorded his impressions of Dagmar in his diary. 'I thought the Empress, whom I had not seen for more than a year, was looking well – better than I expected she possibly could, although a little thinner. She walked with a firm step over a very muddy, slippery road and down a steep hill. The Grand Duchess [Xenia] appeared ill, tired, and very sad. Her daughter [Irina Youssoupov] ... told me she was in indifferent health and much upset by recent events'.[12]

At the end of June Dagmar received some letters from Alix. The Dowager Empress could now send letters through the British Embassy and the Danish Legation but, by early August, the only letter the Queen had received was one smuggled out of Russia by Bertie Stopford. A letter addressed to Princess Victoria reached England that month. It was 'a very sad one. She is kept like a criminal, not allowed to leave the place, or even drive, and they send people from Sevastopol to watch them'.[13]

By July Prince Lvov had resigned and Kerensky was Prime Minister and Minister of War. Irina and Felix, concerned at the way things were developing in the Crimea, went to Petrograd so that Irina could try and see Kerensky. He was living in some style at the Winter Palace with all the old servants, the guards and a red flag flying when he was in residence. Felix and Irina stayed at the Moika Palace for two months, buying food on the black market. Every day there was shooting in the streets. Eventually Irina's persistence paid off and Kerensky received her in the study of Alexander II, her great-grandfather. Bravely she asked him to ensure that her grandmother, the Dowager Empress, was well-treated. Then, as the old servants cried, she left the Winter Palace forever.

Through Monsieur Niquille, the children's Swiss tutor, Dagmar sent a message to Buchanan saying she was nervous about her safety. When Felix told him the Dowager Empress was under arrest, he protested to the Minister of Foreign Affairs about the treatment of the King's aunt. The Minister replied that, due to the pleas of Princess Irina, Kerensky had promised to improve the Dowager Empress' conditions. When Irina and Felix returned to the Crimea they did not tell Dagmar that Kerensky was living in Alexander III's rooms at the Winter Palace.

Not everybody in Petrograd supported the revolution. When a

member of the Duma tried to remove the life-size portrait of the
Dowager Empress from the wall of one of the Institutes, the pupils formed
a bodyguard around it. Shortly afterwards the Institutes were disbanded
and a Charitable Board was established to take the place of the Department of the Empress Marie.

In July a telegram arrived from the Royal Danish Life Guards in
Copenhagen for Dagmar's Name Day. A few weeks later the Commanding Officer, Colonel Friesleben, received a message from Prince Dolgoruky.
'I have been instructed by H.I.M. the Empress Marie Feodorovna to
convey to you her sincere thanks ... for the congratulations and good
wishes that you have sent to her ... Her Majesty was very touched ...'[14]

The Provisional Government's hold was becoming increasingly insecure
and that month the Bolsheviks very nearly pulled off a successful coup.

On 19th August Bertie Stopford reported that the Dowager Empress
was no longer under arrest but she was not permitted to leave the house.
Soon afterwards came the news that Nicholas and his family had been
moved to Tobolsk in Siberia. This gave Dagmar a real shock, as they had
originally hoped to be sent south to Livadia. She now had no idea where,
or under what conditions they were living or if they had more freedom.
Feeling sick with sorrow and despair, she could only tell Queen Olga that
she could find no comfort and expected nothing good from the hands of
those wicked people. She was almost too depressed to write about it.

That evening, 25th August, while Dagmar was in the depths of despair,
Olga's first baby was born. Olga was thirty-five and, not wishing to be
the cause of any further anxiety, did not tell Dagmar when her labour
commenced. At eleven o'clock the Dowager Empress was informed that
Olga had given birth to a son. Dagmar's breaking heart was filled with
joy and she told Queen Olga of Greece how she hurried to Olga's room
to share the happiness of the new mother. The doctor arrived when everything was over. The baby was christened Tihon and, to commemorate
his birth, Dagmar gave Olga a huge sapphire ring. 'My new grandson ...
is a source of joy to us all', Dagmar wrote. To Count Benckendorff she
confided that Olga's baby was the only good news.[15]

Her pleasure was spoilt by the lack of definite news about Nicholas and
his family. She hoped they would be rescued and expected to be closely
involved with any plans. Peter Raevsky, a thirty-four-year-old officer from
the Life Guard Hussar Regiment whose wife had been a lady-in-waiting,
delivered a letter from Dagmar to Bishop Hermogene, who presided over
the church in Tobolsk. It was a Bishop Hermogene who appealed to the
Russians to drive out the Polish invaders during the Time of Troubles.
Now Dagmar felt sure another Hermogene would save Russia and she
begged him to take charge of the plans to free the Tsar and his family 'as

a preliminary to the restoration of the monarchy'. 'My Lord, you bear the name of St Hermogene who fought for Russia', she wrote. 'It is an omen ... The hour has come for you to save our Motherland, all Russia knows you; appeal, expose, condemn'.[16] Hermogene conducted a secret corres-pondence with Nicholas but the monarchists' plans were channelled through Boris Soloviev (now married to Rasputin's daughter), who betrayed them and pocketed the funds.

In August General Kornilov attempted to rout the Soviet and replace the Provisional Government with a military dictatorship. Kerensky turned to the Soviet for help in return for the release of Trotsky and other prom-inent Bolsheviks. The attempt failed when Kornilov's men fraternized with the Bolsheviks who then refused to return the weapons issued to them by Kerensky.

On 15th September Kerensky declared Russia a republic and Dagmar worried about Michael's safety in Petrograd. In the Crimea the situation worsened and the atmosphere at Ai-Todor grew more tense. Xenia's high-spirited sons were becoming hard to discipline, the members of the Household and the servants were more discontented, and Dagmar loudly regretted that she had not gone to Petrograd to support Nicholas after his abdication.

Entry to Ai-Todor was now restricted to only the family's closest relatives. Life had settled into a dull routine. Food was short and they were often hungry but sometimes crabs and butter were sent from Koreiz. They were running out of kerosene and faced being without light. As they had so much room, people were occasionally billeted on the estate. When Xenia and Sandro protested they were given a lecture about the common workers' duty. During the autumn Prince Schervashidze returned from Petrograd. Dagmar's household now consisted of ten people – two ladies-in-waiting, her secretary, the Chief Steward, three maids, one manservant and two Cossack bodyguards. The news of Nicholas' removal to Tobolsk had caused so much upset that by the end of August there was concern for her health. Despite this, she said that the hardships were nothing in comparison with those of the Tsar in Siberia.

In September Reuters reported that the Dowager Empress was gravely ill with influenza and bronchitis. By the end of October she was fully recovered but was still very weak and unable to leave the house. A new Commissar had arrived and conditions had improved. The Crown Princess of Sweden told a friend that 'the Empress Minny is better but she has been very ill a long time and has apparently grown so old. No wonder!'[17] In the low winter temperatures, often only three degrees, the old Empress became depressed and frequently suffered from the cold.

In October Sergei Kostritsky, the Imperial dentist, returned from

Tobolsk with first-hand news of Nicholas, some letters and a few small gifts. Dagmar became so emotional she was unable to calm down for the rest of that day.

The new commissar, Vershinin, described by Xenia as 'a pleasant and kind man', would not make any decisions without the approval of the Sevastopol Soviet. As many of the sailors had returned to Sevastopol on leave, their guard was now removed. They apparently saw no point in guarding people who were neither criminals nor counter-revolutionaries.[18]

In Denmark, the King was worried by news of his aunt's weak condition. On 10th September the Foreign Minister, Erik Scavenius, sent a coded telegram to his cousin Harald in Petrograd, saying the government had agreed that the Dowager Empress ought to return to Denmark. A date for her arrival should be agreed as soon as she was well enough. Harald thought that, although no longer a member of the Russian Imperial family, she remained a Danish princess and therefore the Danish government could request the return of a member of the Danish Royal family. The matter had to be kept secret. The Danish government were reluctant to act, afraid their approach would be seen as interference in Russian internal affairs and compromise government ministers. This attitude coloured all their dealings with her in the years to come and they were always somewhat cool towards Dagmar. They wanted her to request the Provisional Government's permission herself but the Dowager Empress was too proud to approach what she considered an illegal regime. It was hoped that the Provisional Government would suggest that she should leave. Although they did not object to her departure in principle, everything depended on the Petrograd Soviet, in which the Bolsheviks had now gained a majority, and no date could be set. Scavenius saw Kerensky but he was unsympathetic. 'Political considerations' (Scavenius could not imagine what these were) prevented Kerensky from raising the matter with the government. Scavenius found him 'cold and haughty'. It appears that no concrete permission was ever given.[19]

Although letters were often slow in coming ('I long for news', Dagmar said), she managed to stay in touch with Michael, who told her about his last painful meeting with Nicholas in Kerensky's presence. She was also able to maintain contact with Tobolsk. All correspondence had to be submitted to the commissar for censoring. The first letter she received from Nicholas was dated 19th September/2nd October and was followed by a second one. 'God is merciful – He will give us strength for this terrible ordeal', she replied. 'Thank goodness you are all well and that you live together in comfort ... I live only in my memories of the happy past and try as much as possible to forget the present nightmare ... God bless you, send you strength and peace of mind, and may He not allow Russia to perish ...'[20] This is the last of the published correspondence but was not the last contact between Dagmar and Nicholas.

With the aid of two loyal officers, a young girl and various friends along the route, letters and parcels were smuggled to and from Tobolsk at great personal risk. These letters did not go through the hands of the censor. One of these couriers was 'Domna', or 'Domnouchka', a thirty-five-year-old Russian peasant with long blond plaits which earned her the nickname of 'little tresses' among the Imperial family. She carried letters sewn into a chiffon pouch on her breast. Sometimes she managed to hitch a ride on a cattle truck or goods wagon but most of the time she walked. Through these couriers contact between the Crimea and Tobolsk was maintained until the following spring. Dagmar was in touch with Michael at least until the autumn of 1917 and he also managed to keep in contact with Nicholas.[21]

But things were about to get worse. In Petrograd the Bolshevik Central Committee voted for an immediate insurrection. The Yalta men tightened their grip, carrying out daily searches for bourgeoisie and counter-revolutionaries, who were rounded up and shot. The fall of the Provisional Government could only be a matter of time.

CHAPTER 23

Citizeness Marie Feodorovna Romanova

'GIVE PATIENCE, LORD, TO US THY CHILDREN,
IN THESE DARK STORMY DAYS TO BEAR,
THE PERSECUTION OF OUR PEOPLE,
THE TORTURES FALLING TO OUR SHARE'
     – Prayer found in the Ipatiev House

In November the Romanovs learnt of the Bolshevik revolution. Stealthily, and with few casualties, Lenin became master of Petrograd and began to consolidate his position. The nationalisation of the banks and the freezing of private bank accounts was followed by the abolition of army ranks, private ownership of land and the rights of inheritance; the only titles were 'citizen' and 'comrade'. The Black Sea Fleet went over to the Bolsheviks, naval officers were massacred and gangs of unruly sailors roamed the countryside looting and murdering. In the Red Terror that followed, a man's class would seal his fate more than his political sympathies. Although the Crimean Tartars were mostly still loyal to the Tsar they had little taste for fighting and the communists met with scant resistance.

At Ai-Todor the family were completely isolated. Vershinin was still in charge but no-one was now allowed in or out except Dr Malama and Irina Youssoupov, which at least meant that Xenia could see her daughter. Some of the guards were quite friendly and the family addressed them by the familiar 'thou' instead of the more formal 'you'. This situation did not last.

In December Vershinin was dismissed and a representative of the Sevastopol Soviet, a six-foot-four inch giant called Zadorojny, moved into Ai-Todor with new guards. When the prisoners were assembled for a roll-call Dagmar appeared at the top of the stairs but refused to come down. As the guard commander cocked his revolver everyone held their breath. Finally he turned, called the roll and strode out.

The Romanovs were placed under house arrest, watched by their loutish guards and under constant threat from the Yalta and Sevastopol Soviets, who were arguing over who had the right to execute the family. In a letter to Grand Duke Nicholas Michaelovitch, Prince Schervashidze remarked on the Dowager Empress' calm, dignity and courage. She never complained, he said, and her example made their confinement easier for the others to bear.

26th November 1917 was Dagmar's seventieth birthday but what should have been a celebration was a sorrowful occasion. Although her granddaughter Olga Nicholaievna wrote from Tobolsk that things could be worse, Dagmar had not heard from Misha for over a month. There were rumours that he had gone missing from Petrograd at the same time as Kerensky fled from the Bolsheviks. They had little news, even Dagmar's Danish newspapers were returned marked 'addressee unknown', and little money. They began to make a list of their gold, silver and valuables and Dagmar agreed to allow Prince Dolgoruky to send a telegram to Lenin outlining their plight.

Early in 1918 Lenin published The Decree on the Separation of the Church and State. All church property was now state property. Bolshevik soldiers roamed the countryside plundering the silver and holy icons, many of them studded with precious stones, from monasteries and churches. Priests or parishioners who resisted were branded as counter-revolutionaries and arrested. Many were later shot.

Scavenius very quickly saw the ruthlessness of the new regime and he warned the Danish government that the Dowager Empress was now in great peril.

In February he received a desperate letter from Prince Schervashidze, brought to Petrograd by the children's tutor Hr Jurgensen, telling him that they had been completely isolated since 26th October. They were forbidden to go beyond the confines of the estate and only acquaintances were admitted. Because trains were not running from the local station, newspapers, telegrams and letters were only received occasionally. They knew nothing of what was happening outside – not even whether there was peace or war.

The prince said that the banks in Yalta refused to pay any money from their accounts. He asked that the Dowager Empress' journey out of Russia be accomplished 'officially', accompanied by a representative of the Bolshevik government and a member of the Danish diplomatic corps but he stressed that she would not leave without Grand Duchess Xenia and her family. The details of the route would also have to be worked out, he had no idea how it could be accomplished. 'I am in despair to find myself in such a sorrowful situation', he continued, 'and I am happy to know that H.M ... possesses in you an energetic and chivalrous protector who is always ready to defend her interests'.

'In your capacity as Denmark's Minister you are at the moment the only person who one can ask for help and support in our endeavours to lighten Her Majesty's lot ...'[1]

Prince Schervashidze waited impatiently for Scavenius' answer. His letter did not mention Olga, because she and her husband had already decided that they would remain in Russia.

*

On 3rd March 1918 Russia signed a separate peace with Germany at Brest-Litovsk. The terms were harsh but Lenin needed peace at any price. A quarter of Russia's territory, including some of the richest crop lands, was surrendered as the Ukraine, the Baltic States, Finland, Poland, the Caucasus and the Crimea all came under German rule. As German troops marched into Kharkov, Odessa and Taganrog one-third of the population of Russia now found themselves in German-occupied territory. The Ukraine became an independent republic and the other areas were either incorporated into Germany or became German protectorates. Russia was left defenceless as, overnight, Germany trebled in size.

In the Crimea a local government was formed with its seat at Simferopol but, in reality, power was in the hands of the local Soviets. Although the war was over, Dagmar was depressed, realising that millions of Russian lives had been lost in vain.

The Bolsheviks had seized all the residences and personal belongings of the Imperial family and they were left wondering how they would be able to manage when things settled down again. (Sandro thought of opening a hotel.) On 22nd March 1918, by order of the People's Commisssariat for the Republic's Valuables, the former Chancellery of the Dowager Empress was closed. All the officials, including the Head, A.A. Kulomzin, were dismissed without compensation. Catalogues of the collections were compiled, including the Crown and personal jewels, and inventories were taken of all the palaces. Many of these treasures, including belongings of the Imperial family, were later sold.

The Danish newspapers reported that the Dowager Empress would soon be leaving for Denmark. A Danish diplomat in Vienna told the Foreign Ministry in Copenhagen that the Duchess of Cumberland was worried about her sister's safety and she hoped the reports in the newspapers were true. He requested them to send a cypher telegram if they heard anything so that he could let the Duchess know.

The rumours proved to be false. On 21st February the occupants of Ai-Todor were told they would be moved. Dagmar was certain they would be taken to Petrograd.

In fact their destination was Djulber, the nearby villa of Grand Duke

Peter Nicholaievitch, his wife Militza and their younger children Marina and Roman. With its white towers and Moorish-style minarets it resembled something from the Arabian Nights but it had the advantage of high, stout walls. The decision was prompted by the Soviet rivalry. Yalta wanted to execute the Romanovs immediately. Zadorojny, a secret supporter of the Imperial family (he had served under Sandro at the Military Aviation School), had orders from Sevastopol to protect them, at least until Petrograd decreed otherwise and felt he stood more chance of this inside Djulber's fortress-like walls. His own situation was precarious. He told Yalta that he was under orders from Sevastopol and refused to let them help guard the Romanovs. Consequently, the Yalta men were deeply suspicious.

On 11th March Dagmar, Xenia and Sandro were driven to Djulber, where they found that Nicholasha and Stana had already arrived. Although Dagmar said she would take the simplest room, she was given Militza's own suite with a large balcony and a wonderful view up to the mountain of Ai-Petri. Xenia and Sandro were next door and the rest of the party fitted in wherever they could find room. Irina, Olga, and Peter's elder daughter Nadejda (all married to 'commoners') were free.

They were guarded by sixty men with machine guns. The only visitors were Felix and Irina's two-year-old daughter Bébé, who toddled in and out with letters pinned inside her coat, and Dr Malama. They were allowed no further than the lawn in front of the house and, with all the retainers and servants, conditions were cramped. Dagmar had no liking for the Montenegrins and they all protested against their enforced proximity. There was a tense, uncertain atmosphere. Every second week a detachment from Yalta arrived but Zadorojny always refused to surrender the prisoners without proper orders. They never knew if and when these would come.

They were all given a ration card for sugar. Signing her first one 'Marie', the old Empress was told it was insufficient. 'I have been signing "Marie" for fifty years', she replied proudly, 'if it is not sufficient I can do without the sugar'.[2] She ate her meals alone with Xenia. Food was scarce. Sometimes a vegetarian meal of Wiener Schnitzel was made from carrots and cabbage; once they had donkey for lunch and billy-goat for dinner. The bread was of poor quality and filled with straw and other dirt. They lived mainly on buckwheat and pea soup, enlivened by wine from Djulber's cellar. Occasionally they were permitted to receive presents of cake, sugar or bread to relieve the monotony. Dagmar's age and uncertain health made the food indigestible but the chef sometimes prepared special dishes for her with the guards' complicity.

On 12th March Scavenius sent a dramatic telegram to the Danish

Foreign Ministry telling them of the dreadful conditions the Dowager Empress was living under and the acute danger she was in from bands of local Bolsheviks. He also reported that Grand Duke Michael was being treated badly, the Tsar's guards in Tobolsk were hostile and the Imperial family had no money. He had arranged for money and provisions to be sent to the Dowager Empress. The King was immediately informed. King Christian telegraphed to the Kaiser in Berlin, asking if he could put pressure on the Bolsheviks to improve things for his relatives. German military might had crushed the Russians and Germany had recognised the Bolshevik government. William was the one person who could help.

The Kaiser's reply was disappointing. Although he wanted to assist, he was worried about the reaction of the German Socialists. German intervention could be misinterpreted as a move in favour of the restoration of the monarchy which, in turn, could endanger the Tsar. William suggested 'the only practical way' would be a humanitarian appeal by the three neutral Scandinavian monarchies. 'Can not feel able to have anything to do with those swine [the Bolsheviks]', the Kaiser noted in the margin. William, of course, had no idea that the Bolsheviks would have laughed at the idea of a humanitarian appeal from the small Scandinavian kingdoms. There was little Scavenius could do. 'A representative from a small country like Denmark had nothing to offer the Bolsheviks in return for more humane treatment'.[3]

Desperate appeals were beginning to reach Queen Alexandra via her Scandinavian relatives, saying 'Aunt Minny' was nearly dying of starvation, could 'Aunt Alix' not help?[4] Dagmar's situation was relieved when a French governess arrived with 25,000 roubles from Count Benkendorff.

Harald Scavenius raised the matter with Adolf Joffe, the Russian envoy in Berlin, who said that the Romanovs would be provided with everything necessary for their stay in the Crimea. He knew exactly what conditions in Djulber were like but the Bolsheviks had no wish to let Dagmar leave Russia and they made sure the German government were also opposed to her return to Denmark. In response to Prince Schervashidze's desperate appeal the earlier plan for a Red Cross delegate to visit the Dowager Empress was revived and Scavenius enlisted the help of Carl Krebs.

Dr Carl Immanuel Krebs was a twenty-nine-year-old former Guards officer and a member of the Danish Red Cross delegation, occupied with Austro-Hungarian prisoners of war. Scavenius told him that the Empress wished to leave Russia, he had tried to contact Lenin but failed. Krebs 'possessed great courage, resourcefulness and energy. He had a phenominal physique and great experience of travelling in Russia under difficult conditions ... He saw it as his duty and an honour to help a Danish princess in need'.[5]

Krebs went to Bolshevik headquarters at the Smolny Institute and eventually managed to see Trotsky. He asked permission for the Dowager Empress to go home, as she was now just a Russian citizen. 'The Empress Marie Feodorovna is just an old reactionary lady who we couldn't care less about', Trotsky said. 'She has to send in an application for a pass just like anybody else'.[6] If Denmark recognised the government in Russia, he said, and released the frozen money belonging to the Russian State, he would be prepared to discuss the Dowager Empress.

On 27th February Krebs left Petrograd for the Crimea without permission, carrying provisions and 50,000 roubles (about £5,000). The money was provided by Scavenius and later reimbursed either by the Royal family or by Hans Niels Andersen of the East Asiatic Company. Krebs had no official position with the Danish Legation or the Red Cross. If anything went wrong they would be able to deny all knowledge of his mission and it could be passed off as his own idea. The Danish government did not tell King Christian that the trip had been organised by the Danish Foreign Service.

With the help of Carl Nielsen, the Danish Consul in the Ukraine, Krebs reached Yalta. The money, provisions and a letter were secretly taken to Djulber by Hr Jurgensen, the tutor. Shortly afterwards Krebs received a receipt from Prince Schervashidze and a letter of thanks from Dagmar.

He then told the commissar in Yalta that, as he knew the Dowager Empress' Danish family very well, he would like to see her and take news back to Copenhagen. This was granted on condition that only Russian was spoken, the guard commander was present and any letters given to, or received from, her were censored.

Krebs saw Dagmar on 20th March. Xenia and Sandro distracted the guard commander, so that they could have an undisturbed meeting. Krebs reminded her that they must speak in Russian. 'I don't accept that', she replied in Danish, according to the official report. In his memoirs he quotes a more colourful reply: 'By Hell I won't!' The conversation proceeded in Danish.

Krebs reported that Dagmar looked the same as ever but very pale. They sat down by one of the large windows overlooking the sea. Dagmar thanked him for the money and the food, saying it had arrived not a moment too soon. She then spoke of the loutish behaviour of the Bolsheviks and the theft of her private papers, none of which had been returned. Krebs assured her of the concern of the Danish people and the presence of a fellow-countryman seemed to help. She expressed her gratitude to Scavenius and his wife but she did not want to discuss the Tsar ... His official report quotes several instances of her state of mind: 'No, I will not go out. I will not see those beasts', adding that she did not wish to be misunderstood. 'I did love those people' [the Russians]. 'No, you must not leave. It is not until now that my mind has recovered ... It was so surprising'.[7]

Krebs brought back a letter for Alexandra. 'From Darling Aunt Minny I had at last a letter of February 29th ...', she told King George. 'Her life there already was too awful and they nearly starved and have not got a *penny* left – and were never allowed to leave the place for a moment even and her beautiful *motor* confiscated ... She says she has already grown into a perfect skeleton and has no flesh left on her bones!! And God only knows *where* she is at this moment. Oh it makes me quite ill ...'[8]

*

The signing of the peace treaty brought more danger for all the members of the Imperial family, as the Bolsheviks now feared the possibility of a restoration of the monarchy. To forestall this all the male Romanovs residing in Petrograd were ordered to register. They were then exiled to Perm, Viatka or Vologda. Later that month Lenin moved the capital of Russia back to Moscow. Scavenius had been very active on behalf of the Romanovs. Besides looking after the interests of the Dowager Empress he assisted Queen Olga of Greece in her departure from Russia and made repeated appeals on behalf of her brother Grand Duke Dimitri Constantinovitch and Grand Dukes George and Nicholas Michaelovitch, who were all under arrest.

Michael had tried to escape just before the Bolshevik takeover. He and Natasha obtained a permit to go to Finland and they sent George and Tata to wait for them at Batova, an estate fifteen miles south of Gatchina. The car then returned to Gatchina for more luggage. Unfortunately, before the Grand Duke and his wife could join the children, the Bolsheviks seized power and commissars were sent to Batova to arrest what they suspected were fleeing members of Kerensky's government. A warning was telephoned to Michael from the local hospital, so that he did not fall into a trap. When the car returned to Batova an armed sailor was sitting beside the chauffeur. The children were brought back to Gatchina and Michael and Natasha were placed under house arrest.

In March 1918 Scavenius telegraphed that Michael had been arrested again and sent to Perm. The Danish Legation there reported that he was in prison. Later he and his secretary, Johnson, lived in the town in comparative freedom. Michael's seven-year-old son George was in hiding in Petrograd while Scavenius found a way to get him out of the country.

Dagmar was sustained by her natural optimism and her deep religious faith. Early in April she suffered a bitter blow when Prince Schervashidze died. 'Too awfully sad', Alexandra wrote to King George. 'Her only faithful friend, companion, support and guide taken from her *now* in the midst of all her trials and horrors would really be too much for her to bear!! and I quite tremble to think of her future'.[9] At the funeral Dagmar moved among the courtiers as if she was at a palace reception. The Bolsheviks stood aside and took off their hats.

Sometimes her sense of fun came to the fore. All the family, Citizeness Marie Feodorovna Romanova included, had to answer their names at roll-call with a loud 'here!' One evening Dagmar lifted up her small dog and remarked laughingly, 'you have forgotten someone – put his name down'.[10]

As the Germans marched towards the Crimea the Yalta Bolsheviks descended on Djulber under the pretext of collecting gold 'for the revolution' and searching for hidden weapons. Luckily, Dagmar and Xenia's jewels were still with Olga at Ai-Todor. Most of Militza's jewellery was in the Credit Lyonnais Bank in Petrograd. Some of the other pieces were deliberately sawn up to make them easier to hide and to protect the gold. Zadorojny refused to let the Yalta men in and they departed, threatening to return. On their way back they beat the steward of Harax to death.

With the imminent arrival of German troops Zadorojny was warned that the Yalta Soviet planned to eliminate the Romanovs before they could be saved by the Kaiser's army. Terror raged in Yalta. It was impossible for Zadorojny to defend Djulber against an armed band. He proposed to the Grand Dukes that they drive to Alupka that night, where he could hide them in a wine cellar. Nicholasha, Peter and Sandro decided that all the family would remain at Djulber and trust in God. Zadorojny then returned their weapons and advised them to be prepared. They organised the defences, manned the watch in shifts and for several days lived in constant readiness for action.

At this point King Christian and Prince Waldemar decided it was time to bring Dagmar back to Denmark. They arranged for two Danes to travel to the Crimea under the guise of a Red Cross mission to negotiate with the Bolsheviks and organise the journey by ship from Yalta to Constanza in Roumania. Hans Niels Andersen agreed to advance the equivalent of £6,000 for the undertaking. The idea was abandoned when it was over-taken by events.

As the Germans grew nearer Zadorojny's scouts reported that a large party of sailors was coming the next day to take the prisoners to Yalta and shoot them before the Germans arrived. He decided to be away, knowing that his men would bar the gates. Faced with machine guns, the Yalta contingent left uttering threats.

All around the area houses were searched and ransacked, their inhab-itants arrested or murdered. At Harax an attempt was made to kill Prince

Orlov. Grand Duchess Olga and her husband, seriously alarmed, snatched up their baby son and fled towards Djulber where they begged to be admitted.

Dagmar and Xenia, standing at one of Djulber's windows that day, suddenly saw Olga and her family outside and delightedly imagined that they had been moved from Ai-Todor. Unknown to them the guards refused to let Olga in. She and her husband went to the nearby estate of Countess Elizabeth Kleinmichael, who gave them shelter for the next few days.

Zadorojny now moved into Djulber to defend the gate with his most reliable men. All that day the guards prepared for a massive attack, Sandro even helped them place the machine guns. It could only be a matter of time before the Yalta men returned and Zadorojny decided to go to Sevastopol to fetch help. It would be a race to see who arrived first – the firing-squad from Yalta or the reinforcements from Sevastopol.

That evening Nicholasha personally guarded Dagmar's door. She sat up nearly all night playing bezique with Zina Mengden. When Countess Mengden finally decided to snatch some sleep in the Empress' sitting-room at six in the morning she had a small knife under her pillow.

They were saved by a totally unexpected development. An advance German column led by Field Marshal von Eichhorn and despatched personally by the Kaiser arrived at Djulber. Ironically, the fiercely anti-German Dowager Empress was saved by Russia's enemies. 'Regarding the Russian Imperial Personages ...', read a secret report the Empress Augusta of Germany showed the Duchess of Cumberland. '... A couple of days ago their guard was taken over by Germans. The living conditions of the Imperial Personages are, considering the conditions, good. A change of dwelling is not at present envisaged. At the most they will be more dislocated, but for the moment there is no danger'.[11] Although Thyra told her relatives in Denmark that Dagmar was safe and under German protection, the German government did not inform them officially. In all probability, Zadorojny had telegraphed the Germans asking them to rescue the Empress.

The German General asked permission to speak to the Empress and Grand Duke Nicholas to convey the Kaiser's personal invitation to come to Germany. Militza told him they would deliver the answer to Yalta the next day. Dagmar was delighted at her action. She adamantly refused to go to Germany. She would perhaps consider returning to Denmark, but without any help from the Germans. In fact, the Danish Minister in Berlin, Count Carl Moltke, reported that in conversation with a German officer, the Dowager Empress had expressed a wish to return to Denmark but still insisted that any journey out of Russia must be accompanied by a representative of the Russian government and the Danish Legation. The German government and the Bolsheviks were united in their wish that she should remain in Russia. Members of the Imperial family abroad could become a rallying point for émigré monarchist factions, which would also weaken Germany's position. The Soviets wanted the Romanovs to remain inside Russia where they could be controlled. The Germans knew this. They also knew that the Bolshevik government would not last out the year without their help. They need not have worried. Insisting that Germany was still at war with Russia, Dagmar steadfastly refused to receive the German officer who had saved her from death. The Kaiser's offer was rejected.

Dagmar declined all German offers to guard her and was protected by local Tartars. The Germans set up their own patrols nearby. The occupying forces were very civil, treating her with great courtesy which she barely returned, saying she would rather be killed by Russians. Nicholasha was suffering from hurt pride and his wife once drove a visiting Adjutant-General away at the end of a broom. Only Sandro was prepared to talk to the Germans. Dagmar was very angry, but he was afraid they would all be killed when the German troops withdrew. He was anxious to find out whether he and his family could go abroad.

One of the Kaiser's A.D.C.s offered the Russian throne to any Romanov who would agree to countersign the Treaty of Brest-Litovsk. When they all refused, the Germans tried to approach Felix, but were forbidden to see him by his indignant father-in-law.

The Germans were surprised when the Romanovs asked them to spare their Bolshevik captors. The German general was heard to mutter something about 'diese fantastische Russen' under his breath.[12]

Zadorojny had performed several acts of kindness to the family. When Militza's daughter Nadejda had her first baby he took the Grand Duchess over to see her new granddaughter in his own car. It transpired that he had a friend in the Yalta Soviet named Batjuk who, although a communist, was also a member of the Social Revolutionary Party. Batjuk was able to win the Bolsheviks' confidence and wielded great influence in the area. As commissar for Alupka, it was he who had offered to hide the Romanovs in the wine cellar. When they voted to stay at Djulber Batjuk sent a party of soldiers (who were hostile to the local Bolsheviks) to help Zadorojny defend the place.

Soon afterwards, rumours reached the Foreign Office in London that the Empress and Grand Duke Nicholas had been taken prisoner and removed to Kiev. Mr Lockhart, the British Consul-General in Moscow, reported that the Danish Court had sent a special courier to obtain information. A week later Lockhart heard that the rumours were false.

When Zadorojny left he kissed the Empress' hand and addressed her by her full title. 'My duty to Soviet Power', he had told them, 'is to preserve all of you safe and free from harm'. Whose orders he was acting on (and whose intervention prevented the death sentence from being carried out), remains a mystery.[13]

CHAPTER 24

Imperial Sunset

'I CANNOT ABANDON THEM ...' – The Dowager Empress

After celebrating the Orthodox Easter the Romanovs began moving back to their own homes. Dagmar went to Harax, the English-style property of Grand Duke George Michaelovitch and his wife 'Greek Minny' at Alupka, three miles west of Cap Ai-Todor. The first-floor rooms led directly on to terraces overhung with roses and honeysuckle, cascading down to the Black Sea. It reminded Dagmar of Hvidøre. The interior was very English. The reception rooms, where poker and bridge parties used to be held, were called 'The Clubs'. Olga and her family moved into one of the small houses near the main building, which all had red roofs like an English country village. The estate had one advantage over Djulber – it was nearer to Yalta.

It was now easier for Dagmar to keep in touch with her relatives in Denmark, although communications went via Vienna because of Berlin's 'unfriendly' attitude. Waldemar had tried, through Berlin, to obtain permission for Dagmar to return to Denmark but the request was refused, on the grounds that she was 'safe' in the Crimea. He then approached Thyra. Could she, through her daughter-in-law the Duchess of Brunswick, ask the Kaiser about the German government's position? This approach from Thyra, who had just received the letter Dagmar sent with Carl Krebs, met with no more success. The story reached the newspaper *Nationaltidende* in Copenhagen and the German government denied that they had refused any such request.

The Romanovs in the Crimea now settled down to a more peaceful, although still uneasy existence of tennis parties, fishing, gardening and picnics. The younger members of the family even published a newspaper. On 12th June Dagmar's eldest grandson Andrei married Donna Elizabeta Ruffo di Sant' Antimo in the little chapel at Ai-Todor and they moved to a small house near Yalta. As a wedding present Sandro gave them a plot of land on the Ai-Todor estate on which to build a house. They still believed that the nightmare of the last few months would soon be over and they would return to their palaces and live as before.

311

They were only disturbed by rumours from the north. Moscow and Petrograd were under the reign of the Cheka. There were wholesale massacres of the aristocracy and the Bolsheviks now turned their attention to the Romanovs. Ella, Grand Duke Sergei Michaelovitch, Prince Vladimir Paley and Princes Constantine, Igor and Ivan Constantinovitch, were imprisoned at Alapayevsk in the Urals. Grand Dukes Nicholas and George Michaelovitch, Dimitri Constantinovitch and Paul Alexandrovitch were in a St Petersburg prison.

Michael and his secretary Johnson had been living in comparative freedom in The Korolev Rooms, Perm, since March. Shortly before dusk on 12th June a group of men arrived and took them away. Dagmar refused to believe that they had been shot by the Cheka in the woods. For months rumours spread that Michael had been rescued by monarchists and was in hiding. Many believed that his disappearance from Perm was a deliberate move by officers of Admiral Kolchak's army to get him away from Bolshevik hands and thwart Germany's plans to set him up as a puppet Tsar. When Kolchak came to power as Supreme Ruler and Commander of the White Army in Siberia in November 1918 Britain gave him support. German, British and Swedish agents reported that Michael was living in Omsk (headquarters of Kolchak's White Army) but, although plots for his restoration continued during the autumn of 1918, the reports of his whereabouts remained unsubstantiated. Whatever the explanation, Dagmar never heard from him again.

The most disturbing rumours concerned Nicholas and his family. Dagmar had last heard from him in March, when the family were all at Tobolsk. Then letters arrived from Nicholas' daughters, from which it appeared that they had been separated from their parents. In April Nicholas, Alicky and Marie were moved to Ekaterinburg in the hostile Urals and imprisoned in the house of the merchant Ipatiev, ominously designated 'The House of Special Purpose'. Conditions were bad. The other children remained at Tobolsk while Alexis recovered from a haemorrhage, his worst illness since Spala. Early in May, Olga told her parents that 'tresses' had disappeared. Ten days later there was still no news of her whereabouts. During the spring she had left the Crimea with letters and some Holy relics; by the time the package reached Tobolsk the children had rejoined their parents. The link with the Crimea was broken.

By the end of July the uncertainty about Nicholas was becoming unbearable for Dagmar. On 1st August telegrams from Kiev broke the first official news that Nicholas had been shot on the night of 16th/17th July but Alicky and the children had been 'sent to a safe place'. Dagmar had by now completely broken down. She had stomach pains, dysentery and was unable to sleep. Xenia wrote in her diary that her mother was exhausted and wanted to die. Xenia and Sandro tried to prevent a memorial service taking place in order not to cause her further distress. They also tried to stop Dagmar hearing about the memorial services held in the European capitals, but Zina Mengden told her what she read in the newspapers and similar news came from Thyra or other relatives. Dagmar refused to attend the Requiem at Ai-Todor and, out of deference to her, no other members of the family attended. She made Prince Roman promise not to participate in any panikhida for the Tsar during her lifetime. She insisted Nicholas was alive and that the picnic organised for the following day should go ahead. Soon afterwards, they learnt of the deaths of Ella and the other members of the family who had been imprisoned at Alapayevsk.

When the advancing White Army took Ekaterinburg on 25th July they found the Ipatiev House empty. There was only the sinister ground-floor room, with blood on the floor and bullet holes in the walls. The Imperial family had completely disappeared.

It was widely believed that Alicky and her daughters were alive and many of Europe's royalty made diplomatic efforts on their behalf. On 4th August the Spanish Ambassador in London wrote to Madrid regarding Spain's 'approach ... on behalf of the widow and daughters' of the Tsar. Going on to mention the Dowager Empress, he continued, 'would it not be possible to include the case of this august lady in the proposed negotiations? She is, as you know, a sister of Queen Alexandra ... and an intervention in her favour would make more acceptable to the British Royal family and to British public opinion the move being prepared to obtain the release of the Empress Alix'.[1]

King Alfonso XIII of Spain offered to maintain the Dowager Empress for the rest of her life. He was understood to have requested German assistance to enable them all to leave Russia. King George and Queen Mary were anxious for Alfonso to use his influence. Pope Benedict XV made a humanitarian appeal to the Austrian and German governments and also offered Dagmar a life annuity. These initiatives petered out when it was learnt that the family had in all probability died with the Tsar and that Dagmar was in no hurry to leave Russia.

On 7th September Dagmar was visited by a former Finnish officer in the Russian Imperial Guards, Waldemar Spare, who now worked for the Finnish War Ministry. He returned to Copenhagen on 27th September and reported that the Dowager Empress was well, living in relative freedom guarded by Germans (whose Lieutenant was very tactful) but complained of a shortage of butter and coffee. She did not believe the Tsar was dead and expected Empress Alexandra and the children to be sent to the Crimea. He offered to take messages back to Harax and at the end of

October brought Dagmar a case of provisions from her relatives in Denmark.

By October several members of Europe's royal families showed concern for Dagmar's safety. Turkey was on the verge of collapse and the Kaiser was anxious to bring the Romanovs to Germany to prevent them falling into Allied hands. Although the Germans tried to persuade Dagmar and her family to go to Germany the Empress played for time, saying she would prefer Denmark, Sweden or Courland on the Baltic.

Denmark had recognised the new Russian government in May 1918. No protest was made about the Tsar's murder. When King Christian wrote to express his sympathy at the news Dagmar replied on 9th October:

Thanks be to God that the most terrifying rumours concerning my poor beloved Nicky seem to be untrue. After several weeks of terrifying suspense and proclamations, I have been assured that he and his family have been released and brought to a place of safety. You can well imagine how I thank the Lord with all my heart.

'I have heard nothing from him myself since last March when they were still in Tobolsk, so you can imagine the terrible time I have experienced through all these long months even though, in my heart of hearts, I have never given up hope or believed the dreadful rumours. Now that I have heard from several sources [that Nicholas was alive], I have to hope that it is true, so help me God.[2]

On the following day she wrote to Harald Scavenius:

I hope that you and your gracious wife have not suffered too badly as a result of the terrible state of affairs in Petersburg and that you are both well. At present, we live in some peace and freedom, always hoping for better times and trusting in the grace and compassion of Our Lord. I would be very pleased if you would write to me at your leisure and tell me what is happening and how you live. It is a very long time since I have heard from home and I have received no letter from my sister in England since February. It is dreadful to be separated from everyone and to be cut off from the rest of the world.[3]

She asked him to try and trace Prince F. Wiasemsky, who had been dragged off to Kronstadt with a fellow-officer. His brother, Admiral Prince Wiasemsky, was with her in the Crimea and was very worried about his safety.

In response to this letter Ingeborg Larsen, sister of an employee of the Transatlantic Company, arrived at Harax in November. Officially she was working for the Red Cross but when she approached the door of the villa where the two Cossack bodyguards were standing she told them that sewn into her clothes were letters from the Danish Royal family. 'You must believe that I yearn for Denmark and particularly after my beloved Hvidøre', Dagmar told her as they drank coffee.[4] The Transatlantic Company now offered to act as couriers between Dagmar and the Danish Royal family.

Dagmar was not at all worried for her own safety but, as the German Empire collapsed, it was obvious that they could no longer guard the family in the Crimea. The Germans asked the Danish government whether they would be willing for the Dowager Empress to return to Denmark. The reply was positive.

After the signing of the armistice on 11th November the mighty Hapsburg and Hohenzollern dynasties were toppled and numerous Grand Dukes and Princes lost their thrones. The Germans now had to evacuate the Crimea. Civil war raged between the Red and White armies and King George V became extremely worried about his aunt. The Commander-in-Chief Mediterranean, Vice Admiral the Hon. Sir Somerset Gough-Calthorpe, received a 'very secret' order to send a warship to rescue the Dowager Empress. Further information followed. Harax was said to be situated behind what the Admiralty called 'a house' named the 'Swallow's Nest'. As its name suggests, it was perched right on the edge of the cliff at Cap Ai-Todor and was in reality a Gothic pavilion, which looked like a fairy-tale castle. A description of Harax was also provided. They were to use 'the greatest care and tact', avoid armed force, or clashes with any guards who might be protecting Harax. This delicate mission was entrusted to Commander Turle and Lieutenant Commander Korostovzoff, a White Russian naval officer.[5]

Harax was guarded by twenty-eight officers of the Russian Volunteer army (many wounded or shell-shocked) commanded by Captain Paul Bulygin of the Imperial Life Guards. Bulygin had arrived in the Crimea on 5th October. He had been in Ekaterinburg in July hoping to rescue the Tsar but his cover was blown and he had to talk his way out of prison. He told Dagmar that, according to a Danish journalist from *Politiken*, Nicholas was dead. When Bulygin arrived he found that General Denekin, Commander of the White Army in Southern Russia, had left Harax defenceless and he immediately organised a guard. Dagmar arranged for them to be provided with warm jumpers, gloves and socks for night patrols. When winter came she would not allow them to stand outside – they sheltered in her dining-room where tea and sandwiches were provided. The retreating Germans did not interfere because they did not want the Dowager Empress to fall into Bolshevik hands.

This was the situation when Turle and Korostovzoff arrived on 21st November bringing a letter from Admiral Calthorpe, outlining King George's concern and his offer to take her by ship to Constantinople. Dagmar laughed. She rejected any idea of leaving secretly or, indeed, leaving at all unless she was attacked – then it would be openly and only if order had been restored to the region. Turle could do nothing in the face of her obstinacy and, after ensuring that her security was adequate, he returned to Constantinople. Dagmar gave him letters and a jubilant telegram for Alexandra: 'Hurrah. Delighted at last to wire. Such joy to see one of your Captain's kind proposal. [*sic*] Hope that more ships will come openly and soon. Love to you all. Sister Dagmar'.⁶

As the German army withdrew, it was feared that Bolshevik forces would surge forward and take their place. Dagmar and her relatives would be at the mercy of the approaching Red Army. The Empress' sang-froid was not shared by her entourage.

Dagmar's next visitor was a very colourful character. Colonel Joseph Whiteside Boyle, a fifty-one-year-old Canadian, had been a sailor and a prize-fighter before making his fortune in the Klondike Gold Rush. When Canada entered the war he raised a machine-gun detachment at his own expense and offered his own services to the Allies in London. He organised the Russian railway system although he did not speak the language and then went to Roumania to arrange relief for the food crisis. Over six feet tall, powerfully built and absolutely fearless, he soon became involved in British Military Intelligence in Russia and Roumania, where he became a close friend of Queen Marie. He had received information of a Bolshevik rising in the Crimea to coincide with the German withdrawal. The Romanovs would then be killed. Similar information had reached Queen Marie.

The Queen was very concerned about her Russian relatives. Born Princess Marie of Edinburgh, she was the eldest daughter of Prince Alfred and his Russian wife Grand Duchess Marie Alexandrovna. Her sister Ducky, who had already escaped from Russia, was married to Grand Duke Cyril. The Roumanian Queen was thus the niece of the Dowager Empress and the cousin of the Tsar.

Boyle had already brought another cousin of the Queen, Grand Duchess Marie Pavlovna the younger, out of Odessa. Now he and Queen Marie urgently discussed the possibility of rescuing Dagmar. Marie promised a ship and said she would make the Palace of Sinaia available to any members of the family who wanted to leave.

Boyle and a Roumanian naval officer, Commander Basil Pantazzi, left Roumania with an armed force of 200 soldiers, a hand-picked crew, guns, provisions and a car. They arrived in the Crimea on 24th November, where they heard about plans for a local Bolshevik uprising. After foiling this by spreading false reports about the armed strength of their ship, Boyle left for Harax with a Russian guide.

Although Dagmar was grateful for Queen Marie's concern she still refused to leave. 'Here I am able to help in organising some resistance to the Bolsheviki. You cannot take with you all those who have sacrificed everything for me and my family. I cannot abandon them'.⁷ She was determined to remain until she knew where Nicholas and Michael were and if they needed her help. Boyle said the reports of his own undercover agents were inconclusive.

A few days later Commander Turle and Captain Royds returned with newspapers, cigarettes and an offer of hospitality from the King of Italy. The Italian King's yacht was available and King George had also offered a British battleship. Although the Red Army was still approaching, Dagmar was reassured by the Allied presence. She said that, although King Ferdinand of Roumania had sent a boat and begged her to leave, '*Nothing* would induce her to go to Roumania in that little ship'. She had encouraged the other Russians to remain, how could she leave now? 'It was so hard', the Empress repeated, maintaining that the Bolsheviks were such cowards, it only needed a flag to be shown.[8] After an hour of earnest pleading they were convinced Dagmar was wavering.

Commander Turle visited Dagmar again on 13th December. She still did not make a decision. She had sent a message to General Denekin in Yalta, offering to leave if her continued presence was awkward. No reply had yet been received.

Early in January, Dagmar sent Bulygin to try once more to find out what had happened to the Imperial family. For the moment their fate remained vague. No bodies (or photographs of bodies) were produced during Dagmar's lifetime and, although rumours persisted that they were in hiding, Nicholas and his family were never seen again.

*

That winter was exceptionally hard throughout the Crimea. Russia was in the grip of civil war; by March 1919 the Red Army had overrun the Ukraine and was threatening French-occupied Odessa. In an undated telegram to Queen Alexandra, Dagmar said that life in the Crimea was almost too hard to bear. Sandro left for Europe on H.M.S. *Forsyth* with Andrei and Elizabeta, to try and convince the Allied governments of the seriousness of the situation in Russia. Nobody would listen.

A small unit from the White Army was posted to the Crimea. The Romanovs now feared that the retreating Germans would take Nicholasha, former Commander-in-Chief of the Russian army, with them as a prisoner of war and some officers organised a guard of Tartars from the Crimean Regiment.

As the Bolsheviks moved closer and closer, Dagmar was frequently visited by Admiral Calthorpe. The indomitable Empress rejected any proposal that sounded like flight, adamantly declaring that 'it was her duty to remain' and that her presence 'would have a steadying effect on the people'.[9]

Grand Duchess Olga, who was expecting her second child, had decided to leave for the Caucasus, where the Bolsheviks had been driven back. Dagmar angrily insisted that Olga must put her duty to her mother first and blamed Colonel Kulikovsky. She was adamant that she would never leave Russia and refused to move from Harax. 'It was a sad and bitter way to say goodbye ...', wrote Olga. 'And I, knowing what the dangers were, wondered if I would ever see her again'.[10]

*

The French had evacuated the Crimea and the Bolsheviks were closing in. Panic reigned everywhere and Dagmar's situation was now desperate. This could be her last chance to escape.

The Romanovs were celebrating Xenia's birthday when Captain Charles Johnson of the battleship H.M.S. *Marlborough* arrived. He stressed the seriousness of the situation and produced instructions to evacuate the Dowager Empress and her family that very evening. He also brought an offer of asylum from King George and a letter from Alexandra, begging Dagmar to leave while there was still time. He returned to his ship to await her decision.

Even now, with all hope of escape overland cut off, Dagmar still refused to go. Exile would mean living off the charity of her relatives but, if she did not leave, nor could anyone else. Finally, after several hours of persuasion, she admitted defeat. On one condition. The British must evacuate the rest of the family, her retainers and the scores of refugees who were in danger from the Bolsheviks.

This gave the officers quite a headache and the *Marlborough* was hastily rearranged to accommodate many more people than originally planned. Lieutenant Commander Pridham had the unenviable task of satisfying the demands of both rank and comfort. Meanwhile, the Romanovs' servants hastily packed the most valuable possessions for loading at Yalta the following day.

It is said that, before she left Russian soil, Dagmar wanted to pray for Russia's future in the small church at Harax. She refused to be dissuaded by talk of Bolshevik forces in the area. Everyone else could remain behind in safety. She would go alone.

Dagmar asked to embark at secluded Koreiz cove and the ship's carpenter hastily improvised a jetty. Marines and sailors landed on the beach-head, to defend it from the approaching Red Army and escort them to the ship. Speed and secrecy were vital. Any move that betrayed the evacuation to the Bolsheviks could be fatal. A few minutes later the family made their way down to the beach. As they walked across the shaky pier Captain Johnson changed his mind and ordered them to be ferried aboard. The Dowager Empress, accompanied by her dogs, took her last steps on Russian soil and boarded a pinnace.

She was given the Captain's quarters; her maid occupied the cabin next door. Extra bedding was brought from the Imperial estates and spare mattresses were arranged in the officers' cabins for the older people. The younger passengers crammed themselves in where and how they could. Conditions were cramped and uncomfortable. There were nineteen members of the Imperial family with their maids, manservants, governesses and officials of their households; in addition to 1,170 crew, 200 tons of luggage and a fortune in jewels. Peter's daughter Princess Marina acted as interpreter and helped to identify the luggage.

After dark they sailed for Yalta, where the ship's guns covered the port as the evacuation continued for another three days. When the rumour spread that the Dowager Empress was leaving panic set in. People abandoned all their possessions and hurried to the waterfront to try and get on the Allied ships. Dagmar insisted that the *Marlborough* must be the last to leave and said she would personally explain to Admiral Calthorpe why they were late arriving in Constantinople. Later, sitting on deck, she could just see Livadia with its park stretching down to the sea ...

As the Bolsheviks closed in, Dagmar was besieged by people begging to be taken on board which, to her distress, she found was impossible. People streamed onto Yalta pier in ever-increasing numbers. In the chaos and panic families became separated and many of the refugees had only the clothes they stood up in.

It was 11th April 1919. As the *Marlborough* prepared to sail Dagmar stood on deck looking at the land where she had spent fifty-two years of her life, where her husband and two of her sons were buried and where Olga, Michael and Nicholas remained, their fate unknown to her. As she stood silently, tears streaming down her cheeks, a troopship carrying soldiers of the Imperial Guard on their way to fight the Bolsheviks passed close by. When the men spotted the tiny, black-clad figure of the Dowager Empress, the very symbol of Imperial Russia, standing under the White Ensign with the former Commander-in-Chief Grand Duke Nicholas in his Cossack uniform behind her, they began to sing the Russian Imperial Anthem.

As the strains of 'God Save the Tsar' floated across the water Dagmar stood on deck waving, until the troopship had passed from sight. 'The memory of those deep Russian voices, unaccompanied, but in the perfect harmony which few but Russians can achieve, has surely never faded from the minds of those who were privileged to witness this touching scene. Until long after the sloop had passed there was silence. No one approached the Empress ...'[11] It was the last time the Tsarist National Anthem was sung for a former reigning member of the Imperial family within the Russian Empire.

Late that afternoon as the *Marlborough* moved silently into the Black Sea Dagmar stood on deck, watching the coastline until she could see it no more. She had lost her country, possessions and many of her family but she had her life. Now, at seventy-one, she would spend the rest of her life in exile.

PART 5

EXILE
(1919-1928)

CHAPTER 25

The Old Icon

'TOUJOURS Y PENSER, JAMAIS EN PARLER'
('ALWAYS THINK OF IT, NEVER SPEAK OF IT') – Leon Gambetta

A s H.M.S. *Marlborough* left the Black Sea and sailed through the
Bosphorus, Dagmar telegraphed to Alexandra that she was
heartbroken.

On 13th April they anchored near Constantinople and Prince
Dolgoruky advised King Christian that his aunt had arrived safely. The
Legation brought her the Danish newspapers, food was taken on board
and Admiral Calthorpe came to discuss their future. The British government would only allow Dagmar, Xenia and her sons to live in England
and there was a two-day delay while Grand Dukes Nicholas and Peter
transferred to H.M.S. *Lord Nelson*, bound for Genoa.

The *Marlborough* left for Malta on Good Friday and the officers
organised a traditional Russian Easter. Icons, Holy pictures and candles
were placed in one of the larger cabins for the Easter Service. Afterwards
there was cake, wine and the Easter greeting. Hand-painted eggs were
even provided for Dagmar to give to the children. As a gesture of
thanks she gave Lieutenant Commander Pridham a small pearl Easter
egg. Many years later he recalled his impressions of the Dowager
Empress. 'She was very gentle and dignified, very sweet and obviously
unhappy ... that she was leaving her country ...' She was sure the Tsar
and his family were still alive. 'I'm perfectly certain if they had been
murdered we should have been told by our faithful servants', she told
him.[1]

The *Marlborough* was due to return to the Black Sea after discharging
her passengers but this upset Dagmar. She immediately telegraphed to
King George. 'Cannot say how grateful I am for hospitality and remarkable kindness from everybody here on board [.] My one wish is to go in
the *Marlborough* to join you as soon as possible in England ...'[2] The Admiralty informed Admiral Calthorpe that H.M.S. *Lord Nelson* would transport
the Empress to England, if she wished; but, they added, she should be
warned that another opportunity might not occur quickly. The following

day it was reported that the Empress had agreed, details of her entourage would follow.

News of the Empress' imminent arrival in Malta was kept with 'strict military secrecy'.[3] On 12th April, a 'Secret' telegram from the Colonial Secretary to the Governor of Malta, Lord Methuen, underlined the political complications. 'Please receive them with as little ceremony as possible and unofficially, and you had better not meet them yourself. They will arrive practically destitute without clothes or money. Pending decision as to where they are to go, temporary accommodation will be required, but it is not considered desirable to house them where the Governor is in residence ... Do not allow arrival or any reference to it to appear in the local papers. All proper expenses of maintenance and clothing will be refunded to you'.[4] These instructions were later changed and Dagmar was welcomed with the honours due to the King's aunt.

They arrived at Malta on 20th April. When Dagmar was informed that she would occupy the San Antonio Palace, the Governor's lovely seventeenth-century summer residence at Attard, she hesitated, refusing to be hustled off the ship without waiting for the King's reply in case he had changed his mind. Lord Methuen had to use all his persuasive powers.

She finally disembarked the following morning, leaving £125 to be distributed among the crew. 'Let me once more express to you the most ... grateful thanks for all your kindness shown by you and your officers aboard your beautiful *Marlborough* ...', she wrote to Captain Johnson afterwards from London. 'My only regret is that you could not bring us all here'.[5]

At San Antonio Palace, which had been hastily vacated, cleaned and re-equipped, the Empress was greeted by Lady Methuen and a guard of honour. Dagmar occupied Lord Methuen's room and her Cossack bodyguards insisted on sleeping outside the bedroom door. Everything had been done for her comfort, including refitting an old chapel as an Orthodox church. After lunch Lord and Lady Methuen returned to Valletta leaving a young A.D.C., Captain Ingham, in charge.

Dagmar remained in Malta for eight days. She had tea with Lady Methuen at Valletta Palace, visited the barracks where the Russian refugees were accommodated and went on excursions to other parts of the island. One afternoon she went to Verdala Palace near Citta Vecchia, which she had visited with Bertie and Alix exactly ten years before in happier times.

Thoughts of Russia and her sons were never far from her mind. On 23rd April she was visited by Major William Peer-Groves, a liaison officer with the Air Ministry in Japan. Major Peer-Groves' son said that, in 1918, his father 'was in Southern Russia ... on one of the two expeditions which

... went north from Odessa, and one of which reached ... Kiev ...' At that point he separated from the rest of the mission and returned to Odessa alone some time later. He brought back two pieces of jewellery. One was given to the Dowager Empress and the other to an unidentified member of the family in France. It is not known what he told Dagmar. Later, he told two of his children that the Imperial family did not die at Ekaterinburg but were rescued with the help of the British.[6] Other rumours had them spirited to the Far East with the help of Japan. Among Dagmar's visitors in Malta was the Imperial Japanese Consul.

At lunch on 27th April the Empress spoke animatedly about the terrible time she and her relatives had experienced during the last months in Russia. 'I was rather surprised when Her Majesty began to talk about ... the Tsar', Ingham wrote, 'and told me that she was careful not to let others know, but that she knew where he was. H.I.M. was fully convinced that he had escaped and was in hiding at a certain place'. This belief was at first shared by Xenia. Sandro recalled 'exhausting my supply of logic and patience in talking to my wife ... and my mother-in-law who maintained with all the fervour of real devotion that ... Nicky had been "rescued by the Almighty" from the hands of the Bolshevik executioners'. Ingham thought the family were encouraging the Empress' belief. 'They looked at me rather pointedly ... so I was careful to let her think we were all convinced she was right'.[7]

Dagmar did not hesitate to express her views. 'Aunt Minnie looks wonderfully well and is most plucky and full of confidence that Nicky and family are alive', the Marchioness of Milford Haven wrote the following month. 'She has heard, I don't know from what source or if it is reliable, that they are in the hands of the Old Believers (loyal, wealthy and secretive folk I know them to be) who have them hidden away in a monastery in the north, only attainable in mid summer each year'.[8]

The gardens at San Antonio were a paradise, with all manner of rare flowering shrubs. Unfortunately, while planting a tree in the private gardens, Dagmar spotted the German Emperor's name on a plaque nearby. 'Why do you keep a tree planted by the Kaiser – horrid man', she exclaimed, prodding it with her parasol. 'Why don't you pull it up?' When Ingham cheekily told her that it 'wasn't the tree's fault', she turned away, laughing.[9]

In the freedom of Malta, Xenia's sons had become very high-spirited. They tickled the servant's legs at mealtimes, tugged at the guards' rifles so that they came crashing to the ground as their grandmother walked past and one evening a couple of the elder ones slipped off into Valletta. Dagmar soon became exasperated.

She had already heard from Alexandra. 'Only just received your dear letter of 31st March', Alix cabled from England. 'Understand all your poor torn miserable feelings ... Please let me know your plans when settled ... Now, only looking forward to happy meeting'.[10] Although she looked forward to their reunion, Dagmar felt the bitter uncertainty of exile.

The Home Office had been requested to grant the Romanovs 'all possible facilities for disembarkation' but there had been some difficulty about Dagmar's entourage. Finally, seventeen males and twenty-six females were permitted to accompany her to England. Nevertheless, none of them could be certain what sort of a welcome they would receive. One of their major worries was money. Xenia was so concerned that she asked Princess Victoria to reserve 'seven bedrooms, two servants rooms, one sitting room and dining-room' in the 'cheapest possible hotel'.[11]

Their departure from Malta was set for Tuesday, 29th April. The officers of the *Lord Nelson* were surprised at the Empress' vitality, finding her 'great fun'. One of the crew described her as 'full of spirits'. Although she was dressed in black there were no other signs of mourning. After breakfast she came up to the quarter deck. 'She was pretty talkative to all and sundry, we had ... two or three dances and she seemed to take part in all the fun', one of the crew recalled.[12] One evening, despite war-time regulations which meant that all the officers were on watch or asleep, the Empress demanded the Marine Band be fetched to play for a dance.

Her weight had dropped to just under 6 stone. She was so delighted to have proper, regular meals again that she kept all the handwritten menu cards from the ship, together with the music programmes. Dagmar wrote the Old Style Russian date on the menu for 16th/29th April, which included Spring Soup, fried bream on an anchovy base, quails and asparagus, consumed to the accompaniment of music from *The Gondoliers* and other popular pieces.[13] The left-wing *Daily Herald* reported the Dowager Empress' passage on 2nd May, describing her as the 'evil genius' of Nicholas II.

The British government, who had recognised the Provisional Government a week after the Tsar's abdication, could not be seen welcoming members of the former ruling family with open arms. Queen Alexandra was therefore informed that her sister's reception would be low-key. It was a 'purely private family affair', *The Times* reported.

There was also another reason – the Royal family was embarrassed. After the Tsar's abdication, King George V was anxious to help his cousin. When the British government was asked if they would offer the Tsar asylum for the duration of the war, the Cabinet agreed. Although at first the Provisional Government pressed for the Imperial family's departure, later they feared hostility from the extremists and made no effort to accept the British offer. Also the Tsar's children had measles and could not be moved.

British public opinion was against the idea. There were also ugly whispers about the Royal family's patriotism in view of their German ancestry. King George became so worried that he asked his government if the offer could be withdrawn. He was afraid for his own throne. Instructions were sent to Buchanan in Petrograd to avoid the subject and it was suggested that perhaps it would be better if the Imperial family went to France or Denmark. A few weeks later they were moved to Tobolsk.

The official version blamed Lloyd George. Both Grand Duke George Michaelovitch and Grand Duke Michael Alexandrovitch had been refused visas by the British when they tried to escape to England in the summer of 1917. Michael was even asked not to send any more money via Princess Victoria to pay the rent for his house in Sussex. In July 1917 the King changed the name of his dynasty from Saxe-Coburg-Gotha to Windsor and the German Tecks, Battenbergs and Schleswig-Holsteins all took British names and titles.

Dagmar knew nothing of all this, as the *Lord Nelson* docked at Portsmouth in the early afternoon sunshine on 9th May. She seemed both excited and distressed as, surrounded by her family, she waited to greet her sister. It was a poignant meeting. So much had happened since that fateful summer of 1914. Even now there was no privacy as she moved forward, Xenia at her side, to embrace Alix. Only after the formalities had been observed – the presentations of the Empress' suite and the ship's officers – could they have an emotional reunion alone.

At Victoria Station there was another low-key reception. No publicity was given to Dagmar's arrival and the small group of Russian exiles had only been notified at the last moment. Among them was Dagmar's niece Grand Duchess Marie Pavlovna. 'The brilliance and the bustle were gone', she recalled, 'and the feeling of welcome, even if only official, was somehow lacking. In the foreground stood the King and Queen with their family ... We kept in the shadow. There were no crowds; the station was empty and very quiet'.

As the royal party moved down the platform Marie stepped forward. The Empress 'did not appear nervous or upset, she was perfectly calm, contained, and even smiling'. If she noticed the difference in her arrival now compared with the past, the uneasiness, or the mixed feelings, she gave no sign.[14] The Empress was now just one of many Royal exiles starting new lives in Europe and even America.

Dagmar and Alix drove straight to Marlborough House and, for the next few months, divided their time between London and Sandringham. Xenia stayed at Buckingham Palace. Her servants fell on their knees before King George, believing him to be the Tsar, miraculously resurrected from the dead. The strong resemblance must have upset Dagmar. George's entry into the room had often given her a jolt. How much worse it was now.

The Dowager Empress received many visitors, among them her nephew Grand Duke Dimitri, whose exile to the Persian front after Rasputin's murder had saved his life, and Dimitri's sister Marie. The Grand Duchess recalled that Dagmar spoke of the Tsar and his family as if they were all alive and was certain that she would hear from them soon.

Although recent experiences had left their mark, Dagmar also began to recover her old zest. On 2nd July she attended the wedding of Zoia de Stoeckl, who had been a maid of honour at the Russian Court. Inspecting the trousseau she and Alix were like children, exclaiming, 'we would never have been allowed to wear such thin things!'[15]

She continued to interview anyone who might have news of Nicholas or Michael. In July she received Natasha Brasova and her son George. When Michael was arrested in March 1918 Natasha contacted Harald Scavenius, who arranged for seven-year-old George to leave Russia. George and his English governess Margaret Neame hid for five weeks in the house of Colonel Cramer, a Dane charged with overseeing the exchange of prisoners of war. On 25th April George, with Miss Neame posing as his mother (her passport showed her to be the wife of a repatriated Austrian officer named Silldorf) and Captain Sorensen, a Danish officer, boarded a Red Cross train packed with German prisoners of war. Neither Miss Neame nor George spoke German but, to their relief, they were passed through the Russian frontier at Pskov without incident.

On reaching Berlin they stayed at the Danish Embassy while the Ambassador discreetly enquired whether they could cross into Denmark. The German authorities informed the Kaiser, who ordered that they were to be passed straight through the German border. A first-class carriage transported them to Copenhagen, where they were met by a Court official and taken to the Amalienborg. There they stayed until George joined his mother in England just after Easter 1919.

Dagmar and Natasha met at Marlborough House. It was the first time they had seen each other since their stormy interview in 1913. Although the Empress was 'very charming' and made a fuss of George, Natasha sensed that Dagmar did not really like her: 'She will never forgive me that I married her son', Natasha told a friend.[16]

British government policy was to refuse entry to Russian refugees 'unless they have strong business reasons'. Unfortunately, Dagmar was always petitioning the Foreign Office on behalf of 'loyal subjects of the late Imperial regime' who were stranded in Malta. 'The Empress is aware of the restrictions which it has been found necessary to impose ... but H.M. hopes that it may be found possible to make an exception in these particular cases', Sir Arthur Davidson wrote yet again from Marlborough House. 'I have impressed upon the Empress and the Grand Duchess [Xenia] ... the difficulty of admitting Russian refugees ...', he continued, a note of exasperation creeping in. 'The Empress ... feels bound to try and help these people ... as they have done all they can to help her in the anxious time through which she has passed'.[17]

Every Sunday Dagmar attended the Orthodox service in the Russian Church in London. One day a small boy fainted and was carried outside to recover. When he came round he found himself in the Dowager Empress' luxurious car, amongst grey leather upholstery and mahogany fittings. He was the young George Ignatiev, whose grandfather had been Minister of the Interior to Alexander III.

Sadly, Dagmar and Alexandra, once so close, now found they had nothing in common except old age. Times had changed but they still clung to the habits and clothes of their youth. The days were gone when they could stun society by dressing alike. Now they seemed quaint, old-fashioned relics of a bygone era. Dagmar became increasingly irritated by Alexandra's unpunctuality. She paced up and down the hall, umbrella in her hand, while her sister changed to go out – only to find that when Alix finally appeared she had forgotten something. Dagmar would be further exasperated while the object was found. Alix, her deafness almost complete and her sight failing, became increasingly vague and complained about the disruption to her well-run household. Dagmar complained of arthritis or lumbago, enforced idleness and lack of money. With no mental resources to fall back on they became increasingly cantankerous, unwell and unhappy. Now they were together all the time they found less pleasure in each other's company. Consequently, Dagmar soon decided to return to Denmark. 'Better number one at Hvidøre than number two at Sandringham', she remarked.[18]

Once again her old friend Hans Niels Andersen, Chairman of the East Asiatic Company, whom Dagmar had done so much to help while she was in Russia, came to the rescue and arranged for passage on their ship *Fionia*. She was accompanied by Prince Waldemar, who came to England to bring his sister home.

When she arrived in Denmark on 19th August the band of a French warship played the Russian Imperial Anthem and Copenhagen harbour was crowded with boats but there were no flags and no guard of honour. 'So strangely poor and alone', wrote a Danish newspaper.[19] Among the representatives of the Russian colony who gave her an enthusiastic welcome were Baron Buxhoeveden and his daughter Sophie, who had been with the Tsar's suite at Tobolsk. King Christian, Queen Alexandrine and other members of the family greeted her, before she left for Hvidøre in her own car. She had not been there since her hasty departure in 1914 ...

Rørdam, her father's old adjutant who had been in charge of the villa, had died in 1916 but otherwise little had changed. She still had the two Cossack bodyguards armed with daggers and revolvers, her chauffeur Axel, and the entourage who had been evacuated from Russia. Many of the latter had no valid entry papers but the Danish authorities raised no objections and just let them in. Two guardsmen manned the sentry boxes outside Hvidøre, receiving dinner at Dagmar's expense. As the King was paying these expenses he objected, so coffee and toasted buns were substituted.

Shortly afterwards a representative of the Bolshevik government, Maxim Litvinov, arrived in Copenhagen. He had been expelled from England in 1918. The British now wanted to negotiate with Moscow but they refused to have Litvinov in the country, so they forced him on Denmark. Dagmar became so alarmed that she spoke to the British Minister about it and also asked the former Chief of the Danish Military Intelligence Service to find out what Litvinov was really doing in Copenhagen.

Dagmar quickly settled into her old social life. Waldemar visited every day, as did various other members of the family. Sometimes as many as fifteen cars were parked outside Hvidøre. The King and Queen called at first but things did not remain as cordial, especially on the King's side. Dagmar complained in her diary of not sleeping well and the slightest thing upset her nerves, just as she had begun to feel better.

In November Dagmar moved to Christian IX's Palace at the Amalienborg, her parents' former home. That month fifteen cases of valuables from the Anitchkov arrived at Buckingham Palace, sent by the Bolshevik government. When they were unpacked in the presence of Nabikov, the Russian Chargé d'Affairs, the 'valuables' proved to be pokers, shovels, tongs, saddlery and other worthless rubbish. Even the case marked 'Books from the Empress' Library' contained only old railway guides, novels and children's books. Nabokov was acutely embarrassed but, when the Foreign Office reported the incident, the Soviet government took no notice. Art treasures from the Anitchkov were among the items later sold to raise money to prop up the Bolshevik regime. However, when some other packing cases arrived from Ekaterinburg, Xenia found some of Alicky's jewels hidden amongst the clothes. Whether Dagmar and her daughters shared these between them is not known.

In April 1920 Dagmar heard that Olga and her family had arrived in Belgrade. After leaving her mother in the Crimea, Olga, her husband and son, her lady's maid Emillie Tenzov and Timofey Yachik, a Caucasian bodyguard, sailed to Novorossisk. A Russian general put them on a train to the Caucasus, where the Red Army had been driven back. When they reached Rostov General Denekin told them they were not welcome. They travelled to Yachik's village, Nova Minskaia where, on 23rd April 1919, Olga gave birth to her second son Guri in a peasant's hut. By October the Reds were closing in and Olga was again in danger. One cold November night she and her family were forced to flee with only what they could carry. After considerable hardship and danger they arrived back at Novorossisk with not a penny to their name and their two children in a pitiful condition. They stayed with the Danish Consul until February 1920, when they left Russia on a British merchant ship bound for Turkey. As refugees they were interned but finally, through the intervention of the British High Commissioner, they reached Constantinople and then Belgrade where King Alexander welcomed them warmly and offered them a home.

Dagmar immediately said that she wanted Olga in Denmark. She was reunited with her daughter, son-in-law and grandsons, one of whom she had never seen, on Good Friday 1920. It was a bitter-sweet meeting. Beneath the pleasure of seeing each other again lay the knowledge that they were now exiles.

The Danish government did not want to put the Dowager Empress on the Civil List and she was forced to depend on the generosity of her relations. King Christian now made no effort to hide his dislike of his aunt and he soon became annoyed at what he considered were her blatant extravagances. Accustomed to a lavish lifestyle, spending large sums on dresses, constantly entertaining and buying expensive gifts for her friends, Dagmar could not understand that all this was no longer possible. She had no idea of the value of money and seemed to think she could go on spending just as she had for the last fifty years.

In 1920 electricity in Copenhagen was rationed. One evening, the King's footman appeared and hesitantly asked her to turn off unnecessary lights. 'His Majesty said to mention ... that the electicity bill he had to pay recently was excessive', he added.[20] Dagmar promptly ordered her own servant to turn on every light in her wing of the palace. The present Queen of Denmark has called Dagmar 'a very determined lady' and doubts that she would have let her nephew get away with such treatment,[21] although he was often tight with money and severe with his relatives.

He also disliked his aunt's obvious popularity in Denmark, where she was always known as 'Kejserinde Dagmar'. Every day when the King was at the Amalienborg the Changing of the Guard took place. The officers always looked to see whether the Empress was standing by her window, so they could salute her with their sabres. The King was furious but his rude comments had no effect on the soldiers. He frequently wandered round Dagmar's rooms casually examining the furniture and ornaments. If he noticed something missing he asked if she had pawned it. In contrast, the Queen was kindness itself and was often reduced to tears by her husband's behaviour.

Despite the help of wealthy Danish friends the problem of money was very real. Her secretary, ladies-in-waiting, Cossack bodyguards and other servants all had to be paid and Dagmar had left Russia with little more than her jewel box. In 1919 Hans Niels Andersen opened a special credit for her at a London bank. In all she had withdrawn 600,000 kroner (about £30,000). The Empress had attracted a substantial following, from destitute émigrés to members of the nobility who had served at Court. Her generosity towards any Russians who asked for financial assistance was legendary and soon more and more people flocked to Denmark. By 1921 there were two thousand Russian émigrés in Copenhagen alone. Her small, black-clad figure was a familiar sight and the émigrés turned to her for help. Many others just wished to express their respect, or thanks for some past service. A Russian in the Caucasus thanked her for advising him to leave Petrograd in 1916 and take all his money abroad. Her secretary Prince Dolgoruky found himself answering more and more enquiries from refugees who had lost touch with their families. Soon so many letters flooded in that King Christian allowed his own private secretary to help with petitions concerning economic support for the émigrés and offers of presents from them to the Dowager Empress.

Her debts soon reached 803,000 Danish kroner – £40,000 (£600,000 today) – with only two-thirds covered by security. One of her friends told her bluntly that this could not continue. The King remarked that she could always sell her jewels. The Danish government also expected them to be sold. Dagmar said that they were to be sold after her death to provide security for Xenia and Olga. The Empress refused to recognise that anything had changed and saw no reason why she should be inconvenienced.

Andersen now settled Dagmar's debts and paid her an allowance from the East Asiatic Company. The Landmandsbank also allowed her a credit of £10,000, but this was terminated in 1920. When the bank crashed, the East Asiatic Company guaranteed her debts. A Finnish citizen also sent a small donation towards expenses. King George V then gave his aunt an allowance of £10,000 a year (about £450,000 today). He also gave £2,400 a year to Xenia and lent her Frogmore Cottage at Windsor.

Commander G.C. Amdrup (from 1927 Vice Admiral Sir George Amdrup), a former Adjutant to Prince Waldemar who had accompanied him on many of his journeys abroad, was appointed to oversee the Empress' finances. He was later joined by Captain Hans Rørdam. Amdrup suggested that she spend the summer at Hvidøre (which was smaller and more economical to run) and move to the Amalienborg only in winter. Alexandra agreed to pay £1,000 a year to help with the upkeep of the villa and retained a half share of the ownership. She also intended to pay an additional £850 but, as Alix was no better at managing money than Dagmar, it was never paid. Amdrup, who always used the official Royal notepaper from Christian IX's Palace for his correspondence to save money, received the allowance in monthly instalments. After deducting household expenses and salaries, he gave the balance to Dagmar, who soon learnt that if she spent less on entertaining there would be more to give to destitute émigrés. In 1926 Amdrup became Head of Her Majesty the Empress Dowager's Household, a post he held until her death.

Although living in her native land, Dagmar was still a member of a foreign Royal house and, as such, the Foreign Ministry distanced itself. Sheltering the Russians, even one who had formerly been a Danish princess, was not in Denmark's economic interest. At first any letters which came for her from abroad were forwarded to Hvidøre by the Danish Foreign Ministry. In 1920-1922 these averaged about twenty-one letters a year. By 1926, with an average of only three letters a year, the Foreign Ministry were refusing to convey letters unless the contents were known. In future, the Danish Legations abroad were instructed to provide enquirers with her address at Hvidøre so that letters could be posted direct. Foreign Legations were asked to refer any requests or enquiries regarding the Empress to Commodore Amdrup.

Dagmar now became even more inconsiderate, insisting on having Olga constantly at her beck and call to act as a combination of companion, secretary and lady's maid. She made no attempt to disguise her feelings about Colonel Kulikovsky. He was treated as a commoner and an outsider, pointedly excluded when there were guests present and rarely allowed into her presence. Only once did Dagmar invite him to attend a meeting, and that was owing to special military matters in Russia. If the Empress attended a formal function Olga was expected to accompany her mother alone.

Dagmar also found Olga's young sons rather too boisterous. Every afternoon at four o'clock they were washed and tidied up for an audience with 'Amama'. One year she was presented with several hundred tulip bulbs, a flower she particularly liked. They were planted in a star-shaped bed at Hvidøre, where the colourful display was admired by everybody. One morning her grandsons hacked off all the petals. She refused to see the boys for several days afterwards.

'It seemed to me that she was more important than everybody else', recalled Tihon. 'The house, the garden, the car, the driver Axel, the two chamber Cossacks with their daggers and revolvers who were on guard in the hall, and even the Danish guardsmen standing on guard by their red boxes, simply everything, everything, everything belonged to my grandmother and only existed for her. Everybody else including me was nothing. That's how it seemed to me and that to some extent is how it was'.[22]

Dagmar was indefatigable in searching for mushrooms in the woods and also liked to wander round the gardens picking flowers. When it was fine she sat outside reading or writing letters. One of the people she wrote to was Sidonie L'Escaille. In a letter of 15th June 1921, sending birthday wishes, Dagmar described the wedding of her niece Princess Margrethe and Prince René of Bourbon-Parma:

She was so pretty in her wedding dress and had a radiant air. ...Several days before the wedding the fiancé arrived with his mother, the Duchess of Parma, with her daughter and three sons, my nephew George of Greece and his wife and his two children ... It was a numerous gathering.

'The Duchess is charming, she is the sister of the Arch-Duchess Marie Thérèse, who was at our coronation in Moscow in 1883 and remembered it well. She appears very young when one thinks that she is the mother of 12 children! ...

'Every day there were family lunches and dinners and on the wedding day we left from here soon after 11 to go to the Catholic church ... Poor Waldemar was very moved, the bride so sweet and natural. The ceremony lasted an hour and a half, the priest spoke in Danish and French and the music was magnificent ... From the church the young newlyweds drove together in a carriage ... through the town lined with an immense crowd who acclaimed them with cheers and threw flowers ... We all followed in cars to the Amalienborg where there was a gala lunch for the numerous guests in ... Christian VII's Palace ...[23]

Dagmar's views were an embarrassment to the Danish government. With Russia in the throes of civil war and Germany in chaos, Denmark was caught between two problematical neighbours. Her hatred of Germany was well-known and she did not bother to hide her feelings about the Soviet government, or Denmark's recognition of it. During Easter 1920 Denmark faced a serious political crisis and the prospect of a general strike. Left-wingers demonstrated outside the Amalienborg and revolution was only averted by the moderates in the Social Democratic party who did not want the monarchy overthrown.

Political complications also did little to smooth the relationship between the King and his aunt. When King Victor Emmanuel III (son of Dagmar's one-time suitor King Umberto) and Queen Elena of Italy paid a state visit to Denmark, King Christian did not invite Dagmar to the banquet. Italy had recently recognised the Soviet government and her presence would have been embarrassing. Instead Dagmar received a telephone message that they would call on her that afternoon. She was furious. Elena had been one of the three Montenegrin princesses who were educated at the Russian Court. When the royal party arrived at Hvidøre they were met by a footman, who announced grandly that the Empress was indisposed.

In 1920, after fifty years, North Schleswig became Danish again, except the town of Flensborg which, to the anger of Dagmar and Alexandra, remained German. The Empress had actively campaigned to have the Danish/German border moved further south. King Christian came to North Schleswig on the Royal yacht *Dannebrog* and, mounted on a white horse, took possession of the Duchy for Denmark. For Dagmar and Alix, justice had been done at last.

∗

In November 1922 Dagmar arrived in England amid rumours that she had lost a considerable amount of money on financial speculation and in the Landmandsbank crash. It was said that since 1919 her expenses had been around 35,000 kroner per month and she now had no means of maintaining herself.

The priest of the Russian Church in Copenhagen, N.N. Popov, who was also Dagmar's confessor, was then quoted in a French newspaper as having accused the Danish government of not looking after the Empress' welfare. He also said that the Empress was going to live in France, as the Danish government would not protect her from Bolshevik death threats. These reports were vehemently denied. 'The paper could now report that the Dowager Empress would remain in Denmark, where she enjoyed the greatest hospitality, respect and love'. But this did not include financial support from the Danish government and the monetary worries continued.[24]

Dagmar remained in England while consultations were held with the Danish King. He finally agreed that she could return to live at Hvidøre for two months. Meanwhile, Dagmar enjoyed herself.

At the Royal Air Force Pageant at Hendon she and Alix were photographed wearing veiled hats and ankle-length skirts, appearing curiously out of step with the roaring twenties. Alix, whose health declined rapidly after the war, soon became much too frail to travel to Denmark but, since she left England permanently in the summer of 1919, Dagmar had been a regular visitor to Sandringham and Marlborough House. Only a few months earlier, in July 1922, the Empress had been among the 1,200 guests at St Margaret's, Westminster for the wedding of Lord Louis Mountbatten and Edwina Ashley. So frequent were her visits that in 1923 the Foreign Secretary granted the Empress, Prince Dolgoruky and Countess Mengden exemption from the provisions of Part II of the Aliens

Order, 1920. The Empress' two maids Miss Greenvelt and Miss Vassiljeva and Poliakoff the Cossack bodyguard were required to register as aliens in the ordinary way.

On 26th April 1923 she was present at a wedding of unrecognised significance when the King's second son Albert, Duke of York, married Lady Elizabeth Bowes-Lyon at Westminster Abbey. Afterwards Dagmar joined the Royal family on the balcony of Buckingham Palace. The eldest child of this marriage became Queen Elizabeth II.

Shortly afterwards Dagmar fell ill and was unable to return home as planned. Alix was obliged to spend the entire summer at Marlborough House keeping her sister company. It was late August before the Empress felt well enough to return to Denmark on the East Asiatic's *Jutlandia*. The sisters were never to meet again.[25]

*

The Dowager Empress, the most senior of the Romanov survivors, appeared a tragic figure. As the surviving Romanovs surfaced one by one, and in the absence of any definite news regarding the fate of the Tsar and Michael, 'The Old Icon', as Russians called her, the 'Lady of Tears' as foreigners called her,[26] became head of the Imperial House.

Of the fifty-two Romanovs living in Russia in 1918, seventeen disappeared during the Red Terror. Grand Dukes George and Nicholas Michaelovitch, Dimitri Constantinovitch, and Paul Alexandrovitch were shot in the SS Peter & Paul Fortress in 1919. Ella, Grand Duke Sergei Michaelovitch, Prince Vladimir Paley and Princes Constantine, Igor and Ivan Constantinovitch were thrown alive down a disused mineshaft at Alapayevsk. The indominatable Miechen escaped on board her own train and died at Contrexeville in France in 1920. Her three sons Cyril, Boris and Andrei also reached safety.

Although the Tsar was generally believed to be dead, in the absence of proof rumours flourished. In December 1918 the *New York Times* reported that, according to Polish officers who had arrived in Warsaw from Sevastopol, the Dowager Empress had been receiving letters from the former Tsar every ten days.

In January 1920 Dagmar received a report from Sergei Markov, a former cavalry officer who had followed the Imperial family to Tobolsk and succeeded in making contact. After first accounts of the Tsar's execution and the family's evacuation, Markov appealed to Grand Duke Ernst Ludwig of Hesse to save the rest of the family. German information indicated that Alicky and her children were moved to Perm on 17th July. The Grand Duke's representative met Markov in Kiev but the Ukraine was then plunged into civil war and they were unable to do anything.

Soon afterwards, rumours circulated that all the family were dead. Dagmar read Markov's report and sent him 6,000 marks but it did nothing to alter her attitude that the family were alive.

Others tried to extract money. In the early 1920s a monarchist officer in Berlin was told by a Cossack that Grand Duke Michael was hidden in one of the Trans-Volga provinces. He offered to bring the Grand Duke across the Soviet border on two conditions: that the officer accompany him into Russia and that he first obtain 30,000 Danish kroner from the Dowager Empress. The officer refused, knowing that the White Investigation under Nicholas Sokolov had established that Michael was dead.

By 1921 Sokolov was in Paris, with Alexis' former tutor Pierre Gilliard and Paul Bulygin. Sokolov and Bulygin had intended to show Sokolov's dossier to the Dowager Empress and continue their work under her patronage. Dagmar was in London and the government refused to grant them visas but Grand Duke Dimitri arranged for them to visit her in Denmark. An urgent telegram from Olga then arrived, entreating them not to go. Dagmar had refused to see either Sokolov or his dossier when she heard he believed that the Tsar and his family were dead. Yet she contributed £1,000 to help the investigation when it ran out of money. Sokolov had already submitted an interim report, brought to her from Siberia by Bulygin, but she never stopped telling people that Nicholas and his family were alive.

Was Dagmar really convinced, or was it a defence mechanism? That year, in an audience with a member of the Danish Legation, the Empress reacted so emotionally when Nicholas' name was mentioned that the official felt she had now lost her illusions. Nevertheless, in an effort to try and find out what had happened, she gave money to Elizaveta Ersberg, a former chambermaid to the Tsar's daughters who had been with them at Tobolsk. 'Lisa' had reached Ekaterinburg with the Whites and, acting on information, hired a boat to search a pond and a swamp. Shortly after Dagmar's death Elizaveta returned to Russia to continue the search.

Sokolov's investigation concluded that the Tsar, Tsarina, their children and servants had been shot in the sinister ground floor room of the Ipatiev House. Their bodies were loaded into a lorry and taken to The Four Brothers Mine, where they were stripped, chopped up, burned and dissolved in sulphuric acid, before being thrown down a disused mineshaft. When the mine was searched jewellery, clothing and personal effects were found, together with a finger and Dr Botkin's false teeth. The body of Tatiana's pet dog was later discovered at the bottom of the mineshaft, implying that her owners had died as well. But the family's bodies were never found.

A box of relics from The Four Brothers later found its way to Dagmar.

Its arrival did nothing to shake her belief. The box was sent to Paris and its present whereabouts are uncertain.

Her attitude could not be put down to the wanderings of an old woman, unhinged by shock. In the 1970s Grand Duke Vladimir Cyrillovitch stated that 'the Dowager Empress died perfectly sane'. In 1927 French Deuxieme Bureau reports emphasised that she was very lucid and her letters confirm this. 'Because of her position in the family', Prince Waldemar explained, 'it is safe to say that all reports reach her sooner or later, and until two reports tally, she refuses to accept any as final'.[27]

She was undoubtedly encouraged by the conflicting accounts of various investigators and foreign agents. For many years afterwards there were rumours of a failed rescue bid involving the British Royal family and the Royal Navy, a last-minute bid by George V to salve his conscience. In the 1920s many people testified to Sokolov that Empress Alexandra and her daughters were imprisoned at Perm during the autumn of 1918. Others said that Anastasia had escaped and spoke of posters announcing that one or more of the Tsar's daughters was on the run. Was it the truth, or Bolshevik disinformation? Nobody knew. Nevertheless, until the Dowager Empress recognised that the Tsar and Alexis were dead there could be no pretenders to the throne.

Dagmar was therefore outraged when Grand Duke Cyril Vladimirovitch, the first Romanov to break his oath of allegiance to the Tsar, proclaimed himself Curator of the Throne and then Emperor as soon as Michael was declared legally dead in 1924. She had never forgiven him for his actions in 1917 and now condemned his declaration as premature.

Cyril's declaration was a direct infringement of the unwritten agreement by which no member of the Imperial family would claim the throne in the Dowager Empress' lifetime. It split the monarchist movement. He gained no support from the Supreme Monarchist Council (who thought that the future of the monarchy must be decided in Russia) and little support from the family. He raised his daughters' rank from princesses to Grand Duchesses and proclaimed his son Prince Vladimir 'Grand Duke, Heir and Tsarevitch'. He also created Natasha 'Princess Brasova' and made her son George a Prince. The latter title Dagmar apparently recognised, perhaps because he was her grandson.

Few émigrés, least of all the Imperial family, thought that they would be in exile for long and confirmed this by maintaining lavish lifestyles. With only the example of the French Revolution to follow, they thought they would soon resume their former lives. The choice of the next Tsar was therefore important and many of them supported Dimitri. The popular Nicholasha avoided making a claim, although he became the leader of the exiled remnants of the Imperial army. He was actively opposed to Cyril and was assured the loyalty of the remaining members of the Imperial family. On 4th October 1924 Dagmar poured out her feelings to him in a letter which was published in *The New York Times* at her request, under the heading 'Mother of the Tsar Denounces Cyril'.

My heart contracted painfully when I read the manifesto of the Grand Duke Cyril Vladimirovitch who has declared himself Emperor of All the Russias ... I fear that this manifesto will create a schism and in so doing will not improve but on the contrary will worsen the position in Russia which is already sufficiently tormented. If it was the Lord God's will according to his unknowable ways to call to Himself my beloved sons and grandson, then I think that His Majesty the Emperor will be indicated by our basic laws in union with the Orthodox Church and the Russian people. I pray God that he will not be angry with us to the very end and will soon send us salvation by paths known only to Him. I am sure you, as the senior member of the Romanov family, share my attitude.[28]

Cyril's wife Grand Duchess Victoria Feodorovna was quoted in *The New York Times* in December 1924 as saying that a copy of the Empress' letter was sent to them at the same time and Cyril 'replied to the Empress direct some months ago'.

Dagmar 'felt it beneath her dignity to take sides, to issue manifestos, to participate in sham battles', Sandro explained.[29] Even so, it was to the Dowager Empress, whose influence could make or break any of their plans, that the monarchists turned. In January 1924 hopes for a restoration were raised by the death of Lenin, only to be quickly dispelled. Lenin's body was embalmed in a mausoleum in Red Square and Petrograd was renamed Leningrad. Then in 1925, rumours circulating among the Royal families of Europe forced the subject of the events at Ekaterinburg, forbidden in the Empress' household, out into the open and caused a rift in the Imperial family which has never healed.

CHAPTER 26

Little Mother of Russia

'MAY HER SPIRIT STRENGTHEN OUR BELIEF IN
THE FUTURE OF THE FATHERLAND'

At nine o'clock in the evening of 17th February 1920 a young woman was pulled from the Landwehr Canal in Berlin after attempting suicide. She carried no identification, refused to answer questions and her body bore marks of violence. It was thought she was Russian.

After six weeks in hospital she was sent to an asylum as 'Miss Unknown'. Gradually, she befriended the nurses. Then, during the autumn of 1921, she confided a secret – she was Anastasia, the sole survivor of the Tsar's family.

A recently-discharged patient then told a monarchist officer that she had recognised Grand Duchess Tatiana among the asylum's inmates. The news that Tatiana might be alive spread quickly through the large émigré community. Among those who tried to identify her was Baroness Sophie Buxhoeveden, who had been with the Imperial family in Tobolsk. She pronounced her 'too short' for Tatiana – but the girl later told one of the émigrés that she was Anastasia.

For the next three years she was shuttled between the émigrés (one of whom said that he expected to receive a lot of money when the Dowager Empress recognised her granddaughter) and various hospitals, where she was treated for tuberculosis of the bones. Other courtiers and relatives of the Tsar's family visited her – but, although they had to admit she knew many intimate details of Court life and the Imperial family, they were unable to reconcile their memories of the plump, lively Anastasia with the thin, anaemic, tubercular girl in the hospital bed and they were puzzled by her seeming inability to speak Russian. By the summer of 1925 she was critically ill. But by now the matter had come to the notice of the Duchess of Cumberland.

Thyra had lived quietly at Gmunden since the war. Her husband, a lifelong enemy of Prussia, had been deprived of his British titles and his Garter banner had been removed from Windsor. After the Duke's death

340

in 1923 Thyra occasionally visited Denmark, although Dagmar complained that her sister seldom wrote. Thyra's eldest daughter was married to Prince Max of Baden, the last Chancellor of Imperial Germany, who had access to German intelligence reports. She may therefore have received privileged news. The Germans had made it their business to be well informed about the whereabouts of all the Romanovs, as was shown by their prompt action in saving the Dowager Empress. Rumours of Anastasia's escape had circulated in 1918; the stories refused to die. Many Germans claimed to have inside information.

Despite Queen Alexandra's increasing vagueness, she was also aware of the rumours about Anastasia. The Hon. Violet Vivian, whose family was very close to the Queen, maintained that 'there was truth in the Anastasia claim';[1] but it was Thyra and Waldemar who raised the subject at the Danish Court during 1925.

The story of 'Anastasia's' escape, told to the monarchists in disjointed fragments, seemed incredible. During the assassination of the rest of her family she had been saved by a soldier, Alexander Tchaikovsky. He and his family took her on a farm cart to Roumania, where she gave birth to his son. They were married in a Catholic church in Bucharest, although she did not recall signing any papers or possessing a wedding ring. Shortly afterwards Alexander Tchaikovsky was killed and, leaving her son in Roumania, she travelled to Berlin to find her aunt Princess Irene of Prussia. A few days later she was pulled from the canal.

No-one had dared to tell the Dowager Empress and shatter her belief in the survival of the whole family. Thyra decided to take a hand. What if it was Anastasia? Dagmar was worried. There were dynastic considerations at stake. The Bolshevik regime would not last long now that Lenin was dead and this young woman had a son by a Polish/Bolshevik soldier – if she *was* Anastasia her son might one day claim the restored throne. The scandal would be immense. The old Empress had spent over fifty years maintaining the dignity of the Russian throne. This 'Frau Tchaikovsky' was not the first pretender, nor, undoubtedly, would she be the last. No, she could *not* be Anastasia. Further discussion of the subject was unwelcome.

Waldemar then instructed Herluf Zahle, the Danish Minister in Berlin, to launch an unofficial enquiry. His letter was delivered by Alexis Volkov, a former Imperial servant, who was asked to report back when he had met Frau Tchaikovsky. Although Volkov was deeply moved, he did not formally acknowledge her as Anastasia. His report remains sealed in the Danish Royal Archives and it is unlikely that Dagmar ever saw it.

Her household were now insistent that she be shielded from anything upsetting. In 1922 some photographs of the Tsar's family taken in Siberia, together with a letter written by Marie from Ekaterinburg to Anastasia in Tobolsk, were sent to Zina Mengden. They had been smuggled out of Russia by a peasant and forwarded by an old friend of the Dowager Empress, Rodion de Boulatcel. Olga returned the package without mentioning it to her mother. She feared its contents would be too distressing. When Dagmar returned to Denmark after her illness in 1923 her staff noticed that the old Empress had become much more frail. Any further shock could prove too much.

Waldemar now instructed Zahle to conduct a thorough enquiry into the Anastasia affair. Meanwhile the prince agreed to pay Frau Tchaikovsky's hospital bills. More visitors followed, including Pierre Gilliard and his wife Shura, Anastasia's nursemaid. They were impressed and returned a few weeks later with Grand Duchess Olga.

Dagmar was anxious to avoid publicity and considered the visit 'imprudent and unnecessary'. Xenia also sent a strongly worded telegram telling her sister not to go. Olga went nevertheless, mainly at the insistence of Thyra, 'just to clear up the case once and for all'.[2]

After her first visit Olga was unable to decide either way but she was excited and, when she left Berlin four days later, Frau Tchaikovsky's supporters maintained she seemed convinced.

The recollections of Olga's stay and her reaction immediately afterwards soon became blurred when she returned to Denmark. There is no doubt that she felt the responsibility and the fear of making the wrong decision. At Hvidøre she had long discussions with Dagmar and Waldemar. Exactly what she told Dagmar is unknown but the Empress made it plain that she was not interested and was angry with her for travelling to Berlin. For once Dagmar shared an opinion with her son-in-law Colonel Kulikovsky who, together with Pierre Gilliard, had been very active in Berlin trying to prove that Frau Tchaikovsky was an imposter.

Olga submitted to pressure. In January 1926 the Danish press printed a statement saying that Grand Duchess Olga had found no resemblance between the unknown woman and the Tsar's youngest daughter. This denial, issued not at Dagmar's insistence but after Olga had been persuaded by Pierre Gilliard (who had now become one of Frau Tchaikovsky's strongest opponents), did not represent the Grand Duchess' true opinion. Members of the family remembered Olga's anguish and her uncertainty even in 1927 that the woman was a fraud. Olga summed up the dilemma in a letter to Prince Dolgoruky. 'Poor Mamma', she wrote, 'how am I supposed to tell her. It will kill her'. It was a situation Olga was totally unable to cope with. As Princess Xenia of Russia spoke carefully of 'seniority' and 'the accommodation of the elder generation on behalf of the younger', her daughter Nancy put it more succinctly: 'One was sacrificed to save the other'.[3]

Strangely, both Olga and the Gilliards stated that the patient resembled Tatiana more than Anastasia; but Tatiana or Anastasia, Dagmar was not interested. 'What do they think?' she exclaimed. 'That I would sit here … and not rush to my granddaughter's side?'[4]

Dagmar alone had the power to decide if she should be formally recognised. If she admitted that Anastasia was the sole survivor, she would also have to admit that the rest of the family had died. Although female succession was barred, it would be unthinkable to acknowledge that the only surviving daughter of the Emperor had 'married' a Bolshevik soldier and borne his child, a son whose very whereabouts were unknown. She had to be realistic. In the 1920s all the exiled Royal Houses still hoped for a restoration, however remote the possibility seemed and such a scandal could only harm the Romanovs. 'Even if she is Anastasia', said one monarchist, 'this affair must be defeated in the interest of the Russian monarchy'.[5]

Dagmar's attitude was made abundantly clear to Herluf Zahle. She listened in stony silence while he related the details of the Ekaterinburg drama and concluded that the rest of the family had died. Dagmar declared icily that the young woman could not be her granddaughter and dismissed Zahle abruptly.

On another occasion, when Zahle asked the Empress what the world would think if she did not do everything in her power to clear up the mystery, she replied only: 'My daughter Olga tells me this woman is not my granddaughter'.[6] This time the Empress' entourage were annoyed with Zahle for trying to destroy her belief that Nicholas' family were alive.

Soon the whole family were taking sides but, at this critical moment, some bad news arrived from England.

On 20th November 1925 Queen Alexandra died after a heart attack at Sandringham.

*

Alexandra's death was an 'irreparable blow' to seventy-eight-year-old Dagmar. 'At first it left her stunned', recalled Olga. 'When she recovered from the first shock she had the air of someone who had lost her way in a wilderness'. Suddenly she began to look and act her age.[7]

The Queen's death also brought complications. Hvidøre was jointly owned by Alexandra and Dagmar; the property would now have to be sold, half of the sale proceeds going to the Queen's heirs. As the villa was not sold until after Dagmar's death, it appears that King George and his sisters agreed to this arrangement so that the Empress could continue living there.

Just before Christmas the Empress wrote to King George. 'Just heard of your *enormous* kindness and can't find words to express all the depth of my gratitude. You are really *too* kind and I feel sure you do it in loving memory of your beloved Mama. But nevertheless I am quite ashamed to be such a *burden* to you. If it was not for your great generosity I don't know what would have become of me, as I could not have continued to live at Hvidøre ... Please excuse this short letter but I don't feel well at all and am *very miserable*'.[8]

Although Grand Duke Alexander says the Queen bequeathed 'most of her jewellery and some money' to her sister, Queen Alexandra made no formal Will so that it is not possible to confirm this.[9] Now, although Dagmar could hardly realise it, there would be no more weekly letters – there had been some three thousand over the last sixty years. As the months went by her thoughts turned increasingly to the past and she spent hours looking at the photographs of her family which were all around her room. But she never spoke about them.

It was now vital that the Empress was spared any further upset and Alexandra's death put an end to any hopes of Frau Tchaikovsky's recognition as Anastasia. In the autumn of 1926 Harriet Rathlef-Keilmann, Frau Tchaikovsky's companion, forwarded her notes on the case to Copenhagen. She asked Olga to read them and try to persuade the Empress to do the same. Olga approved the passage relating to her visit to Berlin but did not bother to read the rest. It was never shown to Dagmar at all. She was already annoyed with Waldemar, who was under pressure to stop paying the hospital bills.

Later that year Grand Duke Andrei, a graduate of the Military Law Academy in St Petersburg, intervened. Realising that, because of Dagmar and Olga's 'negative attitude' any investigation would incur their disapproval, he wrote to Olga drawing her attention to the defects of the investigation and asking the Empress' permission to conduct his own enquiry. He then set to work on an investigation that lasted him beyond Dagmar's lifetime. His records have never been made public.

Others refused to interfere. 'The Dowager Empress believes that she is going to see her son and his family alive again', Nicholasha explained. 'A shock like this could kill her'.[10]

As the recognitions and denials continued, Dagmar lost all interest and she never met the young woman who claimed to be her granddaughter. Olga felt that, deep down, she had already accepted the reality of the situation. In 1928 Frau Tchaikovsky went to America. To avoid publicity she used the alias Anna Anderson, a name that soon became world-famous.

Behind the political aspects – 'Anastasia's' claims would hinder Cyril;

while Grand Duke Ernst Ludwig of Hesse was afraid his 1916 trip to Russia would be revealed – lurked another spectre. The Romanov millions.

The Tsar was one of the wealthiest men in the world and stories that a vast fortune awaited his rightful heirs had been circulating for years. Many people believed that, when Olga and Xenia learnt that Frau Tchaikovsky had spoken about coded bank accounts for the Tsar's children, this destroyed any chance she had of being recognised.

There were rumours of substantial deposits with the Bank of England (although the money inherited from Alexander III was repatriated in 1900) and Baring Brothers in London, and of considerable amounts in banks throughout the world. The Tsar's personal deposits in the National City Bank alone were rumoured to be in the region of $60 million. In theory no member of the family could withdraw any money remaining in these accounts until the matter was resolved.

By October 1923 Dagmar's debts, which were guaranteed by Hans Niels Andersen and the East Asiatic Company, had reached almost one million kroner and were rising steadily.

Together with Count Ahlefelt, Andersen raised 200,000 kroner (about £10,000) by private subscription to enable her to continue living in Denmark. Although the Danish Foreign Ministry refused to allow a public subscription, other private subscriptions followed. The Great Northern Telegraph Company, another concern which Dagmar had done much to promote in Russia, paid her a small annual allowance of 15,000 kroner. They insisted the arrangement be kept secret, in case the Soviet government caused problems.

With Dagmar and her family in financial difficulties they now started a treasure hunt. In 1920 Xenia was granted Letters of Administration as the Tsar's prime heir in England. This included property rights, the relics and damaged jewellery found at Ekaterinburg (valued at £500) which had arrived from Vladivostock, and literary rights, in an effort to stop publication of Nicholas and Alicky's private letters. When extracts from them were printed in an American newspaper it upset Dagmar considerably.

In 1925 Prince Sergei Georgievitch Romanovsky, 8th Duke of Leuchtenberg, intervened. He was the son of Anastasia of Montenegro by her first marriage to George, 6th Duke of Leuchtenberg. Sergei had been under house arrest with his mother and Dagmar at Djulber in 1918 and he left Russia with the Dowager Empress on board H.M.S. *Marlborough*. He now applied for limited Letters of Administration in New York on behalf of the Dowager Empress and over thirty other relatives after reports circulated that there was money in two of the city's banks. Berlin banks also held deposits but, by the time the money was distributed in 1938, the fall of the mark had considerably reduced their value. (Xenia never claimed her share.)

July 1928 saw the tenth anniversary of Ekaterinburg. The Tsar could now be presumed dead and Xenia tried to recover the Langinkoski Fishing Lodge and property in the village of Halila close to the Finnish/Russian border. This included the Halila Sanitorium, which she believed was bought personally by her father in 1892 for 100,000 roubles. In 1918 both Halila and Langinkoski (confiscated from the Romanovs by the Bolsheviks) became part of Finland. The fishing lodge fell into disrepair but, under the Treaty of Dorpat in 1920, it was agreed that Russian state property in Finland would be taken over by the Finnish State and vice versa.

In 1928 the former Russian Minister of Finance Peter Bark arrived in Copenhagen to take Power of Attorney from the Empress and Xenia to enable legal action to be brought against the Finnish State. The action initially failed, as the Finns claimed that Halila had been handed over to the Department of the Empress Marie by Nicholas II in 1900 and this foundation was supported by state funds. They claimed that Halila was bought by the Russian Chancery, therefore both properties were 'Russian state property' legally acquired under the Treaty of Dorpat. Not until 1934 was compensation obtained.[11]

There is no evidence that Dagmar's motives in the Anastasia affair were financial. She had no grasp of monetary affairs, her concern was purely dynastic. It now appears that all the Tsar's money was withdrawn from foreign banks to help the war effort and he had commanded his relatives to do the same. Any money remaining belonged to the Tsarist government, not to the Tsar personally. 'Would my mother have accepted a pension from King George V if we had any money in England?' asked Olga. 'It does not make sense'.[12]

In the 1920s many people had an interest in the affairs of the Dowager Empress and her daughters and, as long as rumours flourished that substantial amounts were waiting to be claimed, they were determined to make sure that 'Anastasia' was never recognised.

*

In the mid-1920s some unpleasant stories appeared in the Scandinavian newspapers. In November 1924 *Ekstrabladet* reported that the Soviet Chargé d'Affairs had demanded the explusion of 150 White Russian émigrés, including the Dowager Empress, from Denmark. The Danish government, aware that any such action would turn the Danish people against them, refused to comply. A Norwegian newspaper described the demand as 'the height of Bolshevik impudence' and the story was soon contradicted.[13]

Norwegian newspapers then printed a sensational story about the Dowager Empress' supposed attempt to murder her grandson Alexis. This information was given to *The New York Times* by General Kommissarov, who was allegedly a former head of the Russian Secret Police. According to Kommissarov, Dagmar hated the Tsarina so much that she planned to murder Alexis in the castle park with the aid of two gardeners, so that Michael could inherit the throne. It is to be hoped that Dagmar did not read this fantastic piece of rubbish.

Then, in January 1925, the Danish Foreign Ministry learnt that a Russian businessman claimed to be in possession of the Dowager Empress' diary for 1916. He said he had bought it in Kiev, at the request of a White Russian officer who wanted it to be eventually returned to its rightful owner. The diary was written in 'not wholly faultless Danish, and with the dates and Holy Days in Russian'. The businessman was asking an 'outrageous' price.[14]

The Danish Minister in Moscow, Schou, had seen a small part of the diary and believed it to be genuine. He was concerned that one or two of the more outspoken comments could cause embarrassment to the Dowager Empress if they were made public. The only way to stop this was buy it. Prince Waldemar was immediately informed.

Dagmar was again in poor health, so Waldemar decided to find out if any of the contents could be damaging or cause a scandal. He did not tell his sister. Meanwhile, Schou met the Russian in a Moscow restaurant and was given the complete diary to read. In February 1925 he reported that most of it concerned family matters, the weather and such mundane things. However, about ten pages were on political matters: 'criticism of the Russian government's politics, worry for the future, aversion to "a very high ranking person" (probably Alexandra), mention of Rasputin's murder plus a single very bitter remark about Denmark's sale of the West Indian Islands'.[15] Nothing, in fact, that wasn't already known.

At this point Thyra proposed to buy the diary. Schou thought it could be obtained for 3,000 kroner. Thyra agreed to pay but negotiations broke down when it transpired that the Russian wanted three times this amount. Dagmar was never told and the diary's present whereabouts are unknown.

Dagmar could still be almost dangerously outspoken. In 1925 the Russian émigrés were broken-hearted when the Soviet government decided that the Russian Church of St Alexander Nevsky in Copenhagen (which the Empress had built and which was attached to the old Imperial Embassy) was Soviet property. When the Danish government then allowed the Soviets to turn it into an extension of their Consulate, Dagmar was furious. Refusing to accept defeat she engaged Esbern Trolle, the solicitor to the Supreme Court (who took the brief without a fee), to fight the case. She expressed her opinion so loudly that Olga feared she would be kidnapped by Bolshevik agents.

Mr Trolle was victorious and Dagmar attended the first service after the reopening despite a crippling attack of arthritis and lumbago. She still insisted on speaking only Russian inside, maintaining that she was still a Russian Empress. It was her last visit to the St Alexander Nevsky Church.

*

During the last few years of her life Dagmar had difficulty walking and used a stick, but she remained active and recovered some of her interest in life. Queen Olga of Greece was a frequent visitor and once brought her six-year-old grandson Prince Philip, now the Duke of Edinburgh. He was 'rather subdued' in the presence of the Empress.[16]

Sending King George greetings for his birthday in June 1927 Dagmar added, 'I can't say *how delighted* I am England had the pluck to send all those horrid Bolsheviks out of the country after all the evil they have done already'. That summer was cold and windy and in June she was still complaining that she was unable to go to her 'dear Hvidøre' yet. 'Such a pity and such a loss of time', she wrote sadly.[17]

Finally she was able to move but by the autumn the doctors pronounced her too weak to return to Copenhagen. They were forced to remain at Hvidøre which was only heated by kerosene fires. As she weakened further Olga's children saw her less and less.

She worried increasingly about her jewel box. At the Amalienborg it was kept under her bed and sometimes it was brought out so that she could run her fingers through some of the magnificent pieces. At Hvidøre she had the box moved so that she could see it. Finally, Amdrup was given a safe with two keys; one for himself and one for Dagmar's dresser. The contents were frequently checked.

Certainly many of Europe's royalty had their eyes on it. King Christian intimated that he expected his share of the estimated half a million pounds sale proceeds. George V suggested that it be placed in a London bank vault and offered to make arrangements for the sale. Sandro asked her to pawn some of it so that they could start up a paper factory. Xenia asked for her share to be sold to solve her pressing financial problems. Dagmar's own finances were no more secure. In 1927 another planned public subscription was abandoned. A public subscription for her 80th birthday ran into difficulties with the Foreign Ministry but she still refused to sell her jewels, either to help herself or her daughters. 'You will have all of it when I am gone', she said.[18] The only item Dagmar wore now was the diamond brooch Sasha had given her on their wedding day.

On 26th November 1927 Dagmar celebrated her 80th birthday. She was now very feeble and saw few people. She maintained her lifelong connection with the Danish Lifeguards and in December wrote the foreword to the Guards' Association Christmas magazine:

My heart has always belonged to the dear Guard … and [I] cannot say how touched and proud I was that day my beloved husband dressed in the uniform of the Guards, when he was appointed Honorary Chief … by my beloved father. A merry and blessed Christmas is wished for you all by, Dagmar.[19]

In 1928 she received two presents from Russia. The first came with a letter from a Russian engineer living in Prague. Nicholas Ipatiev had formerly owned 'The House of Special Purpose' in Ekaterinburg and he now sent Dagmar a petition, asking for the loan of £500 sterling. Also enclosed were two watercolours which he had found in his house when the Bolsheviks moved out. He believed they were painted by Grand Duchess Olga Nicholaievna.[20]

The second item was even more poignant. In 1918 a Guards officer found the Icon of the Most Holy Mother of God of the Three Hands among a pile of debris in Ekaterinburg. Realising its significance, he arranged for it to be sent to the Dowager Empress via Grand Duchess Olga Alexandrovna and her husband. The icon had come from the Ipatiev House. Nicholas and his family had prayed before it on the night of their murder.

*

By October 1928 Dagmar's strength was failing fast. Her health had improved slightly over the preceding few weeks and the collapse was sudden and unexpected. Her family were immediately summoned.

Towards the middle of the month she slipped into a coma. Her daughters maintained a three-day vigil as she lay in her bed at Hvidøre surrounded by icons. Among them a small crucifix stood out. Set into its centre was a picture of Nicholas.

At seven o'clock in the evening of Saturday, 13th October, Dagmar died peacefully without regaining consciousness. Beside her was her Danish bible.

The King, Queen, Prince Viggo, Princess Thyra and Prince Gustav arrived and Father Koltcheff, the priest of the Russian Church, conducted a service. Soon afterwards a wreath arrived from the Royal Life Guards.

Her body lay in state in the Garden Room, surrounded by six guardsmen. A small altar was set up, a lamp was left burning and prayers were read continuously for the Dowager Empress' soul.

At the Amalienborg details of the funeral were discussed with King Christian, who still managed to be petty. As she was only an *ex*-Empress he decided there was no need to give her a state funeral. Olga and Xenia felt this was a great indignity and an insult to their mother's rank. Finally, public opinion forced the King to change his mind, although he forbade the Empress' Private Confessor to appear at the service in his vestments in case the Catholic community later demanded the same rights. Even the outer coffin case of oak in which Dagmar's coffin would stand in the cathedral was not new – it was a spare one which had previously been used for her father and brother Freddie before their coffins were transferred to marble tombs.

On 16th October the Empress' coffin was placed on the Royal hearse and, escorted by the Guards in full-dress uniform, she left Hvidøre for the last time. In death she once more regained the place of honour which had been hers for so long in life.

The plain wooden coffin lay in Copenhagen's Russian Church covered with the Russian Imperial flag and the Dannebrog, guarded by the Empress' Cossack bodyguards and a Danish guard of honour. Twice a day the family gathered for funeral services. Among the mountain of wreaths and flowers was one from the women of Schleswig with a poem describing her as 'South Jutland's dear sister', and one from the President of Finland. More than five thousand people queued to pay their last respects to 'Kejserinde Dagmar'. Afterwards, the icon of the Empress' regiment of the Chevalier Guards was placed on the coffin lid. As the émigré community, royalty, former Tsarist officers and ministers of the Imperial regime converged on Copenhagen, memorial services were held all over Europe.

On Friday, 19th October, flags flew at half-mast and the Royal Guards, in blue ceremonial uniform, lined Bredgade opposite the St Alexander Nevsky Church. Early in the morning the church began to fill with Russian exiles and the largest gathering of the Romanov family since the revolution: Xenia, Sandro (who had arrived too late to see the Empress alive) and their sons Andrei, Feodor, Nikita and Vassili; Irina and Felix; Olga and Colonel Kulikovsky; Dimitri and his sister Marie; Princes Gabriel and George Constantinovitch with their sister Tatiana; and Princess Albert of Saxe-Altenburg. To Olga the sudden appearance of all these relatives, many of whom had scarcely concerned themselves with the Dowager Empress since their exile, was inappropriate. She especially resented the appearance of Cyril, whose claims as pretender had so annoyed her mother.

Mass was celebrated by the Metropolitan Yevlogii before other distinguished guests arrived for the funeral. Among them were the King and

Queen of Denmark with Crown Prince Frederick, Prince Waldemar and the rest of the Royal family, King Haakon of Norway, Crown Prince Gustav Adolf of Sweden, the Duke of York, the Grand Duke of Mecklenburg, Thyra and her son the Duke of Brunswick with his wife Victoria Louise, the Prime Minister, the Foreign Minister, the Presidents of both houses of the Rigsdag, the commander of the garrison in Copenhagen, the former Prime Minister of Russia Alexander Trepov and Peter Bark.

Father Koltcheff conducted the service while the congregation stood holding lighted tapers. He expressed the hope that 'the Little Mother of Russia' would look down from Heaven and see the 'victory of truth and justice', adding 'may her spirit strengthen our belief in the future of the Fatherland'. Metropolitan Yevlogii then gave an 'interminable' address in Russian. Throughout the service a Danish guard of honour and a Russian guard, comprising dignitaries from the Court and the army, the Empress' ladies-in-waiting and her bodyguards, stood alongside the catafalque.

When the four hour service had finished, all the Russians, led by Xenia and Olga, kissed the icon on the coffin lid. Cyril remained for a moment in silent prayer. Then the members of the Danish Royal family knelt by the coffin and kissed the Dannebrog. Thyra, who was as white as a sheet, had to be supported by Waldemar and Prince George of Greece.

As the coffin was carried from the church the Guards presented arms. Over 100,000 people stood bareheaded along the streets in the bright sunshine as the cortège made its way slowly along Bredgade, past the Kastellet (the Citadel) to Gronningen and the Østbanegaden, Copenhagen's Eastern railway station. The hearse was escorted by a guard of honour from the Guard Hussars and the Guards' band playing the funeral march. All the Kings and Princes followed the coffin on foot, the royal ladies rode in carriages. The city's shop windows were draped in black crepe and only the flag on the Soviet Legation was not at half-mast.

A special train was waiting to take them on the twenty mile journey to the twelfth-century Roskilde Cathedral, burial place of the Danish Royal family.

Outside Roskilde station troops lined the route to the cathedral and the pavements were covered with fir twigs. The interior was lit only by thousands of candles as the final, private, funeral service commenced. Danish and Russian Guards officers carried the tiny coffin, still covered with the two flags, into the cathedral and a procession of Russian priests carrying icons preceded the Cossack bodyguards and the royal mourners. The Danish Court Chaplain gave a valedictory address before, in defiance of the King, Father Koltcheff slipped inside with a long coat concealing his vestments and said a final Russian prayer. Then the last surviving Empress of Russia was laid to rest in Frederick V's Chapel.

'The pure wax tapers are burnt down, the flames are finished', said Father Koltcheff earlier. 'Our Little Mother's, the Dowager Empress' life is over. Russia's many million children have become orphans'.[21]

Postscript

In Scandinavia, Dagmar's memory lives on. To the old Danes who still remember her she is Kejserinde Dagmar, 'our unforgettable Empress'.[1] In the autumn of 1997 thousands flocked to Christiansborg Slot in Copenhagen to view an exhibition about her life. In the Russian Church on Bredgade the chair she used during the services is preserved, along with many other relics, including a book of newspaper cuttings about her life collated by Wiojji, her Russian butler. In Finland she is remembered as one of the most popular royal ladies. One museum has a chair from a peasant's cottage in Nyland, where she once sat while she chatted to the family. The fishing lodge at Langinkoski is open to the public. Every year tourists come to see where the Empress of Russia cooked the meals while her husband fished for salmon.

For Dagmar's family, the most pressing concern after her funeral was to read the Will and settle the Estate. King George V appointed Peter Bark as trustee of the Estate in England, King Christian X appointed Vice Admiral Amdrup and Esbern Trolle, Solicitor of the Supreme Court, as Executors for the Danish Estate. Everything was left to Xenia and Olga. There was nothing for Michael's widow or his son George, although Dagmar had made provision for her servants and Cossack bodyguards. King George was still paying pensions to the Russian suite and servants the following year. Her faithful bodyguard Yachik, who went to work in a greengrocer's shop, received £8 a month from the British Court until 1938. Poliakoff rinsed bottles for a wine merchant.[2] Wiojji lived in the gardener's house at Hvidøre for many years. His calendar always remained at 13th October 1928.

Her most potent legacy remained the jewels. Even before the funeral they had been spirited out of Denmark, in the wake of reports that they would be claimed by the Bolsheviks. King George was anxious that Xenia's experiences should not be repeated. Xenia had handed over all her jewels, including some fabulous black pearls, to crooks who went off without paying and then pawned them for £20,000. The story had greatly embarrassed the Romanovs and their relatives when the case came to Court in 1923. Now, aware that other relatives had their eyes on the jewels and alerted to rumours that a gang of international jewel thieves planned to steal them, the King sent Bark to Copenhagen. The jewel box was sealed in Xenia's presence and taken to Buckingham Palace while arrangements were made for the sale.

In November 1928 King George was taken seriously ill and it was not until 22nd May 1929 that the box was finally opened at Windsor. The seventy-six items were all that was left of Dagmar's considerable collection – the Diamond Star of the Order of St Andrew; 'ropes of the most wonderful pearls ... all graduated, the largest the size of a cherry'; brooches, bracelets, hair ornaments and hatpins, all sparkling with diamonds, emeralds, rubies or sapphires; but her spectacular diamond necklaces and tiaras had remained in Russia ...[3]

A week later Mr Hardy of Hennell & Sons, the Bond Street jewellers, was asked to price every item provisionally and take as long as he needed to sell the jewels discreetly. Xenia withdrew items totalling £11,415 but, because of the slump, the remainder were not disposed of until 1933. A few were returned unsold. The final sale price of £135,624 15s 0d was put in trust for Xenia and Olga.

Some of the jewels were bought by Queen Mary who, contrary to popular belief, paid the full valuation figure. When she died in 1953 her jewellery, including pieces from the Dowager Empress' Estate, passed to members of the British Royal family. The cabochon sapphire brooch surrounded by diamonds, with a pearl drop suspended from it – Dagmar's wedding gift from Alix and Bertie – returned to the Kremlin briefly in the autumn of 1994, when the Queen wore it during her State Visit to Russia. The Queen also wears Dagmar's chain-link choker necklace as two bracelets. Another of the Empress' necklaces – a magnificent four-row choker of 164 pearls, with twenty diamond-studded vertical bars and a large sapphire clasp – has been lent to the Princess Royal. Other jewels are worn by Princess Margaret and Princess Michael of Kent. It seems fitting that these reminders of an Imperial past, and of the Empress who wore them to such great effect, should still be worn today.

Hvidøre was sold. On 28th February 1929 Sir Frederick Ponsonby informed Hugh Cassells, the British Consul in Copenhagen (who held Power of Attorney for Queen Alexandra's heirs), that 'Princess Brasova' wished to claim a share of the sale proceeds for her son George, the Empress' grandson. King George V and his three sisters had agreed to give up their half share in favour of Olga and Xenia. The Estate would therefore be divided between Olga, Xenia and George Brasov.

By a Deed of Conveyance dated 1st July 1929, the buildings and the landward portion of the Hvidøre estate were sold to Mr Jacob Koefoed, a retired wine merchant, for Kr120,000. The remainder was purchased in November by Gentofte Municipality for Kr200,000. The tunnel was bricked up. Most of the contents were sold at auction in April 1929. The sale fetched Kr119,494.94, including Kr1,800 for the Bornholm clock. Some items privately purchased by Xenia, Olga and Princess Victoria were ironically shipped to England on the S.S. *Dagmar*, including the Empress' Delauney Belleville, which Xenia kept. Dagmar's personal property fetched Kr8,968 more than Alexandra's.[4] Hvidøre eventually became a diabetic hospital. It is now a conference centre.

On 22nd November 1929 the Executors paid the sum of £11,704 16s 3d to Peter Bark to be invested on behalf of Olga and Xenia. Olga bought a farm at Ballerup, Denmark. In 1948, fearing that she would be extradited to the Soviet Union for helping Russians to escape to western Europe after the war, she and her husband began a new life in Canada. Nicholas Kulikovsky died in 1958; Olga died in relative poverty in 1960 in a Russian émigré's flat over a barber's shop in Toronto. Xenia also died in 1960, still in receipt of a pension from the British Crown. Her Will (first published in 1991) left a net figure of £117,272 16s 2d to be divided among her family.[5] George Brasov received one-sixth of the proceeds of the Hvidøre estate. He died in France in July 1931 after a car crash, just two weeks short of his twenty-first birthday.

Dagmar is largely unknown in Russia. Although many of her personal possessions, including Court dresses, ball gowns, diaries and letters survive, they have seldom been seen by Russians. Gatchina and the Yelagin Palace were both badly damaged during the second world war and are now being restored. The Winter Palace, where Dagmar danced the night away at so many Imperial balls, is now the Hermitage Museum, the world's largest art collection. The Anitchkov became the home of the City History Museum and, in 1989, the City's Centre for School Children. Only a handful of rooms remain as they were in Dagmar's time. The Cottage at Peterhof was a museum of Art and History under the Bolsheviks and is open to the public. In 1994, the ninetieth anniversary of Alexis' birth, a statue of him was erected in the garden.

For seventy years historians and journalists speculated about the fate of the last Imperial family. Then, in April 1989, a former Russian policeman, Gely Ryabov, announced to the world that some ten years earlier he and Alexander Avdonin, a geologist, had discovered the burial place of the Tsar and his family near Ekaterinburg. The secret had been kept until the time was right for it to be revealed. Ryabov, but not Avdonin, thought that this time had now come.

In July 1991 President Yeltsin authorised the excavation of the Romanovs' burial site. Nine skeletons were excavated in the forest near Ekaterinburg. The faces were smashed and drenched with sulphuric acid, the bodies covered with earth and old railway sleepers and driven over by a lorry. It was established that they were the remains of five women and four men. Five were members of the same family but, if they were the Romanovs, two bodies were missing. But which two – and where were they?

The following year the bones were sent to the British Home Office Forensic Science Service at Aldermaston for mitochondrial DNA testing by Dr Peter Gill, Dr Pavel Ivanov and a team of scientists. Among those who provided samples for comparison was the Duke of Edinburgh, Empress Alexandra's great-nephew. When the results were announced in July 1993 the team were quoted as saying they were '98.5% certain' that the remains were those of Nicholas, Alexandra, three of their daughters and their four servants. In July 1994 the body of Nicholas' brother, Grand Duke George Alexandrovitch, was exhumed from the SS Peter & Paul Cathedral for DNA testing, in order to dispel any further doubts about the authenticity of the Ekaterinburg bones. The results proved beyond reasonable doubt that the remains were those of Nicholas and his family.

The whereabouts of the other two bodies remained a mystery. The identity of the missing Grand Duchess was also in dispute. Dr William Maples, an American forensic anthropologist, insisted that all the skeletons were too fully developed to be Anastasia (just seventeen at the time of the murders), a fact that delighted supporters of Anna Anderson. The Russians insisted that the missing body was Marie – or anyone, in fact, other than Anastasia – and that the bodies of Marie and Alexis were burnt.

Then, in 1994, there was a new twist to the story. When Anna Anderson died ten years earlier, on 12th February 1984, her claim was still unresolved. After nearly forty years of litigation in the German courts Anna Anderson's identity as Anastasia was neither proved nor disproved. Since 1920, she had been opposed by powerful members of the Royal families of Europe, who denounced her as an imposter. Within twenty-four hours of Dagmar's death twelve members of the Romanov family issued a statement from the Court of Grand Duke Ernst Ludwig of Hesse pronouncing 'Anastasia' a fraud. Why they had waited for the Dowager Empress to die before doing so is unknown.

At a press conference in October 1994 Dr Peter Gill announced that DNA extracted from a tissue sample preserved in a Charlottesville hospital after a 1979 operation on Anna Anderson did not match the Romanov DNA profile of the Tsar and Tsarina. However, it did match the DNA of relatives of Francesca Schanzkowska, a Polish peasant woman. Francesca, the woman Anna Anderson's detractors always maintained she really was, disappeared in 1920. The *Berliner Nachtausgabe* had published the results of a private investigation into the Schanzkowska affair in 1927 and concluded that she and Anna Anderson were one and the same person. American tests on strands of Anna Anderson's hair matched Dr Gill's findings and confirmed that she was not related to Prince Philip.

This appears to vindicate the Dowager Empress' attitude towards her putative granddaughter but it still leaves many things unexplained. Not the least of which is Anna Anderson's uncanny physical similarities to the historical Anastasia, her knowledge of intimate details of the Russian Court (including the Hesse peace mission) long before they were widely available and the testimonies of various scientific and medical experts that Anna Anderson was Anastasia. The remains of Alexis and the missing Grand Duchess, who the Russians still insist is Marie, were also said to have been discovered near Ekaterinburg and were said to be awaiting DNA testing.[6] The body of Grand Duke Michael, who was said to have been shot in the woods near Perm, has never been found.

On 17th July 1998, eighty years to the day after their murder, the remains of Nicholas II, Alexandra, Olga, Tatiana, Anastasia and their four servants were finally laid to rest in a side chapel of the SS Peter & Paul Cathedral in St Petersburg.

After a requiem in the Cathedral of the Annunciation in Ekaterinburg, the bodies arrived at St Petersburg's Pulkova Airport on 16th July and were driven in procession to the fortress. The flags of Russia and St Petersburg, with black mourning ribbons, hung from lamp posts and the route was lined with troops. At the Winter Palace, where the cortège briefly slowed down, the Russian flag flew at half mast and there were garlands of fir branches where the Imperial garden had formerly stood. By no means all of the people who crowded the pavement outside the palace were tourists, many Russians had gathered to see the hearses pass. At the fortress the coffins were carried in by soldiers, escorted by pipers from the Royal Scots Dragoon Guards, formerly the Scots Greys. Nicholas merited this honour as he had once been their Colonel-in-Chief.

Over fifty members of the Romanov family assembled for the funeral at eleven o'clock the following day. They were joined by President Yeltsin, who made a last-minute unexpected decision to attend. In an emotional speech, the President called for repentance and atonement for this 'monstrous crime'.

After the service at which, to satisfy the Synod, the names of the victims were not even mentioned, the tiny coffins of Caucasian oak, almost child-like in size, were carried one by one to the St Catherine Chapel where they were buried in the same vault. The Imperial standard draped the coffins of the Emperor and Empress; the Tsar's also had a sword, crossed with its scabbard. As Nicholas' coffin was lowered last of all, a 19-gun salute was fired from the banks of the Neva.

On the wall of the St Catherine Chapel, white plaques record the names of all the dead in gold letters, including the missing two, Alexis and Marie. Outside the entrance to the chapel stands a bank of white lilies and a small, handwritten sign. It says, 'FORGIVE US'.

*

In 1958 Dagmar's coffin was moved from Frederick V's Chapel in Roskilde Cathedral to the crypt.

Steep steps to the right of Christian IX's Chapel descend to a locked door, leading to the private burial place of the Danish Royal family directly under the chapel. The crypt is not open to the public, as it is still used for burials, the most recent occasion being in 1995.

On the other side of the door a few more steps lead down into a white-walled vaulted crypt with a tiled floor and candles around the walls. Ten coffins stand here. Four are children of King Frederick VIII – Prince Gustav, Princess Thyra, Princess Dagmar and Prince Harald. Prince Harald's wife, Princess Helena, also rests here. The coffins of their children, Prince Gorm, Prince Olaf Count of Rosenborg and Princess Caroline-Mathilde are covered with the Dannebrog, as is that of Hereditary Prince Knud, husband of Princess Caroline-Mathilde, who lies alongside his wife. But it is the coffin on the south wall, immediately to the left of the entrance steps, which stands out.

The tomb of the Dowager Empress Marie Feodorovna of Russia, with her monogram of 'M.F.' beneath the Imperial crown, is the only one surrounded by icons on the walls. Two were personal icons which came from her bedroom, a third was sent by Russians in America to commemorate the canonization of members of the Imperial family. It shows Nicholas II, Alexandra, their five children and Grand Duchess Elizabeth Feodorovna with halos shining around their heads. An icon lamp hangs on chains from the ceiling and at one end of the huge oak coffin is a small crucifix containing a picture of Nicholas II, which also came from the Empress' bedroom at Hvidøre.

On 26th November 1997, the 150th anniversary of Dagmar's birth, a service was held in the crypt. Among those present were Johannes Hardenburg-Bruhn, Johan Christian Haar and Emil Schlenkert, three former officers from Hvidøre. Johannes Hardenburg-Bruhn was a standard-bearer for the Life Guards at her funeral. To these three men, all nearing one hundred years of age, the Empress always remained 'Her Majesty'.

The small crypt becomes almost cosy when the candles are lit around the walls, a world away from the cold marble tombs of the SS Peter & Paul Cathedral. Yet Dagmar, denied even the solace of knowing she would be buried beside her husband, had made Xenia and Olga promise that, when circumstances permitted, they would return her body to St Petersburg for burial beside Sasha.

Following several years of negotiations, agreement has finally been reached between Queen Margrethe of Denmark (with whom the final decision rested) and President Vladimir Putin, to re-bury Dagmar's remains beside her husband. The initiative has come from Prince Nicholas Romanov, head of the Romanov Family Association, and his brother Prince Dimitri who lives in Denmark. According to reports in the Danish press, the Queen has stipulated that the ceremony be 'carried out in a dignified and respectful way,' the remains must not be touched and no DNA analysis is allowed. Although the re-burial has already been postponed twice, a new date has been proposed and plans have been drawn up.

After an Orthodox service in the crypt of Roskilde Cathedral Dagmar's coffin will be taken to Toldboden in Copenhagen where it will be placed on a Danish ship for the journey to Kronstadt. There it will be transferred to a Russian ship and taken to the harbour at Peterhof, then overland to the SS Peter & Paul Cathedral in St Petersburg. This route is planned to trace Dagmar's journey when she came to Russia as a bride in 1866.

It now seems that, more than seventy-five years after her death, Dagmar's wish is closer to fulfilment.

Sources

RA = Royal Archives
PRO = Public Record Office
NAM = National Archives of Malta
Christiansborg = *Maria Feodorovna, Empress of Russia* Exhibition Catalogue (Christiansborg Palace, Copenhagen 1997)
Kulikovsky = 'Recollections of a Grandmother'. Lecture notes by Tihon Kulikovsky (translated from Russian by Richard Davies, Leeds University)
Leon = *Lettres de Nicolas II et de Sa Mère*
Letters = Bing (ed), *The Letters of Tsar Nicholas and Empress Marie*

Introduction

1. Sablin, *Obituary*.
2. Iroshnikov, Protsaid & Shelayev, p75.

Chapter 1

1. Paget, *Embassies*, I, p141.
2. Poliakoff, pp33/4.
3. Letter from the Rigsarkivet, Copenhagen.
4. 1850 Census for Amaliegard. Rigsarkivet.
5. Teachers – Klausen, p22; 'Scandinavian' – letter from Ragnar Backström; governesses – information from the Rigsarkivet. The Rigsarkivet cannot confirm how many governesses the princess had.
6. 1850 Census for Amaliegard. Rigsarkivet; Klausen, p22.
7. Madol, *Christian*, p46.
8. Madol, *Christian*, p64.
9. Kinloch Cooke, I, p321.

10. Madol, *Alexandra*, p219.
11. Prince Nicholas of Greece, p59.
12. Fulford, *Dearest Child*, p339.
13. Fulford, *Dearest Child*, p313.
14. 'Graceful ...', Battiscombe, p22; 'little Dagmar ...', Paget, *Embassies*, I, p150.
15. Fulford, *Dearest Child*, p341.
16. Fulford, *Dearest Mama*, p54.
17. Fulford, *Dearest Mama*, p54.
18. Fulford, *Dearest Mama*, p55 & p56.
19. *Letters of Queen Victoria*, 2nd Series, Vol I, p43.
20. Ziegler, p2.
21. *Punch*, quoted in Aronson, *A Family of Kings*, p22.

Chapter 2

1. Madol, *Christian*, p232.
2. Description of Nixa – Aronson, FOK, p26; 'it will never ...' – Graham, p38.
3. Fulford, *Dearest Mama*, p186.
4. Madol, *Christian*, p180.
5. Paget, *Embassies*, I, p203.
6. Quoted in Clausen, pp55/6.
7. Contrary to Tisdall and Bramsen, Dagmar did not go to St Petersburg for the Season in January/February 1865 – information from the Rigsarkivet, Copenhagen; Fricero, p9.
8. Madol, *Christian*, p180.
9. Quoted in Madol, *Christian*, p171. Dagmar and Nixa's letters are in Preben Ulstrup in Christiansborg, p112. The following information is taken from their letters.
10. Corti, p154. Other sources say that his condition was aggravated by a fall during a wrestling match with

his cousin Prince Nicholas of Leuchtenberg, or that he was thrown
against a tree-trunk when his horse
bolted. (See also Ferrand, *Compliment*,
p25.)

11. Madol, *Christian*, p172. (Translation
from French.)
12. Fricero, p14.
13. RA Z105/43. Translation from
German. Letter dated 4th May 1865
from Schloss Rumpenheim.
14. All quotations from Corti, pp154/5.
15. Kennedy, p235.
16. Almedingen, *Romanovs*, p272.
17. Alia Barkovets, 'Nixa, Minny &
Sacha', in Christiansborg, p82. 25th
June/7th July 1865.
18. Alia Barkovets, 'Nixa, Minny &
Sacha', in Christiansborg, p84. 23rd
March/4th April 1866.
19. Alia Barkovets, 'Nixa, Minny &
Sacha', in Christiansborg, p84. 15th/
27th May 1866. Sasha's diary entries
describing his farewell to M.E. and
his proposal to Dagmar, and Sasha
and Dagmar's letters, are in Klausen, pp52/74. The following information is taken from these sources.
20. Loubat, pp56/60.
21. Clausen, p55.
22. Information from Det Livgardens
Historiske Samling, Copenhagen;
the Rigsarkivet. (See also Clausen,
p32.)

Chapter 3

1. The peasants – Massie, *Nicholas &
Alexandra*, pp3 & 4.
2. Moscow & St Petersburg – Massie,
Nicholas & Alexandra, pp4/7; lowered from the sky – Massie, *Peter*,
p602.
3. Lincoln, *The Romanovs*, p240.
4. Prince Christopher, p50.
5. Radziwill, *Recollections*, p53. Dagmar's arrival is from *Illusteret Tidende*
& Klausen, pp86/92.

6. Poliakoff, p268.
7. See Millar, p14.
8. *Letters of Queen Victoria*, 2nd Series,
Vol I, p369.
9. Madol, *Christian*, pp181/2.
10. Poliakoff, p68.
11. Alexander, *Once*, pp154 & 151.
12. See Klausen, pp96/7, Sasha's diary,
9th November 1866. The details of
the villa come from private information and the 1914 Baedeker of
Russia. In 1914 it was still possible
to tour the villa.
13. Quoted in Sinclair, p130.

Chapter 4

1. The Anitchkov – Aronson, FOK,
p49 & personal visit.
2. Hamilton, p488.
3. Fulford, *Your Dear Letter*, pp182 &
184.
4. Bramsen, I, p330. (Translation from
Danish.)
5. Julia Kudrina, 'Our Beloved Empress', in Christiansborg, p44. 23rd
February 1867.
6. *The Times*, 18th July 1867. I am
indebted to Marlene Eilers for this
information.
7. RA Z20/39. Letter of 3rd September
1867. The information about Marie
of Flanders comes from the Royal
Archives. Unfortunately, the Rigsarkivet in Copenhagen 'is not able to
confirm or deny whether Princess
Dagmar may have suffered a miscarriage in July or August 1867'
(letter from the Rigsarkivet). Sasha's
diary entry about his hopes of
starting a family is in Bokhanov &
Others, *The Romanovs: Love, Power &
Tragedy*, p18.
8. Fulford, *Your Dear Letter*, p153.
9. RA Z21/24.
10. Fulford, *Your Dear Letter*, p181.
11. Quoted in Tarsaidze, p127*ff*; manifesto – Radziwill, *Nicholas II*, p17.

The account of Nicholas' birth is taken from Dagmar's diary for 6th/18th May, quoted by Preben Ulstrup in Christiansborg, p118.

12. The christening gown is in Ballerup Egnsmuseum, Denmark. Christian & Louise's visit in August was confirmed by the Rigsarkivet.

13. *The Times*, 9th June 1869. I am indebted to Marlene Eilers for this information.

14. RA Z24/53. 6th May 1870. The Crown Princess refers to the death of her son Prince Sigismund on 16th June 1866.

15. RA Z24/53. Both quotations from letter of 6th May 1870.

16. Alexander, *Once*, p186, although the Russian language edition of his memoirs omits it. See Harcave, *Golden Cockerel*, p212*ff* & Chavchavadze, p215. Vorres, p21, Tisdall, pp48/9, & Massie, *Nicholas & Alexandra*, p13, have all followed Grand Duke Alexander's error. The information from the tomb comes from a personal visit to the SS Peter & Paul Cathedral. Details of the baby's death come from Dagmar's diary entry, quoted in Klausen, pp118/20 (no date given).

17. Madol, *Christian*, pp205/6. 10th March 1871.

18. Bent Jensen, 'The Land of Unlimited Potential', in Christiansborg, pp220 & 222.

19. Antrim, p128.

20. Longford, *Darling Loosy*, pp174/5.

21. Fulford, *Darling Child*, p96.

22. Quoted in Lowe, pp28/9.

Chapter 5

1. Tarsaidze, p98.

2. Christiansborg, p406.

3. Julia Kudrina, 'Our Beloved Empress', in Christiansborg, p34.

4. Bramsen, II, pp166/71. The story has been denied by the Rigsarkivet and confirmed by Det Kongelige Bibliotek.

5. See Klausen, p136. According to the Rigsarkivet in Copenhagen, Marie von Flotow's maiden name seems to be von Gerschau but as her writing is difficult to read this is not certain. The family was of German descent.

6. Yermilova, p83.

Chapter 6

1. Cowles, *The Russian Dagger*, p131.

2. Hough, *Louis & Victoria*, p96.

3. Quoted in Harcave, *Golden Cockerel*, p232.

4. Dufferin, p68.

5. Klausen, pp138 & 139. 1880. No date given. Erroneously cited as being written at Gatchina.

6. Graham, p300.

7. Fulford, *Beloved Mama*, pp91/2.

8. de Stoeckl, p115.

9. Naryshkin-Kurakin, pp67/8.

10. Quotations from Alexander, *Once*, p60.

11. Vassili, p112.

12. Naryshkin-Kurakin, pp70/1.

13. Almedingen, *Alexander II*, p332.

14. Pares, *History*, p441; Alexander, *Once*, p71 (see Alexander, *Once*, pp71/4 for an eye-witness account of the Emperor's death). Dagmar's letter of 4th/16th March 1881 describing her reactions is in Klausen, pp140/1 and in Preben Ulstrup in Christiansborg, p140. The information here is taken from Dagmar's letter.

15. Tarsaidze, p253.

16. Dufferin, pp110/11.

17. Quoted in Tisdall, pp97/8.

18. Battiscombe, p159.

19. Tarsaidze, p255*ff*.

20. Hamilton, pp448/9.

21. Dufferin, p122.

Chapter 7

1. Turpentine – Marie of Roumania, I, p85; clean wood – Cyril, p20.
2. Paleologue, pp359/60.
3. Churchill, pp169/70.
4. Poliakoff, p141.
5. Quoted in Lowe, pp324/5.
6. Vorres, p41.
7. Vorres, p41.
8. Diary. 8th/20th September 1888. Christiansborg, p298.
9. Bogoliubov's memoirs. Quoted in Christiansborg, p402.
10. Churchill, p183.
11. Karsavina, p83.
12. Prince Christopher, p66.
13. Vorres, p33.
14. Windsor, p51.
15. Quoted in Battiscombe, p158.

Chapter 8

1. Waddington, p44.
2. Waddington, pp45/6.
3. Waddington, p46.
4. Waddington, pp50/1.
5. Grand Duke Alexander, *Once*, p89.
6. Vassili, p150.
7. Poliakoff, p172. The full list of the Emperor's titles is on page 171.
8. Quoted in Aronson, *A Family of Kings*, p79.
9. Waddington, p70; Poliakoff, p173.
10. Waddington, pp138 & 68/70.
11. Waddington, pp74/5.
12. Quoted in Aronson, *A Family of Kings*, pp79/80.
13. Harcave, *Golden Cockerel*, p255.
14. Fulford, *Beloved Mama*, p140.

Chapter 9

1. Prince Nicholas, p64.
2. Ponsonby, *Empress Frederick*, p392.
3. Madol, *Christian*, p235.
4. Fulford, *Darling Child*, p69; Roma Lister, p43.
5. Madol, *Alexandra*, p136.

6. Fisher, pp106/7.
7. 27th June/9th July 1894. Letters, p86.
8. Clausen, pp33/4. The 'Bjorneborganas March' is now the honorary march of the President of Finland.
9. The visit to Finland is taken from the special edition of *Universal Illustration* (St Petersburg, 1885); *The Calendar of the Society for Educating the People 1886*, (Helsinki, 1885); and Clausen, pp50/4 & 35.
10. 27th June/9th July 1894. Letters, p88.
11. Clausen, p12.
12. *Ekenas Stadhistoria*, III, pp592/3.
13. I am indebted to Ragnar Backström, Curator of the Langinkoski Imperial Fishing Lodge Museum in Kotka, for all the information about Langinkoski.

Chapter 10

1. Vorres, p58.
2. Alexander, *Once*, p174.
3. Witte, p39.
4. Quoted in Listowel, p134.
5. Marie of Roumania, I, p98.
6. Vorres, p57.
7. 26th January/7th February 1891. Letters, p48.
8. Vorres, p58.
9. Vorres, p58; Radziwill, *Nicholas II*, p18.
10. Belyakova, *Maria Nikolayevna*, p230.
11. 15th/27th January 1891. Letters, p45.
12. Suzanne Massie, *Firebird*, pp415/16.
13. 5th/17th March 1891. Letters, p55.
14. Fabergé, Proler & Skurlov, pp102/5. The egg was presented to Dagmar in 1890 and the illustration clearly shows Alexander III's villa at Fredensborg. Hvidøre was not purchased until 1906.
15. 8th/21st April 1914, quoted in von Solodkoff, *Masterpieces*, p78.

16. von Solodkoff, *Masterpieces*, p9.
17. Cyril, p187.

Chapter 11

1. Poliakoff, pp154/5.
2. Madol, *Christian*, p233.
3. Clausen, p58.
4. Madol, *Christian*, p222.
5. Alexander, *Once*, p174.
6. Dagmar's letter to Willie of 6th/ 18th November 1888 giving her account of the accident is quoted in Klausen, pp190/3. Most of the following information is taken from that account.
7. Vorres, p30.
8. Vorres, p30.
9. See Bramsen, I, p355 for the theory that Dagmar may have suffered a nervous breakdown.
10. Naryshkin-Kurakin, p117.
11. Radziwill, *Intimate Life*, p109.

Chapter 12

1. 23rd June/5th July 1887. Letters, p33.
2. 21st June/3rd July 1887. Letters, p31.
3. Kulikovsky, *Recollections*.
4. Alexander, *Once*, p172.
5. 1890, undated. Letters, pp41 & 43.
6. 1890, undated. Letters, p43.
7. 16th/28th January 1891. Letters, p47.
8. 6th/18th May, 1891. Letters, p58.
9. Vyrubova, p38.
10. 24th May/5th June 1891. Letters, p62.
11. Lowe, p268.
12. Quoted in Radziwill, *Nicholas*, p38.
13. Quoted in Pares, *Fall*, p33.
14. Hough, *Advice*, p106.
15. Victoria Louise, p33.
16. Dagmar's letter to Willie of October or November 1893 (no date given in the source) giving her account of this affair is quoted in Klausen, pp212/

13. The information given here is taken from that account.
17. 27th June/9th July 1894. Letters, p87.
18. 27th June/9th July 1894. Letters, p87.
19. Vorres, p84.
20. 20th August/1st September 1895. Letters, pp101/2.

Chapter 13

1. Alexander III's secret drinking – Figes, p16; 'radiant' – diary of Grand Duke Constantine Constantinovitch, quoted in Maylunas & Mironenko, p51; Sasha's letter – Shelayev, Shelayeva & Semenov, p24.
2. 14th/26th April 1894. Letters, p77.
3. 18th/30th April 1894. Letters, p78.
4. Hough, *Advice*, p124.
5. 27th June/9th July 1894. Letters, p86; Alexander, *Once*, p150.
6. 27th June/9th July 1894. Letters, p87.
7. 27th June/9th July 1894. Letters, p87.
8. 27th June/9th July 1894. Letters, p88.
9. Vorres, p61.
10. Prince Nicholas, p116.
11. Vorres, p64.
12. St Aubyn, *Edward*, p296.
13. Naryshkin-Kurakin, p143.
14. Lowe, p287.
15. Madol, *Alexandra*, p75.
16. Mlle L'Escaille Collection, Hoover Institution Archives, 74109-10-V. 20th October/1st November 1894.
17. Lowe, p288.
18. Mlle L'Escaille Collection, Hoover Institution Archives, 74109-10-V. 20th October/1st November 1894.
19. Vorres, p65; Prince Nicholas, p117.
20. Alexander, *Once*, p169; Nicholas II, *Journal Intime*, p107. 20th October/1st November 1894.
21. Battiscombe, p205.

22. RA Z499/79. Translation from German.
23. Battiscombe, p205.
24. Dangerfield, p309.
25. Vorres, p69.
26. Gilliard, p48.
27. Pope-Hennessy, *Queen Mary*, p309.
28. Lowe, p301.
29. Quoted in St Aubyn, *Edward*, p297.
30. Pope-Hennessy, *Queen Mary*, p309.

Chapter 14

1. RA Z106/67. Translation from German.
2. RA Z106/67. Translation from German.
3. Poliakoff, p236.
4. 24th May/5th June 1895. Letters, p93.
5. Victoria Louise, p33.
6. Oldenburg, I, p188, note 15.
7. Vorres, p72.
8. 24th May/5th June 1895. Letters, pp92/3.
9. Poliakoff, p237.
10. Vorres, p82.
11. 3rd/15th August 1895. Letters, p96.
12. 3rd/15th August 1895. Letters, p96; 20th August/1st September 1895. Letters, p101.
13. Information from *Genealogica Gotha*, p396. Provided & translated from Swedish by Ted Rosvall.
14. 28th September/10th October 1895. Letters, p106; undated from Gatchina. Letters, p109.
15. Undated from Gatchina. Letters, pp108/9.
16. Buxhoeveden, *Alexandra*, p49; Vorres, p72.
17. Vorres, p73.
18. *Letters of Queen Victoria*, 3rd Series, Vol 3, p39.
19. Hough, *Advice*, pp182/3.
20. 22nd May/3rd June 1897. Letters, pp127/8; 8th/20th August 1897. Letters, pp132/3.
21. Mossolov, pp35/6.
22. Maud, p28.
23. Vorres, p80.
24. RA H48/74. Telegram delivered on 11th July 1899.
25. Xenia's diary. 14th/26th July 1899. Quoted in Maylunas & Mironenko, p188.

Chapter 15

1. Xenia's diary. 26th May/7th June 1896. Quoted in Maylunas & Mironenko, p149.
2. Undated. Letters, p148.
3. Xenia's diary. 5th/18th June 1901. Quoted in Maylunas & Mironenko, p206.
4. Salisbury, p205.
5. Maylunas & Mironenko, pp217/9; Paleologue, p188. (See Buxhoeveden, p136; Radziwill, *Intimate Life*, pp119/20.)
6. 5th/18th November 1901. Letters, p159.
7. 5th/18th November 1901. Letters, p159.
8. 23rd October/5th November 1902. Letters, p171.
9. Crawford, p8.
10. Chavchavadze, p150.
11. Abrikossow, p234.
12. 1st/14th October 1902. Letters, p162/5.
13. All quotations from Poliakoff, p242.
14. 29th December 1905/11th January 1906. Letters, pp208/9.
15. 1st/14th October 1902. Letters, p163; Clausen, p36.
16. Lieven, p106; Witte, p180.

Chapter 16

1. Xenia's diary. 25th January 1904. Quoted in Maylunas & Mironenko, p239.
2. Princess Eugenie, p27; Mossolov, p30.

3. Pares, *Fall*, p132.
4. Lieven, pp134/5; Julia Kudrina, 'Our Beloved Empress', in Christiansborg, p38.
5. Lieven, pp134/5; Schememann, p150.
6. Dagmar's telegram to Grand Duchess Marie, sent from Tsarskoe Selo palace, is in the Mainau archives.
6a. Diary of S.R. Mintslov, 7th February 1905. Quoted in Fabergé, Proler & Skurlov, p59.
7. Xenia's diary. 18th August 1905. Quoted in Maylunas & Mironenko, p280.
8. 6th/19th October 1905. Leon, pp66/9.
9. 1st/14th November 1905. Letters, p194.
10. 16th/29th October 1905. Letters, p183.
11. 1st/14th November 1905. Letters, pp192/3.
12. 2nd/15th December 1905. Letters, p198.
13. 29th December 1905/11th January 1906. Letters, p208.
14. 16th/29th January 1906. Leon, p144.
15. Alexander, *Once*, p252.
16. Vassili, pp345/6.
17. Mlle L'Escaille Collection, Hoover Institution Archives, 74109-10-V. 12th/25th May 1906.
18. Fisher, H H (ed), pp130/1.
19. 16th/29th August 1905. Letters, p216.
20. 16th/29th January 1906. Leon, pp142/3.
21. Wolfe, p409.

Chapter 17

1. 26th October/8th November 1906. Letters, p220.
2. Vorres, p82.
3. Kulikovsky, *Recollections*; Poliakoff, p13.
4. Abrikossow, p124.
5. Deed of Conveyance – PRO FO749/13. The Estate of the Late Empress Marie Feodorovna.
6. 9th/22nd September 1906. Leon, pp178/9.
7. Madol, *Alexandra*, p212.
8. de Stoeckl, p114; C. Hardinge, p153.
9. Battiscombe, p267.
10. Madol, *Alexandra*, p212.
11. Information from Det Livgardens Historiske Samling, Copenhagen.
12. 5th/17th August 1906. Letters, pp214/15.
13. Maylunas & Mironenko, pp301 & 306, quoting Xenia's diary for 3rd/16th May & 30th July/12th August 1907; Crawford, pp10/16.
14. 26th October/8th November 1908. Letters, p237.
15. Crawford, p60.
16. Alexander, *Once*, pp260/1.
17. 28th February/13th March 1907. Letters, pp221/2.
18. Ponsonby, *Recollections*, p196.
19. 12th/25th March 1909. Letters, p239.
20. 25th March/7th April 1909. Letters, p241.
21. 30th March/12th April 1909. Letters, p243.
22. 5th/18th November 1910. Letters, p260.
23. 29th April/12th May 1909. Letters, p242; Abela, p144.
24. 29th April/12th May 1909. Letters, p241.
25. Dagmar's letter to Willie of 23rd November/6th December 1909 describing Marie's death and funeral is quoted in Klausen, pp268/71. The following information is taken from that account.
26. Edwards, p81.
27. Pope-Hennessy, *Queen Mary*, p422.
28. 7th/20th May 1910. Letters, p254.
29. Pope-Hennessy, *Queen Mary*, p423.

30. 25th July/7th August 1910. Letters, p256.

Chapter 18

1. 'The Nursery', Pares, *Fall*, p16; 'Poor boy ...' – 7th/20th March 1908. Letters, p231.
2. Princess Eugenie, p36.
3. Princess Eugenie, p60.
4. Birth Registers, Pokrovskoe. BBC *Timewatch*, January 1995.
5. H.H. Fisher (ed), pp266/7.
6. 9th/22nd September 1911. Letters, pp263/4.
7. H.H. Fisher (ed), pp296/7; the prophecy is in Bokhanov & Others, *The Romanovs: Love, Power & Tragedy*, p237.
8. de Jonge, pp205/6; Rodzianko, pp37/8.
9. Gilliard, p177.
10. Pares, *Fall*, p150.
11. Vyrubova, pp87/8.
12. Vyrubova, p94.
13. 20th October/2nd November 1912. Letters, p277.

Chapter 19

1. 4th/17th November 1912. Letters, p283.
2. Vyrubova, p96.
3. 7th December 1912. Quoted in Maylunas & Mironenko, p363.
4. M. Buchanan, p36.
5. M. Buchanan, p41.
6. Grand Duchess George, p146.
7. 27th July/9th August 1913. Letters, pp287/8.
8. Xenia's diary. Quoted in Maylunas & Mironenko, p379.
9. 27th July/9th August 1913. Letters, p285.
10. 8th/21st August 1897. Letters, p132.
11. All quotations from H.H. Fisher (ed), p470.
12. Christiansborg, p470. September 1903.

13. Christiansborg, p474. 10th November 1913.
14. 27th July/9th August 1913. Letters, p287.
15. Xenia's diary. 11th April 1913. Quoted in Maylunas & Mironenko, p374.
16. Dobson, p30.
17. Dobson, p43.
18. Youssoupov, *Lost Splendour*, p167/8.
19. The Archduke's words – Dedijer, pp13, 9 & 16.

Chapter 20

1. Pares, *Fall*, p188.
2. Madol, *Alexandra*, p265.
3. Duff, *Alexandra*, p267.
4. Rodzianko, p337.
5. Julia Kudrina, 'Our Beloved Empress', in Christiansborg, p40. 7th/20th September 1914.
6. Cantacuzene, p58; Bariatinsky, p156.
7. 3rd/16th December 1915. Letters, p295.
8. Rev. A. Clark (James Munson, ed), pp39/40. By permission of Oxford University Press.
9. Dagmar to Grand Duke Nicholas Michaelovitch. Quoted in Maylunas & Mironenko, p401.
10. M. Buchanan, p108.
11. 3rd/16th December 1914. Letters, p290.
12. Diary. 11th/24th January 1915. *Poslednie Novosti*, July 1933.
13. Diary. 28th March/10th April 1915. *Poslednie Novosti*, July 1933.
14. 1st/14th February 1915. Letters, p292.
15. Bent Jensen, 'The Land of Unlimited Potential', in Christiansborg, p222.
16. Diary. 6th/19th July 1915. *Poslednie Novosti*, July 1933.
17. Diary. 8th/21st July 1915. *Poslednie Novosti*, July 1933.

18. Diary. 28th July/10th August 1915.
Poslednie Novosti, July 1933.
19. Diary. 8th/21st August 1915. *Poslednie Novosti*, 1933.
20. Diary. 12th/25th August 1915.
Poslednie Novosti, July 1933.
21. Vyrubova, p126; Salisbury, p285.
22. Diary. 13th/26th August 1915.
Poslednie Novosti, July 1933.
23. Diary. 17th/30th August 1915.
Poslednie Novosti, July 1933.
24. Diary. 18th/31st August 1915.
Poslednie Novosti, July 1933.
25. Diary. 20th August/2nd September 1915. *Poslednie Novosti*, July 1933.
26. Diary. 21st August/3rd September 1915. *Poslednie Novosti*, July 1933.
27. Stopford, pp21/2.
28. Diary. 23rd August/5th September 1915. *Poslednie Novosti*, July 1933.
29. Diary. 24th August/6th September 1915. *Poslednie Novosti*, July 1933.
30. Salisbury, p285.
31. Diary. 24th August/6th September 1915 & 27th August/9th September 1915. *Poslednie Novosti*, July 1933.
32. Diary. 28th August/10th September 1915. *Poslednie Novosti*, July 1933.
33. Salisbury, p285.
34. Diary. 2nd/15th September 1915. *Poslednie Novosti*, July 1915. A curious fact, in view of what was to come later, was that among the visitors recorded in the Dowager Empress' diary on 22nd December 1915 [OS] were the Duma member Vladimir Purishkevitch and a Doctor Lazovert, who were both involved in the murder of Rasputin.
35. 3rd/16th November 1915. A to N, p207.
36. Lieven, p226; Sir G. Buchanan, I, p175.
37. Paleologue, p482.
38. Rodzianko, pp56/7; Bulygin, pp33 & 42.
39. Letter to the author, 17th July 1992. (See King, p231.)

40. 1st/14th November 1916. A to N, p430.

Chapter 21

1. 5th/18th May 1916. Letters, pp296/7.
2. Alexander, *Once*, p302.
3. Crawford, p229.
4. 22nd May/4th June 1916. Letters, p297.
5. Quoted in Paleologue, p131.
6. 30th October/8th November 1916. N to A, p286; 16th/29th September 1915. A to N, p170.
7. 16th/29th November 1916. Letters, p298.
8. Youssoupov, *Lost Splendour*, p187; 4th/17th December 1916. A to N, p443.
9. Alexandrov, p120.
10. Summers & Mangold, 1987 paperback edition, p358. From verbatim notes made by G. Nicholas Tantzos from the Empress' war diary in Moscow. The dates are New Style. See also Occleshaw, p88. Dr Occleshaw says he could find no trace of the Dowager Empress' diary in either Moscow or St Petersburg, nor had anybody ever heard of it. According to the Christiansborg Exhibition Catalogue the Dowager Empress' diaries for 1915 and 1916 are missing. See also my chapter 26 for more about the 1916 diary.
11. Jensen, p28.
12. 6th/19th December 1916. Letters, p299.
13. Alexander, *Once*, pp307/8.
14. Stopford, p88.
15. Vulliamy, p119.
16. Anon, *Fall*, p69. (See also Youssoupov, *Lost Splendour*, pp249/51 & Pipes, *Revolution*, p267*ff*.)
17. 17th February/2nd March 1917. Letters, p300.
18. Dagmar's letter to Xenia of 28th

December 1916/10th January 1917 is in Klausen, pp296 & 298. The information given here is taken from that letter.

19. de Grunwald, pp329/30; Rodzianko, pp246/7.
20. de Grunwald, p329.
21. Stopford, p131.
22. Dagmar's diary. 28th February/13th March 1917. Julia Kudrina, 'How Terrible to Think that it is Only the Beginning', in *The Poppy & the Owl*, No. 24, November 1998, p89.
23. Alexander, *Once*, p319.
24. Dagmar's diary. 1st/14th March 1917. Julia Kudrina, in *The Poppy & the Owl*, p89.
25. Dagmar's diary. 2nd/15th March 1917. Julia Kudrina, in *The Poppy & the Owl*, p89.
26. Vorres, pp151/2.
27. Dagmar's diary. 3rd/16th March 1917. Julia Kudrina, in *The Poppy & the Owl*, p89.
28. Dagmar's diary. 4th/17th March 1917. Julia Kudrina, in *The Poppy & the Owl*, p89.
29. Alexander, *Once*, pp320/1.
30. Grand Duchess George, p181; Dagmar's telegrams – Bokhanov & Others, *The Romanovs: Love, Power & Tragedy*, p288.
31. Dagmar's diary. 4th/17th March 1917. Julia Kudrina, in *The Poppy & the Owl*, p89.
32. Dagmar's diary. 5th/18th March 1917. Julia Kudrina, in *The Poppy & the Owl*, p89.
33. Vulliamy, pp273 & 277/8.
34. RA GV Q722/48.
35. Dagmar's diary. 8th/21st March 1917. Julia Kudrina, in *The Poppy & the Owl*, p90.
36. Battiscombe, p291.
37. Vorres, p152.
38. Jensen, pp23 & 25.
39. Alexander, *Once*, pp328/9.
40. Jensen, p32.

Chapter 22

1. Vorres, p154.
2. Stopford, p143.
3. William Clarke, p264. I am indebted to William Clarke for generously sharing information about the Dowager Empress' finances which he was unable to use in his own book.
4. Benckendorff, p124.
5. Xenia's diary. 2nd/15th May 1917. Quoted in Klausen, p316.
6. Dagmar's letter to Queen Olga of Greece (cited in the source as dated 4th/17th May 1917) describing the search of Ai-Todor, and her letter of June or July (no date given) describing the enquiry, are in Klausen, pp317/19. The information given here is taken from these accounts.
7. Youssoupov, *Lost Splendour*, p25.
8. Klausen, p319, letter to Queen Olga as above. June or July 1917 (no date given).
9. Jensen, p35. 4th/17th May 1917. Information also taken from the same letter, quoted by Ulstrup in Christiansborg, pp196/8.
10. Jensen, p37.
11. Dobson, pxiii.
12. Stopford, p165.
13. PRO FO800/205. Sir Arthur Davidson to FO. 30th August 1917.
14. 14th/27th July 1917. Det Livgardens Historiske Samling, Copenhagen. Translation from French.
15. Dagmar's letter to Queen Olga written in August 1917 (no date given) mentioning the birth is in Klausen, pp322/3. The information given here is taken from that letter; 21st November/4th December 1917. Letters, p302; information from William Clarke.
16. Bykov, p48.
17. RA Add. C22/206. To Lady Egerton, widow of the Duke of Connaught's Comptroller. 24th January 1918.

18. Xenia to Nicholas. 15th/28th October & 30th November/13th December 1917. Quoted in Maylunas & Mironenko, pp587 & 592.
19. Jensen, pp41/4.
20. 21st November/4th December 1917. Letters, pp301/5.
21. See Princess Eugenie, pp258/9*ff*, 266*ff* & 271 for the contact between the Crimea and Tobolsk.

Chapter 23

1. Jensen, p56. 23rd January/5th February 1918.
2. Pantazzi, p270.
3. Jensen, pp52/4.
4. Jensen, p57.
5. Jensen, pp57 & 59.
6. Clausen, p18.
7. Summary of the Report to the Danish Foreign Office by Carl Immanuel Krebs, May 1918. Det Livgardens Historiske Samling, NAI-C.X-1879. Translated from Danish by the Curator.
8. RA GV AA35/19. 15th June 1918.
9. RA GV AA 35/19.
10. Poliakoff, p306.
11. Victoria Louise, p111.
12. Alexander, *Once*, p347.
13. Iroshnikov, Protsaid & Shelayev, p339.

Chapter 24

1. Quoted in Ferro, pp268/9.
2. Jensen, p100.
3. Jensen, pp124/5.
4. Neerbek, p118.
5. PRO FO371/3329. War Cabinet, No. 502. 14th November 1918; Occleshaw, *With the Greatest Care & Tact*.
6. PRO ADM137/953. C-in-C to Admiralty, No. 747Z. 23rd November 1918.
7. Pantazzi, p270.

8. RA GEO V. M1344A/55.
9. Vorres, p162; Pridham, p50.
10. Vorres, p163.
11. Pridham, pp73/4.

Chapter 25

1. Interview transcript kindly provided by Anthony Summers.
2. RA GV M1344A/112.
3. Letter from National Archives of Malta to the author.
4. Secretary of State to Governor of Malta, 12th April 1919. N.A.M.
5. Pridham, p133.
6. Interview transcripts kindly provided by Anthony Summers. See also Occleshaw, p131.
7. Ingham, p61; Alexander, *Always*, pp7/8.
8. The Marchioness of Milford Haven to Mrs Richard Crichton, 22nd May 1919. Broadlands Archives.
9. Ingham, p51. The Empress' tree still stands in the private garden of H.E. The President of Malta.
10. Quoted in Ingham, p78.
11. PRO HO 45/11549. Foreign Office to Under Secretary of State, Home Office. 3rd May 1919; Ingham, p79.
12. Interview with Mr Douglas. Interview transcript kindly provided by Anthony Summers.
13. The full menu is in Klausen, p339.
14. Marie of Russia, *Princess in Exile*, pp98/100.
15. de Stoeckl, p179.
16. George's escape – Crawford, pp344/5; meeting with Natasha – Gray, pp136/7. Neither Pauline Gray nor the Royal Archives are able to confirm the date of this meeting, which seems to have taken place around 26th July.
17. PRO HO45/11549. Sir Arthur Davidson to F.O. 19th May & 28th May 1919.
18. Dagmar and Alexandra – Aronson,

A Family of Kings, p213; 'Better number one …' – Bramsen, I, p394.
19. Jensen, p130.
20. Vorres, pp169/70.
21. Quoted in Van der Kiste, *Northern Crowns*, p81.
22. Dagmar and her grandsons – Kulikovsky, *Recollections*.
23. Mlle L'Escaille Collection, Hoover Institution on War, Revolution & Peace, 74109-10.V. 5th June 1921.
24. Jensen, p139.
25. Last meeting – letter from the Royal Archives.
26. Botkin, p254.
27. Summers & Mangold, p370, note 2.
28. Letter kindly provided by the late Tihon Kulikovsky-Romanoff. Translated from Russian by Richard Davies of Leeds University.
29. Alexander, *Always*, p212.

Chapter 26

1. Occleshaw, *Romanov Conspiracies*, p131.
2. Vorres, p174.
3. Kurth, *Anastasia*, pp120 & 121/2.
4. Alexander, *Always*, p212.
5. Kurth, *Anastasia*, p145.
6. Kurth, *Anastasia*, p410, note 89.
7. Vorres, pp179/80.
8. RA GV AA43/364.
9. Alexander, *Always*, p212; information from the Royal Archives.
10. Dagmar's 'negative attitude' – quoted in Kurth, *Anastasia*, p147; Nicholasha's remark – *ibid*, p145.

11. I am indebted to Ragnar Backström, who conducted further research for me in Finland; see also William Clarke, pp114/15 & 271/2.
12. Vorres, p180.
13. Jensen, p140.
14. Jensen, p143.
15. Jensen, p143.
16. Information from H.M. Queen Ingrid of Denmark and H.M. Queen Anne of Roumania; Prince Philip – Vorres, p172.
17. RA GV AA43/367.
18. Vorres, pp180/1.
19. Letter provided by Det Livgardens Historiske Samling, Copenhagen. Translated from Danish by the Curator.
20. Jensen, pp134/5.
21. Jensen, p153.

Postscript

1. Clausen, p78.
2. Letter from Pauline Gray to the author; Henrik Bertelsen, 'Russiske flygtninge i Danmark 1917-24'.
3. Ponsonby, *Recollections*, p340; list of jewels (without sale prices) kindly provided by Hennell of Bond Street Ltd.
4. PRO FO749/13. The Estate of the late Empress Marie Feodorovna.
5. Lovell, pp461/5.
6. A Russian newspaper report which subsequently proved to be erroneous.

Bibliography

Abela, Major A.E. *A Nation's Praise*. (Progress Press, Valletta, 1994.)

Abrikossow, Dimitri I. *Revelations of a Russian Diplomat*. (University of Washington Press, Seattle, 1964.)

Alexander, Grand Duke. *Once a Grand Duke*. (Cassell, 1932.)

— *Always a Grand Duke*. (Cassell, 1933.)

Alexander, Helene. *Imperial Fans from the Hermitage*. Exhibition catalogue. (The Fan Museum, Greenwich, 1998.)

Alexandra, Empress of Russia. *Letters of the Tsaritsa to the Tsar, 1914-1916*. (Duckworth, 1923.)

Alexandrov, Victor. *The End of the Romanovs*. (Hutchinson, 1966.)

— *The Kremlin*. (1963.)

Almedingen, E.M. *The Emperor Alexander II*. (Bodley Head, 1962.)

— *The Romanovs: Three Centuries of an Ill-Fated Dynasty*. (Bodley Head, 1966.)

— *The Empress Alexandra, 1872-1918*. (Hutchinson, 1961.)

— *An Unbroken Unity: A Memoir of Grand Duchess Serge of Russia, 1864-1918*. (Bodley Head, 1964.)

Anon. *I, Anastasia*. (Michael Joseph, 1958.)

Anon. *The Fall of Romanovs*. (Ian Faulkner, 1992.)

Antrim, Lady Louisa Jane. *Recollections of Louisa, Countess of Antrim*. (The King's Store Press, 1937.)

Arch, Nigel & Marschner, Joanna. *Royal Wedding Dresses*. (Sidgwick & Jackson, 1990.)

Aronson, Theo. *A Family of Kings*. (Cassell, 1976.)

— *Grandmama of Europe*. (Cassell, 1973.)

— *Crowns in Conflict*. (John Murray, 1986.)

— *Princess Alice, Countess of Athlone*. (Cassell, 1981.)

Arthur, Sir George. *Queen Alexandra*. (Chapman & Hall, 1934.)

Ascher, Abraham. *The Kremlin*. (Reader's Digest Association Ltd, 1972.)

Baedeker's Russia 1914. (David & Charles and George Allen & Unwin, London, 1971.)

Balfour, Michael. *The Kaiser & His Times*. (The Cresset Press, 1964.)

Balsan, Consuelo Vanderbilt. *The Glitter & the Gold*. (George Mann, 1953.)

Bariatinsky, Princess Anatole Marie. *My Russian Life*. (Hutchinson, 1923.)

Barkovets, Alia & Tenikhina, Valentina. *Nicholas II. The Imperial Family*. (Abris Publishers, St Petersburg/Peterhof, 1998.)

Barkovets, Alia. 'Nixa, Minny & Sacha', in *Maria Feodorovna, Empress of Russia*, exhibition catalogue. (Christiansborg Palace, Copenhagen, 1997.)

Battiscombe, Georgina. *Queen Alexandra*. (Constable, 1969.)

Beal, Erica. *Royal Cavalcade*. (Stanley Paul, 1939.)

Belyakova, Alla. *Across the USSR – Leningrad, A Guide*. (Novosti Press Agency Publishing House, 1990.)

Belyakova, Zoia. *Grand Duchess Maria Nikolayevna & Her Palace in St Petersburg.* (Hazar, 1995.)
— *The Romanov Legacy. The Palaces of St Petersburg.* (Hazar, 1994.)
Benckendorff, Count Paul. *Last Days at Tsarskoe Selo.* (Heinemann, 1927.)
Bergamini, John. *The Tragic Dynasty.* (Constable, 1970.)
Bing, Edward J. (ed). *The Letters of Tsar Nicholas & Empress Marie.* (Ivor Nicholson & Watson, 1937.)
Bokhanov, Alexander & Others. *The Romanovs: Love, Power & Tragedy.* (Leppi Publications, 1993.)
Botkin, Gleb. *The Real Romanovs.* (Putnam, London, 1932.)
Boulay, Cyrille & Paoli, Dominique. *Nicolas II et Sa Famille. L'Album de Souvenir.* (Editions Flamarrion, Paris, 1992.)
Bradley, John. *The Russian Revolution.* (Brompton Books, 1988.)
Bramsen, Bo. *Huset Glucksborg: 150 år.* (Forum, Denmark, 1992.)
Brayley-Hodgetts, E.A. *The Court of Russia in the 19th Century.* (Methuen, 1908.)
— *Moss from a Rolling Stone.* (J.M. Dent & Sons, 1924.)
Brooke-Shepherd, Gordon. *Uncle of Europe.* (Collins, 1975.)
— *Royal Sunset.* (Weidenfeld & Nicolson, 1987.)
— *Victims at Sarajevo.* (Harvill Press, 1984.)
Brown, Douglas. *Doomsday 1917: The Destruction of Russia's Ruling Class.* (Readers Union Ltd, 1975.)
Bruce Lockhart, R.H. *British Agent.* (Putnam, 1933.)
Buchanan, Sir George. *My Mission to Russia.* (Cassell, 1923.)
Buchanan, Meriel. *Dissolution of an Empire.* (John Murray, 1932.)
Bulygin, Paul. *The Murder of the Romanovs.* (Hutchinson, 1935.)
Buxhoeveden, Baroness Sophie. *The Life & Tragedy of Alexandra Feodorovna.* (Longmans, London, 1928.)
— *Left Behind. Fourteen Months in Siberia during the Revolution.* (Longmans Green & Co, 1929.)
Bykov, Paul. *The Last Days of Tsardom.* (Martin Lawrence, 1934.)

Cantacuzene, Princess Julia. *Revolutionary Days.* (Chapman & Hall, 1920.)
Carmichael, Joel. *A Short History of the Russian Revolution.* (Nelson, 1966.)
Cercle d'Etudes des Dynastes Royales Européennes. (Paris, 1980-1998.)
Cerwinske, Laura. *Imperial Russian Style.* (Barrie & Jenkins, 1990.)
Charques, Richard. *The Twilight of Imperial Russia.* (Oxford University Press, paperback, 1965.)
Chavchavadze, Prince David. *The Grand Dukes.* (Atlantic International Publications, N.Y., 1990.)
Christmas, Walter. *The Life of King George of Greece.* (Eveleigh Nash, 1914.)
Christopher, Prince of Greece. *Memoirs.* (Hurst & Blackett, 1938.)
Churchill, Lady Randolph. *Reminiscences.* (Edward Arnold, 1908.)
Clark, Rev. Andrew. *Echoes of the Great War.* Ed. by James Munson. (Oxford University Press, 1985.)
Clarke, William. *The Lost Fortune of the Tsars.* (Weidenfeld & Nicolson, 1994.)
Clausen, H.C. *Kejserinde Dagmar.* (Paul Kristensens Forlag, Denmark, 1991.)
Conway, Sir Martin. *Art Treasures in Soviet Russia.* (Edward Arnold, 1925.)
Corti, Count Egon. *The Downfall of Three Dynasties.* (Methuen, 1934.)

Cowles, Virginia. *The Last Tsar & Tsarina*. (Weidenfeld & Nicolson, 1977.)
— *The Romanovs*. (Collins, 1971.)
— *The Russian Dagger*. (Collins, 1969.)
Crankshaw, Edward. *The Shadow of the Winter Palace*. (Penguin Books, paperback, 1981.)
Crawford, Rosemary & Donald. *Michael & Natasha*. (Weidenfeld & Nicolson, 1997.)
Cyril, Grand Duke. *My Life in Russia's Service, Then & Now*. (Selwyn & Blount, 1939.)

Dangerfield, George. *Victoria's Heir*. (Constable, 1942.)
de Grunwald, Constantine. *Le Tsar Nicolas II*. (Berger-Levrault, France, 1965.)
de Jonge, Alex. *The Life & Times of Gregorii Rasputin*. (Collins, 1982.)
de Stoeckl, Baroness. *Not All Vanity*. (John Murray, 1950.)
Dedijer, Vladimir. *The Road to Sarajevo*. (MacGibbon & Kee, 1967.)
Dehn, Lili. *The Real Tsaritsa*. (Butterworth, 1922.)
Dobson, Christopher. *Prince Felix Yusupov. The Man Who Murdered Rasputin*. (Harrap, 1989.)
Dolgoruky, Prince Paul. *Tattered Banners*. (Seely Service, 1947.)
Dolgoruky, Princess Stephanie. *Russia Before the Crash*. (Herbert Clarke, 1926.)
Drozdov, George. *A Tour of Moscow, An Illustrated Guide*. (Planeta Publishers, Moscow, 1990.)
Duff, David. *Alexandra, Princess & Queen*. (Sphere, 1981.)
— *Hessian Tapestry*. (Frederick Muller, 1967.)
— *Victoria Travels*. (Frederick Muller, 1970.)
Dufferin & Ava, Hariot, Dowager Marchioness of. *My Russian & Turkish Journals*. (John Murray, 1916.)

Eagar, Miss Margaretta. *Six Years at the Russian Court*. (Hurst & Blackett, 1906.)
Edwards, Anne. *Matriarch*. (Hodder & Stoughton, 1984.)
Eilers, Marlene A. *Queen Victoria's Descendants*. (Atlantic International Publications, N.Y., 1987.)
Enache, Nicholas. *La Descendance de Pierre le Grand, Tsar de Russie*. (Sedopols, Paris, 1983.)
Essad-Bey, Mohammed. *Nicholas II, Prisoner of the Purple*. (Hutchinson, 1936.)
Eugenie, Princess of Greece. *Le Tsarevitch, Enfant Martyr*. (Perrin, Paris, 1990.)
Eulalia, Infanta of Spain. *Court Life from Within*. (Cassell, 1915.)

Fabergé, Tatiana, Proler, Lynette G. & Skurlov, Valentin V. *The Fabergé Imperial Easter Eggs*. (Christie's Books, London, 1997.)
Ferrand, Jacques. *Romanoff – Un Album de Famille*. (Paris, 1989.)
— *Romanoff – Un Album de Famille, Complément*. (Paris, 1990.)
— *Il est Toujours des Romanov!* (Paris, 1995.)
— *Descendances Naturelles des Souverains et Grands-Ducs de Russie de 1762 à 1905*. (Paris, 1995.)
Ferro, Marc. *Nicholas II, The Last of the Tsars*. (Viking, 1991.)
Field, Leslie. *The Queen's Jewels*. (Weidenfeld & Nicolson, 1987.)
Figes, Orlando. *A People's Tragedy*. (Johnathan Cape, 1996.)
Finestone, Jeffrey. *The Last Courts of Europe*. (J.M. Dent, 1981.)
Fisher, H.H. (ed). *Out of My Past: The Memoirs of Count Kokovtsov*. (Stanford University Press, California, 1935.)

Fisher, J.R. *Finland & the Tsars, 1809-99*. (Edward Arnold, 1899.)

Fitzlyon, Kyrill & Browning, Tatiana. *Before the Revolution*. (Allen Lane, Penguin Books, 1977.)

Fjellman, Margit. *Louise Mountbatten, Queen of Sweden*. (Allen & Unwin, 1968.)

Florinsky, M.T. *Russia: A History & an Interpretation*. (Macmillan, 1947.)

Frankland, Noble. *Crown of Tragedy: Nicholas II*. (William Kimber, 1960.)

Freeman, John & Berton, Kathleen. *Moscow Revealed*. (Abbeville Press, 1991.)

Fricero, Emmanuel. *The Grand Duke Nicholas Alexandrovich, Crown Prince of Russia*. (Association Cultuelle Orthodoxe Russe, Nice, 1958, recently re-issued.)

— *The Russian Orthodox Cathedral of St Nicholas in Nice*. (Casa Editrice Bonechi, Florence, 1994.)

Fulford, Roger (ed). *Dearest Child*. (Evans, 1964.)

— *Dearest Mama*. (Evans, 1968.)

— *Your Dear Letter*. (Evans, 1971.)

— *Darling Child*. (Evans, 1976.)

— *Beloved Mama*. (Evans, 1981.)

Fulop-Miller, René. *Rasputin: The Holy Devil*. (Fontana, 1967.)

Galitzine, Prince George. *Imperial Splendour*. (Viking, 1991.)

Gaynor, Elizabeth & Haavisto, Kari. *Russian Houses*. (Stewart Tabori & Chang, N.Y., 1991.)

Gendrikov, Vladimir & Sen'ko, Sergei. *The Cathedral of SS Peter & Paul, the Burial Place of the Russian Imperial Family*. (Liki Rossii Publishing, St Petersburg, 1998.)

George, Grand Duchess. *A Romanov Diary*. (Atlantic International Publications, N.Y., 1988.)

Gilliard, Pierre. *Thirteen Years at the Russian Court*. (Hutchinson, 1921.)

Glenny, Michael & Stone, Norman. *The Other Russia*. (Faber & Faber, paperback, London, 1991.)

Grabbe, Count Alexander. *The Private World of the Last Tsar*. (Collins, 1985.)

Graham, Stephen. *The Life & Reign of Alexander II*. (Ivor Nicholson & Watson, 1935.)

Gram-Andersen, Major Jesper. *Pro Rege et Grege. The Royal Danish Life Guards 1994*. (The Royal Arsenal Museum, Copenhagen, 1994.)

Grant, N.F. (ed). *The Kaiser's Letters to the Tsar*. (Hodder & Stoughton, 1920.)

Graves, Charles. *Royal Riviera*. (Heinemann, 1957.)

Gray, Pauline. *The Grand Duke's Woman*. (Macdonald & Janes, 1976.)

Habsburg-Lothringen, G. von & Solodkoff, A. von. *Fabergé: Court Jeweller to the Tsars*. (Alpine Fine Arts, 1979.)

Hamilton, Lord Frederick. *The Vanished World of Yesterday*. (Hodder & Stoughton, 1950.)

Hammer, Dr Armand. *The Quest of the Romanov Treasure*. (Williams & Norgate, 1937.)

Hanbury-Williams, Maj. Gen. Sir John. *The Emperor Nicholas As I Knew Him*. (Arthur L. Humphreys, 1922.)

Harcave, Sidney. *The Years of the Golden Cockerel: The Last Century of Romanov Tsars*. (Robert Hale, 1968.)

— *The Russian Revolution of 1905*. (Collier-Macmillan, 1964.)

Hardinge, Sir Arthur. *A Diplomatist in Europe*. (Jonathan Cape, 1927.)

Hardinge, Charles. *Old Diplomacy*. (John Murray, 1947.)

Haslip, Joan. *The Lonely Empress*. (Weidenfeld & Nicolson, paperback, 1987.)
Hibbert, Christopher. *Edward VII: A Portrait*. (Penguin, 1982.)
Hindley, Geoffrey. *The Royal Families of Europe*. (Lyric Books, 1969.)
Hingley, Ronald. *The Tsars, 1533-1917*. (Corgi, 1973.)
Hough, Richard. *Louis & Victoria, the First Mountbattens*. (Hutchinson, 1974.)
— (ed). *Advice to a Granddaughter*. (Heinemann, 1975.)
— *Edward & Alexandra*. (Hodder & Stoughton, 1992.)

Imperial St Petersburg. Pages from History, 1703-1917. (Various.) (Art-Lux, St Petersburg, 1996.)
Ingham, Robert. *What Happened to the Empress*. (Booklet.) (St Joseph's Institute, Hamrun, Malta, 1949.)
Iroshnikov, Mikhail, Protsaid, Liudmila & Shelayev, Yuri. *The Sunset of the Romanov Dynasty*. (Moscow, 1992.)
Izvolsky, Alexander. *Memoirs*. (Hutchinson, 1920.)

Jackman, S.W. *The People's Princess*. (Kensal Press, 1994.)
Jensen, Bent. *Zarmoder blandt Zarmordere*. (Gyldendal, Denmark, 1997.)
— 'The Land of Unlimited Potential', in *Maria Feodorovna, Empress of Russia*, exhibition catalogue. (Christiansborg Palace, Copenhagen, 1997.)
Judd, Denis. *Eclipse of Kings*. (Macdonald & Janes, 1976.)

Karsavina, Tamara. *Theatre Street*. (Constable, 1947.)
Kennedy, A.L. (ed). *My Dear Duchess*. (John Murray, 1956.)
Kennett, V. & A. *The Palaces of Leningrad*. (1973.)
Kent, H.R.H. Princess Michael of. *Crowned in a Far Country*. (Weidenfeld & Nicolson, 1986.)
King, Greg. *Empress Alexandra*. (Atlantic International Publications, N.Y., 1990.)
— *The Last Empress*. (Birch Lane Press, N.Y., 1994.)
Kinloch Cooke, C. *A Memoir of H.R.H. Princess Mary Adelaide, Duchess of Teck*. (John Murray, 1900.)
Klausen, Inger-Lise. *Dagmar, Zarina fra Danmark*. (Lindhardt & Ringhof, Copenhagen, 1997.)
Kleinmichael, Countess Marie. *Memoirs of a Shipwrecked World*. (Brentano, 1923.)
Klier, John & Mingay, Helen. *The Quest for Anastasia*. (Smith Gryphon, 1995.)
Kschessinska, Mathilde. *Dancing in Petersburg*. Translated by Arnold Haskell. (Gollancz, 1960.)
Kudrina, Julia. 'How Terrible to Think that it is Only the Beginning', in *The Poppy & the Owl*, the journal of the Friends of the Liddle Collection. (November 1998, No. 24)
— 'Our Beloved Empress', in *Maria Feodorovna, Empress of Russia*, exhibition catalogue. (Christiansborg Palace, Copenhagen, 1997.)
Kurth, Peter. *Anastasia: The Life of Anna Anderson*. (Little, Brown, 1983.)
— *Tsar: The Lost World of Nicholas & Alexandra*. (Little, Brown. 1995.)

Lee, Sir Arthur Gould (ed). *The Empress Frederick Writes to Sophie*. (Faber & Faber, 1955.)
Leroy-Beaulieu, Anatole. *The Empire of the Tsars*. (Putnam, 1894.)

Levine, Isaac Don. *Eyewitness to History*. (Hawthorn, N.Y., 1973.)
Lieven, Dominic. *Nicholas II, Emperor of All the Russias*. (John Murray, 1993.)
Lifer, Serge. *Diaghilev*. (Putnam, 1940.)
Lincoln, W. Bruce. *The Romanovs, Autocrats of All the Russias*. (Weidenfeld & Nicolson, 1981.)
— *In War's Dark Shadow*. (Oxford University Press, paperback, 1994.)
— *Passage Through Armageddon*. (Oxford University Press, paperback, 1994.)
Lister, Roma. *Reminiscences*. (Hutchinson, London, no date.)
Listowel, Judith. *A Hapsburg Tragedy: Crown Prince Rudolf*. (Ascent Books, 1978.)
Loftus, Lord Augustus. *Diplomatic Reminiscences, 1862-79*. (Cassell, 1894.)
Longford, Elizabeth. *Louisa, Lady in Waiting*. (Jonathan Cape, 1979.)
— *Darling Loosy: Letters to Princess Louise*. (Weidenfeld & Nicolson, 1991.)
Loubat, J.F. *The Mission to Russia in 1866 of the Hon. Gustavus Vasa Fox*. (Appleton, N.Y., 1879.)
Louda, Jiri & Maclagen, Michael. *Lines of Succession*. (Orbis Publishing, 1981.)
Lovell, James Blair. *Anastasia, the Lost Princess*. (Regnery Gateway, Washington, 1991.)
Lowe, Charles. *Alexander III of Russia*. (Heinemann, 1895.)
Lyons, Marvin. *Nicholas II, the Last Tsar*. (Routledge, Kegan Paul, London, 1974.)

Maclean, Fitzroy. *Holy Russia*. (Weidenfeld & Nicolson, 1978.)
Madol, Hans Roger. *Christian IX*. (Collins, 1939.)
— *The Private Life of Queen Alexandra*. (Collins, 1940.)
Magnus, Sir Philip. *Edward VII*. (Penguin, paperback, 1967.)
Majolier, Nathalie. *Step-daughter of Imperial Russia*. (Stanley Paul, 1940.)
Malcolm, Sir Ian. *Trodden Ways*. (Macmillan, 1930.)
Maria Feodorovna, Empress of Russia. Exhibition catalogue. (Christiansborg Palace, 1997.)
Marie, Grand Duchess. *Things I Remember*. (Cassell, 1930.)
— *A Princess in Exile*. (Cassell, 1932.)
Marie, Queen of Roumania. *The Story of My Life*. (Cassell, 1934/5.) 3 vols.
Markov, Sergei V. *How We Tried to Save the Tsaritsa*. (Putnam, 1929.)
Martin, Ralph G. *Lady Randolph Churchill*. (Sphere, 1974.)
Massie, Robert K. *Nicholas & Alexandra*. (Gollancz, 1968.)
— *Peter the Great*. (Gollancz, 1981, Abacus paperback edition.)
Massie, Suzanne. *Land of the Firebird*. (Hamish Hamilton, 1980.)
— *Pavlovsk: The Life of a Russian Palace*. (Hodder & Stoughton, 1990.)
Matveyev, Dr Vladimir. *The Hermitage, Selected Treasures from a Great Museum*. (The State Hermitage Museum, Leningrad, 1990.)
Maud, Renée Elton. *One Year at the Russian Court*. (John Lane, The Bodley Head, no date.)
Maylunas, Andrei and Mironenko, Sergei. *A Lifelong Passion*. (Weidenfeld & Nicolson, 1996.)
McNaughton, Arnold. *The Books of Kings*. (Garnstone, 1973.)
Menkes, Suzy. *The Royal Jewels*. (Grafton Books, 1985.)
Michael, Maurice. *Haakon, King of Norway*. (Allen & Unwin, 1958.)
Michael, Prince of Greece. *Crown Jewels of Europe*. (Dent, 1983.)
— *Nicholas & Alexandra: The Family Albums*. (Tauris Park, 1992.)
— *Imperial Palaces of Russia*. (Tauris Park, 1992.)

Millar, Lubov. *Grand Duchess Elizabeth of Russia. New Martyr of the Communist Yoke*. (Nikodemos Orthodox Publication Society, California, 1991.)

Milner-Gulland, Robin & Dejevsky, Nikolai. *Atlas of Russia & the Soviet Union*. (Phaidon, 1989.)

Minney, R.J. *Rasputin*. (Cassell, 1972.)

Monkswell, Lady Mary. *A Victorian Diarist*. Vol 2: 1895-1909. (John Murray, 1946.)

Moorehead, Alan. *The Russian Revolution*. (Collins, 1958.)

Morton, Andrew. *Theirs is the Kingdom*. (Michael O'Mara, 1989.)

Mossolov, Alexander A. *At the Court of the Last Tsar*. (Methuen, 1935.)

Mouchanow, Marfa. *My Empress*. (John Lane, N.Y., 1918.)

Nadelhoffer, Hans. *Cartier, Jewellers Extraordinary*. (Thames & Hudson, 1984.)

Naryshkin-Kurakin, Elizabeth. *Under Three Tsars*. (Dutton, N.Y., 1931.)

Neerbek, Hans. *Søstrenes Slot*. (Hernovs Forlag, Copenhagen, 1990.)

Nelson, Nina. *Denmark*. (Batsford, 1973.)

Nicholas II, Tsar of Russia. *Journal Intime de Nicolas II*. (Payot, Paris, 1925.)

— *Journal Intime de Nicolas II, juillet 1914-juillet 1918*. (Payot, Paris, 1934.)

— *Lettres de Nicolas II et de Sa Mère*. Ed. by Paul Leon. (Simon Kra, Paris, 1928.)

— *Letters of the Tsar to the Tsaritsa, 1914-1916*. (Bodley Head, 1929.)

Nicholas & Alexandra, the Last Imperial Family of Russia. Exhibition catalogue. (Booth-Clibborn Editions, London, 1998.)

Nicholas, Prince of Greece. *My Fifty Years*. (Hutchinson, 1926.)

Nicholson, Sir Harold. *King George V*. (Pan, paperback, 1967.)

Noel, Gerard. *Princess Alice, Queen Victoria's Forgotten Daughter*. (Constable, 1974.)

Nun Nectaria. *A Gathered Radiance: The Life of Alexandra Romanov, Russia's Last Empress*. (Valaam Society of America, 1992.)

Oakley, Stewart. *The Story of Denmark*. (Faber & Faber, 1972.)

Obolensky, Serge. *One Man in His Time*. (Hutchinson, 1960.)

Occleshaw, Dr Michael. *The Romanov Conspiracies*. (Chapmans, 1993.)

O'Connor, John. *The Sokolov Investigation*. (Souvenir Press, 1971.)

Oldenburg, S.S. *The Last Tsar: Nicholas II, His Reign & His Russia*. (Hattiesburg Miss, Academic International Press, 1975.)

Ometev, Boris & Stewart, John. *St Petersburg: Portrait of an Imperial City*. (Vendome Press, N.Y., 1990.)

Onassis, Jacqueline (ed). *In the Russian Style*. (Thames & Hudson, 1976.)

Ovsianikov, Yuri. *Invitation to Russia*. (Conran Octopus, 1989.)

Paget, Lady Walburga. *Embassies of Other Days*. (Hutchinson, 1923.)

— *Scenes & Memories*. (Smith, Elder & Co., London, 1912.)

Pakula, Hannah. *The Last Romantic: A Biography of Queen Marie of Roumania*. (Weidenfeld Paperbacks, 1984.)

— *An Uncommon Woman*. (Weidenfeld & Nicolson, 1996.)

Paleologue, Maurice. *An Ambassador's Memoirs*. (Doran, 1925.)

Paley, Princess. *Memories of Russia, 1916-1919*. (Herbert Jenkins, 1924.)

Pantazzi, Ethel Greening. *Roumania in Light & Shadow*. (The Ryerson Press, London, 1921.)

Pares, Sir Bernard. *The Fall of the Russian Monarchy*. (Johnathan Cape, 1939. Cassell, paperback, 1988.)
— *A History of Russia*. (Jonathan Cape, 1949.)
Pipes, Richard. *Russia Under the Old Regime*. (Weidenfeld & Nicolson, 1974.)
— *The Russian Revolution, 1899-1919*. (Collins Harvill, 1990.)
Poliakoff, Vladimir. *The Empress Marie of Russia & Her Times*. (Thornton Butterworth, 1926.)
Polynina, Irina and Rakhmanov, Nicolai. *The Regalia of the Russian Empire*. (Red Square, Moscow, 1994.)
Ponsonby, Sir Frederick. *Recollections of Three Reigns*. (Eyre & Spottiswoode, 1951.)
— *Letters of the Empress Frederick*. (Macmillan, 1929.)
Pope-Hennessy, James. *Queen Mary*. (George Allen & Unwin, 1959.)
— *A Lonely Business*. (Weidenfeld & Nicolson, 1981.)
Potts, D. M. & W. T. W. *Queen Victoria's Gene*. (Alan Sutton, 1995.)
Poutiatine, Princess Nathalie. *Princess Olga, My Mother*. (Gulf Publishing, Valletta, Malta, 1982.)
Pridham, Vice Adm. Sir Francis. *Close of a Dynasty*. (Allan Wingate, 1956.)

Radzinsky, Edvard. *Nicholas II. The Life & Death of the Last Tsar*. (Hodder & Stoughton, 1992.)
Radziwill, Princess Catherine. *The Intimate Life of the Last Tsarina*. (Cassell, 1929.)
— *My Recollections*. (Isbister, 1904.)
— *Nicholas II: The Last of the Tsars*. (Cassell, 1931.)
— *Russia's Decline & Fall*. (Cassell, 1918.)
— *Those I Remember*. (Cassell, 1924.)
Ramm, Agatha. *Beloved & Darling Child*. (Alan Sutton, 1990.)
Raleigh, Donald J. (ed). *The Emperors & Empresses of Russia: Rediscovering the Romanovs*. (M.E. Sharpe, New York, paperback, 1996.)
Rathlef-Keilman, Harriet von. *Anastasia, the Survivor of Ekaterinburg*. (Putnam, 1928.)
Reed, John. *Ten Days That Shook the World*. (N.Y. Modern Library, 1935.)
Richards, Guy. *The Hunt for the Tsar*. (Peter Davies, 1971.)
Rodney, William. *Joe Boyle, King of the Klondike*. (McGraw-Hill Ryerson, Toronto, 1974.)
Rodzianko, M.V. *The Reign of Rasputin*. (Philpot, 1927.)
Romanov, Prince Roman. *Det var et rigt hus, et lykkeligt hus*. (Gyldendal, Copenhagen, 1991.)
Rose, Kenneth. *King George V*. (Weidenfeld & Nicolson, 1984.)
Rutherford, Ward. *The Russian Army in World War I*. (Gordon Cremonesi, 1975.)

Sablin, E. 'Obituary of Empress Marie Feodorovna', in *The Slavonic & East European Review*, Vol 12, No. 19.
Sagovsky, Hilary. *Boobi's Memoirs*. (The Book Guild Ltd, Sussex, 1989.)
Salisbury, Harrison E. *Black Night, White Snow*. (Da Capo, paperback, 1977.)
Schmemann, Serge. *Echoes of a Native Land*. (Little, Brown & Co., 1997.)
Seton-Watson, H. *The Russian Empire, 1801-1917*. (Clarendon Press, Oxford, 1967.)
Shelayev, Yuri, Shelayeva, Elizabeth & Semanov, Nicholas. *Nicholas Romanov: Life & Death*. (Liki Rossii Publishing, St Petersburg, 1998.)
Shulgin, V.V. *The Years*. (Hippocrene Books, N.Y., 1984.)

Sinclair, Andrew. *The Other Victoria: The Princess Royal & the Great Game of Europe*. (Weidenfeld & Nicolson, 1981.)

Snowman, A. Kenneth. *Carl Fabergé, Goldsmith to the Imperial Court of Russia*. (Greenwich House, 1983.)

Solodkoff, Alexander von. *Masterpieces From the House of Fabergé*. (Harry N. Abrams, N.Y., 1984.)

Sotheby's. *The Romanovs. Documents & Photographs Relating to the Russian Imperial House*. (1990.)

Spiridovich, A. *Les Dernieres Années de la Cour de Tzarskoie Selo*. (Payot, Paris, 1925.)

Stanley. *Later Letters of Lady Augusta Stanley, 1864-76*. (Jonathan Cape, 1929.)

St Aubyn, Giles. *Edward VII, Prince & King*. (Atheneum, 1979.)

— *Queen Victoria: A Portrait*. (Sinclair-Stevenson, 1991.)

Stone, Norman (ed). *The Russian Chronicles*. (Random Century, 1990.)

Stopford, Hon. Albert. *The Russian Diary of an Englishman*. (Robert M. McBride, N.Y., 1919.)

Storfyrstinde Olga. (Various.) (Published by Ballerup Historiske Forening, 1994.)

Summers, Anthony & Mangold, Tom. *The File on the Tsar*. (Gollancz Paperbacks, 1987.)

Tantzos, G. Nicholas. *King by Chance*. (Atlantic International Publications, N.Y., 1988.)

Tarsaidze, Alexandre. *Katia, Wife Before God*. (Macmillan, 1970.)

Thompson, G.M. *The Twelve Days*. (Hutchinson, 1964.)

Tisdall, E.E.P. *Marie Feodorovna, Empress of Russia*. (Stanley Paul, 1957.)

Treasures of the Czars: From the State Museums of the Moscow Kremlin. Presented by Florida International Museum, St Petersburg. (Booth-Clibborn, London, 1995.)

Trewin, J.C. *The House of Special Purpose*. (Scarborough, paperback, N.Y., 1982.)

Troyat, Henri. *Daily Life in Russia Under the Last Tsar*. (George Allen & Unwin, 1961.)

Tuchman, Barbara. *August 1914*. (Constable, 1962.)

Ulstrup, Preben. 'Marie Feodorovna through Diaries & Personal Letters', in *Maria Feodorovna, Empress of Russia*, exhibition catalogue. (Christiansborg Palace, 1997.)

Van der Kiste, John. *Queen Victoria's Children*. (Alan Sutton, 1986.)

— *Victoria Melita, Grand Duchess Cyril of Russia*. (Alan Sutton, 1991.)

— *Edward VII's Children*. (Alan Sutton, 1989.)

— *Crowns in a Changing World*. (Alan Sutton, 1993.)

— *Northern Crowns: The Kings of Modern Scandinavia*. (Alan Sutton, 1996.)

Van der Kiste, John & Jordaan, Bee. *Dearest Affie: Alfred Duke of Edinburgh, Queen Victoria's Second Son*. (Alan Sutton, 1984.)

Vassili, Count Paul. *Behind the Veil at the Russian Court*. (Cassell, 1913.)

Victoria, Queen. *The Letters of Queen Victoria*, 2nd Series, 1862-78. (John Murray, 1926.)

— *The Letters of Queen Victoria*, 3rd Series, 1886-1901. (John Murray, 1930.)

Victoria Louise, Duchess of Brunswick & Luneburg. *The Kaiser's Daughter*. (Prentice-Hall, 1977.)

Vorres, Ian. *The Last Grand Duchess*. (Hutchinson, 1964.)

Vulliamy, C.E. (ed). *Red Archives (Krasny Arkhiv)*. (Bles, 1929.)

Vyrubova, Anna. *Memories of the Russian Court*. (Macmillan, N.Y., 1923.)

Waddington, Mary King. *Letters of a Diplomat's Wife, 1883-1900*. (Smith, Elder, 1903.)
Whittle, Tyler. *The Last Kaiser*. (Heinemann, 1977.)
Wilkenschildt, Merete. *Kongelige Leksikon*. (Lindhardt & Ringhof, Copenhagen, 1998.)
Wilson, Colin. *Rasputin & the Fall of the Romanovs*. (Panther, paperback, 1966.)
Wilton, Robert. *The Last Days of the Romanovs*. (Thornton Butterworth, 1920.)
Windsor, H.R.H. Duke of. *A King's Story*. (Putnam, 1947.)
Witte, Count Sergius. *Memoirs*. (Heinemann, 1921.)
Wolfe, Bertram. *Three Who Made a Revolution*. (Thames & Hudson, 1956.)
Wonlar-Larsky, Nadine. *The Russia That I Loved*. (Elsie MacSwinney, 1937.)

Yermilova, Larissa. *The Last Tsar*. (Parkstone Planeta, 1996.)
Youssoupov, Prince Felix. *Lost Splendour*. (Jonathan Cape, 1954.)
— *Rasputin*. (Dial, N.Y., 1927.)
— *En Exile*. (Librairie Plon, Paris, 1954.)

Zemlyanichenki, Marina & Kalinin, Nikolai. *The Romanovs and the Crimea*. (Trans. Yekaterina Tabidze.) (Russian Nobility Descendants Union, Kruk, Moscow, 1993.)
Ziegler, Sir Philip. *Edward VIII*. (Collins, 1990.)

Articles

Occleshaw, Dr Michael. 'With the Greatest Care and Tact'. In *Royalty Digest*, March 1993.
Zeepvat, Charlotte. 'Poor Dear Aunt Thyra'. In *Royalty Digest*, August 1994.

Public Record Office

ADM53/48558 – Log of H.M.S. *Marlborough*.
ADM53/47287 – Log of H.M.S. *Lord Nelson*.
FO749/13 – The Estate of the late Empress Marie Feodorovna.
FO800/205 – Russia & Siberia 1916-19.
HO45/11549/380030 – Entry of the Dowager Empress into England.
FO371/3329 – Political Russia files 1918.
ADM137/952.
ADM137/933.
ADM137/953.
FO371/3977 Part A.

National Archives of Malta

'Pratique Deposition of the HMS *Marlborough*', Register of Arrivals of the Customs Department. Vol K1191/916.
'Secret' telegram – Secretary of State for the Colonies to the Governor of Malta, 12th April 1919.

The Hoover Institution on War, Revolution and Peace

The Mlle L'Escaille Collection. 74109-10.V.

Guide Books

Baedeker. Moscow, St Petersburg, Copenhagen.
The Peter & Paul Fortress. (Aurora Art Publishers, Leningrad.)
The Moscow Kremlin. (Aurora Art Publishers, Leningrad.)
Petrodvorets: The Grand Palace.
Petrodvorets Cottage.
Roskilde Domkirke.
Tsarskoe Selo.

Periodicals

Illusteret Tidende. 21st October 1866.
Point de Vue.
The Imperial Quarterly.
The Imperial Russian Journal.
Royalty.
Royalty Digest.
The World of Interiors.
Majesty.
Vanity Fair.

Newspapers

The Times.
The New York Times.
The Daily Herald.
The Morning Herald.
Poslednie Novosti. July 1933.

Index

Marie Feodorovna, Empress (*General References* contd)
— helps South Jutland prisoners of war: 261
— upset by the suffering of war: 262
— becomes a great-grandmother: 262
— passes on intelligence from Alix: 262/3
— receives Hans Niels Andersen: 263/4
— helps refugees from Poland: 263
— & Nicholas' decision to become C-in-C: 264/5
— & dismissal of Prince Orlov: 265
— blames Alicky: 265/6
— visits Olga in Kiev: 266/7
— fails to break the power of Alicky & Rasputin: 267
— rumours of involvement in plots: 268
— moves to Maryinsky Palace, Kiev: 269/87
— 50th anniversary of her arrival in Russia: 271/2
— Tsar & Alexis visit Kiev: 271/2
— demands Sturmer's dismissal: 272
— attends Olga's remarriage: 272/3
— confides fears to Nicholas Michaelovitch: 273
— & German peace offers: 275/6
— reaction to Rasputin's murder: 276/7
— travels to Kursk: 277
— concern over Alicky's influence: 278/80
— learns of disturbances in Petrograd: 281/2
— learns of Nicholas' abdication: 282
— meets Nicholas in Moghilev: 282/4
— sees Sir John Hanbury-Williams: 284
— revolution reaches Kiev: 284/6
— agrees to go to Crimea: 287
— at Ai-Todor: 288/302
— no letters from England: 289
— fate of her palaces during revolution: 290
— financial situation: 290/91
— & search of Ai-Todor: 292/3
— feelings about revolution: 293/4
— under house arrest: 294, 297
— attends funeral of Princess Dolgoruky: 295
— sends letter to Buchanan: 295
— & birth of Olga's baby: 296
— appeals for Tsar's rescue: 296/7
— serious illness: 297/8
— contact with Michael & Nicholas: 298/9
— Danish efforts to secure her release: 298, 307
— Sevastopol Soviet takes over Ai-Todor: 300
— 70th birthday: 301
— confiscation of assets & properties: 302
— moved to Djulber: 302
— under arrest at Djulber: 303/10
— receives money from Count Benckendorff: 304
— visit from Carl Krebs: 304/6
— & Prince Schervashidze's death: 306/7
— rescued by the Germans: 308
— refuses to receive German general: 308/9
— rumours of her transfer to Kiev: 309
— lives at Harax: 311/18
— rumours about Nicholas & Michael: 312/13
— visit from Waldemar Spare: 313/14
— refuses to believe Nicholas is dead: 314
— visit of Ingeborg Larsen: 314
— George V offers to evacuate her: 315/16
— concern of Queen Marie of Roumania: 316
— visit from Joe Boyle: 316/17
— refuses to leave Russia: 317
— Olga leaves for the Caucasus: 318
— embarks on HMS *Marlborough*: 318/19
— leaves Russia: 319/20
— arrives in Malta: 323/4
— stay in Malta: 324/6

Marie Feodorovna, Empress (*General References* contd)
— journey to England: 326/7
— arrival in England: 327
— receives Natasha Brasova: 328
— petitions on behalf of Russian refugees: 328/9
— at Marlborough House: 326/8
— arrives back in Copenhagen: 329
— at Hvidøre: 330
— reunion with Olga: 330/31
— relationship with King Christian X: 331/2, 334/5
— debts: 332/3, 335, 345
— attitude of the Danish government: 333
— relationship with Olga's children: 333/4
— attends Princess Margrethe's wedding: 334
— attends wedding of Lord Louis Mountbatten: 335
— attends Duke of York's wedding: 336
— as senior survivor of the Romanovs: 336
— & Sokolov's dossier: 337
— conflicting accounts of investigators: 336/8
— outraged at Cyril's declaration: 338/9
— & the Anastasia claimant: 341/3, 344
— death of Alix: 343/4
— hunt for Tsar's assets: 345/6
— reports that she was to be expelled from Denmark: 346
— her supposed attempt to murder Alexis: 347
— 1915 diary: 347
— fights for Russian Orthodox Church: 347/8
— failing health: 348
— refuses to sell jewels: 332, 348/9
— 80th birthday: 349
— receives two items from Ekaterinburg: 349
— death: 349
— funeral: 350/52
— Will: 353
— sale of jewels: 353/4
— sale of Hvidøre: 354/6
— fate of her homes: 355
— coffin moved to the private crypt: 358/9
Marie Feodorovna, Empress (Princess Sophia-Dorothea of Württemberg) (wife of Emperor Paul): 86, 140, 177
Marie Louise of Cumberland, Princess: 195
Marie Nicholaievna, Grand Duchess (later Duchess of Leuchtenberg & Countess Stroganoff) (daughter of Nicholas I): 126/7
Marie Nicholaievna, Grand Duchess (daughter of Nicholas II) (granddaughter):
— mentioned: 185, 240, 244, 251, 312, 342
— body missing: 356
Marie of Orleans, Princess: 118, 134, 230/31
Marie Pavlovna, Grand Duchess (Princess Marie of Mecklenburg-Schwerin, Grand Duchess Vladimir) ('Miechen'):
— mentioned: 101, 156, 267, 272
— marriage to Grand Duke Vladimir: 62
— as rival leader of society: 97, 117, 178, 247/8
— hopes Michael will marry her daughter: 194
— & Cyril's marriage: 209
— patron of Cartier: 225
— converts to Orthodoxy: 230
— conversation with Dagmar: 265
— leaves Petrograd: 279
— fate of: 336
Marie Pavlovna the younger, Grand Duchess (later Princess William of Sweden) (niece):
— mentioned: 145, 327/8, 350
— birth: 144
— under guardianship of Sergei & Ella: 193, 207